LENIN LIVES!

Nina Tumarkin

LENIN LIVES!

The Lenin Cult in Soviet Russia

Harvard University Press

Cambridge, Massachusetts, and London, England   1983

Publication of this book has been aided by a grant from
the Andrew W. Mellon Foundation.

This book is printed on acid-free paper, and its binding materials
have been chosen for strength and durability.

Library of Congress Cataloging in Publication Data

Tumarkin, Nina.
    Lenin lives!

    Bibliography: p.
    Includes index.
    1. Lenin, Vladimir Ilich, 1870–1924—Influence.
2. Soviet Union—History—1917–   . 3. Statesmen—
Soviet Union—Biography. I. Title.
DK254.L46T85   1983   947.084'1' 0924 [B]   82–15665
ISBN 0–674–52430–6

947.084
T925

To Adam Ulam

Acknowledgments

Looking back on my years with Lenin, I am struck by the enormity of my debt to the Russian Research Center of Harvard University. It provided the community of colleagues, office, library, kind words and great expectations that I needed in order to write this book. I thank Mary Towle, Susan Gardos, Rose DiBenedetto, and the rest of the staff for their patience and good cheer. My greatest thanks go to the Russian Research Center's current director, Adam Ulam, who always encouraged and inspired me.

Wellesley College was most generous, supplying me with funds to print the microfilm I brought back from the Soviet Union and to help with the cost of typing the manuscript. Above all I thank the College for the Early Leave that enabled me to spend the spring semester of 1978 in the USSR doing the most important piece of my research. I should like to thank the International Research and Exchanges Board for sponsoring that trip, and Robert C. Tucker, Stephen Cohen, and Mark Kuchment for helping me to prepare for it. My thanks also go to the staff of Moscow's Museum of the Revolution for their unfailingly courteous cooperation.

I am deeply grateful to the many friends and colleagues who read my manuscript and offered advice and support of all kinds: Steven Fosburg, Richard Pipes, Adam Ulam, Abbott Gleason, Brenda Meehan-Waters, Mark Edwards, Robert C. Tucker, Robert Bathurst, Jon Ackerman, David Binder, Daniel Field, Norman Naimark, Richard Stites, and Robert V. Daniels. Norman Naimark, in addition, kindly shared with me his expertise on Russian revolutionaries in the 1880s. Jerold Auerbach and David Powell made illuminating comments on a paper that summarized a major portion of the book. Sidney Monas put the idea of this book into my head a long time ago. Barbara Sindriglis has been a splendid typist. Nancy Deptula was an excellent proofreader. My warm thanks to all of them.

viii Susan Rosbrow-Reich and Kenneth Reich gave me their own special kind of encouragement, and David and Barbara Powell literally sheltered me while I was writing most of this book. To the four of them I would like to express my enduring and loving gratitude.

Wellesley, Massachusetts
December 1982

Contents

Illustrations

following page 164

Sources of illustrations: 1, 2, 4, 5, 6, 8, 13, 14, 19a—Poster Collection, Lenin Library, Moscow; 3, 7—*Lenin: Sobranie fotografii . . . 1874-1923* (Moscow, 1970), pp. 180, 423; 9—*Lenin* (Moscow, 1961); 11—*Leninu, 21 ianvaria 1924* (Moscow, 1925), pp. 371, 411, 437; 15, 16, 17, 18—A. N. Kotyrev, *Mavzolei V. I. Lenina, proektirovanie i stroitel'stvo* (Moscow, 1971), pp. 44, 52–53, 146, 145; 19b—Iu. M. Sokolov, ed., *Samoe dorogoe* (Moscow, 1939), p. 25; 20a, 20c—Photos by the author; 20b—L. R. Varshavskii, *Obraz V. I. Lenina v narodnom i dekorativno-prikladnom iskusstve* (Moscow, 1969), p. 37; 20d—*Doshkol'noe vospitanie,* no. 4 (1979), cover; 20e—November 7 greeting card, Moscow 1977.

Prologue

"And when will Lenin be alive?" said a child's voice behind me. I turned around to face an elegant woman in a fur coat arranging the muffler on a boy of about eight. I looked at her questioningly. "This is his first visit," she explained, "and I told him that sometimes, when good little children come to see him, he wakes up." I nodded, drawing my own scarf more closely about my neck, and glanced at the huge line of people in front of us. At least two more hours of icy slush and gray March wind loomed ahead before we would reach the Lenin Mausoleum.

As a foreigner I had the option of a short line, but I was in Moscow to study the history of the Lenin cult, and deliberately chose to share the experience of ordinary Russian tourists. The long winter wait, it turned out, was an integral part of the visit, a most uncomfortable ordeal that made its end all the more welcome and dramatic. The sight of so many people ready to endure the cold increased my anticipation; their general mien was respectfully subdued, with none of the grumpiness sometimes visible on long food lines. This felt like a slow-motion pilgrimage to a holy place, which in a way it was. For the organized cult of Lenin celebrates the leader as an immortal, accessible to the people through his writings, his ubiquitous portraits, and his embalmed flesh, on permanent display in the mausoleum.

Some twenty-five feet from the entrance, young guards in smart gray uniforms began looking us over very carefully; no objects of any kind may be brought into the mausoleum. Two by two we entered a dark marble chamber. Suddenly a guard grabbed my right arm and squeezed it tightly. "What do you have under your coat?" I remembered the big wallet I had stuffed into the back pocket of my slacks. "Money," I said, for some reason feeling very frightened. "Really?" he persisted. "Yes." "All right," he muttered, and let go of my arm. The line started to move again and a man in front of me turned around and asked, with evident eagerness, "What *do* you have in your pocket?" The guards hushed us both and we descended into the tomb.

A soft, roseate light shone on Lenin, who lay in the middle of a large darkened room. At a disappointingly great distance from the body we walked along the cold marble walls of gray and black in which a red geometric design was embedded. Guards kept the line moving quickly, giving us no time to pause, so we stared as we walked. There, in an ordinary suit and tie, lay the first head of the Soviet state. He seemed neither dead nor alive. The hands were too shiny to be fleshlike but his head looked real, although, perhaps because of the lighting, his color was a bit more pink than that of an ordinary corpse. He looked quite good, considering; in fact, he seemed almost livelier than did Leonid Brezhnev, who was still almost five years away from his own death. But then this was 1978—Brezhnev was seventy-one years old and suffering from advanced arteriosclerosis—whereas Lenin had died of the same disease more than a half century earlier at the much younger age of fifty-three.

The sullen gray sky appeared very bright indeed as we left the mausoleum by its rear door, which deposited us near Stalin's grave (decorated with fake red carnations) and the spot where Brezhnev now reposes. Three Soviet leaders have died in office, but only Brezhnev's funeral culminated in burial. Stalin's body was embalmed and displayed together with Lenin's for eight years before political circumstances prompted a quick burial beside the Kremlin wall. Lenin's remains have never left the mausoleum, except for four years during the last world war, although the building is periodically closed for repairs.

Other visitors to the Lenin Mausoleum might come away wondering whether they had in fact seen Lenin or some bogus reproduction of the dead leader. I left with a different set of questions. Why was Lenin's body preserved and displayed in a mausoleum? Did it have something to do with the succession crisis that followed his premature death? How did it relate to the widespread Lenin cult that exploded nationwide when he died? How and why did the first state to call itself socialist give rise to the first significant ruler cult of the twentieth century?

The cult of Lenin's memory that dominated Communist Party ritual in the 1920s developed early in Soviet history, coming at a time when public politics and rhetoric in Russia were neither ritualized nor standardized, as they are today. The cult was built gradually during Lenin's lifetime and just after his death by people at all levels of Soviet political life. *Lenin Lives!* provides a glimpse of the variety of political expectations and aspirations held by party and nonparty members during these first years of Soviet rule, when the elements of a new political culture were still in flux. The emerging official veneration of Lenin tapped the talents of dedicated party zealots, factory workers, soldiers and sailors, reverent peasants grateful to the ruler who let them keep a bit of land, unsuccessful sculptors who sought some subject that might guarantee sales of their work, professional propagandists, party sharpies who thought up ways to please their superiors—and a host of others, including Lenin's closest lieutenants. Some produced enduring cult artifacts and rituals, and others, kitsch.

I invite the reader to peer into the kaleidoscope of a postrevolutionary regime and to witness the way in which the broken pieces of old Russia were rotated by historical imperatives and formed into new patterns that could legitimate the state. A political system that justified its troubled present with the promise of utopia was well served by the secular deification of Lenin as a revolutionary hero whose struggle to liberate Russia had earned him a glorious death and everlasting life.

The true freedom of the people is only the freedom of their imagination. Life is not a blessing to them and will never be a blessing, but it will be for ever and ever an expectation, a hope that it will become a blessing. The people need a hero, a saint ... And the more remote, the more vague, the less accessible the hero, the more freedom for the imagination, the easier it is to live. There must be a "Once upon a time there lived" about it—something of the fairy tale. Not a God in heaven, but here, on our dismal earth. Someone of great wisdom and monstrous power ...

Maxim Gorky, "The Monarchist," *Fragments from My Diary*

Note: Nowhere in the rhapsodic literature about Lenin published in the Soviet Union do its authors use the term "cult" (*kul't*) or "cult of personality" (*kul't lichnosti*) to describe the organized reverence for Lenin. In the Soviet Russian lexicon these terms stand for excessive vanity and abuse of real power combined with the systematic use of political terror. Thus Stalin and Mao Zedong had personality cults, but Lenin did not. I use "cult of Lenin" in the sense familiar to the Western reader, to mean organized venerational worship.

In transliterating Russian words and proper names I have used the Library of Congress system in the notes and bibliography, and a slightly modified form of that system in the text. Translations are my own unless otherwise indicated.

1 Russian Roots of the Lenin Cult

"Alas," the Roman Emperor Vespasian uttered on his deathbed, "I suppose I am becoming a god."[1] The emperor could make light of his posthumous pilgrimage to godhood because, by the time of his death in 79 A.D., the deification of emperors was a regular practice. It had grown out of the inability of the republican state religion to meet new imperial needs. The deification of emperors contributed to the growth and stabilization of the empire, with the deified emperor providing sanction for the imperial system.[2]

The idea of the divinity of Roman emperors came from the East. It originated in Egyptian ruler worship brought to the Hellenistic world by Alexander the Great. Both in Greece and in Rome cults of emperors found fertile soil in their polytheistic pantheons, which admitted new gods and demigods and blurred the clear distinction between men and gods characterizing monotheistic religions.[3] The cult of Alexander in particular thrived amid older Greek traditions of hero cults and of the cults of founders of cities (Alexander was accorded divine honors in the Egyptian city of Alexandria).

Just as the deification of Greek and Roman rulers was rooted in older conceptions of power and divinity and stimulated by current needs of state, so too later revolutionary cults were generated by political imperatives and were, at the same time, based on existing traditional forms and symbols. Such cults included elements of spontaneous devotion to revolutionary symbols and leaders, as well as self-conscious artifice provided by the designers, managers, and

2   publicizers of the cults. In all cases, new political rituals evolved to mobilize popular loyalty and demonstrate the legitimacy of regimes that claimed to represent a hitherto oppressed populace.

The French revolution gave rise to a complex of symbols, rites, and myths, many of which revolved around an idealized vision of republican Rome; some were taken from rituals deeply rooted in French culture, including those of the Catholic church. Thus there was a "republican Ten Commandments" and a credo: "I believe in a Supreme Being, who has made men free and equal."[4] The revolution also spawned numerous cults of revolutionary leaders, such as Marat and Robespierre, whose likenesses in the form of miniatures and busts proliferated for a decade until they were replaced by the artifacts of the organized cult of Napoleon Bonaparte. The American revolution was in part legitimated by a cult of George Washington, the most elaborate cult of a revolutionary leader prior to Lenin's, and the most similar. The mythical Washington of paeans, odes, and Parson Weems's famous (and largely fictitious) biography became an exemplar for citizens of the new American nation. In 1800 the British ambassador to the United States observed that "the periodical recital of the feats of their Revolutionary War, and the repetition of the praises of Washington" inspired the people and "contribute[d] to the formation of a *national character,* which they consider as much wanting in this country."[5] The adulation of Washington was so widespread that in 1815 a Russian visitor remarked that every American feels it his "sacred duty" to have a portrait of Washington in his home "just as we have the images of God's saints."[6]

The Russian revolution was a process of mounting anarchy that called for new symbols to confer meaning upon the chaos, and as the Communist Party moved to dominate Russia it increasingly centered its claims to legitimate rule on an idealization of Lenin as the revolution's author and guiding force. The cult of Lenin took shape gradually and piecemeal, acquired an institutional base in 1923, when illness had removed Lenin from power, and crystallized into a secular religion of national proportions immediately after his death in 1924. The full-blown cult of Lenin was an organized system of rites and symbols whose collective function was to arouse in the cult's participants and spectators the reverential mood necessary to create an emotional bond between them and the party personified by Lenin.[7] Stylized portraits and busts of Lenin were its icons, his idealized biography its gospel, and Leninism its sacred writings. Lenin Corners were local shrines for the veneration of the leader, and its central shrine was the mausoleum in Red Square displaying Lenin's preserved remains. This formalized veneration of Lenin persisted until the end of the 1920s, when the emerging cult of Stalin began slowly to eclipse it.

The cult of Lenin was followed in Russia by the extravagant Stalin cult, and subsequently by the many cults of personality that have played a role in the evolution and preservation of virtually every Communist regime. This suggests that the Lenin cult reflected or provided a model for some wider pattern of behavior. But there is a big difference between the Lenin cult and those that succeeded it. Later cults, like those of Stalin, Mao Zedong, and Tito, were cults of a living leader, serving to legitimate the leader's enduring personal domination in his party. In some of them, the leaders themselves actively contributed to their own enshrinement. The cult of Lenin undoubtedly served as an example for the later cults of living Communist leaders, but it reveals less about Communism in general than it does about Russia and about the process of forming a new political culture in the wake of revolution.

Although the cult of Lenin had a commonality of purpose with its historical antecedents in revolutionary history, its forms and trappings were peculiarly Russian. Its genesis is explained by the political exigencies of postrevolutionary Russia in combination with Lenin's own history and with particular elements of prerevolutionary Russian political culture or, rather, cultures—that of the mass of the Russian people toward whom the Lenin cult was geared and the culture of the Russian revolutionary intelligentsia, some of whose Bolshevik exponents were especially active in the creation of the Lenin cult. The cult served the needs of the Soviet state and indeed, as a standardized complex of activities and symbols, was a government and party enterprise concocted for the delectation of the untutored masses. But its derivation is deeply rooted in Russia's past, and its history demonstrates the pull of the irrational in the formation of Soviet political culture and shows how the new Bolshevik order, seeking to impose itself upon Russia, was itself molded by precisely those elements of old Russian culture that Lenin so desperately sought to destroy.

4   **Saints and Princes**

In the early eighteenth century, Peter the Great began the western-ization of elites continued by his successors, but the bulk of the Russian population, the peasantry or *narod,* retained its indepen-dent traditional culture. Religion and ritual were central to the life and experience of the narod. Rituals of birth, marriage, and death were Christian. The church calendar divided the peasant year into working days and religious holidays. Fasts were taken seriously, as were the drunken binges preceding and following them, especially at Easter time. Peasants routinely uttered prayers and incantations in their everyday speech, and their icon corners, placed diagonally across from the stove in their houses, were the focus of religious rit-ual within the home. Icon corners derived from earlier forms of an-cestor worship. Pagan elements had survived in the religious prac-tices of the Russian peasantry, including a highly developed demonology of spirits and devils who were thought to influence all aspects of human life.[8]

Besides Jesus Christ and Mary, the many saints of the Or-thodox church were objects of veneration and figured in elaborate, stylized iconographic representations. The calendar was filled with the names of hundreds of saints, some of Greek or Bulgarian ori-gin—since Russia had, in the tenth century, adopted Byzantine Christianity—but most of them were Russian. The first to be canon-ized were Boris and Gleb, the martyred sons of Prince Vladimir who had made Christianity the official religion of the new Kievan state, and the last was St. Serafim of Sarov, canonized in 1903.

Canonization always occurred after the saint's death, sometimes after the passage of centuries. Church commissions would examine evidence of sanctity and make recommendations; saints of the entire Orthodox church were canonized by the highest church officials.[9] Miracles constituted a necessary proof of sanctity and could occur during or after a saint's life. The most renowned of all Russian saints, Sergius of Radonezh (1314–1392), exhibited powers to heal the sick and even to resurrect the dead. He also caused the appear-ance of water in the wilderness, a classic miracle, for it associates the saint with founts of energy, of life sources.[10] But a true Orthodox saint also performed miracles after death. Often the followers of a man believed to be a saint during his lifetime would spontaneously flock to his graveside for the thaumaturgic powers of his remains and for his purported ability to act as an intercessor between people and God. Official canonical investigations typically followed this spontaneous popular veneration. There was, as well, a popular belief that the body of a true saint was incorruptible, and many a canonical commission was summoned because the remains of some holy man or other had been unearthed accidentally to reveal an undecayed body. The incorruptibility of remains was neither a canonical requirement for sainthood nor sufficient evidence for canonization; most popular claims of sanctity were rejected by church investigatory commissions.[11] Yet the conviction that the body of a saint does not decay after death continued to be widespread, and this belief provided the basis for Dostoevsky's famous scene of the death of Father Zosima in *The Brothers Karamazov*. The elder Zosima was revered as a saint while he lived and, when a crowd gathered in his small cell to pray before the body and someone asked to open a window, the question was dismissed: "to expect putrefaction and the odour of corruption of the body of so great a saint was an utter absurdity, deserving pity (if not a smile) for the frivolity and lack of faith of the man who asked that question."[12] To the dismay of his followers, decay set in rapidly, forcing the conclusion that Zosima had not been a saint after all.

The relics of a saint were important sites of pilgrimage, but the veneration of saints most frequently took the form of prayers before icons depicting the revered figures, either in scenes from their lives or in stylized portraiture influenced by Byzantine iconography. An especially popular iconographic style showed the saint in the center of the icon and, along its edges, a series of tableaux portraying in consecutive order important moments in his life. Icons themselves were not objects of worship, but it was generally believed that the icon served as a vehicle through which a saint, Mary, or Christ himself could keep in constant touch with this world. Miracle-working icons were direct expressions of God's grace. Icons were kept not only in homes but in churches and shrines as well, and were prominently displayed in religious processions. Besides icons, the saints' *vitae* circulated orally and in writing, detailing their wondrous lives and deaths. Well into the nineteenth century saints' lives were the preferred reading of the people, more so even than the Bible.

6   Russian saints were revered not only for their miracle-working gifts but also for their humility and asceticism, their other-worldliness. However, the category of Russian saints particularly relevant here has been called "the canonized princely passion-sufferers." An impressively large proportion of early Russian saints were princes canonized not for traditional reasons, such as martyrdom for the faith, but for having encountered early deaths simply because they were princes and warriors—for fulfilling their duties as princes. St. Andrei Bogoliubsky, for example, Grand Prince of Suzdal and Vladimir in the twelfth century, was a cruel man, but he offered no resistance to murder by his boyars in 1175 and was ultimately canonized. "Andrew died a saint because he accepted the consequences of becoming a prince," writes Michael Cherniavsky. He died not *for* Jesus Christ but *like* him, accepting violent death because being a prince had brought about an inevitable end. The saintly prince, like the others in the calendar, was not immortal but remained an eternally active protector of Russia. "In this sense, the saintly princes performed the same function after death that they did in life—the protection and care of their subjects and land. They were admitted to this role, however, only because their death was a result of their participation in the Christlike passion possible only for princes; they accept, 'voluntarily,' the death that comes to them by virtue of their being princes, and through this acceptance, they are able to remain princes after death for all time."[13] In this view, political assassination becomes sacrificial and the victim a holy martyr. Thus in 1801 the court assassination of Paul I prompted a local cult, with the faithful coming to venerate his remains.[14] This tradition may partially explain the spontaneous popular adulation of Lenin that followed his wounding in an assassination attempt in 1918, the incident that spurred the development of his cult.

The People and the Little Father

With the gathering of the Russian lands by the Grand Principality of Moscow in the thirteenth through the sixteenth centuries, and the assumption by Prince Ivan the Terrible of the title of tsar (the Russified form of "caesar") in 1547, the cult of saintly princes was gradually transmogrified into the myth of a tsar who was at once secular and yet ruled by divine right. It was analogous to the contemporary

English notion of the king's two bodies, "the Body natural," which was mortal and "subject to all Infirmities that come by Nature or Accident," and the "Body politic," which "cannot be seen or handled, consisting of Policy and Government." The person of the king incorporated both bodies.[15] The Russian concept showed the influence of the sixth-century Byzantine thinker, Agapetus, who held that while the emperor was a man in his sinfulness, he was Godlike in his power: "Though an emperor in body be like all other, yet in power of his office he is like God, Master of all men . . . Therefore, as God, be he never chafed or angry; as man be he never proud."[16] Sixteenth-century Russian monarchs emphasized their divine investment, adding to their burden the awesome charge of acting as intercessors for the souls of their subjects. Until the end of the seventeenth century, tsars spent many of their waking hours praying, visiting monasteries, and participating in other religious rituals, regardless of their personal religious views.

With Peter the Great this changed. He became not tsar but "Imperator" and swept away the religious rituals that had consumed so much of his predecessors' time, along with the old caftans and beards worn by Russian tsars and boyars. From Peter's accession until Nicholas II's abdication in March 1917, Russian empresses and emperors looked and in many respects acted like their Western European counterparts. Most of the Russian monarchs were personally religious but, while an elaborate etiquette was required of those who attended court, court life was for the most part secular in nature. Important moments in the lives of emperors—their births, coronations, namedays, funerals—were observed with magnificent pomp as public holidays.

Notwithstanding the secularization of rulership after Peter, the narod clung to the pre-Petrine conception of the monarch. To them he remained, at least until 1905, their *batiushka* (little father), who was kindhearted, connected with God, and through this divine link bound personally to each of them. Soviet historians call this concept "naive monarchism."[17] We lack the kinds of written sources about peasant conceptions of political power that are available for the political formulations of supporters of the emperors. But peasant petitions, proverbs, folk tales, as well as patterns of peasant revolts, demonstrate a deeply held conviction that the tsar was good, that he desired to give the peasants what they most wanted—land—and

8 that only the tsar's officials and the landowners prevented the tsar from realizing his will. *Tsar' dast* (the tsar will give) ran the popular adage. As Daniel Field has observed, naive monarchism was completely misguided; oppressive serfdom was supported and subsidized by the emperor. Nonetheless, after the emancipation in 1861 that tied peasants to the village commune and forced them to pay the landowner for the land they tilled, the peasants predictably vented their anger on officials and landlords, not on the emperor who had signed the emancipation manifesto.[18] The peasants believed he had meant to give them freedom and land. Some took great personal risks by rebelling or by simply petitioning the little father himself for the expected land and freedom. Petitioners, invariably punished for their efforts, continued to believe that if the tsar only knew of their plight, he would rectify injustice and liberate them.

If the tsar did not do so, there were two alternative explanations: either he was beguiled by advisers and nobles, or he was not the true tsar but an imposter. Peasant revolutions, at least through the end of the eighteenth century, followed pretenders who claimed to be the true tsar. In the Pugachev rebellion of 1773–1775, one eighth of Russia's population—peasants, cossacks, miners, workers, ethnic tribesmen—rose up to slaughter their masters, all in the name of the "true tsar," a pretender claiming to be Peter III. The leader was in reality a cossack named Emelian Pugachev; Peter had been murdered in a palace coup by his wife, the Empress Catherine II (the Great), more than a decade earlier. Calling himself Peter, Pugachev liberated the peasants from bondage and gave them that which they most desired: "Verily did I grant you all these rewards: the land, the fisheries, the forests, the beehives, the beaver-trap lines, and other good things, and also freedom."[19] "The tsar will give," and Peter (Pugachev) gave.

If the true tsar revealed himself among his people, who was sitting on the throne in St. Petersburg? Before that, if the true tsar had a beard, as the Bible demanded, and a traditional embroidered caftan and led his subjects in prayer, who was that giant with the nervous tic in his eye, dressed like a Dutchman, who indulged in every form of immorality and called himself "Petrus Primus Imperator Russorum"? A radical answer to this question was provided by the Old Believers, the schismatics who had broken with the established church after it had imposed changes in ritual in the second half of the seventeenth century. For the Old Believers, Peter the Great was not the tsar at all, but the Antichrist. This was a desperate conclusion, for if the Antichrist were reigning, then the end of the world was at hand. For many Old Believers, the entire Romanov dynasty after Peter represented the Antichrist.[20]

The basis for identifying the true tsar was not the demonstrated personal goodness of the monarch. The tsar, in the traditional peasant conception, was not supposed to be Christlike. In fact, the monarch who figures most prominently in old Russian songs is Ivan the Terrible; the Russian epithet, *groznyi,* connotes not terror but something akin to awe and dread. Ivan IV's long rule (1553–1589) was unusually brutal, not only to the staggering number of boyars and members of other privileged orders whom he had tortured and killed but also to the peasants whom he systematically bound to the lands of his servitors, precipitating an important stage in the development of full serfdom in Muscovy. Nonetheless, historical songs described him as a "just" tsar, terrible in his wrath but good to those who had faith in him.[21] Seventeenth-century folk tales about Ivan depict him as a friend of the peasant and an enemy of the boyar. Peter the Great was also the subject of historical songs and tales. For the Old Believers he may have been the Antichrist, but to many he was the just tsar, loving his people and wreaking vengeance on their oppressors.[22] The peasants maintained their traditional view of the tsar despite Peter's westernization, by simply ignoring the changes he had wrought: "In folklore and in other expressions of naive monarchism, dating from the eighteenth and nineteenth centuries, the monarch is not the emperor; he is still the tsar, and surrounded not by ministers and senators but by boyars and *voevody;* and he rules, as of old, over *Rus',* not Peter's *Rossiiskaia imperiia.*"[23]

"God is on high, the tsar is far away," went a peasant proverb. Yet a striking element in the characterization of the tsar in Russian folk tales was that he was not only sympathetic to the peasant, but was very like him in his style of life. The narod depicted their batiushka as living simply. One typical tale concerns a tsar's son who cannot find an acceptable bride among all the girls invited to his father's feast for that purpose, and so he leaves home to find a wife, first asking his father and mother to bake him some bread to take on

10   the road.[24] In another tale a tsar "steamed himself in his steam bath, and he went with his working people to the lake to bathe."[25]

Russian emperors did not go swimming with peasants, but peasant mythology continued to maintain that tsars wished to live among them. A striking example of this belief was the legend about the death of Alexander I which had gained currency by the time his body had been transported to the capital from Taganrog, where the emperor had died on December 1, 1825. A story was circulated that Alexander was not dead but had chosen to wander the Russian land among his people, suffering with them, and that the corpse sent to St. Petersburg was that of a sailor. The legend gathered strength in the next decade when the belief became current that he had been seen in Siberia as Fedor Kuzmich, a hermit who lived a simple pious life and died in 1864.[26]

Peasant faith in the tsar was a source of exasperation to the populists of the 1870s whose efforts to organize the peasantry in revolt foundered, at least in part, on naive monarchism. The peasants refused to abandon their conviction that the tsar would ultimately deliver them and give them their land. The monarchy was well aware of the people's loyalty and did its best to capitalize on it. Thus in 1898, seventeen years after Alexander II was assassinated by terrorists, the government of Nicholas II sought to continue his myth by publishing a popular biography of the slain emperor, *Tsar Liberator, Tsar Martyr,* an illustrated book designed for the growing number of literate peasants in Russia. It was published in two editions totaling 106,000 copies—enormous for the time—and, in simple language, portrayed the tsar as devoted to his people and as a martyr for that love.[27] The government also attempted to put to use the popular veneration of saints. St. Serafim of Sarov was canonized at the insistence of Empress Alexandra in 1903. This was a time when national movements were straining the bonds holding the empire together. An official publication discussing the canonization made a point of observing that the relic of the saint attracted all nationalities, that he united them all into one family.[28] The peasants tried to use naive monarchism in their own way, most notably to escape harsh punishment after engaging in subversive activities by asserting that they had been misled by a pretender.[29]

The last great public display of naive monarchism was Bloody Sunday, January 9, 1905. On that day many thousands of workers—men, women, and children—marched in slow and ceremonial procession to the Winter Palace in St. Petersburg, to present their grievances to Nicholas II. The petitioners sang prayers and the national anthem, "God Save the Tsar," and carried icons and portraits of the emperor. They were seeking higher wages and better working conditions and, having failed to gain their ends by striking, they appealed directly to the sovereign. Their petition begins with a preamble:

> Here we seek the final salvation. Do not turn Thy help away from Thy people. Lead them out from the mire of lawlessness, poverty and ignorance. Allow them to determine their own future; deliver them from the intolerable oppression of the officialdom. Raze the wall that separates Thee from Thy people and rule the country with them. Thou reignest in order to bring happiness to Thy people, but this happiness is torn out of our hands by Thy officials, and there is nothing left for us but grief and humiliation.

The form was traditional but not the content. The workers asked the sovereign to grant them popular representation: "Russia is too vast, and her needs are too great and manifold to be dealt with exclusively by the bureaucrats. *Popular representation is essential;* it is essential that the people help themselves *and govern themselves.*"[30] The obvious conclusion is that either the workers themselves or their political leaders had used the myth of the tsar to couch revolutionary demands. The autocrat was not even there to receive the petitions, the petitioners were met with volleys of gunfire, and hundreds were massacred by imperial troops.

Bloody Sunday was the prelude to the revolution of 1905 and was viewed by contemporary liberal society as evidence of the growing spiritual and political bankruptcy of the Romanov dynasty. The autocracy was unable to use the narod's naive monarchism to maintain itself after 1905.[31] Most striking is the absence of popular protest after Nicholas' abdication in 1917 and even after his murder the following year.

Naive monarchism was not entirely innocent. It was an accepted formulation for peasant demands utilized by peasants, government authorities, and finally revolutionaries. Those members of the radical intelligentsia who sought to influence rural Russia would have to learn to capitalize on popular perceptions of power. Only two decades after 1905 the new rulers of Russia would demonstrate this im-

12 perative in the cult of Lenin. Some Russian people were waiting for a true deliverer. "They say that Lenin isn't the real one," a worker remarked cryptically to the writer Ivan Bunin in 1918, "they killed the real one long ago."[32] Others were ready to accept Lenin as the "real one" once he had given them land and had been incorporated into their vision of Russia.

Saints and Heroes of Pen and Pistol

The Russian intelligentsia had its own calendar of saints and warrior-heroes and heroines parallel to and separate from those of the narod. The cult of Lenin was the culmination of a gradual process of evolution within the radical intelligentsia. The process began with the Byronic cult of Pushkin, continued with the cult of Chernyshevsky as a radical wing of the intelligentsia looked to a politicization of its writer-heroes, and moved to the simultaneously spectacular and ascetic heroism of the Russian terrorists. In the first years of the twentieth century, when religious concerns pervaded social thought, a current within Bolshevism known as "god-building" sought to found a new religion. Twenty years later, the god-builders Leonid Krasin and Anatoly Lunacharsky were to help deify Lenin by supervising the preservation of his body and the construction of its final resting place in Red Square.

For educated society under Nicholas I (1825–1855), intellectual and political life was dominated by an oppressive censorship, bureaucracy, and police. Under an autocratic regime that allowed for no political activity except that directed by the crown, and no freedom of political expression through writing or even through systematic reading of subversive writings (all literature so deemed was of course banned from Russia), literature played an immense role in the lives of educated Russians. It presented the only vehicle for the public expression of the "truth" in Russia, with poetry its most sublime form. The social and political context in which the thought patterns and value systems of the intelligentsia developed is, of course, extremely complex. To talk in general terms about "an intelligentsia" does not really do justice to the variety of personalities encompassed in such a term and the spectrum of philosophies they espoused. It is, however, possible to delineate some common denominators, to provide something analogous to a "national charac-

ter" for that small community of individuals at mid-century who so
influenced the broader literate society and out of which developed
the late nineteenth-century revolutionary movements.

An intense passion for ideas gripped the intelligentsia of the Russia of Nicholas I. It had a striking propensity to accept new ideas in
their totality.[33] Many were especially receptive to German idealism,
which posited that the moving forces of history were in the realm of
the spirit and were accessible to the discerning spirits and minds of
philosophers who possessed the requisite greatness of soul to commune with the Spirit (*Geist*) of history. You could participate in the
process of historical development without leaving Russia, St. Petersburg, or even your own parlor. The receptivity of the Russian intelligentsia to the idealistic philosophies of Hegel, Fichte, and
Schelling reveals a yearning to escape the reality of their lives,
to blot out the sense of isolation that oppressed them, and to ease
the frustration of their inactivity and ineffectualness by infusing
the spiritual with all the drama and power of the externally perceptible world.

A creator of new ideas, a man with the talent to reach others when
the way to communication was blocked by censors and police and
the depressingly dull provincialism that seemed to characterize
Russian life even in the capital cities—such a man was certain to be
recognized and revered. Such a man was Alexander Pushkin, the
first figure to achieve apotheosis within the broadest circles of the
Russian intelligentsia. The great poet has been an object of love and
worship in Russia from his lifetime (1799–1837) until the present
day. Russians still memorize his poems, gaze at statues depicting his
graceful form and youthful face, and flock to the places he frequented, such as the lyceum at Tsarskoe Selo (renamed Pushkin)
and the apartment on the Moika Canal in Leningrad where he died
at the age of thirty-seven. The Russian love for Pushkin is intensely
personal and alive. "A swarthy youth wandered along the trails
[near the lyceum] and we still cherish the sound of his steps," wrote
the poet Anna Akhmatova in 1911.[34]

One of the creators of the cult of Pushkin was the literary critic,
Vissarion Belinsky. For him, Pushkin gave the Russian national
spirit a vocabulary with which it could express itself in all its painful
reality and glorious potential. Belinsky's literary criticism was
deeply moral, singling out for judgment not simply the writer's work

14   but also his life, politics, morals, and character. This concept of criticism was enthusiastically received in society and turned Belinsky himself into something of a cult figure after his death. It is consonant with Russian receptivity to genius and morality that when Dostoevsky delivered his famous speech on Pushkin to the Society of Lovers of Russian Literature on June 8, 1880, in honor of the unveiling of the big Pushkin monument in Moscow, the great novelist was hailed as "more than a genius" and greeted with shouts of: "You are our saint, you are our prophet."[35] The notion that the writer of genius must lead the life of a moral exemplar was to resonate in the Lenin cult when Lenin's biography was idealized and Lenin's writings were elevated to scripture. Furthermore, we shall see that Lenin wished to be judged and emulated by his followers just as he himself had emulated his own model, N. G. Chernyshevsky.

The three greatest men the world has produced are Jesus Christ, St. Paul, and Nikolai Chernyshevsky, wrote a Russian publicist of the 1860s.[36] Chernyshevsky, a priest's son with theological training, from the provincial town of Saratov on the Volga, was a cult figure for generations of Russian radicals and had a profound effect on Russian revolutionary history. A critic and novelist, Chernyshevsky (1828–1889) lived the life of an ascetic and, during his long term of penal servitude in Siberia, became the great martyr of Russian radicalism.

Chernyshevsky's novel *What Is To Be Done?* (1863) inspired generations of populists and populist sympathizers and, as Lenin later remarked, "plowed me over completely."[37] It is a utopian novel that many critics have dismissed on its artistic merits, which are thin. But it describes a generation of "new people" (revolutionaries) who dedicate their lives to preparing themselves to liberate the oppressed people. They dream of small communes and establish cooperative workshops. The book was a source of inspiration to many young people who were moved by its voluntarism, by the idea that improving *themselves*—by being moral and selfless and strong—they could ultimately transform Russia. It is this message of Chernyshevsky's—the potential of individual human will—coupled with his implacable hatred of liberalism that must have appealed to the young Vladimir Ulianov. The faith in will, so appealing in a world that appeared to harbor no source of salvation, and the shining optimism in the face of a bleak reality made the novel a blueprint for a happy future. It was the inspiration and comfort provided by the Russian saints of pen that brought them the adoration of their contemporaries and of future generations.

Perhaps the greatest appeal of *What Is To Be Done?* to its nineteenth- and early twentieth-century readers is that it described women and men of action. These figures contrasted sharply with the contemporary picture of the typical Russian. Four years before the book was published, I. A. Goncharov published his celebrated novel *Oblomov* (1859), in which the main character represents "the dangerous Russian illness which militated against work, activity, struggle, aspirations—the ideal of sleepy, imperturbable peace, of immobility, of lazy, fruitless holiday daydreaming, of idleness, of lying around in a dressing-coat."[38] The radical critic N. A. Dobroliubov rejoined with an essay in which he took Oblomovka, Goncharov's estate, to be a microcosm of all Russia. "There is a part of Oblomov in every one of us. Who will liberate us from this torpid stagnation and peace?"[39]

Goncharov had, of course, caught something very characteristically Russian. Can it be that the capacity for action ultimately atrophies if it is not given channels for expression? Whatever the reason, the excitement of the possibility of action inspired many members of the intelligentsia and was strengthened by the astounding faith in science that characterized the nihilists of the sixties, the radicals of the seventies and eighties, and the Marxists of the nineties. This was the age of Darwin, Comte, and Marx—that glorious half century of hope in man and faith in the perfectibility of life.

Although the term "nihilism," introduced by Turgenev in *Fathers and Sons* (1862), comes from the Latin word meaning "nothing," the nihilists, influenced by positivism, believed not in nothing but in science. In science could be found the key to action, for it could provide the basis for deciding which course of action to take. This faith in science, called scientific materialism, first came at a time when, after the bitter disappointment in the reforms of the 1860s, there could be no expectation of salvation from the monarchy. After the spectacularly unsuccessful "to the people" movement of 1874, when thousands of young Russians streamed into the countryside hoping to agitate and educate the peasants, only to be beaten, turned over to the authorities, or at best ignored by the understandably suspicious peasants, faith in the narod appeared misplaced as well. Radicals were going to have to rely on their own strength of will and on rigorous social analysis that would come from a scientific approach to society and politics.

The ultimate statement of radical self-reliance was terrorism, which was the path chosen by a small number of Russian revolutionaries at the close of the 1870s. In January 1878 a young woman, Vera Zasulich, shot and wounded the governor of St. Petersburg to avenge his flogging of a jailed political prisoner. The aftermath of the shooting was more striking than the act itself: when tried, Zasulich was acquitted by a jury, making her trial a cause célèbre in Russia and Europe. Among Russian radicals, Zasulich became a heroine of the highest order for her dedication and courage. Her example served to encourage a wave of terrorist acts.

In the three years after the Zasulich pistol shot, terrorists succeeded in killing a number of important government figures. These murders were meant to demonstrate the vulnerability of the leading lights of government, and the daring and strength of the revolutionaries who carried them out. But the climactic act was to be the assassination of Alexander II himself, for only with the murder of the little father would the narod understand the baselessness of their belief in him and develop a consciousness of their power to forge a populist utopia. After a number of unsuccessful attempts by the underground revolutionary organization, the People's Will (Narodnaia Volia), the goal was finally achieved on March 1, 1881. Alexander II was killed by a bomb on a Petersburg street. The regicide was condoned only by the most radical among the intelligentsia. Its main political effect was to usher in a reaffirmation of autocracy and a regime of extreme reaction.

Still, a stream of radical young people, mostly students, continued to believe that terrorism was necessary—the only possible revolutionary act—in an autocracy. One of these terrorists was a retiring, serious, brilliant, gentle young man—Alexander Ilich Ulianov, Lenin's older brother, a prize-winning biology student at St. Petersburg University, hanged in 1887 at the age of twenty-one, for conspiring to assassinate Alexander II. While Soviet historians have predictably canonized Alexander Ilich (just as they have turned all of Lenin's family into a holy family), Alexander Ulianov *was* saint-like, a young man of enormous talent, integrity, courage, selflessness, and humility. He came to join the conspiracy against the emperor reluctantly, for he was by temperament opposed to violence. He became a terrorist because he felt he had no other choice as a morally responsible person.[40]

Although as the twentieth century approached, the hardnosed politics of Marxism appealed to many members of the intelligentsia, many others, including the terrorists, persisted in their perversely rigorous moral code, which forced them to sacrifice themselves for their cause. Zasulich had actively invoked the suffering Christ in a phrase from Ryleev that she found especially inspiring: "There are times, indeed whole epochs, when there can be nothing as beautiful as a crown of thorns."[41] While traditional peasant culture had turned the *victims* of assassination into Christlike figures, the terrorists depicted the *assassins* as the passion-sufferers. This was articulated by Egor Sazonov, who in 1904 assassinated Plehve, minister of internal affairs:

> Remember my youthful dreams about peaceful activity for the good of the unfortunate people. And suddenly a terrible task stood before the shy and peace-loving person that I was. I could not throw it off my shoulders. My conscience, my religion, my gospel, and my God required it from me. Could I disobey? Yes, my dear ones, my revolutionary and socialist beliefs became fused with my religion. *I feel that we socialists are continuing the cause of Christ, who preached brotherly love among people and died for the people as a common criminal.*[42]

Sazonov, Alexander Ulianov, and Vera Zasulich exemplify the Russian saints and heroes of pistol, who were willing to die like Christ for the long-suffering people. For them, Russia was perishing from the paradoxical combination of barrenness and decay, spiritual sterility and social decay, and only spectacular deaths—those of the oppressors and their own, if need be—could affirm life and achieve for the Russian people a shining immortality.

The radical intelligentsia had canonized its saints and heroes from its own ranks. It had also developed its concept of a higher morality and higher truth that all self-conscious Russians must serve. Lenin was to absorb this revolutionary tradition under dramatic cir-

18 cumstances following the death of his brother. He rejected saintly terrorism and chose to be a writer of genius, the author of Bolshevism. Paradoxically, many of his own followers, who had been steeped in this revolutionary tradition, were to turn Lenin into a Christlike martyr after his own death.

The Heavenly City of the Intelligentsia

The period from the late 1890s through the revolution was a time of deep spiritual crisis for the Russian intelligentsia, many of whose most creative members turned to religion to find an identity for themselves and for Russia. "An apocalyptic mood, and that with a pessimistic tinge, supervened in Russia at the end of the nineteenth century," observed the philosopher Nikolai Berdiaev.[43] In no other country in Europe was there such a sweeping literary preoccupation with apocalyptic imagery as in Russia under Nicholas II, particularly in the work of the great symbolist poets of the Silver Age. The most important literary exponent of the apocalyptic theme was Andrei Belyi, the novelist and poet. Like many thinkers of his generation, Belyi sought to link his spiritual regeneration with the creative energies of the narod and thought that the narod could conceive of revolutionary change only in apocalyptic terms.[44] His novel *Petersburg,* published during the first world war, was full of apocalyptic imagery, as was his poem of the revolution, "To the Motherland" (*Rodine*) written in 1917, which ends with a dramatic quatrain:

> And you, fiery element,
> Rage on, consume me with flames,
> Russia, Russia, Russia—
> Messiah of days to come![45]

The most famous of all revolutionary poems is also the most famous Russian poem of the apocalypse and the Second Coming. Alexander Blok's "The Twelve" (1918) describes twelve armed revolutionaries who set out to "give Holy Russia a taste of shot." And with them,

> With gentle step upon the snow,
> Through a pearly snow cloud,
> In a white crown of roses—
> Marches in front—Jesus Christ.[46]

A widely read philosopher of the nineties, N. F. Fedorov (1828–1903) was deeply steeped in this apocalyptic mood.[47] His work appeared to have profoundly influenced Leonid Krasin, the man who supervised the preservation of Lenin's body and construction of the original mausoleum. Fedorov believed that technology, before very long, would find a means to eliminate death and that mankind ultimately would achieve physical immortality. He saw as the Christian duty of the living community to join together and to resurrect the flesh of its ancestors; thus would eternal life be achieved without the terrible judgment day. Resurrection, he said, "is the personal business of each man, as a son and descendant."[48]

The resurrection of Christ had long been a prime concern of Russian sectarians, who had suffered a long history of persecution by the imperial government. At the beginning of this century a number of Russian Marxists sought to tap the sectarians' hatred of the autocracy and win them over to Social Democracy. In 1903, the Russian Social Democratic Labor Party passed a resolution stating that political activity among sectarians was to be intensified.[49] To this end, the Bolsheviks began publishing *Rassvet* (Dawn) in Geneva in 1904. "A Social-Democratic Leaflet for Sectarians," its function was to depict Marxism to Russian sectarians in concepts and language that they would find comprehensible and compelling. Its editor, V. D. Bonch-Bruevich, who was to play an important role in the Lenin cult, was an expert in Russian sectarianism and published widely in the field. It took the expertise and talent of a Bonch-Bruevich to compose the mellifluous and dramatic prose that characterized this remarkable journal. His opening editorial attacked all the Russian tsars for their persecution of sectarians and Old Believers, and stated that the journal's goal was to inform the reader of events occurring in the wide world, in "various corners of our vast motherland, and among the ranks of Sectarians and Schismatics."[50] The first issue of *Dawn* also contained the rousing Polish workers' song "Red Banner." The vision of revolution it contains combines Marx and St. John; it is Communist and apocalyptic. It begins:

> The boundless world is drowned in tears,
> All our life is arduous toil,
> But the inevitable day will dawn,
> The judgment merciless and terrible!

20   And ends:

> Down with tyrants! Away with fetters!
> We need not tread old paths of slavery!
> We will show the world a new path,
> Labor will rule the world!

Bolsheviks also engaged in face-to-face propaganda among sectarians. Nikolai Valentinov, whose comrades were involved in these efforts, recalled that the sectarians completely confounded the Social Democratic propagandists with their "unorthodox" questions. "What is the connection between body and soul?" "Is there another world beyond the visible one, which we cannot know?" "What did Saint John the Divine want to show and teach in Revelations?"[51]

The search for spiritual regeneration that inspired many members of the intelligentsia in fin-de-siècle Russia found a resonance within Bolshevism. It crystallized in the "god-building" movement (*bogostroitel'stvo*). Maxim Gorky was the most prominent literary exponent of the movement, and its main theorist was the young Anatoly Lunacharsky, who was to become the Soviet government's first Commissar of Enlightenment (Education) and one of the main architects of the cult of Lenin.[52]

Lunacharsky became a revolutionary very early, at the age of fifteen. In 1892, at seventeen, he left Russia for Zurich, where he studied philosophy with the "empirocriticist" Richard Avenarius, and then moved to Paris. In 1898 he went to Moscow where he became a member of a Social Democratic group, was arrested shortly thereafter, and exiled to Kaluga for a brief period and then to Vologda where he befriended the philosopher A. A. Bogdanov (Malinovsky) whose sister he married.[53] Following Bogdanov, at the time the most prominent Bolshevik within Russia, Lunacharsky joined the Bolshevik faction of the Russian Social Democratic Labor Party, and in 1904, not long after the termination of his exile, he once again left the country for Europe, this time to work with Lenin who came to Paris to meet him.[54]

Lunacharsky's interests tended toward the philosophical and the aesthetic; in later years he was to refer to himself as a "poet of the revolution."[55] He was passionately interested in art but, as a Marxist (he was careful to point out), was also concerned with religion.[56] For Lunacharsky, religion was the key to the realization of human potential, and socialism was bound to shape a new religion, one that would be totally humanistic. Marxist religious faith was to be a faith in future man, man unfettered by the shackles of class and individualism. In 1904 he first articulated the vision of a socialist religion, a deification of human potential: "The faith of an active human being is a faith in mankind of the future; his religion is a combination of the feelings and thoughts which make him a participant in the life of mankind and a link in that chain which extends up to the superman ... to a perfected organism ... If the essence of any life is self-preservation, then a life of beauty, goodness and truth is self-realization."[57] In 1908 and 1911 he published a two-volume work, *Religiia i sotsializm* (Religion and Socialism) in which he expounded his theory of god-building.

Lunacharsky called Karl Marx one of Judaism's "precious gifts to mankind," along with Isaiah, Christ, St. Paul, and Spinoza.[58] Feuerbach and Marx after him had "helped human consciousness to become human religion." Lunacharsky was deeply impressed by Feuerbach's *Essence of Christianity* and felt that its author had caught the heart of religion, unlike Plekhanov, who had caught "only its clothing."[59] While the Bolsheviks emphasized the creative powers of the human will, rejecting Plekhanov's more traditionally deterministic view of history, their philosophy was no different from Plekhanov's arid rationalism. Marx had bid his followers to change the world, but this they could accomplish only as a result of the religious impulse, for religion was the emotional bond that linked human beings together.[60] And religion provided the only prism through which the world could be understood: "religion is enthusiasm and 'without enthusiasm it is not given to people to create anything great.' "[61] Bolshevism was to create a new religion, with a god who was human, who was all future humanity. "Scientific socialism," Lunacharsky wrote in 1907, "is the most religious of all religions, and the true Social Democrat is the most deeply religious of all human beings."[62] When we consider the wonder of human genius, when we witness "the miracle of the victory of human reason and will over nature," he remarked, "do we not feel how the god born between the ox and the donkey is becoming strong?"[63]

Lunacharsky's eschatology promised a universal "development of the human spirit into an 'All-Spirit.' " This he called the process of god-building, and the "greatest and most decisive act" in that pro-

22   cess was to be revolution.[64] The Marxist religion was even destined to overcome death, in his view, through its capacity to link human beings to future generations, through man's perception of "the universal connectedness of life, of the all-life which triumphs even in death."[65]

Lunacharsky's brother-in-law, A. A. Bogdanov, against whom Lenin wrote an angry book entitled *Materialism and Empiriocriticism* (1909), was also a proponent of god-building. He saw that task as one of creating a living community of people which would transcend individualism and achieve immortality. Whether or not Bogdanov had been directly influenced by Fedorov's writings on physical immortality, he believed that eternal life could be achieved through transfusions of blood; experiments in transfusions resulted in his own death in 1928.

Lenin attacked Bogdanov not for his religious views but for his epistemology, which indicated that reality was dependent on our perception of it and was not absolute and independent. But the fight between Bogdanov and Lenin was intensely political as well. Between 1907 and 1910 Bogdanov was the center of a Bolshevik group that was influenced by syndicalism, inspired by the ideas of god-building, and above all not centered on Lenin.[66] Leonid Krasin, at the time an electrical engineer who manufactured bombs, smuggled arms, and raised money for the Bolsheviks, was an important member of this group. Threatened by Bogdanov's circle, Lenin broke with it and, after many attacks on its philosophy, politics, and on god-building, he helped to destroy it.

Lenin's shrill attacks on the Bogdanov circle were largely political. But apart from this, he was enraged by god-building, especially as expressed by his friend Gorky. Lenin wrote Gorky two letters in which he reminded the writer that the god of the god-builders is no different from any other god; the belief in every god is "necrophilia," he wrote.[67] Gorky's god-building seemed even more dangerous than traditional religion because it was more difficult to expose and oppose.

God-building—and the later immortalization of Lenin—sought a true deification of man. This Promethean impulse is implicit in Marxism, which claims that conscious and free men will be the creators of a new world, and is implicit as well in the Russian revolutionary tradition, which was alternately fused with a faith in the

greatness of the Russian narod and in the revolutionaries themselves, who were to transform Russia and, ultimately, the world according to a vision of equality. Marxism, Russian revolutionary
thinking, and profound apocalyptic stirrings all help to explain the
emergence of the god-building movement. It is an irony of history
that the god-builders acted to deify human genius in the person of
Lenin, for whom all religion was anathema and god-building particularly repugnant, and that Lenin should have become, by the efforts
of some of his oldest friends, the man-god of Communism.

2 Vladimir Ilich Ulianov-Lenin

Lenin lived only fifty-three years and died not long after assuming the premiership of Soviet Russia. He bore a peculiar relationship to the symbolic figure celebrated by his cult biography, a gospel located at the center of sacred party history. Some pieces of the idealized cult persona coincided with the real Vladimir Ilich Ulianov-Lenin; others did not. And then the symbol itself went through many shapes and guises: the standard cult figure of the mid-twenties—the martyred hero of genius—was quite distinct from the benign dimpled gentleman in soft focus that was peddled by the managers of the Lenin cult during the Khrushchev era. The real Lenin was neither hero nor gentleman, but he was a genius in revolutionary politics.

Lenin the cult figure was later lauded for his enormous modesty that prevented him from tolerating any manifestations of a cult during his lifetime. This is partly true and partly false. Lenin did hate to hear himself lauded in odes and speeches, disliked being the recipient of flattery and extravagant gifts, and avoided photographers, painters, and sycophants. But this was not really because of his modesty, although he was a man of modest tastes. His concept of the rewards of power was simply different from that offered by the frequently empty conventions of ceremonial praise. Lenin was neither greedy nor vain; he coveted neither material possessions nor the luxury of enjoying the knowledge that tens of millions of people might admire an inflated version of his biography. He was supremely self-confident and had no need of such vanities. What he sought throughout his life was the means to impose his will on a populace that bore little resemblance to him in temperament or talent. As revolutionary and head of state, he demanded from his followers submission in the form of obedience, dedication, and hard work; ritualized praise was, for Lenin, not an acceptable alternative expression of political submission.

One might therefore conclude that the real Lenin had no bearing on the generation of the symbol around which a cult developed after his death. Paradoxically, this too is false. The object of his cult—an immortal Lenin who personifies the Communist Party and is the author of the guiding line to socialism—is the reflection of Lenin's conception of himself evident in his writings, in the organization of the party he founded and led, and in his style of leadership. Lenin had no intention of turning himself into a cult figure, but the party and government that created the cult did bear the profound imprint of his personality and life experiences.

Volodia Ulianov

Vladimir Ilich Ulianov was born on April 10, 1870, in Simbirsk, the Volga town that was the birthplace of Ivan Goncharov, author of *Oblomov*. It was "a picture of slumber and stagnation," Goncharov wrote in 1888. "Thus one wants to fall asleep, looking at this calm, at the sleepy windows with lowered blinds, at the sleepy physiognomy of the people sitting in the houses or chancing to be met in the street. We don't have anything to do, all of these people think, yawning and looking lazily at you."[1] But sleepiness and laziness had no place in the Ulianov household.

Vladimir's father, Ilia Nikolaevich Ulianov, was a hard-working man whose career testifies to the opportunities for social and economic advancement available to men of talent and perseverance in postemancipation Russia. Ilia's mother was of Kalmyk ancestry (a Mongolian ethnic group, hence Vladimir's slanted eyes and high cheekbones); his father was a serf who had managed to buy his freedom and subsequently earned his living as a tailor. Thanks to an older brother who worked to pay for his schooling, Ilia received a good education. He became a teacher of mathematics and science, and later an inspector of schools in Simbirsk province. With each career advancement came the privileges and titles in accordance with the table of ranks that governed the imperial civil service. By 1874—when little Vladimir was four years old—Ilia Nikolaevich had become director of schools, with the corresponding rank of Actual State Councilor and the title of Excellency. With this rank the senior Ulianov attained hereditary nobility, which prompted Lenin, thirty years later, to refer to himself as a child of the landed gentry.[2] Vladimir's mother, Maria Alexandrovna Blank, who was at least partly of German origin, came from a far more refined family than her husband; her father was a physician who retired to become a landowner in the region of Kazan.

During much of Vladimir's childhood, the Ulianovs lived in a modest but pleasant house with a large yard, located in a respectable neighborhood. Though the family was not wealthy, it was comfortable. Ilia Nikolaevich employed a nurse, a cook and her daughter, an errand man, and occasional workers to help with the garden and orchard. Summers were spent in Kokushkino, Maria Alexandrovna's family estate not far from Kazan, where swimming, boating, hiking, and similar pleasures engaged the Ulianov children.

Volodia, as Vladimir was called, was the noisiest of the six Ulianov children, a redheaded, chubby, and rowdy little boy who craved and got attention. He was also a domineering child who teased his siblings and cousins, thought up new games, dictated the rules, took charge. He was an accomplished athlete—not typical for a Russian youth of his class or time. He was a formidable swimmer, skater, and cyclist, and loved to hike and row. He later became an excellent hunter. Volodia was an exemplary student, but from his father received little praise for his accomplishments. The eldest daughter, Anna Ilinichna, later wrote that her father had been right; the boy's consistently superior grades and his enormous self-confidence made the father's lack of praise a "healthy corrective."[3]

His parents loved Volodia, although the memoirist Valentinov asserts that his older brother Alexander (Sasha) was the darling of the family. "Alexander was revered as a special creature," wrote Valentinov. "His oldest sister loved him with a kind of hysterical love." But Volodia was the favorite of the children's nurse, Varvara Grigorevna, who used to say that all the Ulianov children were gold, "but my Voloden'ka is a diamond."[4] Evidence on the relationship between Sasha and Volodia is scanty. Soviet biographers and tour guides in the restored Ulianov home in Simbirsk (now Ulianovsk) are fond of repeating that Volodia greatly admired his older brother and wanted to imitate him in everything. That may be but, according to their sister Anna, the feelings were not mutual. Sasha apparently confessed to her that he disliked those features of Vladimir's character which "cut": his arrogance, his tendency to mock, and his insolence.

The two brothers were very different in character and, Sasha told his sister, they were not at all close.[5] Among the other differences separating the introspective, gentle zoology student from his younger brother was the older boy's interest in political and social questions, to which Vladimir gave little thought. Vladimir's greatest love was literature, which along with Latin was his favorite subject at school. He especially loved the novels of Turgenev, which he read many times over and knew thoroughly. Years later Vladimir could still quote phrases from *Rudin* or *Smoke,* and his frequent references to their characters seemed to assume they were well-known to everyone.[6] His intimate relationship with Turgenev's fiction was hardly unusual in his milieu; indeed, it is a striking illustration of the Russian intelligentsia's view of literature dominating life. This tendency to imbue literary creations with all the living import of actual experience was to have an important bearing on Lenin's later development as a revolutionary and Marxist. But that was all in the future in the summer of 1886, the last the boys spent together in Kokushkino. Anna recalled that Volodia paid no attention to the stack of books on political economy that Sasha brought with him from St. Petersburg. In the room they shared, Sasha read Marx while his sixteen-year-old brother lay on his cot rereading Turgenev.[7]

The political views of the Ulianov family are a particularly delicate issue for Soviet biographers of Lenin attempting to explain why Volodia Ulianov of Simbirsk became the greatest revolutionary the world has ever known. The recent cult of Lenin has idealized his parents and siblings, requiring Soviet biographers to posit in the Ulianov family a general sympathy for radical politics. Some have argued that Ulianov senior expressed support for revolutionary activity and terrorism, and even insist that the Ulianov family welcomed political dissidents exiled to Simbirsk. Ilia Nikolaevich was certainly no reactionary but, a loyal servant of Alexander II, he believed reform should be generated within the autocratic system.[8] His eldest daughter Anna was most emphatic in insisting that, because

28 of his position, Ilia Nikolaevich did not—and could not—befriend political exiles. He was totally opposed to terrorism and deeply chagrined by the assassination of Alexander II in 1881. "He had never been a revolutionary," did not discuss political issues with his children, and if anything, she wrote, wished to "protect" them from revolutionary ideas.[9] In this he succeeded as long as he lived. But in January 1886, at age fifty-four, he died of a cerebral hemorrhage. The following fall Sasha joined a conspiracy against Alexander III; his role in it was the manufacture of bombs. The police learned of the planned assassination just before it was to occur, and on March 1, 1887, Sasha, with some thirty other people, was arrested. He had hidden his brief involvement with terrorism from the family, and so his arrest came as a violent shock to his mother and brothers and sisters, who were still mourning the death of Ilia Nikolaevich.[10]

At his trial, Alexander Ulianov displayed a nobility of spirit noticeable to all present (and even to the emperor, who read the trial transcript). He did everything he could to take as much blame upon himself as possible in order to spare his comrades and, after his death sentence, refused his mother's repeated entreaties that he beg the emperor for mercy. In the end he took pity on her and asked for clemency, although he made it apparent in the letter that he did not deserve it.[11] His mind seemed quite clear that he should sacrifice his life to the struggle for freedom in Russia, and his only deep regret appeared to be the pain he was causing his mother. The timing of his turn to terrorism—so soon after his father's death—would suggest that he was in part courting death. He was hanged on the morning of May 8, 1887, along with four other conspirators.

The Power of the Pen

At the time of Sasha's execution, Vladimir was studying for his final examinations at the gimnazium. His superior academic performance (he received the highest grade in all subjects but one—logic) demonstrated his enormous powers of concentration and ability to sustain productive energy in times of emotional stress. At graduation, the director of the gimnazium, Fedor Kerensky (father of the future head of the 1917 Provisional Government) awarded Vladimir a gold medal. Kerensky also wrote on his behalf a glowing recommendation to the University of Kazan. In view of the fact that Vladimir's

brother had just been executed for attempted regicide, this was an
act of integrity and kindness which contrasted sharply with the rejection of the bereaved Ulianov family by many members of Simbirsk society.

In the absence of trustworthy sources, conclusions on Vladimir's
reaction to his brother's death must be speculative, but there is no
reason to read Vladimir's success at school as an indication of cal-
lousness. Indeed, the lack of intimacy between the two brothers may
have made the loss of Sasha even more painful for Vladimir. Apparently he had not understood Sasha, characterizing him as a
withdrawn scientist forever peering into a microscope, and may well
have felt some measure of regret and even self-hate for his own nar-
rowness of vision. Vladimir tried to achieve a fuller understanding
of his dead brother by reading some of Alexander's favorite books.
Thus the stage was set for the decisive encounter between the future
Lenin and one of Sasha's most beloved novels, Chernyshevsky's
What Is To Be Done?

Vladimir had in fact read the book three years earlier but, he admitted later, had understood it only superficially. Given the book's
popularity among the young, he probably would have rediscovered
it on his own; yet the circumstances in which he now read it
prompted him to ponder it intensely. He pored over its pages, fired
by the conviction that the "new" people Chernyshevsky described
really did exist, that his very own brother, unbeknownst to him, had
been one of them, and that he could and must be one of them as
well. The book "captivated my brother, and captivated me," he later
told Valentinov. "It transformed me completely" because, Lenin
explained, Chernyshevsky demonstrated that the life of a revolutionary was the only possible one for a person of integrity, and "he
also showed—even more importantly—what a revolutionary should
be like, what his principles should be, how he must achieve his
goals, what methods and means he should employ to realize
them."[12] Sensitized by his brother's death, young Ulianov found in
What Is To Be Done? an animate world that he was able to experience as profoundly and intensely as he did real life—perhaps even
more intensely.

Sasha's execution also exerted a more immediate and practical influence on Vladimir's future: it caused an interruption of his legal
studies that led to four years of enforced idleness during which the

30   young man was able to articulate his own concept of the ideal Russian revolutionary. He had begun his studies in the juridical faculty at the University of Kazan in the fall of 1887 and, shortly thereafter, because of Alexander's reputation as a terrorist—and a martyr—was invited to join a revolutionary group that, in December of that year, took part in a student protest against the university administration. Vladimir was arrested, jailed for two days, expelled from the university, and then ordered to Kokushkino where he remained for almost a year. While living at Kokushkino, Vladimir Ilich combed the shelves of its library, locating the volumes of Chernyshevsky's journal *Sovremennik* (The Contemporary) Sasha had read not long before. Vladimir read them passionately, taking extensive notes. With his astonishing capacity for total intellectual engagement, he absorbed Chernyshevsky's essays on Belinsky, Hegel, philosophical materialism, aesthetics, Mill's political economy, and the peasant question. Lenin later said it was these essays that first interested him in economic questions, especially those dealing with rural Russia. Vladimir Ilich was so taken with Chernyshevsky that he got hold of his address and wrote him a letter, but received no response. He was greatly saddened to hear of the author's death the following year.[13]

"Chernyshevsky's encyclopedic knowledge," Lenin later said, "the brilliance of his revolutionary views, his merciless polemical talent—conquered me."[14] Ulianov was deeply impressed by Chernyshevsky's unyielding detestation of liberalism, by his profound commitment to revolution, by his voluntarism and faith in the ability of the new men and women to realize that revolution for the sake of the suffering Russian people. He sensed in Chernyshevsky a revolutionary optimism, a conviction that the promised day of revolution was within sight and could be reached through the will of conscious revolutionaries. Most important, Ulianov was awed by the power of Chernyshevsky's pen—which enabled Chernyshevsky to communicate his revolutionary faith to his readers. This power above all else made Chernyshevsky the model for Vladimir Ilich's career as a revolutionary. He was to be a revolutionary who would inspire, persuade, and mobilize by the written word.

This was hardly a surprising decision for the youth who saw Turgenev's characters as more real than life and who tried to understand the one real revolutionary he had known—his brother—by investigating the fictional heroes on whom he believed Sasha modeled himself. Those models, and especially Chernyshevsky himself, were now Vladimir's; their revolutionary style and commitment had become his own; and like them, he would conquer souls by the force of his pen and through the example of his own life. For Vladimir Ulianov, the pen was mightier than the bomb.

Routes of Revolution

Cult biographers of Lenin represent Russian radicalism in the 1880s as consisting of two separate wings, terrorism and Marxism. Vladimir Ulianov is incorrectly depicted as marching resolutely toward the Marxists. Not only did his route take him in a quite different direction, but it did so almost inevitably, given the fluidity that characterized the Russian revolutionary movement in the 1880s—a time when the socioeconomic fabric of Russia was rapidly changing. The most important of these changes was the steady growth of capitalism and industrialization in Russia during the 1880s and the attendant emergence of a working class, numbering some 1.3 million in 1887.[15] At the same time, an unprecedented growth in population and the deleterious effects of the unjust land distribution that had accompanied emancipation combined to push the Russian peasantry, idealized by populists for its revolutionary potential, into a seemingly hopeless economic and spiritual decline.

Despite the massive police crackdown following the People's Will's assassination of Alexander II in 1881, dedicated men and women repeatedly attempted to resurrect its spirit in movements that resembled it in a reliance on terrorism and conspiratorial organization. Confronted with the stark contrast between a decaying peasantry and the burgeoning urban proletariat, the Narodovoltsy[16] gradually came to pin their hopes for revolution on industrial workers who, however small in number, tended to be concentrated in large factories and were therefore receptive to organization and propaganda. A further influence on this change in outlook was volume one of Karl Marx's *Capital,* translated into Russian in 1872 and widely read.[17]

Despite other differences, the Narodovoltsy were united in their faith in the efficacy of terror, and even more by their conviction that violent revolution was essential. Freedom could never be achieved within the autocratic system. Only a conspiratorial organization of

32 dedicated revolutionaries could overthrow that system. Perhaps their most salient characteristic was an enormous voluntarism, a profound faith in their own abilities—their own will—to create in Russia the opportunity for total social equality. Alexander Ulianov had held these convictions and so, following him, apparently did Vladimir Ulianov.

Narodovolchestvo was not the only revolutionary route for radical youth at the end of the 1880s. Coexisting with the People's Will were groups of Social Democrats who considered themselves to be fully Marxist. Like the Narodovoltsy, Russian Social Democrats believed in the necessity of a political struggle, and that the working class should be educated to consciousness and relied upon to help carry out that struggle. Russian Social Democrats who followed Georgy Plekhanov, the emigré Russian Marxist theoretician, envisioned a two-phase revolutionary process: in the first, all anti-autocratic elements of society would join to topple the autocracy; in the second, the working class would declare its opposition to all others and work steadily toward a socialist revolution. Objective, scientifically determined processes, said the Social Democrats, ensured that the working class would develop the requisite sociopolitical consciousness to effect a socialist revolution and, ultimately, Communism. This Marxian faith in the laws of historical development contrasted sharply with the voluntarism of the Narodovoltsy. Social Democrats rejected terror as a political tactic. They tended to see tutoring workers in Marxism as their immediate task and concentrated on making contact with workers' circles and on publishing and distributing Marxist literature. Because of these relatively apolitical activities, Social Democrats suffered a good deal less at the hands of the police than did the Narodovoltsy. How could men who sought out workers on Sunday afternoons to lecture them on astronomy or Darwin and read to them from *Capital* worry the *okhrana* (police) officers who had to contend with the real danger of terrorist attacks on bureaucrats and on the person of the Most Gracious Sovereign?

Even though Plekhanov strove, in his 1885 pamphlet *Our Differences,* to depict the two main revolutionary tendencies of the period as diametrically opposed, the Russian revolutionary movement of the late 1880s was in fact characterized by an extraordinary complexity, diversity, and fluidity. Radical circles often contained members who differed wildly on major issues (the day when "factionalism" was impermissible in revolutionary brotherhoods was still far away). Radicals moved from circle to circle, changed their minds on basic issues, and responded to new polemics and new realities as they learned about them.

The biggest difference between Social Democrats and Narodovoltsy was one of tone. The sense of urgency, of voluntarism, and the commitment to the selective use of terror—all these were alien to the Social Democrats. They trusted in the historical inevitability of socialism and eschewed terror as romantic, foolishly adolescent, and counterproductive. But this condemnation of terrorists was permeated with a profound ambivalence. Those brave men and women of the late 1870s who had exposed themselves to the ultimate risk continued to inspire virtually all Russian radicals. Abandoning faith in heroic terrorism meant, for most Social Democrats, shedding the ideals of their youth. This was the case with Vladimir Ilich Ulianov. In a famous passage in his own *What Is To Be Done?* (1902), a statement his wife, Nadezhda Krupskaia, would later call autobiographical, he expressed a deep attachment to the People's Will: "Many of them [Russian Social Democrats] had begun their revolutionary thinking as Narodovoltsy. Almost all had, in their early youth, enthusiastically worshiped the terrorist heroes. To abandon the captivating impression of that heroic tradition required a struggle."[18]

During the fall and winter of 1888–89, Ulianov first studied the work of Karl Marx. He read *Capital* as well as Plekhanov's influential *Our Differences,* presumably from the point of view of a Narodovolets convinced of the necessity of a violent revolution through terror.[19] Although these powerful Marxist texts stimulated Ulianov, much as the works of Turgenev and Chernyshevsky had in the past, he does not seem to have tried to strengthen his Marxist connections or to abandon the convictions of a Narodovolets. He did not, for example, make contact with the leading Marxists then residing in Kazan, Nikolai Fedoseev and M. L. Mandelstam.[20]

In Samara, to which he moved with his family in 1889, Vladimir Ilich became involved with a group of Narodovoltsy led by A. P. Skliarenko.[21] At the same time he continued his efforts to complete his legal studies interrupted by his expulsion from the University of Kazan. In 1890, the Ministry of Education granted him permission to take the examinations required for a degree in

34 jurisprudence, which he did the following year (passing every subject with the highest grades), whereupon he took up the practice of law while continuing to devote his energies to the calling he had found during his years of enforced idleness.

V. V. Vodovozov, a St. Petersburg acquaintance of Sasha's who frequented the Ulianov household in 1891–92, recalls that Vladimir had embraced Marx's writings with great enthusiasm and considered himself a confirmed Marxist: for Vladimir "Marxism was not a conviction, but a religion."[22] He was also a self-assured and independent thinker; this manifested itself in his relations with the revolutionary circle of which he was a member during this period. Vladimir Ilich was the "undisputed authority" within that circle, all of whose members worshiped him for his intellectual abilities and accomplishments. His knowledge of history and political economy was impressive. He read German, English, and French, was a skilled debater, and did not allow any concern for the self-esteem of those around him to prevent him from showing off his skill and knowledge, in particular his remarkable mastery of Marxist literature.[23]

However, Ulianov was still a "transitional Marxist."[24] He combined faith in Marxism's capacity to explain the world with a belief in his own ability to change it—a legacy of the Narodovoltsy tradition. What is clear from his role in the Samara circle is that he had the power to communicate his beliefs to others, to overwhelm them with facts supporting his positions on social and economic development, and to convince them of his own unusual talents as a revolutionary. Vodovozov, a liberal whose memoir of Lenin is in general not complimentary, nonetheless recalled that "even then I was convinced—and openly spoke about this—that Ulianov's role would be significant."[25]

During the Samara years Vladimir Ilich became the head of the Ulianov family. His mother, his sisters, and even his brother-in-law (Anna's husband) "all but prayed" to the twenty-one-year-old Vladimir, whom they had come to regard as a genius.[26] The reverence in which Sasha had been held by Maria Alexandrovna and her daughters when he was alive and the subsequent transfer of similar feelings to Vladimir, the next oldest boy, hints at a tendency of the family's women to imbue one of its male members with the status of a "star." Vladimir assumed that role after Sasha's death and never lost it. The child and adolescent who had always yearned for attention and had never received sufficient reinforcement from his father for his excellent work at school, who had seen Sasha become the scientist, the moralist, and finally the revolutionary of the family, was now, as a young lawyer and radical, the adored center of the Ulianov household.

The undoubted satisfaction Vladimir received from his new role may well have been mixed with a measure of guilt or anxiety, for he had gained the desired adulation of his family over the dead bodies of his father and brother. When we later consider Lenin's ambivalence about the praise heaped upon him as chairman of the Council of People's Commissars, praise that helped lay the earliest structural foundations for the postrevolutionary Lenin cult, we would do well to remember the grim circumstances under which he attained the leadership of his own family.

Determined to be for others what Chernyshevsky had been for him—an exemplar of genius—young Ulianov had taken giant strides toward his goal since his brother's execution. Within both his family and his small circle of radical sympathizers, he was the acknowledged leader. Ulianov could instill his voluntaristic revolutionary faith in others. But if he were to prove himself within the movement as a whole, he had to leave Samara, which had no industry, no proletariat, not even a university. So, in the fall of 1893, when his younger brother Dmitry entered Moscow University and the rest of the family moved to Moscow with him, Vladimir Ilich left for St. Petersburg, the center of Russian Social Democracy during the 1890s.

The St. Petersburg circle Ulianov joined shortly after his arrival in the capital was led by Stepan Radchenko and Herman Krasin, both students at the Technological Institute, and included among its members Gleb Krzhizhanovsky, future chairman of Gosplan (the Soviet State Planning Commission), and Nadezhda Konstantinovna Krupskaia, whom Lenin was eventually to marry. The Radchenko circle was led exclusively by members of the intelligentsia, and its conspiratorial organization was reminiscent of the old People's Will.[27] At the same time, however, the group defined itself as Marxist and practiced, in the words of Krzhizhanovsky, "a specific cult of Marx." Krzhizhanovsky later recalled with some embarrassment how in 1893 he assumed that no one could have a sensible approach toward politics without having read *Capital* two or three times. He

36 and his friends expected this not only of the intelligentsia but also of the workers with whom they were trying (with little success) to establish political ties.[28]

One of Ulianov's first recommendations to the Radchenko circle was that it include among its activities discussions of papers presented by its members.[29] The role of revolutionary writer was to be his path, and it was as a writer that Ulianov made a name for himself within the small but rapidly growing ranks of Russian Social Democrats. The aspiring revolutionary critic quickly succeeded in gaining the attention of his fellow radicals with his first major work, *Who Are the "Friends of the People" and How Do They Fight Against the Social Democrats?* (1894), an anti-populist polemic. Ulianov's temperament and style, simultaneously contentious and pedantic, were perfectly suited to polemics. He subjected the populists to his own special brand of derisive sarcasm coupled with a barrage of detailed information about the Russian peasant economy—a technique reminiscent of Chernyshevsky's essays.

His status within the movement was greatly enhanced during the summer of 1895 when, during his first trip to Europe, he made the acquaintance of the two great luminaries of Russian Social Democracy, Pavel Akselrod and Georgy Plekhanov. In the fall of 1895, Lenin first met Iuly Martov, future leader of the Mensheviks, and soon after they formed a new revolutionary organization, the "Group of Social Democrats," which included Krzhizhanovsky, Radchenko, and Nadezhda Krupskaia. It engaged in agitation among St. Petersburg workers. On December 8, 1895, most of its members were arrested and jailed, including Vladimir Ilich.

Lenin spent two years in a St. Petersburg jail and three more in exile in western Siberia, continuing his earlier pattern of productivity when in enforced isolation. When his exile terminated, Lenin left for Europe to publish *Iskra* (The Spark), a newspaper that he and Martov hoped would bring cohesion to an increasingly fragmented Russian Social Democratic movement.

A Lesson in Love and Leadership

His *Iskra* years (1900–1903) completed the period in which Vladimir Ilich became Lenin, the acknowledged leader of the Bolshevik faction of the Russian Social Democratic Labor Party. In 1900, however, he was only a junior member of the editorial board of *Iskra*, to be published in Munich and smuggled into Russia. The other junior members were Martov and Alexander Potresov; the senior trio included Akselrod, Vera Zasulich, and the grand old man of Russian Social Democracy, Plekhanov, a man whom Ulianov revered.

Ulianov's belief in Plekhanov as the ideal revolutionary teacher led to a personal debacle that contributed significantly to Lenin's concept of revolutionary politics. From the beginning of the *Iskra* board-organizing conference held near Geneva in August 1900, Plekhanov behaved in a petty, autocratic manner, insisting he have his way on each issue. His young admirers, Potresov and Ulianov, were offended. The full measure of Plekhanov's arrogance only became apparent, however, when he demanded a dominant position on the editorial board by threatening to resign, thus intimidating his comrades into giving him an extra vote on all editorial questions. Now effectively editor-in-chief, Plekhanov began to order everyone about, while the two "youngsters" looked on, dumbfounded.

Ulianov and Potresov were devastated. A week later Ulianov wrote:

> Had we not been so in love [with Plekhanov] . . . we would not have experienced such a crash in the literal sense. This was the most severe, the most painfully severe, painfully brutal life lesson. Two young comrades "courted" an older comrade because of their great love for him, and, all of a sudden he injects into this love an atmosphere of intrigue, and makes them feel—not like younger brothers—but like idiots who are being led around by the nose, like pawns that can be moved around at will . . . And the enamored youth receives a bitter lesson from the object of his love: to regard all persons "without sentimentality," to keep a stone in his sling.

"Blinded by our love," he added, "we had actually behaved like *slaves,* and to be a slave is a humiliating thing."[30] Usually silent about his emotions, Ulianov described his feelings of loss on the morning after Plekhanov's coup as completely disorienting.

> I simply could not make myself believe it (just as you cannot make yourself believe it when you have just learned that someone close to you has died)—could it be I, the fervent worshiper of Plekhanov, who now speaks of him with such malice and walks with clenched

teeth and a devilish chill in my soul to tell him cold and sharp words . . . ? Is this really not some horrible dream? Is this reality?[31]

While Vladimir Ulianov's genuinely traumatic reaction may be somewhat out of proportion to Plekhanov's insult, it can be explained both by his personal history and by the timing of the confrontation. Plekhanov was the last of several heroes whom, like Chernyshevsky, Vladimir had worshiped at a distance, and the only one he had met. Possibly some residue of unexpressed love for the others had inflated his already strong feelings for Plekhanov, making the rejection even more painful. Perhaps the sense of loss brought back some of the feelings he had experienced as an adolescent when both his father and his brother died without having given Vladimir the reassurance and expressed admiration he evidently wanted. (Even Chernyshevsky died without answering the letter Vladimir had sent him the previous year.)

The "bitter lesson" Ulianov learned from Plekhanov's abuse was part of a larger course life was teaching him. He was developing an approach to politics based on the absence of trust. The bourgeoisie could not be trusted as allies in the impending overthrow of the autocracy. Heresies within the movement had badly shaken his faith in the Social Democratic intelligentsia. Finally, by 1902 Lenin had lost faith in the revolutionary capacities of the Russian proletariat. While the Plekhanov episode alone did not inspire Ulianov's broad skepticism, it undoubtedly quickened it. But that trauma was only a part of a general crisis of faith that he experienced during the first two years of the twentieth century. The result was predictable: Ulianov moved from disillusionment to self-reliance, not to despair. This faith in himself became the lodestar of his revolutionary path.

Armed with Marx and a pen, Ulianov grew into Lenin. He no longer looked to others for leadership, but provided it himself as the author of a cogent revolutionary theory and the head of a revolutionary party. In 1902, he expounded his convictions in a dry, polemical pamphlet that earned him a position of independent leadership within the Social Democratic Party. He named it after Chernyshevsky's *What Is To Be Done?*

Its main point provides the foundation of Lenin's theory of party organization. Lenin declared that the working class could never develop a revolutionary consciousness independent of a revolutionary party, that in its absence the proletariat would develop a "trade-union consciousness," which would seek only to fulfill economic needs. All of the other elements of his political construct flow from this premise, which violates Marx's fundamental conviction that the proletariat would inevitably act in its own best interests, that it would take only time for the industrial proletariat to develop a revolutionary consciousness and rise up against its bourgeois oppressors. According to Lenin, the proletariat was dependent on the party, which had to play a dynamic role in the revolutionary process by providing theory, consciousness, organization, leadership, and strategy for the struggle. The party would need a tight, centralized organization of professional revolutionaries. "Give us an organization of revolutionaries, and we shall overturn the whole of Russia!" he declared. He proclaimed his faith in the "miracles" that can come from the actions "not only of circles, but even of individual persons," and challenged his readers to become heroes, inviting them to join the ranks not of martyrs, but of saviors. It was time to raise the sadly diminished *prestige* of revolutionaries. The Narodovoltsy, the "circles of heroes" of the seventies with "their seething energy," were to serve as a model and an inspiration.[32]

Both the novel and the brittle polemic appealed to individual Russian revolutionaries to prepare themselves, dedicate themselves, and rely on no one but themselves for the realization of the great task ahead. Lenin wanted his book to have the same effect as the novel. Hundreds of people, Lenin believed, became revolutionaries as a result of reading Chernyshevsky's book and he hoped his *What Is To Be Done?* would provide the same inspiration. If Chernyshevsky's novel had the power of captivating Alexander and Vladimir Ulianov, then its namesake could captivate a following for its author. In this it was successful.

Valentinov described the enthusiasm with which Lenin's book was received by his Social Democratic circle in Kiev: "He put forward the image of the 'professional revolutionary,' a St. George the Dragon-killer, responding to 'all instances of injustice and brutality toward any class.' We liked this . . . It was ablaze with violent voluntarism . . . and its calls to 'will,' to act, to fight . . . aroused in us the most heartfelt response."[33] Lenin succeeded not only in making his pen a conquering weapon to mobilize an army, but in turning his writings into the *key* to revolutionary activism. "Without a revolu-

40   tionary theory," he wrote, "there can be no revolutionary movement."[34] Only a cogent theory can convince the best people to devote their lives to full-time revolutionary activity, and only on the basis of strong theory can an effective organization be created and maintained.

With *What Is To Be Done?* Lenin came to a turning point in his political development. The lawyer from Simbirsk had become a revolutionary leader with his own theory and his own following, particularly after the 1903 split between the Bolshevik and Menshevik factions of the Russian Social Democratic Labor Party. Lenin had become the founder and leader of Bolshevism.

Bolshevik Leader

Leadership takes constant work. As leader, first of a revolutionary party and then of the new Soviet state, Lenin illustrated this axiom with particular force. He demonstrated that his talents were suited to leadership as he conceived it; throughout his career he revealed a prodigious capacity for working with concentration and self-discipline, under the most trying conditions. Bruce Mazlish has argued that Lenin was a classic example of the "revolutionary ascetic" type of leader.[35] He contends that Lenin had few libidinal ties and that his libido was bound up completely with himself. Although it is true that his emotional attachments were few and limited, particularly after Plekhanov's insult in 1900, the concept of the ascetic does not accurately capture Lenin's style; nor does it characterize his cult image, since Communists viewed asceticism as part of the adolescent pose struck by the idealistic Narodovoltsy.

What struck contemporaries was that Lenin was so orderly in his work, his appearance, and his surroundings, this last a startling contrast to the legendary messes in which most Russian revolutionaries lived. The London commune that Martov and Zasulich called home was notoriously chaotic,[36] and by comparison Lenin's tidiness, his simple tastes, seemed all the more impressive. The juxtaposition of radicalism with utter self-control, an unusual blend for his milieu, made him appear at once revolutionary and responsible.

Krzhizhanovsky wrote that in exile Lenin exuded an air of "purity." He did not drink or smoke. He loved brisk walks, chess, ice skating, and hunting.[37] In his work Lenin was organized, self-disciplined, and especially productive in isolation, as in 1890-91 when he prepared for his law examinations, or in the last years of the decade when he continued to write and write well, in prison and in Siberian exile. Once his European emigration had begun, Lenin took great care to avoid the time-consuming society of his fellow emigrés, avoiding the cafés they frequented. In this there was no self-deprivation. He really disliked their chatter, which invariably enervated him. Lenin was less an ascetic, one who deprives himself of pleasure in order to achieve some higher goal, than he was a "workaholic" in a society that hardly knew the type.[38]

Lenin had another character trait that proved especially crucial to exercising his particular type of leadership; he had the toughness to break, sometimes irrevocably, with those who did not support him on his terms. This was the dynamic behind all the splits and schisms that figured so prominently in the history of Bolshevism before the 1917 revolution. "Split, split, and split," he wrote at the beginning of 1905 to the secretary of the Bureau of Committees of the Majority in St. Petersburg, warning him of wily Mensheviks.[39]

Sometimes the split took a supreme effort to sustain, as it did after the break with Martov.[40] But in all these cases Lenin's unshakable conviction that his leadership was essential, and that he alone understood the path to revolutionary power, gave him the strength to sustain his course, even if this meant accepting a drastic reduction in the number of his followers. Potresov, the *Iskra* editor who later broke with Lenin, wrote that there was an aura of "chosenness" about Lenin, that "he was the will of the movement concentrated into one person."[41] Lenin might not have been comfortable with Potresov's way of putting it, but the history of the Bolshevik Party from 1903 until 1917 suggests that, indeed, Lenin saw himself as the custodian of the political vision toward whose realization other comrades must work. And if they would not be persuaded, Lenin was willing to remain with only a few faithful followers, the self-embodied consciousness of what Russia must become.

One wonders how often Lenin thought of Chernyshevsky during those years after the 1905 revolution when Bolshevism fragmented into querulous factions and the entire revolutionary movement seemed depressed and without direction, for throughout this dispiriting period, Lenin held with remarkable fidelity to the image of that hero of his youth. He bristled at those who chided him for his bookishness, but he was in fact a remarkably literary leader. With a pen that had unusual powers of persuasion, he stubbornly worked to establish the consistency of his vision, to make them see it through the sometimes bewildering series of tactical reversals he himself so often ordained.

Belinsky had believed that in Russia the writer presented his total self—his background, his morality, his style of life, as well as his written work—for judgment by his peers. The author of Bolshevism asked no less of himself and his followers. His concept of the professional revolutionary was the logical culmination of the elements that had formed him, and the same is true for his developing notions of leadership. In his every act the leader must evince the qualities that had been defined as prerequisites for party membership. He must be the exemplar, establishing the guiding line for others while scrupulously observing it himself. In the process of combining elements from the Russian revolutionary tradition in a new, more rigorous and demanding way, Lenin was marking out a style of leadership that would be one of his major contributions to the politics of the century he did so much to shape. He was also, inadvertently, helping to lay the complex foundations for his own cult.

Lenin's real initiation as a revolutionary leader occurred in the summer of 1903 at the tiny (43 voting delegates) Second Congress of the Russian Social Democratic Labor Party (RSDLP). There Lenin adroitly maneuvered to split the party on the issue of membership. He advanced a formulation that was much more narrow than Martov's, reflecting his vision of an exclusive party comprised of professional revolutionaries. Although the congress endorsed Martov's broader definition, Lenin manipulated events to prompt a walkout by delegates representing the "economist" position and the Bund (General Jewish Workers' Union), temporarily leaving his supporters in the majority position (*bol'sheviki*) and Martov's in the minority (*men'sheviki*), thus giving rise to the names of both factions.[42]

Throughout the congress Lenin comported himself as if his standing as a leader were already recognized. Trotsky later claimed that the *stariki* (the old ones) of the movement (Akselrod and Zasulich) were incredulous when it was all over: "Was it so long ago that he came abroad as a mere pupil and behaved as a pupil?" "Where,

then, did he get that supreme self-confidence?"[43] The stariki were   43
not the only ones surprised by Lenin's performance. Back in Russia,
exiled Social Democrats like Anatoly Lunacharsky and his comrades in Vologda thought the schism was sheer madness. "The first
paragraph of regulations? Is that worth a split? The distribution of
chairs on the editorial board? Have they gone crazy over there,
abroad?" Upset by the news of the event, the group of exiles was
buzzing with rumors "that Lenin is a troublemaker and a schismatic
and no matter what the cost wants to establish an autocracy in the
party, and that Martov and Akselrod did not want, so to speak, to
swear an oath of allegiance to him as all-Party khan."[44]

There is evidence that the Social Democrats who placed themselves in Lenin's camp did so not so much because they preferred his
wording of the party statute, but because they wanted to declare
themselves for Lenin's "nerve."[45] Thus it was not surprising that
Lenin attracted individuals excited by strong leadership. Some of
the Geneva Bolsheviks were former Narodovoltsy, men who admired bold, risk-taking revolutionaries. They were undoubtedly attracted by Lenin's voluntarism and his praise of the heroes of the
seventies that reverberated through his early writings.

Lunacharsky observed that the majority of the Marxist intelligentsia in St. Petersburg and Moscow were drawn to Menshevism,
while the Bolsheviks attracted professional revolutionaries from the
provinces.[46] The provincial revolutionaries were probably more
comfortable with Lenin's unpretentious bearing and ordinary appearance than they were with the intellectual arrogance and man-
nered airs of leaders like Plekhanov. Krzhizhanovsky said that
Lenin looked like a peasant from the Volga, and we can assume this
was important to provincial Russians new to the movement.[47] Lenin
was one of them. He was a Russian from the Volga region, the heart
of Russia (not a Jew, like Martov, Trotsky, or Akselrod); he had
never been a student in one of the capitals. His speeches were powerful but without a hint of polish or elegance. He was confident but
never haughty, refined, or pretentious.

The source that most vividly describes the relationship between
the new faction and its leader is Nikolai Valentinov's memoir. One
of the professional revolutionaries from the provinces who had been
attracted to Bolshevism, Valentinov recalled that when he arrived in

44 Geneva from Russia in January 1904, he had been greatly struck, even "shocked" by the "atmosphere of worship" with which the Bolsheviks had surrounded Lenin. Lepeshinsky, for one, "adored Lenin almost like sentimental schoolgirls who 'worship' some of their teachers." He believed with all his heart that some day Lenin would do great things: "Everybody will see then what a great, very great person he is," Lepeshinsky told Valentinov. "'Our old man is wise, '" he often intoned, and Valentinov recalled that "at such times his eyes filmed over with tenderness and his whole face expressed adoration."[48]

This religious veneration of Lenin by the Geneva-period Bolsheviks disturbed Valentinov, and he was determined to resist the development of similar feelings in himself. He failed, however, and later wrote that he "fell in love" with Lenin.[49] Lunacharsky described this as a general pattern. "People who come close to his orbit not only become devoted to him as a political leader but in a strange way they fall in love with him."[50] Potresov explained the leader's "hypnotic" effect on people in terms of his enormous will, faith, and self-confidence:

> Plekhanov was esteemed, Martov was loved, but only Lenin was followed unquestioningly, as the only undisputed leader. For only Lenin embodied ... a personage of iron will, indomitable energy, combining a fanatical faith in the movement, in the cause, with as great a faith in himself. Louis XIV could say: I am the state; so Lenin without unnecessary words invariably felt that he was the party, that he was the will of the movement concentrated into one person. And he acted accordingly.[51]

It was natural that his strong supporters would have been most devoted to Lenin during this founding period, when the enthusiasm he had inspired by his bold prosecution of the split was still alive. But it is difficult to make definitive statements about his charisma when the only available sources are memoirs on a subject that lends itself so readily to hyperbole. Even the best recollections, possibly including Valentinov's, may be distorted. Besides, Lenin's charisma came and went; his leadership was not always effective, despite the unrelenting work he devoted to it. Ironically, his first encounter with a genuine revolutionary situation led some of his supporters to question his leadership and initiated a period of fragmentation within Bolshevik ranks.

When mounting popular discontent culminated in the massive general strike of October 1905 that precipitated autocratic Russia's short-lived period as a constitutional monarchy, many emigré revolutionaries hurried home to participate in the dramatic events. Lenin arrived in St. Petersburg late, only in November. "He worked mostly with his pen," recalled Lunacharsky who, in his 1919 memoir, made little attempt to conceal his disappointment: "It seemed to me that Lenin was not the genuine revolutionary leader I had thought him to be. It began to seem as though emigré life had somewhat diminished Lenin, that the inner party struggle against the Mensheviks had for him pushed into the background the mighty struggle against the monarchy, and that he was more a journalist than a genuine leader."[52] In Lunacharsky's assessment Lenin was continuing the struggle on the "emigré scale," and was not showing himself capable of actively functioning on the level called for by the reality of actual revolution. Lunacharsky "began to fear that the revolution had no genuine leader of genius."[53]

After 1905 Lenin remained the leader of the Bolshevik movement, but it was scattered by factional strife that increased after 1907, the year that marked for Lenin the beginning of a decade of emigration. Abroad, Lenin's most vocal opponent was Bogdanov, who strongly criticized what he saw as Lenin's authoritarian domination of the party. Throughout this period Lenin's remarkable confidence in the correctness of his vision endured. He made it clear that he would continue to split, even if this meant the most drastic reduction in the number of his supporters. Thus, when he convened a party conference of his followers in Prague in January 1912, there were only twenty delegates, with Grigory Zinoviev the only other person of any prominence attending. This situation did not prompt Lenin to compromise; instead he claimed that the Prague conference represented all of Russian Social Democracy. He meant it and, given Lenin's terms, he was not exaggerating. After all, Social Democracy could espouse only one general line; all others were by definition incorrect, their authors heretics. It was only World War I, which erupted in the summer of 1914, that provided the context in which Lenin's leadership again galvanized the Bolsheviks, carrying them in a rising arc of energy and cohesiveness toward their historical climax in the year 1917.

Characteristically, from the beginning of the war, Lenin adopted

46   a position that clearly marked him off from most of his socialist comrades, both Russian and European. While most Russian socialists either supported the nation's war effort ("defensists") or demanded an immediate cessation of hostilities without victors or vanquished ("internationalists"), Lenin seemed to sense the war's tremendous potential for exacerbating social conflict in all the participating countries. He was convinced that the war was the terminal stage in the development of capitalism and signaled the advent of an international economic crisis leading to an international socialist revolution. Thus the duty of true Social Democrats was to quicken the revolutionary mood that lay dormant in the popular consciousness, "to help the masses become conscious of these moods, deepen them and give them shape. This task finds correct expression only in the slogan: convert the imperialist war into a civil war."[54]

Lenin repeated the slogan with that furious consistency so characteristic of him. But this time Lenin was jousting not only with his Russian rivals, but with the gods of European Social Democracy. At the international socialist conferences held at Zimmerwald in September 1915 and Kienthal in April of the following year, Lenin stubbornly pressed his radical position despite overwhelming opposition. The man who in 1903 had had the "nerve" to split the infant Russian socialist movement now proclaimed the bankruptcy of the Second International and called for the founding of a Third International to unite the world socialist movement and lead it resolutely to its rendezvous with the decisive revolutionary moment provided by the imperialists in their greedy war. Ironically, however, Lenin was convinced that not Russia, but Europe and particularly Germany, would take the lead in sparking the international socialist revolution. In January 1917 he addressed a group of Swiss working-class youth in the Zurich People's House, reviewing the events of 1905 and terming that Russian revolution the *prologue* to the coming European revolution.[55]

Only one month later striking workers and mutinous soldiers toppled the Russian autocracy. There is something appropriate in the fact that the author of Bolshevism was in Zurich, forced to sift the course of events from newspapers, conservative ones at that. He seethed with impatience to return to Russia where unimaginable events were occurring with dizzying speed, to Russia where, as he

saw it, a socialist revolution awaited those who had the courage and   47
clarity of vision to see what needed to be done.

Lenin in 1917

The February revolution produced no leaders of great talent either
in the Provisional Government, a self-constituted body consisting
mainly of Duma dignitaries, or in the Petrograd Soviet of Workers'
and Soldiers' Deputies, a spontaneously formed organization that
claimed to represent "the people." But the people increasingly chose
to represent themselves in that year of revolution. In a gradual process of atomization, local committees and soviets (councils), sprang
up like mushrooms throughout the empire as the revolution spread
outward from the capital cities. Bonds of loyalty, custom, and fear
that had held together the vast multinational empire melted away as
Russia disintegrated into its smallest parts.

Standard Soviet histories of 1917 describe the mounting anarchy
as a background to the role of V. I. Lenin, a *deus* emerging quite literally *ex machina,* from the train at Petrograd's Finland Station on
the night of April 3, to save the revolution from the specter of a
tsarist restoration. Undoubtedly Lenin's leadership in 1917 is difficult to evaluate. The October revolution is unimaginable without
Lenin's tactical genius and furious energy. But these must be
weighed against some of the other factors explaining the successful
coup: the numerous mistakes of the Provisional Government; the
organizational and oratorical genius of Trotsky, who came to Petrograd in May and only then formally joined the Bolshevik faction;
the efficacy of the party's military organization; and, of course, sheer
luck. Moreover, although Lenin put all of his will and authority in
the party toward persuading his followers to support his positions
even as they underwent shifts with bewildering speed, he met with
only varying success—until the end.

The Bolshevik Party in 1917 was characterized by open debate.
The views of right and moderate Bolsheviks often won majority
support at the expense of Lenin's. Despite the reversals and seeming
defeats, both within his party and in the wider arena of revolutionary Russia, Lenin maintained confidence in his ability to steer
his party to revolutionary victory, and he proved remarkably suc-

48   cessful in communicating that confidence to others. Lenin's greatest strength in 1917 lay in his determination to maximize the political potential of each new circumstance and his willingness to tailor his slogans to the shifting moods of the masses. He did not hesitate, for example, to enlist the energies of the peasantry to hasten the advent of the dictatorship of the proletariat. With cold consistency he subordinated every means to his goal, the seizure of revolutionary power in order to realize his vision of a socialist Russia. Time and again in the course of that crowded year his consistency provided a line against which the chaos of circumstance could be judged. As Russia reeled toward political atomization and social chaos, Lenin's confidence in the validity of his vision provided the sharpest possible contrast to the vacillation and trepidation of less bold politicians. His pen struck many moods, from the almost utopian musings of *State and Revolution* to the sharp letters in which he alternated between persuasion, scorn, and shame to convince his followers to support his call for armed insurrection. In the end it is but a slight exaggeration to say that Lenin achieved power because he alone insisted on having it. It was his ultimate triumph over what appeared to be overwhelming odds that would later inspire his lieutenants to imbue him with magical qualities and make of him a cult figure.

Lenin had come to Petrograd as the party's main spokesman and leader. In the capital he found no real competition. Zinoviev, a renowned orator and party leader of the first rank, was with Lenin, and the other two great speakers and leaders, Lunacharsky and Trotsky, had not yet declared for the Bolshevik camp. Besides, Trotsky was still out of the country. Automatic acceptance of his political views did not accompany Lenin's acknowledged leadership of the party. On the contrary, he had to fight and persuade. That he eventually won all the battles with his comrades does credit to his extraordinary powers of persuasion as well as to his ability to assess the absolute minimum on which to compromise when necessary.[56]

Lenin's stated goals, expressed in his famous "April Theses," revealed full-blown his enormous voluntarism. Although Russia had just entered its "bourgeois" phase, Lenin called for the renunciation of any cooperation with the "bourgeois" Provisional Government, insisting that the power it shared with the Soviet be transferred to the latter body. The theoretical premise underlying Lenin's speech was that the period of bourgeois political hegemony in Russia was already coming to an end after six weeks, rather than the several decades originally envisioned by Social Democrats. To wait for the bourgeois stage to pass on its own would mean to allow capitalism and a parliamentary democracy to become entrenched and strong, thus ensuring that he and his generation would not live to see the socialist revolution to which they had devoted their lives. Besides, what if Marx's prediction was not to be trusted? How close had the democratic nations of the West come to socialist revolutions? Was it not possible that allowing a bourgeois republic to mature would in fact prevent Russia from ever moving in a socialist direction? And if the socialist revolution were to be delayed, who would lead the revolutionary vanguard in thirty or fifty years? Surely not Lenin. These concerns are evident in Lenin's writings and speeches of the next seven months. Lenin also took the unpopular stand of opposing Russia's continued participation in the war, tempering his original (even more unpopular) demand voiced in the speech he made to a Bolshevik audience on the very night of his arrival in Petrograd, a demand for an immediate cessation of hostilities. In time he was able to convince the party organization to come over to his side.

On the domestic front, the revolution was moving left at its own swift pace determined not—as Lenin had predicted—by the revolutionary vanguard, but by the largely spontaneous actions of those very elements on whom Lenin had counted least in his earlier theoretical constructs: peasants who were seizing estates and the soldiers, sailors, and workers who were increasing the ranks of Bolshevik supporters exponentially during the summer of 1917. Their impatience for immediate and radical social change erupted on July 3 in the July uprising, a culmination of days of urban rioting that hardened the government's stand toward the Bolsheviks.

Bolshevik leaders were rightly alarmed by the Provisional Government's call for loyal troops and its stated intention to expose Lenin's traitorous connection with the Germans.[57] Lenin's opponents had accused him of this ever since his arrival in Petrograd, but the campaign intensified in the wake of the abortive "July days" when Alexander Kerensky, head of the Provisional Government, issued warrants for the arrest of Lenin and other prominent Bolsheviks. Trotsky, Lunacharsky, Kamenev, and Alexandra Kollontai, the most prominent female Bolshevik, were actually arrested; Lenin and Zinoviev fled to Finland. The fortunes of the Bolsheviks rose

50   again at the end of August, partly as a result of their continuing propaganda but even more because an attempted mutiny by the popular commander-in-chief of the army, Lavr Kornilov, prompted Kerensky, who now needed the Bolsheviks' support, to release their leaders from jail. Lenin and Zinoviev, however, remained subject to arrest. So Lenin stayed underground, at a remove from the revolution he aspired to lead, until the very eve of his coup and relied, as always, on his pen to imprint the rush of history.

In August and September he wrote *State and Revolution,* an anarchist pamphlet that reflected precisely the Russian revolutionary process during these months. While Russia was becoming progressively ungovernable, with spontaneously formed committees taking charge in the army, the villages, and the factories, Lenin was urging his readers to destroy the state. The essay began with a defense of the "revolutionary soul" of Marxism, which prophetically sketched the fate of his own theory.

> During the lifetime of great revolutionaries, the oppressing classes constantly hounded them, received their theories with the most savage malice, the most furious hatred and the most unscrupulous campaigns of lies and slander. After their death, attempts are made to convert them into harmless icons, to canonise them, so to say, and to hallow their *names* to a certain extent for the "consolation" of the oppressed classes and with the object of duping the latter, while at the same time robbing the revolutionary theory of its *substance,* blunting its revolutionary edge and vulgarising it.[58]

Lenin sought to restore the fighting edge of Marx, little realizing he himself would become a "harmless icon" after his own death. In *State and Revolution* his aim was to legitimize the call for the total destruction of the old order and its replacement by a dictatorship of the proletariat. By September he was ready for the final push: armed insurrection.

Bolsheviks were now in the majority in the soviets of Petrograd and Moscow. Bolshevik support among the soldiers, sailors, and workers of both capital cities had never been greater. This was due as much to the failure of the Provisional Government to meet the problems of inflation, food supply, and transport as it was to the intense propaganda campaign waged by Lenin and his supporters. Total anarchy was inevitable, with Bolshevism losing out to "spontaneity" if the party did not seize the moment. In September Lenin

wrote to the Central Committee, pleading with them to begin immediate preparations for an armed insurrection. In Lenin's view the
abortive Kornilov coup assured the army's support of a Bolshevik
seizure of power, since it had to look over its right shoulder for enemies of the revolution and embrace those on its left.

Lenin's letters produced a general feeling of dismay. As in April,
Lenin had taken a position directly counter to the prevailing mood
of the party leadership. His comrades' reception of the letters was so
negative that the Central Committee planned to destroy the letters
lest they reach the Petrograd workers and inspire another July uprising, which could land them all in jail again. In the end they kept the
letters but at the same time moved to ensure that no mass appeals or
preparations for an insurrection were made. A week later at a meeting of the Central Committee, Lenin's demand for an armed uprising was not even discussed.[59] This was just six weeks before he became chairman of the Council of People's Commissars.

Lenin had decided it was time to seize power, and from his hide-
outs in Finland and, as of mid-September, in nearby Vyborg he had
only his pen with which to win over the means to that end, his own
party organization. Week by week, in articles and letters, he
hounded the Central Committee into supporting his position. He
heaped shame and scorn upon those—like Zinoviev and Kamenev—who let fear (and sensible judgment) stand in the way.
While virtually all of his followers in some way or another tem-
porized, deeming an armed insurrection superfluous in view of the
impending Second All-Russia Congress of Soviets (scheduled first
for October 20 and then eventually postponed until the 25th),
through which some peaceful transfer of power might be effected le-
gitimately within a coalition, Lenin alone was convinced that the
kind of government he envisioned could never be realized except
through an armed coup. The crucial vote was held in the Central
Committee on October 10. By ten to two, with Zinoviev and Kamenev against, the motion for armed insurrection passed. After this
Lenin continued his exhortative role, hectoring his comrades into
transforming that vote into action, even as a rising river of anarchy
rapidly eroded the last vestiges of popular support for the Provisional Government.

Lenin in October. Throughout Soviet history, books, articles,
poems, paintings, and films have celebrated this dramatic confron-

52   tation between the man and the moment. "And in future times,/looking back/at these days,/Lenin's head/is what you'll first see," Vladimir Maiakovsky solemnly declared in the epic poem he composed shortly after Lenin's death.[60] And indeed Lenin's energy and determination during those weeks between the failed Kornilov mutiny and October 25 were crucial to the coup and to the eventual development of the Lenin cult.

All of Lenin's talents were uniquely suited to the crisis: his extraordinary sense of timing; his uncanny ability to gauge correctly the weakness of his opponents; and something else that was a combination of rage, courage, and hysteria. In retrospect it might seem odd to suggest that through his barrage of angry and urgent communications demanding the overthrow of the government Lenin managed to bully a recalcitrant Military Revolutionary Committee (of the Petrograd Soviet), under Trotsky's dynamic supervision, into taking over the capital's main points of communication and finally, on the night of October 25, into overwhelming the Provisional Government in the Winter Palace—but that is in fact more or less what happened. On the night of the 24th in full disguise (his face swathed in bandages, his bald head sporting a wig), Lenin ventured out of hiding and made his way to Bolshevik headquarters at the Smolny Institute. On the morning of the 25th Lenin issued a proclamation declaring the overthrow of the Provisional Government and the assumption of power by the Military Revolutionary Committee of the Petrograd Soviet of Workers' and Soldiers' Deputies. It did not bear his signature, but his writing and thinking were henceforth to shape Russia as the power of his pen was supplemented by an army, a navy, and a political police.

Ruler of Soviet Russia

"The fish rots from the head," says a Russian peasant proverb—which aptly describes what happened to the Romanov dynasty. By the time Nicholas II assumed the throne in 1894, the autocracy had been languishing for a long time. Its entire operating system eliminated the possibility of dynamic leadership that the empire so desperately needed. Not since Nicholas I had there been a Russian ruler who took charge of imperial administration and ran it with energy and perseverance. The subsequent monarchs were increasingly content to function as mere referees among warring bureaucratic agencies.

Nicholas II failed to meet even these modest expectations. Envisioning himself as a tsar of old who ruled by benevolent decree, he abandoned the role of bureaucratic mediation and gradually isolated himself from his own government, thus accelerating the paralysis that became evident by 1915.[61] The old regime had ceased to function as an effective governing force, even before its capitulation in the face of mounting strikes and food riots in February 1917. The dramatic last days of his reign displayed Nicholas' utter lack of comprehension of the events about to force his abdication: "I order you to stop the disorders tomorrow, since they are impermissible in a difficult time of war," he wired the governor-general of Petrograd from general headquarters on February 25, when 240,000 strikers had taken to the streets of the capital and the revolution had begun to move on its own inevitable leftward course.[62]

When Lenin took power in October 1917, the challenges he faced were even greater than those confronting Nicholas. The Bolshevik slogan "Bread, Peace, Land" encapsulates the three most pressing needs and omits the fourth: imposing political order on the chaos. Atomization continued through the summer of 1917, and by the fall tiny villages were sewing their own flags and proclaiming themselves republics. Lenin's party had staged successful coups in Petrograd and Moscow but, although its support had grown appreciably since the spring, particularly in the capital cities where Bolsheviks dominated the Soviets, it was still a minority party. Contemporary observers did not expect the "insane adventure," as the Bolshevik seizure of power was called in *Izvestiia* (the organ of the Petrograd Soviet) to last more than a week. Yet despite the anarchy, despite the disastrous war, despite the opposition of all political parties except the left wing of the Socialist Revolutionaries, the Bolshevik Party not only retained but extended and consolidated its power.

Much of the credit is Lenin's. He had played a central role in the seizure of power, although the events of October could not have happened without Trotsky's brilliant direction of the Military Revolutionary Committee or, more important, without the escalating anarchic surge engulfing Russia in the autumn of 1917 and the political bankruptcy of the Provisional Government. But when it came to creating the Bolshevik system of government and directing it

54   through the incredible trials of its first years, Lenin's contribution was quite extraordinary. For almost five years, until illness forced him out of the Kremlin in 1922, Lenin ruled Russia as chairman of the Council of People's Commissars, providing the country with its most dynamic leadership since the death of Peter the Great. He was the primary architect of the new government and the author of its policies.

Once in power, time and again Lenin was pitched in battle not only against White armies and foreign interventionists, but also against reputable Communists who opposed his policies. At the end of the civil war, opposition groups within the party complained vociferously against *edinonachalie* (the growing domination of the party by its center) and demanded a greater measure of political independence. Lenin struggled as well for the adoption of his views by the party's Central Committee, within which he was but the most authoritative member.

The first of these battles was the hardest—that of ending the futile military struggle against Germany. Lenin forced the humiliating Treaty of Brest-Litovsk on a resistant party, insisiting that the Russian armies were no longer capable even of retreating. Lenin summoned all his authority and talent to force the treaty's ratification. His most unpopular creation, it cost him the support of the Left Socialist Revolutionaries as well as the backing of many members of his own party, with Nikolai Bukharin at their head, who feared for the survival of Bolshevik power in Russia if it should cede large parts of its territory to Germany.

In the end, of course, the outcome of the war nullified the treaty, and Lenin's decision was vindicated. This was often the case with his policy shifts, so much so that in Lenin's case the old adage may be inverted to "right makes might." Lenin did have a remarkably acute sense of timing, a feel for what at any given moment was necessary for political survival. This talent—or genius—did not fail to impress itself on his lieutenants who were close enough to appreciate how unimaginably difficult the job was.

With humble representatives of the narod, Lenin's style was homely.[63] He was accessible, simple, attentive, and concerned. In short, he seemed like the simple "just tsar" of the peasants' naive monarchism. The poor came mostly with complaints, petitions, and sometimes gifts of food (which he donated to orphanages and day-care centers). Peasants occasionally bowed low upon entering his office. Lenin was careful to show respect to the poor and uneducated, something he did not always do for his comrades and government officials. His manner demonstrated trust. What distance was put between him and peasant petitioners came from his staff, who on their own initiative set up a disinfection room in the Kremlin through which visitors were supposed to pass and wash themselves before seeing the leader.[64]

Of his entire complex of behavior toward the populace, only one aspect appears not to fit his temperament: he refused bodyguards when he traveled or spoke in public. It is unlikely that he felt safe without bodyguards; courage had never been his forte, as evidenced by his quick efforts to hide both in 1905 and in 1917. Yet he needed to *show* trust along with the dedication for which he so quickly became famous. It was this that left him open to the gunfire that nearly cost him his life in 1918 at a gathering he had been advised to avoid. That morning the head of the Petrograd secret police had been assassinated, but Lenin kept his appointment and paid the consequences.

There were times when he consciously acted to inspire the people by means of symbolic gestures. A dramatic example was the first *subbotnik* in the Kremlin, a free work day granted "voluntarily" as a gesture of solidarity with the regime. The first so designated was May Day, 1919. From early morning, bands saluted the revolutionary holiday. In the courtyard of the Kremlin a military unit was doing construction work (a common practice during War Communism). At exactly nine in the morning Lenin walked out into the square and said to the military commander: "Comrade Commander, permit me to join your unit for participation in the subbotnik." This aroused worries for Lenin's health, for not a year had passed since the shooting of 1918. Nonetheless, the order was given to move, and to the strains of music the participants proceeded to their work. The task involved moving and sorting the debris left by construction. The soldiers attempted to jolly Lenin into transporting some light materiel, but he immediately began to lift a heavy log onto his shoulder and set to earnest work, humming a revolutionary march. "From the Kremlin the news then traveled by telephone to all Moscow that Vladimir Ilich was participating in the subbotnik, working with all the others." He continued to work all

56 day, breaking only to make a short speech to his coworkers.[65] He was building his own myth as he sought to inspire the nation of Oblomovs to learn how to work. His own work, however, was the relentless effort of leadership.

In many respects Lenin's leadership of the new Soviet state is consistent with his leadership of the prerevolutionary Bolshevik Party. Again and again appear the signs of his firm conviction that only he could discern the correct path socialist Russia must follow through the trials of its formative years. In policy matters he exhibited the same potent combination of tactical flexibility and a fixed vision of the goal toward which Russian and world history were inexorably advancing. Like the earlier party, the structures that emerged to guide the successful completion of the revolution were fashioned in the image of Lenin's leadership style. This was at once their great strength and, in the long run, their weakness.

Lenin held no office that invested him with formal party leadership; technically he was simply another member of the Central Committee and the Politburo (the five-man bureau organized in 1919). In practice, he was unquestionably the party's most authoritative voice—a role he assumed because he was determined to play it and which he retained through energy and skill. His determination to get his way at party congresses coupled with his skillful manipulation of his comrades (a talent Trotsky lacked) enabled him to gain victory after victory within the party, which in any event held a position inferior to the government during this early period of Bolshevik rule. In the words of Osinsky, a critic of Lenin's dictatorial conception of democratic centralism at the Ninth Party Congress in March 1920, "Lenin constantly pushed everybody, directed everybody ... he was in fact the one director and leader."[66] His all-consuming job as head of state aside, Lenin from the very beginning sought a personal domination of his party while permitting a free exchange of opinions. (This was to be a short-lived luxury at party congresses which disappeared even before Lenin's death.) But Lenin could not be everywhere at once, and when the unwieldy Central Committee was restructured in 1919 to include a Political Bureau and an Organizational Bureau, his comrades directly confronted the question of Lenin's all-encompassing leadership style. They could not allow Ilich himself to carry out all the duties of the Central Committee, "to have the burden on one pair of shoulders," said one delegate. "And although Ilich has a head like no other on earth, it is still necessary that around that head there be people."[67]

While Lenin shaped and directed the party by force of his "head," by his concentrated, focused energy, and his remarkable powers of persuasion, he was both the author and the *formal* head of the Soviet governmental structure. Just as he had been the founder and leader of the Bolshevik faction fifteen years earlier, so now he was the creator and supervisor of the Council of People's Commissars (Sovnarkom). The circumstances of the first weeks of Bolshevik rule were chaotic, as government officials found housing and dragged in furniture and recruits. There are stories of Lenin literally grabbing people in corridors and stairwells and appointing them to jobs, often against their vain protests.[68] It was some time before the government could settle into a routine, particularly with the disruption of its move to Moscow in March 1918.

In 1918 the council met almost nightly, with sessions lasting from early evening often until 1:00 or 2:00 in the morning. In the years following, as its organization grew more complex, it met less frequently, with only fifty-one meetings in 1921. Throughout the period, government and not party affairs claimed most of Lenin's time. In 1921, 60 percent of Lenin's published or recorded correspondence was addressed to employees of the central government.[69]

Although the commissars and their deputies seemed to prefer the informal style of meeting to which they had become accustomed in the party, Lenin imposed a businesslike formality, strictly limiting the number of minutes allowed to reporters and commentators and checking the Russian propensity for lateness with a system of fines. He simultaneously conducted several items of business during meetings—writing, reading notes, carrying on conversations—yet seems to have had no difficulty in imposing his authority.

Lenin's imprint on the council came from his position as chairman but even more from his penetrating manner of management: "What cannot be indicated in any diagram was that Lenin pervaded the whole Sovnarkom system, his activity constantly entering it at all the nodal points, his methods stamped on its very structures and procedures and his attitudes and expectations 'internalised' to a greater or lesser extent in the working personalities of most of the individuals active in the system."[70] Lenin was a "dynamically

58   effective *chief executive"* with a "highly activist style." He was involved in the daily affairs of the commissariats and frequently intervened to make judgments and take action.[71] He also had a talent for mediating between agencies, the role so frequently assumed by his imperial predecessors.

Gradually between 1919 and 1922, the year of Lenin's physical deterioration, the government was subordinated to the party, which came to dominate political affairs even before Lenin's death. One factor in this shift was the sudden death in 1919 of Iakov Sverdlov, the brilliant organizer who had headed the Congress of Soviets and functioned as the secretary of the party's Central Committee. These twin posts had made Sverdlov the real linchpin between party and state. In general, however, this increase in the political power invested in the Central Committee and Politburo was a function of the tendency to centralize political authority in the wake of Red victories in the civil war. It was facilitated by the fact that local party committees tended to be more effective than the often more independent local soviets.

As long as Lenin remained chairman of the Sovnarkom, however, it continued to issue main directives that were then administered through the soviets. The increasing responsibility of the party did relieve the council of some of its burdens, but it remained plagued by too much work. In part the fault for this lay with Lenin, since his executive style invited officials to look directly to him for speedy resolutions to their problems. Of course he knew how to delegate power; how could he have been an able administrator otherwise? But his distrust of his fellow workers, often justified, led him to spend time devising ways to check on them—and then check on them again. The countless letters and notes with which he had deluged his organization until October 1917—questioning, threatening, cajoling his comrades into carrying out the tasks entrusted to them—were now repeated in numerous memoranda and telephone calls to central government officials directing every stage of their work. Other commissars could and did limit their attention to their specific areas of responsibility, but as Lenin's sister pointed out, "Ilich alone, as chairman, was obliged to listen to everything . . . to find the most appropriate decision in confused and often labyrinthine disputes, with passions running high. He was required to be an expert on all matters."[72]

In taking so much upon himself, Lenin created a council that could not function properly without his constant, active participation. Thus the first stages of the arteriosclerosis that was to end his life crippled both the leader and the government he directed. It is a striking testimony to Lenin's style of leadership that the measures he put forward to aid his government, even after the onset of serious illness in 1922, were proposals "whose chances of success depended on his personal involvement in carrying them out."[73] As for designating a replacement chairman of the council, Lenin did produce his famous "testament," which he dictated on January 24, 1923, just six weeks before a massive paralytic stroke permanently incapacitated him. In this memorandum he evaluated his most influential lieutenants and found them all wanting. Lenin's intention, conscious or not, was to sabotage the possibility of his replacement. He simply could not conceive of his regime functioning without him and was unable to envision himself incapable of continuing concentrated work.

The very structure of Soviet rule thus reflected the leadership style that Lenin had evinced since at least 1903; in fact the new institutions were fitted so completely to Lenin's leadership that they seemed a direct extension of his person. It is no surprise that he, who was childless, often spoke about Soviet Russia in language filled with images of the infant or child in need of nurturing and direction. Lenin's close identification with the party and his conviction that he alone could draw the blueprint for the new social order demonstrates at once his profound self-confidence and his disdain for what he perceived as the limited capacities of most other Russians, including many of his own comrades. He needed to teach them, to enlighten them, and during that process to direct their activities. Part of that enlightenment was to be self-knowledge. In 1904 in Geneva Lenin expressed a wish to "lock up" some of his comrades in a room and force them to read *Oblomov*. "Have you read it? Well, read it again. And when they fall down on their knees pleading, we cannot stand it, then they should be examined: have you understood the essence of Oblomovism? Have you sensed that it resides within you? Have you resolved to rid yourselves of this illness?"[74]

As ruler of Russia, Lenin found it exasperating to work with people who did not know how to use their capacities productively and who could not see their own weaknesses and limitations. In most re-

60 spects, Lenin had a remarkably acute understanding of his own capabilities and few illusions about himself. It is certainly to his credit that, despite his manifold accomplishments as the builder of the new Soviet state, he understood that his genius was confined to one realm: politics. By contrast, Stalin in the heyday of *his* personality cult wished to be recognized as superlative in everything—philosophy, linguistics, military strategy—like an omniscient deity. Lenin was more like a Greek or Roman god who was master in only one field of activity. He pretended to nothing more. Lenin, for example, was sensible enough to leave the purely military conduct of the civil war to Trotsky, avoiding any claims to the military leadership of the Red army.[75] He never wore a uniform, nor did he take to dressing like a worker in the style later affected by some of his comrades. As head of state Lenin continued to wear the same suits and ties he had worn in European emigration.

Still, within the realm in which he excelled, Lenin had his blind spot; he was unable to separate himself from his creations, the party and the government, and thus he could not protect them from being orphaned at his death. After all, the author of Bolshevism, the activist revolutionary writer, had become just that at least in part because the act of writing itself is a controlling and masterful endeavor. It transcends time and space and can move those unseen by the author and unknown to him. Lenin had struggled to move events according to the imperatives provided by his literary and ideological mentors, the world around him, and his own past history. And he had been successful in erecting a system that enabled him to put his stamp upon Russia not merely through writings that might persuade his recalcitrant countrymen, but through directives that could haul them out of the morass of old Russia. It was apparently beyond him to contemplate the possibility that he might construct an edifice through which the actual course of historical events appeared to be within his control—and then be forced to leave it before the real work had even begun. But it was precisely this loss of the indispensable leader in 1922 that prompted the creation of an immortalized Lenin to replace the living one, and in the process paved the way for the establishment of the basic institutions of a cult.

As for Lenin's blindness to his own mortality, the explanation may have quite another source. Common sense tells us that although Lenin was still in early middle age, his father's death from a

cerebral hemorrhage at fifty-four ought to have alerted Vladimir
Ilich to a possible danger to himself. It apparently did not. It is entirely possible that Alexander's execution at twenty-one, following
on the heels of his father's death, evoked in Vladimir an inability to
consider his own eventual death. "No, this path will not be ours.
This is not the path to take." These are the words that young
Ulianov allegedly uttered upon learning of his brother's execution,
according to his younger sister Maria, who was nine at the time.[76]
Maria Ilinichna's intended message was that then, at the age of seventeen, Vladimir had already believed that Marxism and not
Sasha's conspiratorial terrorism must liberate Russia. If this incident
actually occurred, it cannot be an illustration of Ulianov's early
Marxist convictions. He first read Marx more than a year after
Sasha's death. But it is possible that Vladimir made some dramatic
statement to reassure his mother (and himself) that her other children were not going to get themselves killed for the revolutionary
cause. He may have developed a profound investment to live life to
the end.

These speculations are not meant to suggest that Lenin thought
himself superhuman or immortal. The only immortality he envisioned was through his writings and his transformation of Russia.
This was a far from modest projection, and in fact it provided the
cornerstone for the cult that followed his death. "Lenin has died, but
Leninism lives!" "Lenin has died, but his cause lives on!" were the
watchwords of the massive agitation campaign that spread the
Lenin cult throughout Russia in 1924. His very identification with
his writings, his palpable conviction in their correctness and their
power, helped transform them into sacred writings. Difficult as it is
to speculate on any individual's sense of self, few aspects of Lenin's
personality are more apparent than his confidence in his own ideas
and his determination to communicate them to others with the full
force of their power and clarity. He, and only he, would forge the
true path to socialism by means of his teachings, his directives, his
constant supervision, and his personal example.

This last was the characteristic of Lenin's that was to be transformed into the most enduring aspect of the Lenin cult: Lenin as the
exemplar, as the ideal model of behavior for all Soviet citizens. His
continuing function as a paradigm for political socialization in the
Soviet Union, particularly of children, remains even today the most

active manifestation of his cult. The image of Grandpa Lenin is imprinted on the minds of schoolchildren, who are inundated with stories and poems about the leader, especially about his exemplary childhood. Emphasis is placed, as would be expected, on his outstanding schoolwork and, even more to the point, his excellent study habits. Lenin's institutionalized persona as an embodiment of the highest socialist virtues is rooted in Lenin himself. His self-conscious and developed role as exemplar provides the strongest link between Ulianov the man and Lenin the cult figure.

From his early childhood Volodia Ulianov exhibited the traits of someone who needed to show others how to do things. He was a rowdy, bossy boy who dictated the rules of games and needed to be regarded by his peers and superiors as the best. He became a model student, and was moved by the extraordinary men he encountered in his reading, first of Turgenev and later of Nikolai Chernyshevsky. Young Ulianov's receptivity to idealized exemplars put him into the pattern common to the Russian intelligentsia of his time. Its heroes were politicized, but the intensity of hero worship had not diminished, from the reverence for Pushkin in the second quarter of the nineteenth century to the adulation of Chernyshevsky in the third and fourth. What distinguished Ulianov from many others and what marked his transformation into Lenin was his compulsion to become *himself* an exemplar and to create a party that, infused with his ideas and directives, would serve the crucial inspirational and supervisory role in effecting revolution in Russia. Part of the work of leadership was that of providing a model for his followers, who were to be the revolutionary vanguard. It may be far-fetched to say that his style of leadership before the revolution was consciously tailored to what he hoped would be imitation by others; he did not want a party of independent thinkers like himself. On the other hand, he was too intelligent to ignore the inspirational appeal of the style that appears to have come naturally to him. His hard work, self-discipline, the unusually high standards he set for himself, allowed him to expect the same of others and helped make him an effective leader.

As ruler of Soviet Russia Lenin consciously behaved even more than before as the ideal model of the new citizen. His work style as chairman of the Council of People's Commissars showed how desperately he wanted to be imitated. He demanded that his officials work longer, harder, and more efficiently, in addition to the basic requirements of sobriety and honesty. The Russian penchant toward Oblomovism was his omnipresent bête noire.

His modest style of life in the Kremlin was legendary. His apartment was small and his salary was low. The cult literature invariably touches on the angry note he sent to Bonch-Bruevich when the latter raised Lenin's salary from 500 to 800 rubles per month without his approval.[77] He preferred to avoid photographers, sculptors, portraitists, flatterers. All this was in tune with his natural inclinations, but he was also setting an example for his staff. He needed above all to distinguish himself and them from the repellent style of the corrupt, vain, self-indulgent tsarist bureaucrats whose vanity made them ineffectual. Fawning and praise were dangerous and could only deflect from the real goal—that of transforming Russia into something new, that of rooting out Oblomovs and replacing them with Fausts and Henry Fords. If a new model was necessary for the vanguard, it was even more imperative for the nation at large.

"We do little to *educate the people* by living, concrete examples and models taken from all spheres of life, but that is the major task of the press during the transition from capitalism to communism," Lenin wrote in September 1918.[78] The mythical Lenin *vita* created by the cult was intentionally normative; its function was precisely to educate the people into exhibiting a desired mode of behavior, one consonant with the values personified by a Vladimir Ilich who was larger than life, who through his writings had bent history to his will and had achieved for himself the death-defying role of perpetual guide to socialism.

3 Lenin in Bolshevik Myth, 1917–1922

The foundation of the Lenin cult was laid during the years of Lenin's active rule. Its elements and builders were diverse. Workers, peasants, party agitators, and the highest party dignitaries came to laud Lenin as a leader of genius. This development was not an organized progression. It was a response evoked in part by Lenin's leadership, but to a greater extent by the political imperatives that called for dramatic images and symbols to legitimize the Bolshevik regime. Published agitation about Lenin began to spread his idealized image across Russia. That image was varied during the years he ruled Russia and provided the basis for the myth his later cult was to celebrate. Early Soviet agitation gave rise to a demonology and hagiography of Soviet Russia. It was within this fantastic creation that the myth of Lenin gradually emerged. The party built on that myth and contributed to it in the effort to strengthen the acknowledged authority of the new political order.

Early Soviet Agitation

Authority cannot be permanently maintained by fiat. It is a relationship between ruler and ruled, based on faith. The ruled must perceive their rulers as legitimate and worthy of trust. Lenin's first decree as chairman of the Council of People's Commissars was to earn him more popular trust than any other until the introduction of the New Economic Policy in 1921. This was the decree on land. Signed by Vladimir Ulianov-Lenin, it was published in *Pravda* and *Izvestiia* and also circulated on individual flysheets, reproduced in huge quantities.[1] With a stroke of his pen and the endorsement of the Congress of Soviets on October 26, 1917, Lenin abolished noble and monastic landholdings for future distribution by peasant land committees. The actual mechanics of land transfer were left vague, but the decree was widely understood to mean one thing: the Bolshevik government headed by Lenin was giving peasants the land they so coveted. If any single act could have put Lenin into the role of tsar-deliverer, it was his signing of the land decree, for it echoed the old peasant formula, "the tsar will give."

Lenin gave land with one hand but took away bread with the other. The harsh policy of War Communism was the bane of the Russian countryside from its adoption in 1918 until its dissolution in 1921. It brought packs of armed workers into the villages to requisition food for the army and urban population. The civil war was a two-year bloodletting whose outcome was to determine the political leadership of Russia. Armed clashes raged across the vast expanse of Russia from Siberia to the Ukraine, but the ultimate struggle was for the loyalty of the civilian population. White promises vied with Red promises. How could Red promises outshine the realities of War Communism, with its attempt at strict control over the production and distribution of all goods? How could Red promises mobilize the loyalties of a populace that suffered from shortages of everything but disease and death? Coming after three years of war and revolution, the civil war ravaged most of what was left of Russian industry, transport, and food production. Reminiscent of the "Time of Troubles," the prolonged civil war of the early seventeenth century, this war depopulated Russian villages and towns through famine and epidemics of cholera and typhus. Predictably, many peasants expressed hostility toward the grain requisition squads, and some thought that the Bolsheviks who had given them the land were different people from the Communists who were taking their food (the party changed its name to Communist in March 1918).[2] Yet for the most part they continued to support the Communists. For this the credit is largely due to the vast agitation-propaganda work carried out in myriad forms by members of the party and their supporters during the civil war years. It was within the context of this agitation that the cult of Lenin began to emerge.

In *What Is To Be Done?* Lenin had defined agitation as a concen-

66 trated emotional appeal geared toward the untutored masses and calculated to arouse their indignation against the injustices perpetrated by the autocracy and by capitalism. Agitators were to give speeches, while propagandists were to use the printed word to explain more complex ideas to sophisticated readers.[3] After the revolution, agitation was adapted to the new conditions of Soviet Russia. The spoken word was supplemented by the entire range of available spectacles and modes of communication. Festivals, street theater, film, radio, posters, paintings, poems, songs, bric-a-brac, hastily erected busts and statues, emblems, badges, flags, banners, monuments, and printed flyers carried simple messages comprehensible even to the illiterate. Capitalists, imperialists, Nicholas II, landlords, priests, illiteracy, the Entente, all were evil; they were the enemy. Workers, poor peasants, and Communists were the champions of good and the friends of the people.

Although agitation was of primary importance to the new regime, particularly during the civil war, it had no centralized organization until the fall of 1920 when the Central Committee established Agitprop, its department of agitation and propaganda, and the Commissariat of Enlightenment formed its political education department, Glavpolitprosvet. During the war the main agency in charge of agitation aimed both at the army and at the civilian population was PUR, the Central Political Administration of the Red army. At the same time, much agitational material streamed out of local party committees and nonparty organizations—workers' clubs and soviets.[4] The first great agitational events were the grand revolutionary festivals of May Day (May 1) 1918 and the first anniversary of the October revolution in Moscow and Petrograd. Petrograd was festooned in red for May Day, and a decorated Roman chariot symbolizing Freedom led an organized procession of massed workers. The central figure in the festival was the personified hero of the revolution—a worker standing against a background of the rising sun. In Moscow a new symbol of the Soviet state appeared among the May Day decorations—the crossed hammer and sickle, which in the summer of 1918 became its official emblem.[5]

Lenin took great interest in every aspect of agitation. On April 12, 1918, the Council of People's Commissars issued a decree ordering the removal of tsarist monuments (except national treasures) and their replacement with monuments to revolutionary leaders. It also

called for new emblems and inscriptions on buildings and the renaming of streets to reflect the ideals of revolutionary Russia.[6]
Lenin was particularly eager to have a monument to Marx and
Engels. It vexed him that the construction even of temporary statues
took such a long time. "I am exasperated to the depths of my soul,"
he wrote Commissar of Enlightenment Lunacharsky on September
12, 1918. "There is no outdoor bust of Marx . . . I scold you for this
criminal negligence."[7]

The temporary monument to Marx and Engels, a remarkably
ugly statue, was finally completed in time for the celebration of the
first anniversary of the revolution. At its unveiling, Lenin made a
speech in which he lauded the great historical role played by the
founders of Communism. He also presided over the unveiling of a
large bas-relief on the Kremlin wall commemorating victims of the
revolution buried in a fraternal grave. After cutting the ribbon that
held the sheet draped over the bas-relief, Lenin suggested that the
scissors he used be saved and placed in a museum—testimony to his
acute sense of ritual.[8] Again he made a speech, this one urging his
listeners to strive for the same heroism exhibited by those who had
died for the revolutionary cause.[9]

In insisting on monumental symbols to inspire the Russian people
and give them direction, Lenin was willy-nilly helping to lay the
foundations for his own cult. Nothing in his behavior indicates that
this was his intention; there is no evidence that he gave any thought
to the glorification of his memory after his death or, indeed, to his
death at all. Nonetheless it was Lenin who strove to people the new
Soviet temple with gods to inspire enthusiasm and emulation, and in
part it was Lenin's example that showed the party and people how
to revere their heroes and leaders.

To Lenin, Karl Marx was the most important inspirational symbol. His palpable feelings of reverence for Marx were doubtless
shared by many of his comrades. If Krzhizhanovsky recalled that
his Petersburg revolutionary circle of the mid-1890s had practiced a
"cult of Marx," it is likely that some of this awe for the founder of
Communism was revived and enhanced by the Bolshevik success at
seizing and maintaining power in the name of Marxism. Marx was
to help provide legitimation for the new regime. It was his portrait
that was carried in the Moscow procession of November 7, 1918.[10]
But there were other heroes as well. On May Day 1919, Lenin pre-

sided over the unveiling of a temporary monument to the seventeenth-century cossack rebel, Stenka Razin, erected at the site of his execution. Three years later Maxim Gorky wrote: "The Russian peasantry does not know its heroes, its leaders, its champions of love, justice and vengeance." According to Gorky, even Razin, whose peasant army fought against the government of Alexei Romanov for almost three years, was remembered in a few songs and nothing more. Pugachev, the eighteenth-century rebel, had left no mark at all.[11] Lenin worked to make the Russian popular mind responsive to its heroes. These included Bolshevik victims of natural deaths, such as Iakov Sverdlov, who died of influenza in March 1919. At a memorial service, Lenin vowed that Sverdlov's memory would serve as a symbol of revolutionary devotion, a model of organizational skill, and an example to guide increasing numbers of workers toward the worldwide spread of Communism.[12] This speech was reproduced on gramophone records for mass distribution.

As agitational weapons in the struggle for socialism, Lenin was interested in more than just monuments to revolutionary heroes. Once the civil war began it was necessary that modes of agitation be mobile, following the Red army into newly conquered areas. Monuments, statues, and occasional festivals would not suffice to mobilize a populace that was bombarded with agitation from every front. The press had always been the central vehicle of propaganda and agitation, but the fighting and a shortage of newsprint during the war made the distribution of newspapers difficult.[13] In wartime there were only two ways for the Bolshevik government to reach the people: by train and by ship. So agit-trains and agit-ships moved through the countryside as representatives of the new regime. The first of these was a train dispatched from Moscow under the auspices of the All-Union Central Executive Committee in mid-August 1918. It was called the Lenin Train. Bearing on its roof the slogan "Workers of the World, Unite," it was entirely covered with frescoes depicting heroic workers and soldiers. It was the first of several trains that went to the front laden with books, brochures, newspapers, posters, films, and projectors—and trained agitators.

Although Lenin never rode the Lenin Train, in the summer of 1919 he sent his wife traveling on the agit-ship *Red Star* even though Krupskaia was not well (she suffered from a goiter) and the trip would doubtless be tiring and possibly dangerous.[14] The *Red Star* was gaily decorated with frescoes and red flags and was accompanied by a small red barge carrying a printing press, movie projector and films, a store, and a library with books, newspapers, and posters. Krupskaia later reported to her husband that some soldiers she had met on the trip had been told by a priest that "Bolsheviks were like the apostles, going to the people to bring light and truth." Lenin responded that the form of the simile was wrong, but its idea was correct.[15]

Lenin erred. The analogy of Bolsheviks and apostles was perfectly correct, given the imagery of the Russian popular mind. Agitation in the civil war years gave free rein to the imagination of its numerous and varied creators.[16] The influence of religious forms and themes is strikingly evident in the posters and leaflets of the period. A "Proletarian Ten Commandments" was published by the Central Executive Committee of the All-Russian Congress of Soviets.[17] Many posters of the period took their form from old Russian icons. It was common, for example, for them to depict workers or soldiers as dragon slayers on stylized red horses, that is, as modern-day St. Georges killing dragons of imperialism. One of the most beautiful posters of the period is captioned "Long Live the Red Army" and shows two soldiers on a winged horse suspended above a fortress and an army; the graphic representations are unmistakably iconographic. Winged horses figure prominently in civil war posters, and their riders are invariably heroic men holding sacred texts or killing beasts. One such rider holds an open book on which the letters resemble biblical Old Slavonic and spell out: "Workers of all Nations, Unite!"[18]

The presence of religious images in Soviet agitation has several possible explanations, each of which is likely to be necessary but not sufficient for a comprehensive understanding of the phenomenon. Some agitators and graphic artists were doubtless moved by a genuine iconoclasm and meant their creations to be deliberate and cutting parodies of icons. For others, in contrast, the revolution had inspired deep feelings of religious veneration, which they expressed through the only symbols that could adequately convey them. Indeed, the very power of symbols lies in their ability instantly to communicate emotion and attitude. Still other artists and agitators may have been intentionally attempting to create works that would effectively move the peasant viewer and reader who were reared on saints' lives and the Bible, calculating that religious symbols were likely to resonate in the peasant soul and transfer deep-seated feelings of reverence for holy images to equally profound stirrings of devotion to the Communist Party. The element common to all these explanations is the importance of symbols in the war for popular loyalties and, indeed, their enormous significance in traditional Russian culture. Even a passing acquaintance with Russian folklore and the most sensitive literary portrayals of peasants (Turgenev's *Sketches from a Hunter's Album* provides a ready example) reveals that the Russian peasant thought, or in any event expressed his thoughts, symbolically. This had less to do with religion than with a language through which one could approach the world. Many of the common symbols animating peasant speech were quite ordinary and at the same time threatening—such as the bear or the shrewish wife. But more generally, in the Russian popular mentality, the vocabulary of real power drew upon images of the supernatural. In traditional peasant culture the miraculous and phantasmagoric were a regular part of daily life. As in every Christian country (and maybe more so), vestigial pagan elements thrived within Russian Christianity. Saints, devils, imps, goblins, and other creatures constantly vied for control of every aspect of quotidien existence. Spirits, both Christian and pagan, guarded household and crops and controlled the forces determining success and failure, life and death.

The trauma of revolution and civil war had intensified the most basic emotions, tearing the fabric of civilized life with promises of ancient hopes realized and primal vengeances satisfied, and brought into high relief the fantastic expectations of the oppressed. What could justify total risk but total salvation?

The tone of civil war agitation was generally fantastic or violent, often both. A 1918 leaflet publicizing the Red army spun a gentle fantasy, but one in which the stakes were ultimate—universal truth against total evil. The characters are not Christian but folkloric. On the top of the leaflet a black hand points a finger to a big red five-pointed star emblazoned with a hammer and a plow. (This emblem coexisted with the hammer and sickle in 1918.) "The red star is the emblem of the Red army. Why does the Red army wear a red star?" The answer reads as follows:

Because every army wears the picture of that which it serves. **71**
What did the cockade of the old army represent?

It represented a ribbon from the tsarist flag in radiant beams.

And it represented the fact that the soldier served the tsar.

And the previous army served the tsar and by his decrees slaughtered peasants and workers and helped landlords and the bourgeoisie to oppress the narod . . .

What does the red star represent?

Listen, comrades!

Do you know the story of how once upon a time there lived on earth a beautiful maiden named PRAVDA? [truth].

She was beautiful beyond words and on her forehead had a burning star. The beams from that star brought light to the world, all people lived by truth, all lived well, everyone had enough, no one murdered or insulted anyone.

And once upon a time there lived on earth black KRIVDA [falsehood].

She wanted to disturb people and take away their happiness. She carefully stole up to PRAVDA and took her star and hid it. And right away the white earth became dark. And in the darkness, dark people began to do their dark deeds . . .

KRIVDA began to rule the whole world.

"Good people, find my star. Return my star. Return the light of truth to the world."

And a goodly youth appeared, went to search for the star of truth, battled with KRIVDA . . .

Finally, wounded and bloodied, he conquered KRIVDA and took from her the hidden star . . .

He fastened this star to his forehead and went to PRAVDA.

And evil people, KRIVDA'S supporters . . . tried to take the star away and extinguish it.

But the brave lad conquered them all, chased away all the enemies, and came to PRAVDA and brought her the star.

And once again it became light on the earth, and the evil people, KRIVDA'S supporters, ran away from the light like owls or bats and disappeared into the darkness.

And once again people lived by truth.

And once again life became good . . .

HAD YOU HEARD THIS STORY, COMRADE?

So, the Red Star of the Red army is the star of Pravda. And red soldiers are the brave lads who are fighting Krivda and her evil supporters so that truth should rule the world and that all those oppressed and wronged by Krivda, all the poor peasants and workers, should live well and in freedom . . .

ALL MUST JOIN THE RED ARMY, FASTEN THE RED STAR ONTO THEIR FOREHEADS, AND FIGHT THE SUPPORTERS OF KRIVDA—TSARS, PRINCES, LANDLORDS AND THE BOURGEOISIE!

ALL UNDER THE RED STAR, COMRADES!

BECAUSE IT IS THE STAR OF PRAVDA!

IT IS THE STAR OF THE EMANCIPATION OF ALL TOILERS FROM HUNGER, TOIL, WAR, POVERTY AND SLAVERY.

IT IS THE STAR OF THE HAPPINESS OF ALL POOR PEASANTS AND WORKERS.

THIS IS WHAT THE RED STAR OF THE RED ARMY REPRESENTS![19]

This leaflet shows the imaginary world that agitational creations could promise their readers. Not all the leaflets read like fairy tales, but they all appealed to strong emotions. Some appealed to hope. A 1918 flysheet for peasant women urged them to join the party: "In this terrible (*groznyi*) hour one must not be, cannot be outside the party. Only the blind and deaf may be outside the party now. The blind do not see the sun of freedom, the deaf do not hear the voice of their own conscience, of class interests, the voices of children resurrected from the dark and from slavery."[20] But most appealed to hate. Overwhelmingly civil war agitation attempted to arouse rage against the enemy. This was particularly true in posters that, like leaflets, were a call to action and could move everyone, including the illiterate. Some showed proud workers brandishing their tools like weapons, and others portrayed fierce soldiers with burning eyes and fearsome bayonets running to the front. The most effective depictions, however, were of the enemy—fat, smirking capitalists, fat, toothless priests, fat White generals in uniform. The enemy was almost invariably fat. Sometimes it was monstrous. A piglike capitalist wallows in his coin-filled spiderweb. A worker swings a club at a many-headed serpent representing the old order. A hideous swollen face representing the Entente powers tries to hide behind a serene mask of peace.[21] Occasionally the army itself took the form of a dread creature—the winged angel of death or the skeleton of the grim reaper himself, putting to flight the Romanov doubleheaded eagle. Good and evil were depicted in battle with each other most frequently, and the violence of their imagined confrontations only faintly reflected the actual brutality unleashed in Russia during the civil war.

Agitation served to mobilize both the army and the home front, and party propaganda, the exposition of the party line, was transmitted through the Moscow and Petrograd press, which, with only limited success, attempted to set the tone for the entire nation. The political concerns of the party and government changed with the termination of fighting. Agitation and propaganda were placed under Agitprop and Glavpolitprosvet. The demilitarization of political education was a tremendous undertaking. Krupskaia was head of Glavpolitprosvet and in 1922 complained that the civil war had made such a deep imprint on the nation that even civilian agitators took the same strident tone as did military ones, and that new personnel in her section after the war knew and valued only wartime agitation.[22] Wartime agitation has so influenced our work, wrote one Glavpolitprosvet official in 1922, that the only campaigns we launch consist of seeking out the enemy and then throwing everything at him, screaming at him in full voice on gramophones, posters, and wall newspapers.[23] The new agitation needed to reflect the new times.

War Communism was followed, in 1921, by the more popular New Economic Policy, a partial reversion to capitalism that allowed private trade within the country and substituted a tax in kind for forced food requisitions. At the close of the civil war the social base of the party was dangerously weak. War, the movement of workers into the party and Soviet administration, and the dislocation of industry had brought about a sharp numerical decline in the industrial working class—the new society's purported vanguard. The government bureaucracy was quickly filled with demobilized soldiers who had neither the experience nor the education necessary for administration. Party membership increased during the New Economic Policy, but many of the newer members lacked the dedication and zeal of the original revolutionary cadre and were seeking the elevated political and social benefits conferred on members of the Communist Party.[24]

The Tenth Party Congress of 1921 charged Glavpolitprosvet and other organs with the task of intensifying agitational work as part of the struggle against the "petty-bourgeois counterrevolution," dangerously inherent in the New Economic Policy.[25] Agit-trains and ships were no longer necessary; they were replaced by permanent centers of agitation—clubs, libraries, special reading rooms, theaters.[26] There was a consensus in Glavpolitprosvet that mass audiences were no longer interested in the old type of meetings, posters, and leaflets that tried to rouse their anger. New forms were necessary, new subjects that would inform the people as well as interest and move them.[27] At the same time, there was a need to organize and standardize agitation, all under difficult financial constraints.

Glavpolitprosvet and Agitprop ultimately were successful in unifying and standardizing agitation and propaganda in 1924 and 1925, when they found a *positive* symbol around which to structure their work: the idealized memory of V. I. Lenin. The agitational campaign these organizations launched shortly after Lenin's death was to spread a cult of Lenin across the land and to turn its trappings and rituals into a pervasive part of Soviet political practice.

Lenin's publicized image was an increasingly important focus of agitation and propaganda even throughout the years of his active rule. His authority as leader of Russia and his heroic stature in the popular imagination were in part a spontaneous revival of naive monarchism. They derived also from the posters, poems, paeans, and biographies dedicated to him during these years. Adulation of Lenin was also the work of his closest comrades—Zinoviev, in particular—who strove to demonstrate to the party and the populace the respect and reverence due the man who was attempting to rule Russia in their name.

The Lenin Myth Begins

Between Lenin's arrival in Petrograd in April 1917 and the October revolution, no hint of the Lenin cult that would begin to emerge the following year was in evidence. Although he was the acknowledged head of the party, in practice this meant little because his positions were judged largely on their merits with no special weight given to his status. At the Sixth Party Congress, held while Lenin was still in hiding, he was hailed by his comrades as the dominant theorist of Bolshevism; his writings were cited as authoritative and even prophetic.[28] But, though the Provisional Government's charges of treason against him provoked much discussion and though the delegates uniformly supported him, they showed no reverence for their leader. He was not singled out for praise. Only once did a delegate relay special greetings to Lenin alone, and these came not from the Central Committee but from a group of workers who sent their sympathy to Lenin for his forced absence, along with their wish that his ideas should provide the foundation for the deliberations of the congress.[29] In general, greetings were offered to both Lenin and Zinoviev, who were in hiding together. At the opening of the first session, a delegate moved that Lenin be elected honorary chairman of the congress, a motion that was greeted with applause and unanimously passed. But immediately Sverdlov, a member of the congress' presidium and, along with Stalin, the dominant figure in the Petrograd party organization still at large, added another motion to include as honorary chairmen Zinoviev and those party leaders who were in jail: Kamenev, Trotsky, Kollontai, and Lunacharsky. Sverdlov's proposal was also applauded and the motion was carried. The congress sent greetings to Lenin, Trotsky, Zinoviev, and Kamenev;[30] Lenin was the first among several notable Bolshevik leaders.

To the public Lenin presented himself as simply a member of the Central Committee of the Russian Social Democratic Labor Party (Bolsheviks). He so described himself in his open letter to the All-Russian Congress of Peasant Deputies in May 1917. An accompanying agitational biography specifically states that Lenin heads no party but is a *member* of the Social Democratic Party, which was founded when he was still a boy. In 1903, the party split into Bolsheviks and Mensheviks, and "gradually Lenin came to be considered one of the main leaders of Social Democracy." The biography calls Lenin a writer (*literator*) from a revolutionary family. The author was not certain of Lenin's exact age, describing him as about fifty years old (he was forty-seven). Lenin is portrayed as victimized by the police, who arrested him in 1887 together with Alexander. He took the name Lenin to hide his real name from the police, and the nickname stuck.[31] The rest of the brief biography describes not Lenin's personal history, but that of the party—appropriate for the man who saw Bolshevism as *his* emanation.

Before the coup the Bolshevik press did not, as a rule, single Lenin out for special attention. M. S. Olminsky, an editor of the Moscow Bolshevik daily *Sotsial-Demokrat,* provided an exception—the first self-conscious characterization of Lenin. Olminsky

76   began by explaining that the editors had been asked to publish biographical information about Lenin. "We Bolsheviks are not inclined to push individuals into the foreground," he said, adding that it was customary to write biographies only as obituaries. However, in view of workers' requests and the slander of Lenin in the bourgeois press, he would depart from custom this once.

Olminsky portrays Lenin as a man of extreme modesty and total dedication to the party. Lenin never thinks of food, clothes, or recreation; "his only concern is the party." He does not aspire to glory and wrote under several pseudonyms to protect himself against the censors, but also because he did not care to make a name for himself. Not caring what people think of him, he only does what is right; this makes him many enemies who slander him and distort his words. In order to avoid confusion, adds the author at this point, we exhorted him to make a practice of signing his articles more frequently (Lenin's articles in 1917 were often published without signature). Olminsky closed with the suggestion that those close to Vladimir Ilich publish collections of his past articles. "He himself would never think of doing this; this is the kind of character he has."[32]

Olminsky's is the first known instance of publicity about Lenin in the Bolshevik press, and it came from the pen of a man who, the next year, was to write that while the Socialist Revolutionary Party, as the descendant of the Narodovoltsy, was too caught up in hero cults, Russian Marxists had gone too far in the opposite direction and were paying too little attention to Lenin.[33] It is not surprising that its author was a former Narodovolets and had been part of the circle of admirers that Valentinov described as "reverential" of Lenin.

Another biography of Lenin published in the Bolshevik press at approximately the same time was written by Krupskaia and edited by Lenin. A reprinted version identifies his corrections, making it the closest available approximation of an autobiography by Lenin.[34] The only other is the beginning of an autobiography that dates from the late spring or early summer of 1917 and is a response to a group of soldiers who wrote Lenin asking him about himself. His answer gives his name, date, and place of birth, then mentions his brother's execution, his own arrest in 1887 and exclusion from the university, his exile from Kazan, and his arrest in 1895. There the manuscript stops. It was not published until three years after his death.[35]

Krupskaia's biography, published unsigned in *Soldatskaia pravda*, may well be Lenin's response to the soldiers' request.[36] It portrays Lenin as he apparently wished to be portrayed, not as a star but as a personification of his party and his cause. That is precisely what he became as a cult figure in the 1920s. The title of the biography attests to this leitmotif: "A Little Page from the History of the RSDLP." It describes Lenin's return to Petrograd in April and the festive welcome given him by the workers. For them Lenin was the "personification of the transfer of power to the workers"; the phrase is Lenin's own, a correction of Krupskaia's original statement that Lenin was the "personification of popular power." In this biography Lenin also demonstrates his identification with *Iskra*. Krupskaia had written of Lenin's seminal role in its founding, after which she wrote that "there is no need to speak of *Iskra*'s significance." Lenin did not agree, adding the following sentence: " 'Iskra' laid the foundation for the Russian social democratic labor party." Also in connection with *Iskra*, Lenin showed his aversion to being singled out as a personality apart from the movement. Krupskaia wrote that economism (a fin-de-siècle party heresy) was attacked by the Leninists (*lenintsy*). Lenin crossed out Leninists and replaced it with Iskraists (*iskrovtsy*). As a biographical sketch, this article is fair and modest, although it omits young Ulianov's early connections with the Narodovoltsy and begins the story of his revolutionary activity with his St. Petersburg work in 1894. It does not exaggerate his role in the 1905 revolution and even mentions that, after two days in the capital, Lenin was forced to go into hiding.

Another work that in a more distant way can be considered an authorized biography of Lenin is John Reed's *Ten Days That Shook the World*. This eyewitness account of the October revolution by an American journalist of socialist persuasion greatly appealed to Lenin. The author presented him with a copy in the fall of 1919. Lenin wrote a foreword to it, recommending the book to all workers and expressing his wish to see it translated into "all languages" and published in "millions of copies." He calls Reed's depiction of the events of October "truthful and most vivid."[37]

The heroes of *Ten Days That Shook the World* are the workers and soldiers of Petrograd. The revolution is described as a living organism—moving, growing, literally humming with energy. In this context Lenin appears only rarely, but when he does he is spectacularly heroic, growing progressively larger as he nears the center of activity. First he is the author of the "audacious" "Letter to Comrades," published on October 19, urging immediate armed insurrection. He next appears three days before the coup as a mighty tocsin, summoning his party to action: "On the one side the Monarchist press, inciting to bloody repression—on the other Lenin's great voice roaring, 'Insurrection! . . . We cannot wait any longer!' "[38] He remains audible but not visible until the very day of the coup, causing two of the comrades who had opposed insurrection, Kamenev and Riazanov, to feel "the lash of Lenin's terrible tongue."[39] Lenin finally appears at the extraordinary session of the Petrograd Soviet called by Trotsky on October 25 and is "welcomed with a mighty ovation." Reed describes Lenin in his full stature only once, at the Congress of Soviets in session that evening:

> It was just 8:40 when a thundering wave of cheers announced the entrance of the presidium, with Lenin—great Lenin—among them. A short, stocky figure, with a big head set down in his shoulders, bald and bulging. Little eyes, a snubbish nose, wide, generous mouth, and heavy chin . . . Dressed in shabby clothes, his trousers much too long for him. Unimpressive, to be the idol of a mob, loved and revered as perhaps few leaders in history have been. A strange popular leader—a leader purely by virtue of intellect; colourless, humourless, uncompromising and detached, without picturesque idiosyncrasies—but with the power of explaining profound ideas in simple terms, of analysing a concrete situation. And combined with shrewdness, the greatest intellectual audacity.

When it was his turn to speak, he was greeted with a long ovation that was repeated after his opening sentence: "We shall now proceed to construct the Socialist order!" Only in this instance does Reed portray Lenin as the revered leader, with the audience below "a thousand simple faces looking up in intent adoration."[40] Reed provides no characterization of Lenin of the sort offered by Olminsky. There is simply one description and an assessment of his charisma as coming from the power of his intellect. That undoubtedly pleased Lenin—if he paid attention to it.

In 1919, when Lenin read Reed's book, he had many more pressing matters to occupy his time than that of scrutinizing descriptions of himself. Therefore it is not certain that the description of him as the adored leader was necessarily to his liking. More important, doubtless, was the totality of the account which made Lenin the unseen spirit that impelled the party to revolution and which focused on the party's muscle—the masses for whom he saw himself speaking. To those masses Lenin remained more or less invisible even after he became head of state.

In the first ten months following the October revolution Lenin was barely perceptible as a public figure beyond the speeches he delivered before live audiences. Krupskaia recalled that in the first weeks of Bolshevik rule "nobody knew Lenin's face at that time. In the evening we would often . . . stroll around the Smolny, and nobody would ever recognize him, because there were no portraits then."[41] His first official photographic portrait was made in January 1918, a realistic depiction of a very tired man.[42] It was reproduced on the first published poster of Lenin. Bland and spare, it bore the simple caption of his name and government title.[43] In the same year, 1918, the Petrograd Soviet published an advertisement for its official organ, *Izvestiia,* which showed Lenin's elevated stature as founding father of the new regime: two portraits of identical size were symmetrically placed on the page—one of Lenin, the other of Marx.[44]

In the press, Lenin was not singled out for praise or even special attention, except immediately after the seizure of power when the new leader was honored with a brief biographical sketch in *Izvestiia*[45] and a smattering of verse. On October 29, 1917, *Pravda* published a poem dedicated to the "uncompromising fighter for proletarian ideals, Comrade N. Lenin." This poem lauds Lenin's speeches, which provided both the warmth of a sun's caress and the peal of a mighty tocsin.[46] Another, published three weeks later in *Soldatskaia pravda,* a newspaper aimed at the military, was an early attempt at a formal paean to the new head of state:

> Hail to the Supreme Leader of the People;
> Dedicated to Citizen Ulianov (Lenin)
>
> Hail to you, soul of the people,
> Free, pure citizen!
> Hail to you, freedom's beauty,
> Invincible giant!

> Hail to you, our leader of the people,
> Champion of rights and ideas,
> Pure as crystal, noble,
> The terror of the rich and of tsars!
> The families of workers, of the hungry
> Are in your ranks—your shield in battle;
> Their legion of sons of the free,
> Is on guard—believes—will triumph![47]

The most extravagant example of Leniniana in this period was a poem by Demian Bednyi, soon to become the Bolshevik poet laureate. Entitled "To the Leader" (*vozhdiu*), it was a piece of occasional verse written for May Day, 1918. It is filled with religious imagery. "You were in a distant land,/ But in spirit you were with us always,—/ There grew, page by page,/ The Holy Bible of Labor." Every day was fraught with danger, the poet continues, reminiscing about 1917, the danger of "open assault/ And the crafty designs of a hidden Judas."[48]

No Judas did appear, but there was an open assault on Lenin on August 30, 1918. It was an assassination attempt by a terrorist of Left Socialist Revolutionary persuasion. Its aftermath was a bloody reprisal of arrests and shootings by the Cheka that the Bolshevik press called the "Red Terror." The shooting also spurred the first major concentration of Leniniana and marked the first occasion on which Lenin evoked extravagant praise simultaneously from diverse sources. This was the first event in the gradual emergence of the cult.

On the morning of August 30, 1918, the head of the Petrograd Cheka, Moisei Uritsky, was murdered. Lenin was to give two speeches that day. Despite the attempts of his sister and colleagues to dissuade him from keeping his appointments in view of the possible danger to his life, Lenin made his speeches on schedule. As he was about to get into his car outside the Michelson factory where he had made his second appearance, Fania Kaplan shot and wounded Lenin. Lenin's chauffeur drove the stricken leader to his Kremlin apartment and telephoned the secretary of the Sovnarkom, Bonch-Bruevich, whose first concern was for political security. He ordered a strengthening of the Kremlin guard and alerted Red army units. Then he grabbed some first aid equipment from his apartment (his wife was a physician) and rushed out to help Lenin.[49] He had been shot in the shoulder and neck and was in pain, but the wounds were not mortal.

The central press immediately launched a campaign of agitation, vowing to avenge the treacherous attacks. Uritsky was lauded with eulogies and poems in honor of the "fallen leader."[50] But the agitational focus was on Lenin. The first official response to the shooting came from Iakov Sverdlov, president of the Soviet's Central Executive Committee. Calling him the "genuine leader of the working class," Sverdlov said that "the role of Com. Lenin, his significance for the working movement of Russia, the working movement of the whole world," was "acknowledged among the broadest circles of workers of all countries." He vowed that in response to this attack on its leaders the working class would rally and unleash a merciless mass terror against the enemies of the revolution.[51] Kaplan was speedily executed, and although she had not been connected to any organization, hundreds of people were arrested and shot in reprisal for the shooting.

The country was already in the grip of civil war, and the attack on Lenin was interpreted as an act of war. Trotsky, leader of the Red army, hurried to Moscow from the Kazan front. In an address to the All-Union Central Executive Committee on September 2, he spoke of Lenin's struggle against death as a "new front," for Kaplan's bullets had been a direct attack on the Bolshevik regime. Trotsky affirmed his faith in Lenin's victory, but at the same time observed that no other defeat would be as tragic for the working class as the death of Lenin. Lenin was the "leader of the new epoch" and the "greatest human being of our revolutionary epoch." Trotsky was well aware that "the fate of the working class does not depend on individual personalities." But, he continued, the individual can help the working class to fulfill its role and attain its goal more quickly. Lenin was brought forth by Russian history for the new epoch of "blood and iron" as the "embodiment of the courageous thought and the revolutionary will of the working class." His greatness as a revolutionary leader lay in his unshakable will and in his unusual perspicacity, his acute "revolutionary gaze."[52] Trotsky's speech was an intentional agitational weapon; it was published not only in the press but in pamphlet form, together with a speech of Kamenev, head of the Moscow Soviet, in an edition of one million copies.[53]

On September 6 in Petrograd, Zinoviev, the chairman of its Soviet, made a long address that was also published (200,000 copies).[54] Its tone combines religious fervor and melodrama. He began by saying that for the entire previous week every honest Russian worker had but one concern: would the leader recover? Zinoviev then provided the happy news that Lenin had indeed recovered from his wounds. The speech was purportedly a factual biography of Lenin. But Zinoviev selected his facts carefully. He began, for example, by saying that Lenin's father came from peasant stock; he neglected to add that by the time Vladimir Ulianov was born, his father had achieved hereditary nobility.[55] Zinoviev depicts Lenin as a saint, an apostle, and a prophet. He describes Lenin's long years in emigration as the trial of an ascetic: "He lived like a beggar, he was sick, he was undernourished—especially during his years in Paris."[56] Lenin came to be the "apostle of world communism." *What Is To Be Done?* Zinoviev calls the gospel (*evangelie*) of the Iskraists. Lenin was not only an ascetic, he also displayed the perfect optimism of the true believer and the gift of prophecy. Zinoviev remarked that the years of reaction in Russia were particularly discouraging for the revolutionaries living in emigration. The revolutionary hope encouraged by the 1905 revolution was dashed by its aftermath. But Lenin, in Zinoviev's story, showed courage and hope and inspired his followers. He knew that the revolution would succeed: "Do not lose heart; these dark days will pass, the muddy wave will ebb, several years will pass, and we will be once again on the crest of the wave; the workers' revolution will be reborn." Lenin became a leader of cosmic stature, a mover of worlds:

> Someone powerful and strong has disturbed the petty-bourgeois swamp. The movement of the waters begins. On the horizon a new figure has appeared . . .
> He is really the chosen one of millions. He is the leader by the grace of God. He is the authentic figure of a leader such as is born once in 500 years in the life of mankind.

There is no reason to doubt the sincerity of Trotsky's and Zinoviev's praises of Lenin. The Bolshevik seizure and retention of power had been a remarkable achievement, and Lenin's leadership was a crucial component of its success at every stage. No doubt his lieutenants admired him enormously. But, in addition, their speeches were calculated to show that they perceived the assassination attempt as a declaration of war on the Bolshevik leadership, an attack that warranted mass reprisals. Lenin had been only wounded, not killed, and Kaplan had not been a formal member of the Socialist Revolutionary Party, and yet hundreds of SRs were executed in the "Red Terror" on the grounds that their party had assaulted the embodiment of the entire proletariat. These Communist dignitaries of the highest order had begun to create their myths of Lenin. The process must have been at least partly conscious.

Trotsky and Zinoviev were the most renowned orators in the party. They must have understood the effect and significance of every phrase, every image with which they described the stricken leader. They were setting the tone of respect, reverence, and fervent solidarity that was the official party position on Lenin. As they sought simultaneously to arouse anger toward the Socialist Revolutionaries and to praise Lenin, they were laying down the fundamental tenet on which the Lenin cult would be based: loyalty to Lenin and the party he founded meant death to his opponents and detractors. Fervent love and undying hatred were to accompany each other and were invariably to be expressed together in the flood of articles unleashed by the attempt on Lenin's life.

One of the most striking of these was written by Lev Sosnovsky, a Bolshevik journalist and editor of *Bednota,* a newspaper aimed at the broad mass of peasant readers. (In 1920 Sosnovsky became head of the Central Committee's new Agitprop.) Two days after the shooting Sosnovsky wrote an article in *Petrogradskaia pravda* in which he described Lenin in Christlike terms—a formula he was to repeat after Lenin's death. First he spoke of Lenin as a symbol to workers of the whole world, a symbol of the struggle for peace and socialism. Then he added a corollary inversion common to the Leniniana that followed the attempted murder. Capitalists, he wrote, hate Lenin for that very reason; they see him as their main enemy. He went on to speak of Lenin as a leader of such universal stature that Italian mothers, according to their tradition of naming their children after heroes, were now naming their babies after him. Sosnovsky devised this formula for Lenin: "Lenin cannot be killed . . . Because Lenin is the rising up of the oppressed. Lenin is the fight to the end, to final victory . . . So long as the proletariat lives—Lenin lives. Of course, we, his students and colleagues, were shaken by the terrible news of the attempt on the life of dear 'Ilich', as the Communists lovingly call him." Ilich is the mortal man and Lenin is the immortal leader and universal symbol. "A thousand times [we] tried to convince him to take even the most basic security precautions. But 'Ilich' always rejected these pleas. Daily, without any protection, he went to all sorts of gatherings, congresses, meetings." The mortal man exposed himself to danger, but Lenin cannot be harmed. Again the Christ parallel is striking. Lenin's wounding appears as a voluntary sacrifice of a man who consciously made himself vulnerable.[57]

Lenin's sacrifice and martyrdom was the theme of one of the many poems the shooting inspired:

> You came to us, to ease
> Our excruciating torment,
> You came to us as a leader, to destroy
> The enemies of the workers' movement . . .
> We will not forget your suffering,
> That you, our leader, endured for us.
> You stood a martyr.[58]

Other poems called Lenin a martyr, suffering for the salvation of the poor.[59] He was an "enlightened genius," a "dear father," a "savior."[60] And finally he was a cross between Christ and St. George.

> Great leader of the iron Host,
> Friend and brother of all oppressed people,
> Welding together peasants, workers, and soldiers
> In the flame of crucifixions.
>
> Invincible messenger of peace,
> Crowned with the thorns of slander,
> Prophet who has plunged his sword into the vampire,
> Fulfiller of the fiery dream.[61]

The popular avowals of Lenin's martyrdom were probably not responses to institutional directives. No apparatus existed at this time to indicate the appropriate epithets and images, although the press of Moscow and Petrograd was making an attempt in this direction. Some historical process was turning Lenin into a "passion-sufferer" resembling the medieval saintly princes whose sanctity derived from the tragic ends they met as princes. Like the officially sponsored cult of Alexander II, the cult of Lenin derived its beginnings in the public avowals of his voluntary self-sacrifice for his people. But Lenin's superhuman stature was complicated by the fact that he had martyred himself—and then survived. Some literature immediately following the incident attributed his physical survival to a miracle.

A dramatic example demonstrates the syncretism of ideology and mysticism that came to characterize the later cult of Lenin. An article in a Moscow regional newspaper said that only the joint will of the proletariat had saved Lenin from certain death. "The history of firearm wounds during the last war is full of truly 'miraculous' occurrences . . . when a little notebook, medallion, or even button deflected a bullet and saved a person's life." But those involved shots at a great distance. Lenin's "murderess" fired point-blank. A few centimeters to the left or to the right and the bullet that pierced his neck would have killed him. The bullet in his shoulder could have penetrated his lung. Not a button and not a medallion, but the "will of the proletariat" intervened to save Lenin, whose trust had made him open to attack.[62] This story is reminiscent of those that filled government and church publications in Russia after an unsuccessful attempt on the life of Alexander II in 1866. The gunshots missed the emperor because of the "Divine Hand of Providence" that caused the bullets to whiz past their target. (Most nineteenth-century Russian terrorists were very bad shots.)

Whatever popular rumors there may have been to the same effect, the stories about Alexander were officially generated. What of the stories about Lenin in 1918? What does it mean to have Lenin portrayed as a martyr or a recipient of supernatural grace? Were the authors of poems and eulogies expressing their real feelings, or were they deliberately attempting to create a myth with which to mobilize readers? These questions can have no definitive answers. But it is certain that the flamboyant poetry and prose about Lenin sparked by the shooting were not modeled on what appeared in the central press. Only Zinoviev's writings matched the extravagance of what was published in local newspapers, and his speech was published a full week after the assassination attempt. The mythologizing of Lenin began immediately after the event. Probably some journalists and poets expressed sincere sentiments of sorrow and anger in the vocabulary that came naturally to them. Others may have consciously attempted to paint Lenin in forms and colors they believed

86   would move their readers. And many simply were expressing solidarity with the Bolsheviks in the strongest language available to them. Doubtless all of these elements were at work in this earliest mythologizing of Lenin, but the wish to demonstrate solidarity probably comes closest to an inclusive explanation of the effusive and quasi-religious rhetoric eulogizing Lenin in September 1918. The civil war had begun, and the Kremlin had not waited to unleash its Red Terror as an immediate response to what it perceived as an attempted Socialist revolutionary coup d'état. It was time to demonstrate loyalty clearly and sharply.

Feelings of religious veneration and political loyalty spring from a common source in the human psyche, and no gradual secularization had effected a separation between the two in the minds of the common people. Saints' lives, the favorite reading of the peasantry, had provided a vocabulary of power even for many members of the revolutionary intelligentsia, particularly those from the provinces who were only a generation or two removed from humble origins. Moreover, the highly developed demonology of Russian popular religion included constant tensions between good and bad spirits, saints and devils. The language of this culture provided the earliest vocabulary of the emerging Lenin myth. It was evident in the popular mythologizing about Lenin that counterposed him to a monstrous and demonic enemy. A good example is provided in an article published in a provincial weekly of the Military-Revolutionary Committee of the Moscow-Kiev-Voronezh railroad:

> The counterrevolutionary hydra, as the devoted companion and consistent betrayer of all good, truth, and justice, is extending its poisonous tentacles from the depths of the nether regions, searching for a weak spot on the body of the world revolution ... This sea creature, a marvel of ugliness, a freak of nature, a fright to the world—called octopus at sea and the bourgeoisie on land—is a freak of nature, blind at birth and a result of the demon's own creation in the world ...
>
> And so on August 27, the organized enemy of Soviet Russia—the bourgeoisie—and its devoted companions, the social-traitor "Chernovites" committed an unheard-of crime against the laboring class of the entire world—they shot point-blank at Lenin, the leader of the world proletariat ... the sole idol and divinity of the working class,

the poorest of the peasantry, of every honest man and citizen of the entire world, and all of mankind.

A pitiful and unfortunate parody! A single mad and convulsive hand of a dying humanoid beast directs these senseless, mad shootings in Moscow and Petrograd.

And that hydra or blind eternal "octopus," caught in the eternally dark ocean depths and flung out on the dry sea shore, helplessly twisted its claws and accidentally struck a man who had come imprudently close to it, who was also preparing to deal it a last fatal blow.

No, unhappy hydra! Your days are numbered and your bite can only serve as a signal for the universal fraternal union of all working people.[63]

The author of this powerful if confused prose was an unsophisticated representative of the common folk, most likely a railroad worker. His writing is ungrammatical, and the primitive imagery could only reflect the popular imagination. This kind of literature on Lenin was very short-lived, not surviving Lenin's death. With the very first flurry of Leniniana that followed the attack on Lenin, Bolshevik journalists followed the party leadership in working to standardize Lenin's public persona, to establish an official biographical depiction of Lenin that would make the leader an effective political symbol within the constraints of Marxist ideology. An acceptable standardization of Lenin's image was not effected until after his death in 1924, when the organized cult of his memory was in full force. But the process began immediately after the assassination attempt.

"The cult of personality contradicts the whole spirit of Marxism, the spirit of scientific socialism," wrote Olminsky in 1918. Not individuals, but productive forces move the process of history. However, while Socialist Revolutionaries exaggerate the role of individuals, creating "cults of heroes" and "icons," Russian Marxists have erred in the other extreme by ignoring their leaders. Olminsky himself had begun a myth of Lenin in the brief biographical sketch he published in May 1917. In 1918 his stated purpose was to urge his comrades not to let their ideology prevent them from writing about Lenin, since he was after all more than simply head of state. "Our party is inseparable from Com. Lenin just as he, in turn, is inseparable from the party. And to know, to study Com. Lenin as a literary and political figure means to know and study in one individual the

88 colossal revolutionary proletarian collective." This became a cornerstone of the cult: Lenin is the collective, the party, the working class. It was precisely in the name of this relationship—Lenin as the embodiment of the people's will—that the party was to mobilize the nation with a series of rituals following Lenin's death. "To know Com. Lenin is to know ourselves," wrote Olminsky. "In this lies the legitimate justification of our interest in his personality."[64] Olminsky wrote his piece before the assassination attempt. After the shooting incident Lenin's unique stature was taken for granted, and ideological justifications no longer were included in writings devoted to him. Olminsky's desire for more publicity about Lenin was fulfilled after the shooting, when the Soviet Central Executive Committee rushed into print two biographies of Lenin for mass consumption, one aimed at workers and the other at peasants. These biographies were clear and deliberate attempts to establish Lenin's impeccable credentials as a focus of political loyalty for the Russian people, who, until the shooting, knew little about him.

Emelian Iaroslavsky, who was to head the Institute of Party History in the 1930s, wrote a biography of Lenin, *The Great Leader of the Workers' Revolution,* the day after the shooting. The author promised to give his readers "only the facts" about Lenin, not the slander spread by the bourgeoisie. "Every ass from the bourgeois camp will now try to kick the wounded lion." Iaroslavsky's stress is on Lenin's ties with the proletariat. He predates by two years Lenin's involvement with St. Petersburg workers, stating that it began in 1891 when Lenin entered the University of St. Petersburg (in reality Lenin merely took his examinations there and engaged in no organized political activities in the capital until 1893). Above all else, Lenin is depicted as beloved by the working class. In 1917 when the order went out for his arrest, it was the Petrograd workers who protected him "for the October revolution, of which he was the soul, the brain . . . The Bourgeoisie does not yet know . . . how dear this person is to the working class." And we, the old party workers, wrote Iaroslavsky, know that, even when we disagree with him, he is better than all of us.[65]

The Peasant Department of the Central Executive Committee published a biography of Lenin in which he is—and always was—above all concerned with the peasantry. One hundred thousand copies were published, an enormous edition testifying to the fact that it was destined for a mass readership. The pamphlet's title reflected its theme: *The Leader of the Rural Poor, V. I. Ulianov-Lenin.* "The history of the Russian peasantry has its bright heroes," it begins. "There are not many of them—Stenka Razin, Pugachev, and a few intelligentsia-populists who considered themselves friends of the peasantry." But recent history has brought forth a new hero "whose name is always on the lips of the entire peasantry. In the past two years this hero appeared in the dark Russian countryside with a brightly burning torch and is scattering the blinding sparks of his fiery brain far beyond the borders of Soviet Russia. The wireless radio catches these sparks and sends them out across the surface of the globe. This hero is Vladimir Ilich Ulianov-Lenin." Even though Vladimir Ilich can rightly be called the leader of the socialist revolution in Russia and the world, the Russian countryside considers him above all *"its* leader-hero." The next sentence, which leads directly into the biography, exemplifies the conscious distortion of Lenin's career that was the leitmotif of this agitational pamphlet: "Vl. Ilich's entire life, all his teachings, his literary and political activity, were inseparably linked with the countryside." The first link came from his father, who was of noble background but nonetheless a person close to the peasantry in spirit. This sympathy for the suffering peasantry the father passed on to his family. Lenin grew up to be an exemplary hero. He was bold, publishing *Iskra* despite tsarist censorship (a misleading idea, for *Iskra* was published abroad to avoid the censors). A "prophet of genius," he prophesied the developmental process of the 1917 revolution twelve years earlier, in 1905, when he correctly assessed the necessary agrarian program. He was always the friend of the poor peasant, while the Socialist Revolutionaries are the friends of the landlords. This last is the biography's most important point, for the Socialist Revolutionary Party was *the* party of the Russian peasantry.[66] When the SR party tried to kill him, it was fate that saved him as well as his "iron heart in an iron organism."

The biography ends with a pure fabrication about the shooting. When the would-be assassin fired, the workers began to panic, but "Vl. Ilich shouted to them, 'Comrades, order! This is not important—maintain order!'" This shows Lenin's spiritual nature, concludes the author. "To him it was not important that he was being killed on behalf of the toilers—it was only important that the toilers

90   themselves not cease even for a moment their organized struggle . . . Such is our glorious leader, our dear Vladimir Ilich."[67]

LENIN made a quick recovery from his wounds, returning to work within two weeks of the incident. But Moscow was buzzing with rumors that he had really died and had been carried out of the Kremlin at night and buried in secret. He needed public visibility, but his doctors had ordered him to make no addresses for three months. Consequently Bonch-Bruevich arranged to film Lenin in the Kremlin courtyard.[68] "Vladimir Ilich's Kremlin Stroll," the first documentary film of Lenin, was shown throughout Moscow in the fall of 1918.[69]

With Lenin's speedy convalescence the spate of Leniniana subsided; if Bonch-Bruevich is to believed, Lenin himself must take the credit for this. He asserts that Lenin was appalled by what he read about himself in the newspapers after the assassination attempt: "It is shameful to read . . . They exaggerate everything, call me a genius, some kind of special person . . . All our lives we have waged an ideological struggle against the glorification of the personality, of the individual; long ago we settled the problem of heroes. And suddenly here again is a glorification of the individual!" Lenin then sent for his friends Olminsky and Lepeshinsky, both editors, and ordered them to accompany Bonch-Bruevich to the offices of *Pravda* and *Izvestiia* and tell the editors to "put on the brakes." P. N. Lepeshinsky, an old Bolshevik and former Narodovolets who had been one of Lenin's Geneva worshipers, now chuckled with him and remarked that the patriarch of the church ought to make Lenin a saint.[70] Lenin's response was in keeping with his generally suspicious attitude toward flattery. Public adulation had a dangerous tendency to substitute for real proofs of loyalty—work, discipline, obedience to directives of the party center. Furthermore, since Bolsheviks had heretofore restricted their paeans to *dead* comrades, the published praises might have made Lenin feel he was being turned into the "harmless icon" he described in *State of Revolution*. Lenin's orders were carried out, and the press of Moscow, which set the tone for that of the provinces, stopped its systematic publication of his praises.

But the cult of Lenin had been set on its course, although no one at the time would have predicted its future development. The attempt on Lenin's life had brought forth a new rhetorical convention for expressing solidarity with Bolshevik policies: extravagant adulation of Lenin. This had taken many linguistic forms. Some of the imagery was religious, some was folkloric, and some came from the language of war. All of it was emotional and intense. Its range reflected both the social and cultural heterogeneity of its users and the richness of revolutionary rhetoric in this early, formative period of Soviet culture. More than a decade would pass before the establishment of a standard political rhetoric of uniform formulas, epithets, and clichés. The cult of Lenin played a big role in its formation by providing an official object of Communist enthusiasm whose exalted status ultimately gave the highest authorities in the party the full power to determine the language fit to describe him.

In part, the transformation of Lenin from an object of adulation into a cult figure was marked by the imposed control of the permissible epithets and adjectives that the party dignitaries deemed to be suitable. This occurred after his death and corresponded to the institutional control over his visual portrayals, which also began in 1924 with the formation of a special commission to review all portraits and busts of the leader and pass judgment on their acceptability. Just as Lenin wished *Iskra* to provide the guideline for party workers, so the organizers of his cult were to provide a guideline for the cult edifice. The cult of Lenin was to be a visible construction of one truth, one history, one man—to serve as a model for the Communist Party of the Soviet Union, which sought to establish one line for every significant aspect of life. The cult was an early expression of that endeavor and at the same time contributed to it.

Long before the cult was organized, a variety of myths about Lenin had developed. After Lenin's death those myths were to be standardized into one "story" (with acceptable variations). They were also to be brought together as "literature on Lenin," sacred collectibles that the Lenin Institute carefully catalogued in its inclusive bibliographies.

It was just after Lenin's death, "with Lenin's grave not yet closed" (thus too early for the author to know that his grave would not be closed at all) that the poet and folklorist L. Seifullina hurriedly wrote down the myths of Lenin she claimed to have heard in the winter of 1918 in remote villages of the Ural mountains. The region had a diverse population of peasants, cossacks, Mordvinians, Bash-

92   kirs, Kirghiz. Many religious groups were represented in this distant land—Orthodox Christians, Old Believers, Muslims, and a variety of sectarians. These were people whose folklore demonstrated no engagement with the Russian state. There were no stories about the tsar or his officials, but only about local notables. And yet Seifullina claimed that Lenin's name captured the popular imagination and aroused strong feelings in the narod. Some Old Believers and sectarians "shouted out whole pages of the Bible by heart, attributing to Lenin the number of the beast, the number six hundred sixty-six, the number of the Antichrist." This formulation equated Lenin with the tsar, for Old Believers had traditionally depicted the Romanov emperors as the Antichrist. They wielded the Bible to attack Lenin, but Seifullina described others who used it to defend him, such as one party member who yelled out biblical texts to prove the holy justice of Lenin's political acts. She maintained that even then, during Lenin's lifetime, legends about him were spread in traditional folkloric forms such as *byliny* (epics). Russian peasants tell stories only about people in whom they believe, she maintained, and they believed in Lenin. "Through these stories Lenin penetrated the soul of the peasant."[71]

Were folktales about Lenin spontaneous creations inspired by the appearance of a new hero, a new strong man powerful enough to sweep away the tsar, or were they the products of bards and storytellers with Bolshevik sympathies who used their art to influence the local public? Probably both. But all artists create with the intent to influence and move audiences, and folk artists are no exception. Folklore is fundamentally concerned with power—natural, supernatural, and political power. Bolshevik bards composed stories about Lenin within the folk tradition of making powerful figures accessible by introducing them in stylized and familiar mythic forms.

Some measure of hyperbole may distort Seifullina's rhapsodic description of the peasantry's engagement with Lenin, but it is unlikely that she went so far as to fabricate the tale of Lenin and Tsar Mikolashka,[72] which she claimed to have heard from an old woman in a peasant settlement in Orenburg province. The tsar, Mikolashka, was told by his most important general that there was a certain person, "of unknown rank, without a passport, who goes by the name of Lenin."[73] This Lenin threatened to take away the tsar's soldiers with one word and to grind the generals, commanders, and officers—even the tsar himself—into ashes and let them blow in the wind. The tsar took fright and sent a message to Lenin, offering to divide the country in half with Lenin to prevent him from uttering that word. Lenin agreed but specified that the tsar must take the "white" half—the generals and officers and rich people—while Lenin took the "black"—the soldiers, peasants, and workers. The tsar was overjoyed to keep his riches, but then discovered that Lenin had tricked him. His officers had no soldiers to lead and no people to make the country run. So the tsar's white part of Russia went to war against Lenin's black part to regain the latter. But the white could not survive for long. "So it was that Lenin took the country away from the tsar."[74]

Folk tales about Lenin demonstrate a measure of popular bonding with the leader. In order to strengthen that link, enhance his authority with the populace, and set an example for its readers, the central press published numerous greetings and messages of goodwill to Lenin that poured into the offices of Soviet newspapers after the shooting. They also printed effusive letters to the editor to demonstrate the people's love of Lenin and their belief in his love for them: "Allow me, an old writer not engaged in politics, to express on the pages of your newspaper my indignation against those who raised their hands against the brilliant fighter for equality, Vladimir Ilich Lenin." The author, who sounds very much engaged in politics, noted that Christ died saying, "Forgive them, Father, for they know not what they do." But Lenin's opponents knew well what they were doing. "Do they not know that Lenin is the world beacon, the light of whose love illuminates all the dark corners of human suffering?"[75] Three weeks after the shooting *Petrogradskaia pravda* even reprinted a peasant's letter originally published in a provincial newspaper. "And when the little father [*tsar'-batiushka*] with God's help was overthrown, the SRs appeared but we, the rural poor, waited for the party that would give us the land. After the land decree of November we peasants were overjoyed. 'Who, then, is this good person who did everything so cleverly?' We read the signature on the decree—'Lenin.'" The letter ends, "Faith in the priest has fallen away and interest in and love for Lenin have grown."[76]

This letter is an example of a very early step in the creation of Lenin's cult, for it seeks to arouse positive feelings for Lenin not through direct praise, but through a conscious underlining of his

94 purported strong relationship with the people. Another instance, an article in the literary journal *Tvorchestvo* (Creation), quotes a poem written by a worker that portrays Lenin as simultaneously a protector from above and the embodiment of the people. "You are for Russia a firmament!/ You are the light of truth! You are the people itself!" The author calls Lenin the "brain and heart of the proletariat." The article ends with a playful explanation of the need to enhance Lenin's public image. "When there appeared in Moscow the first rumors about the impending construction of a monument to somebody, evil tongues hatched the story that the first monument Com. Lenin ordered was one to himself. While deliberately slandering him they did not know how close they were to the truth. For his monument is the Freedom he fought for."[77]

The shooting inspired the postrevolutionary Lenin myth. Within months, the effusive public response to the attack was itself incorporated into the mythologizing of Lenin. In March 1919, a journal for railroad workers published a paean to Lenin in which this process is evident:

> All nations have fairy tales about Cinderella, who was persecuted for a long time, oppressed, forced to endure slander, but then truth triumphed and Cinderella was transformed from a sloven into the tsarevich's wife and the future tsaritsa. We were all witnesses to such a "turn of the wheel" in the fate of V. I. Ulianov-Lenin.
>
> Persecuted not only under the autocracy but also after the February revolution, constantly condemned to an illegal existence, working in the underground, unable to mention his own name in order not to ruin his beloved cause, in October 1918 [*sic*] as if by the wave of a magic wand, V. I. becomes the head of government in the Russian republic.
>
> It is a most honored position, but at the same time a most responsible and difficult one . . .
>
> It is a life and death struggle.
>
> It is a struggle which put a revolver in the hands of a woman representative of the left SR party and which only by chance did not cost the life of V. I.
>
> Either—or . . .
>
> The attempt might have taken V. I.'s life.
>
> Or it might have given him what it did give him:
>
> An impassioned outburst of indignation, a fervent expression of alarm, love, wildly enthusiastic greetings not only from all over So-

viet Russia, but from abroad, from representatives of the masses
who are taking up arms against their age-old enslavers . . .

The Leader of the Russian proletariat, V. I. Ulianov-Lenin, is becoming recognized as the Leader of the world proletariat.[78]

In a 1919 essay on Lenin, Lunacharsky also spoke about the love for the leader occasioned by the assassination attempt, but within the rarefied realm of the highest party circles. When Lenin lay wounded, he recalled, and they feared for his life, no one expressed their feelings better than Trotsky who said: " 'When you think that Lenin may die, all our lives seem useless and you stop wanting to live.' "[79]

Lunacharsky's memoir was florid but fair. He had good reason to respect Lenin profoundly, and the qualities in the leader that he singles out for special praise—his will and tremendous vitality—were indeed characteristic of Lenin and are crucial to the success of all leadership. Lunacharsky also had some minor reservations about Lenin. When he first read *The Development of Capitalism in Russia*, he recalls, it left him cold.[80] He was disappointed that Lenin did not exhibit strong leadership in 1905–06.[81] And he would find it "somehow ridiculous" to call Lenin hard-working. "I somehow never saw him immersed in a book or bent over a desk."[82] Some of these observations were excluded from an edition of the essay published in 1923, a time when the cult was building. At a later point in the history of the cult, acceptable defects in Lenin's character would be included in published works about him only for the obvious purpose of making him believable rather than perfect (the failure to include "defects" was one of the weaknesses of George Washington as a cult figure in the United States).

Lunacharsky's 1919 portrait of Lenin was not aimed at a mass readership.[83] But the following year Lenin evoked collective praises from the highest party dignitaries. These were occasioned not by some threat to Lenin either from a political opponent as in 1918 or from illness as in 1923. The event was Lenin's fiftieth birthday, April 22, 1920.

Lenin's Fiftieth Birthday

In the spring of 1920 the eventual Red victory in the civil war was already apparent, and popular discontent with War Communism

96   was making itself felt. The failed socialist revolution in Germany in the fall of 1918 and the gradual restoration of the capitalist economies in Europe after the end of World War I had destroyed the hope—shared by virtually all Bolshevik leaders in 1917—of an imminent westward spread of revolution. Soviet Russia was isolated and faced the difficult transition from war to peace, from revolutionary struggle to the extraordinary task of consolidating power and restoring the ravaged economy. The "nationalities question" loomed progressively larger as the central party organization worked to control the non-Russian areas of the empire. Lenin's personal grip of the party was tightening as its new organizational apparatus moved to replace the soviet rule of Russia.

The Eighth Party Congress in the spring of 1919 had confirmed the creation of the Politburo and the Organizational Bureau (Orgburo) as part of a general centralizing tendency within the Communist Party. Party discipline was defined as adherence to the following maxim: "All decisions of the higher jurisdiction are absolutely binding for the lower."[84] As a wartime measure this ruling was acceptable to the party at large, but in March and April 1920, with the end of hostilities in sight, the growing centralism of the party provoked strident opposition at the Ninth Congress. Lenin, who had as always made the opening speech, was singled out for attack by delegates opposed to what they perceived to be an attempt at dictatorship of the party by its center. Lev Kamenev responded: "Yes, we have administered with the aid of dictatorship . . . We must develop a dictatorship based on complete trust that we have taken the correct line." In 1919 a party faction known as the Democratic Centralists launched a vocal opposition to War Communism and the increasing centralization of the party. At the Ninth Congress one of its leaders, Lev Sapronov, warned of the possible consequences of the continuing domination of the party by its higher bodies: "I then put this question to comrade Lenin: Who will appoint the Central Committee? You see, there can be individual authority here as well. Here also a single commander can be appointed. It does not appear that we will reach this state, but if we do, the revolution will have been gambled away."[85] The acrimonious congress closed on April 5, 1920. Little more than a fortnight later came Lenin's fiftieth birthday. The highest party officials seized on the occasion and turned it into a rally in support of Lenin and his continuing domination of the party. At the same time, Agitprop used his birthday to launch an agitational campaign around Lenin. This marked the next stage in the emergence of the cult.

On April 23, 1920, the central press was filled with greetings, paeans, and poems honoring Lenin's fiftieth birthday.[86] *Pravda* and *Izvestiia* devoted almost all their news coverage to the event and, in particular, published articles praising Lenin written by leading members of the party. Trotsky wrote a piece in which he strove to compensate for the internationalism of Marxism by depicting Lenin as above all a Russian leader. His article, "The National in Lenin," postulated that Lenin was the symbol of the new Russian nation and that those who opposed him opposed Russia. In this piece Lenin was, in a curious way, a Slavophile's dream. "This most indisputable leader of the proletariat has not only the outward appearance of a muzhik [peasant], but also . . . the inner being of a muzhik." Like Platon Karataev, the idealized peasant in *War and Peace,* Lenin in Trotsky's formulation had an instinctive feel for what is good, what is right. Lenin was a combination of Russia old and new; his was the shrewd wisdom of the Russian peasant developed to its highest degree and "armed with the latest word in scientific thought." Lenin embodied the vital forces of Russia and was thus a true national leader. In order to make his point, Trotsky even compared Karl Marx unfavorably with Lenin. Marx wore a formal frock coat; Lenin would never wear such a coat. But then Marx's whole style was rich, elaborate, and German. Lenin's was simple, ascetic, utilitarian, and Russian.[87]

Both Zinoviev and Stalin addressed themselves to Lenin as creator and moving force of the Communist Party. "To speak of Lenin is to speak of our party," said Zinoviev. "To write a biography of Lenin is to write the history of our party." Lenin is to the Communist Party what Darwin was to the natural sciences and Marx to political economy. Zinoviev outlined Lenin's career, beginning with Lenin's appearance on the horizon of the workers' movement in the early 1880s—an obviously deliberate exaggeration. Lenin led a resolute struggle against bourgeois liberals and Narodovoltsy, founded and led Bolshevism, and finally steered his party to power in Russia with his "iron hand," great heart, and intuitive genius."[88] This was a

98   reminder to the party: without Lenin none of them would be where they were. Stalin's praise of Lenin centered on a talent that later proved to be dangerously developed in Stalin himself: the ability to identify enemies early and the resolution to break with them. Stalin approvingly quoted the nineteenth-century German socialist Lassalle as saying, "The party becomes strong by purging itself." "Lenin was a thousand times right in leading the party along the path of uncompromising struggle against the antiparty and anti-revolutionary elements."[89]

Nikolai Bukharin was editor of *Pravda* and the party's most brilliant theoretical spokesman. His piece, "Lenin as Revolutionary Theoretician," reflected his own proclivities. Lenin, he said, must finally be recognized not only for his genius as a revolutionary tactician and leader, but as a great theoretician. Lenin founded a whole new theoretical school, and his April Theses had become the "gospel" of the workers' movement.[90] Sosnovsky's peasant-oriented newspaper *Bednota* sent greetings to Lenin on behalf of all its readers and called his fiftieth birthday "a bright holiday on which all minds and hearts are directed to him who gave his entire life and all his strength to the cause of the emancipation of labor."[91]

The evident purpose of this press campaign was to strengthen the perceived legitimacy of the party's authority by concentrating it in the titanic talent and personal heroism of its idealized ruler. Lenin's supporters self-consciously equated him with the party and its policies, and confirmed the convention of praising Lenin as a desirable expression of solidarity with the direction the regime was taking. They were turning him into a mythical figure within the party and, by celebrating the anniversary of his birth as a holiday, they were making him a focus of party ritual. The tone of the campaign differed markedly from the strident articles bearing a spontaneous stamp of shock and anger after the shooting of 1918. The birthday paeans were formal, ceremonial, and deliberate.

But that did not make them, of necessity, insincere. If Lenin had been a Bolshevik hero in the Geneva days, he was even more likely to inspire awe in his closest collaborators by proving his ability to realize his stated goals. Much of his dynamism had come from his enormous faith in his capacity for leadership, and now, with the civil war nearly over, he had shown that he could indeed lead his party to power and maintain that power, in the face of extraordinary obstacles. Futhermore, Lenin had proven himself to be the most successful of all Social Democratic leaders, even though before 1917 not the Russian but the German Social Democratic Party had reigned supreme in international socialism. In 1920 Lenin was not only the head of the first state to call itself socialist, but was also the acknowledged leader of the international Communist movement. In this Lenin's followers undoubtedly took pride. From the beginning they singled Lenin out as the leader of the world revolution, with emphasis on his global status. The claims for his internationalism may have represented both an effort to bolster national pride in a Russian leader and, at the same time, an attempt to strengthen Lenin as a symbol of political legitimacy in the eyes of the non-Russian peoples of the former empire. This last was to be a major factor in the Lenin cult after 1924, when a flood of Leniniana was produced in every republic, accompanied by avowals that Lenin was beloved by this or that national minority. Even before 1920 some poetry honoring Lenin had come from the pens of non-Russian poets. In 1919 an Armenian poet had lauded Lenin as a "genius, fighter, leader," and in the same year the Kirghiz bard, Toktogul, wrote a poem entitled, "What Kind of Mother Gave Birth to Such a Son as Lenin!" The focus on Lenin's birth gives this poem a classically mythic quality: "Lenin was born for our happiness./ He became leader for our happiness."[92]

Lenin's fiftieth birthday inspired a wave of occasional verse. Demian Bednyi's poem described Lenin as captain of the ship of state, guiding his vessel past dangerous rocks and through turbulent storms.[93] Another poem portraying Lenin as captain was consciously modeled on Walt Whitman's elegy on the death of Lincoln, "O Captain! My Captain!" The poet, a Siberian, dedicated to the sacred memory of Whitman "this joyful hymn to My captain."

> Lenin! O Lenin! Your immutable fate
> Has shown the world a resplendent path! . . .
> O! Then live! Your abundant genius
> We need like the sun in our life and death struggle.[94]

Vladimir Maiakovsky also dedicated a birthday poem to Lenin and began with a dramatic justification of it:

> I know—
> It is not the hero
> Who precipitates the flow of revolution.
> The story of heroes—
> is the nonsense of the intelligentsia!
> But who can restrain himself
> and not sing
> of the glory of Ilich? . . .
> Kindling the lands with fire
> everywhere,
> where people are imprisoned,
> like a bomb
> the name
> explodes:
> Lenin!
> Lenin!
> Lenin! . . .
> I glorify
> in Lenin
> world faith
> and glorify
> my faith.[95]

Maiakovsky's affirmation of faith in Lenin was echoed in the press campaign of April 23, 1920, which deliberately stressed the emotional bonding between Lenin and the people. An article in *Bednota* maintained that "the toiling masses strongly believe in their leader." *Bednota* also published a reminiscence about the peasant response to the decree on land in October 1917. "What a wizard that Lenin is!" a peasant said, on learning of the decree. "The land belonged to the landlords, and now it is ours." "But won't he cheat us?" asked his neighbor. The author of the memoir next recalls explaining that Lenin had dedicated his whole life to the people. Then, he claims, all the twenty or so peasants gathered at the meeting during which the interchange took place "in one voice shouted: 'Such a man won't cheat!' " The same newspaper carried an article by a peasant woman who had been to see Lenin in the Kremlin and had found him "more hospitable and concerned than words can say—just like your own father."[96] Not just the press but also agitational posters stressed the theme of Lenin's link with the narod. A special poster published for his birthday showed a portrait of Lenin and a peasant and a worker gazing up at him. The caption read: "Long live our Ilich!"

As part of its campaign, Agitprop published two popular biographies of Lenin to coincide with his birthday and also with district party conferences scheduled at that time. One of these came out in an enormous edition of 200,000. The author, V. I. Nevsky, was the son of a merchant and had studied at Moscow University. In 1920 he was deputy chairman of the All-Russian Central Executive Committee and head of the party Central Committee's Department for Rural Work. He was to become a noted party historian. But in this book there was nothing scholarly; it was pure politics. It reads like a fairy tale, beginning with Lenin's portentous birth:

> Fifty years ago, when Alexander II was tsar of Russia, when the working people lived a very hard life under the yoke of the landlord and the capitalist, in the town of Simbirsk in a family of modest means there was born a boy whose destiny was to take the land from the landlords together with the workers and peasants, to emancipate the toiler from his enemy—the landlord—and to begin a radical, social rebuilding of the whole world.

From their parents the Ulianov children learned to love the oppressed and disinherited. Alexander Ulianov "went against the tsar and landlords" but he was caught and hanged. Vladimir Ulianov "was not frightened by the tsar's threats and gallows, but thought about the best way to help the people free itself not only from the tsars, but from all oppression." To this end, he applied himself to his studies. He later joined a secret union with "people called social democrats" who wanted to give all land and capital to the toilers. Because of this Lenin was jailed and exiled to Siberia. "But could prison and exile break a person like Vladimir Ilich? There he grew even stronger in his convictions of how to make the people happy." He became a professional revolutionary and encountered many opponents, but always spoke the truth and his prophecies were always realized. "Now everyone knows how Lenin's prophecies have come true, that the landlords' and capitalists' power would be overthrown by workers and peasants, that all power would pass into the hands of the toilers." And in the civil war the enemy was conquered only because the toilers fought bravely for freedom, land, and the soviets, and only because the "Communist Bolshevik Party" itself set an example and because Lenin constantly summoned his people to battle. Just as there is no stronger love for one person than the love the toilers have for Lenin, so there is no hate stronger than the one that capitalists and landlords have for him. Everyone recalls the awful moment when "a crazy woman, a servant of the oppressors, wounded Com. Lenin. Com. Lenin lives, and he will still live a long time, because in his mind are the minds of hundreds of millions of toilers, and in his heart—the blood and love of the whole oppressed and suffering world."

In Nevsky's biography Lenin does not change. He is immutable, knowing from the very beginning what the right path will be, foretelling it, and finally bringing it to pass. Lenin was depicted to the peasant readers as a prophet, a concerned ruler, and an example for emulation. He is selfless; he studies hard.[97] This book is a pure example of the party intelligentsia wooing the people by trying to concoct a fable that would appeal to them.

The other agitational biography published for Lenin's birthday was originally delivered as a speech to the Kazan Soviet at a meeting commemorating Lenin's birthday. Less primitive than Nevsky's piece, it touched on Lenin's relationship to Marx: "Marx founded the communist *teaching;* Lenin leads the transformation of that teaching into *life.*" The biography was illustrated; it contained a drawing of Marx and Lenin, whose faces were already familiar to many. But it also included a drawing of Lenin as an adolescent in his gimnazium uniform. This speech to the Kazan Soviet emphasized Lenin's link to the city, thus attempting to enhance both his appeal there and the status of Kazan.[98] The publication of Lenin's portraits from his childhood and youth was to become an important part of the cult for a different reason; it was to familiarize the Russian populace with not just a leader, but an entire *vita* in which every stage was equally important.

Lenin's Response

The April 22 meeting of the Kazan Soviet was one of many gatherings in honor of Lenin held on that day and the next. The most publicized commemorative meeting was organized by the Moscow committee of the party. One after another the party's most notable members and supporters vied with each other to praise Lenin. Kamenev, Lunacharsky, and Stalin were among the speakers.[99] Lenin conspicuously absented himself from the proceedings. Only when the speeches and poems had all been read did he enter the hall. He thanked the assembly for their greetings and for having spared him from having to listen to them. He expressed the hope that in the future the party would find more appropriate ways to celebrate anniversaries.

Lenin then read a passage from a 1902 article by Karl Kautsky, the prominent German Social Democrat, who had written of Russia's changing place in the world. In 1848 Russia had been a "black frost" in the "spring of the people"; she had no revolutionary movement, and Nicholas I had been the bulwark of reaction in that age of revolutions. By 1902, members of the Russian revolutionary movement were more fiery than their Western counterparts, and "perhaps they are now fated to be that storm which will break the ice of reaction" and bring a new spring. Lenin was reminding his comrades that they were now the guardians of world socialism. They must not lose face and look foolish. But they were in danger of doing just that if they gave themselves airs. The position of a conceited man is "stupid, shameful and ridiculous." Lenin concluded with the hope that "under no circumstances will our party permit itself to be in the position of a conceited party."[100]

Lenin's annoyance at the stylized and elaborate praises was in keeping with his temperament, his vision of the party, and of his role within it. Lenin so identified himself with the Communist Party that in his little speech he equated it with himself; in praising Lenin the party was praising itself. That is why he saw fit to warn it against getting a "swelled head." The head was his, but it was connected to the party's body politic. Public flattery of his personality traits and individual achievements was more than merely distasteful; it was dangerous. The trouble with Russians had always been that they were idle dreamers who lacked the courage to see themselves clearly. Puffing themselves up with pride in having a "leader of genius" could only make them more vulnerable, for hyperbole was inevitably confusing.

Lenin demanded not flattery, but discipline and hard work. In his view, ceremonial adulation was a bribe, an easy way out, a convention that within the Russian bureaucracy had had a long and unproductive history: some flattering phrases about the boss, and he would ignore the fact that you left work an hour early every day. Not this boss; for Lenin such nonsense would not do. Besides, Lenin also may have feared that praise of him might provide a model for the routine adulation of other party leaders as well. It is enough to remember Lenin's horror at Plekhanov's vanity and self-importance to imagine the feelings with which he might have contemplated the Politburo of the current party evoking systematic (and hypocritical) praises from the rank and file.

And yet his attitude toward praise was decidedly ambivalent. He may have felt uncomfortable in its presence, but he allowed it to go on. As a youth, Vladimir Ulianov had earned the wholehearted adulation of his family only after the deaths of his father and brother. This may have inspired the mixed message he consistently sent out to his followers when he became leader of Russia. On the one hand he permitted public praise; on the other he preferred the image of simplicity.

He waited his turn in barbershops and tried to return library books on time.[101] Both Russians and foreigners alike commented on his remarkable lack of ostentation. When Lenin visited the village of Kashino on the occasion of its electrification in 1920, he impressed the villagers with the simplicity of his dress. "Astounding!" remarked one of the peasant women; "such a person, and he has no gold ring, no chain, no gold watch . . . astounding!" Lenin had contributed to his reputation of modesty by introducing himself to each of the villagers individually. Surely they knew who he was, but he behaved as if they had no reason to know his name in advance.[102] As chairman of the Council of People's Commissars he liked to keep foreign dignitaries waiting while he chatted with workers and peasants. The image of "man of the people" was his trademark. The narod, in turn, responded positively to his well-publicized simplicity. After Lenin's death a peasant wrote: "He was simple with us . . . simpler than any of us. It used to be he would come up to a muzhik in a field, start a conversation—ask about everything. He would chew us out for farming the old way; we don't listen to the agronomers. And it was so wonderful that the most important man in Russia would chat with you, like your brother peasant."[103]

Lenin's passive acceptance of publicity doubtless was partly inspired by his perception of the effectiveness of his image in legitimizing the new regime and in publicizing it. As Lunacharsky once observed, "I think that Lenin, who could not abide the personality cult, who rejected it in every possible way, in later years understood and forgave us."[104] In 1919 he recorded a series of speeches for distribution throughout the country, aware of his unique power to impart a strong message to the people. On May Day of that year he stood unperturbed in Red Square, watching the festivities, while behind him on the Kremlin wall there hung suspended two large portraits in identical frames—one of Marx and the other of himself.[105] Indeed, an incident that occurred in 1918 suggests that there were moments when Lenin identified himself with Marx. A factory worker later recalled meeting Lenin and asking him for a photograph of himself as a memento of the event. As she tells the story, Lenin smiled, reached into his pocket, and pulled out for her a small badge embossed with Marx's portrait.[106]

During the years of his active rule Lenin was increasingly becoming an object of public glorification. He infrequently registered mild protests when this irritated him, such as the scolding he gave his comrades on his fiftieth birthday, and his evident unwillingness to recognize the honorific use of his name. In September 1922 the Michelson factory took the name of Lenin in honor of the historic event that had occurred there four years earlier, the assassination attempt by Fania Kaplan. Its workers invited Lenin to attend a rally in honor of the renaming and of the fifth anniversary of the October revolution. Lenin declined the invitation with a note explaining that poor health prevented him from accepting. He addressed it: "To the Workers of the Former Michelson Factory."[107] He could not bring himself to call it "the Lenin Factory." He really was ill, having suffered a stroke some months before, and by refusing to acknowledge the factory's new name he may have been expressing some anxiety about the renaming, assuming that institutions ought to be named after dead people and that he was already becoming a "harmless icon."

Yet he was not ambivalent about playing the role of exemplar, as he did on May Day 1919 when he had worked in the Kremlin courtyard on the first subbotnik. He was also not ambivalent when, in the guise of praise, he was described in language so unbecoming that it was insulting. In 1920 Lenin was aroused to open anger by an editorial and letter that Maxim Gorky published about him in the journal of the Communist International. These so infuriated Lenin that he sent the Politburo a draft resolution:

> I move the following resolution by a *collection of signatures* in the Politburo:
> The Politburo of the C.C. considers the publication in No. 12 of *Kommunisticheskii internatsional* of Gorky's *articles* extremely inappropriate, especially the editorial, since there is not only *nothing* communist about these articles, but a great deal that is *anti-*communist in them. In the future *such* articles must *on no* account be published in *Kommunisticheskii internatsional.*[108]

Gorky's description of Lenin was studded with so many inappropriate statements that it is difficult to identify the ones Lenin must have found most insulting:

> Lenin's mistakes are the mistakes of an honest person, and no reformer in the world has ever operated without making mistakes . . . He always speaks of one thing—getting rid of social inequality. His faith in this is the faith of a fanatic—but an educated fanatic, not a metaphysical or mystical one . . .
> A Frenchman once asked me: "Don't you find that Lenin is a guillotine who thinks?"
> "I compare the workings of his thought to a hammer [Gorky responded], which, possessing sight, shatters into bits precisely that which must be annihilated . . .
> In a religious era, Lenin would have been considered a saint . . . A stern realist, a shrewd politician, Lenin is gradually becoming a legendary figure. This is good.
> Occasionally in this [his] harsh politics there gleams the light of an almost feminine gentleness toward man, and I am sure that the terror [he unleashes] causes him intolerable—although very artfully hidden—suffering . . .
> I once again sing the praises of the holy madness of the brave. Of these Vladimir Lenin is the first and the maddest.[109]

One of Gorky's judgments was strikingly apt: Lenin *was* becoming a legendary figure, and that figure was being infused with an increasing amount of vital force. Early posters of Lenin were little more than blown-up photographs of the leader gazing benignly at his viewers. But gradually he was portrayed with more dynamism. One poster, published in 1920 in Baku, shows Lenin standing atop a Grecian temple, his arm extended, finger pointed ahead, his face full of grim determination. The caption reads: "A specter is haunting Europe, the specter of Communism." In the same year the graphic artist Deni published a playful poster—a cartoon of Lenin perched on top of the globe with a broom, sweeping away capitalists and kings. In 1922 the Moscow Party Committee published a poster in which Lenin stands on a globe with outstretched arm; behind him are the rays of the rising sun.[110] The image of Lenin in posters had shifted from a passive to an active one. He was becoming the subject not of mere portraiture, but of an iconography.

Through posters, photographs, and the many articles by and about him in the press Lenin increasingly became known as the leader of the party, the personification of the new *vlast'*, the new power. Some thought of him simply as the new tsar of Russia. In 1923 a Moscow cab driver, passing by two huge portraits of Marx and Lenin, explained to an American journalist that Comrade Karl Marx was "the chief Bolshevik of the world," and that the "little one with the small beard was Lenin, the bolshevik Tsar of Russia." "The two of them live over there," he added, pointing his whip to the Kremlin.[111] At the time of Lenin's funeral the French journalist Rollin claimed to have heard the rumor that some peasants "talk with awe and reverence of the new Tsar called Leninandtrotsky, who has come from the East to regenerate Holy Russia."[112] But these are isolated examples. It is doubtful that after 1917 the majority of the people remained so ignorant of changing events that they actually thought Lenin bore the title of tsar.

The political atomization of the revolutionary period had dissolved old allegiances; by and large the people behaved as if they believed that power was now to be theirs alone. After the revolution the new regime made itself felt by issuing decrees, setting up local offices with Lenin's portrait on the wall, sending armed workers to the countryside, and above all by the work of thousands of party agitators who sought to win the loyalty of the people in soviet after soviet, village after village. As the populace began to accept the

108 new regime as legitimate, or at least victorious, it is quite natural to assume that they did so in the only political terms meaningful to them. The human mind is conservative and historical, comprehending the new in familiar terms and images. Thus Lenin, as ruler of Russia, evoked a popular response based on previous patterns of behavior and belief. The assassination attempt of 1918 had produced spontaneous portrayals of Lenin as a passion-sufferer, like Saints Boris and Gleb of the eleventh century and Andrei Bogoliubsky of the twelfth. That the persons who articulated this myth may have been Bolshevik sympathizers makes it no less "of the people."

In 1922 Gorky wisely observed that the Russian intelligentsia was being "devoured" by the peasantry and predicted that in the end the peasantry would determine the new culture of Soviet Russia.[113] At the close of the civil war the party apparatus was gaining control over the devastated country, but with the restoration of order, the authority of the past was putting its stamp on new loyalties. For the narod political and religious or supernatural power were closely linked and always personified in identifiable male and female saints or rulers. Naive monarchism had focused upon the little father as a positive figure who personally cared about his people. If the Bolshevik intelligentsia, more self-conscious than the narod, was nonetheless influenced by *its* own historical traditions, then the Russian people, many of whom were now active politically for the first time in their lives, inevitably transferred to the new regime some of *their* old forms of allegiance. They may not have thought Lenin a tsar, but they nonetheless behaved as if he were just that.

The most dramatic instance of this occurred in March 1921 during the Kronstadt rebellion. The rebels were sailors from the naval base near Petrograd. Long-time Bolshevik supporters, they were reacting to War Communism—the harsh discipline, the centralization, the lack of food and fuel—in which they saw a total betrayal of their anarchistic revolutionary vision.[114] Before the rebellion was crushed, its participants had set up a revolutionary commune. They framed their political claims in the traditional popular rhetoric, the language of Razin and Pugachev. They saw Zinoviev, head of the Petrograd Soviet, and Trotsky, Commissar of War, as their main enemies, as evil officials who sought to oppress them. But at least at the start, the rebels reserved a special reverence for Lenin. His portraits were left hanging on the Kronstadt office walls while Trotsky's and Zinoviev's were ripped off. On March 14, the rebel newspaper *Izvestiia* spoke of Lenin as a tsar whose wicked boyars prevented him from acting on behalf of the narod. It reported that during a meeting about trade unions Lenin had expressed the wish simply to resign. "But Lenin's cohorts would not let him flee. He is their prisoner and must utter slanders just as they do."[115] Lenin also aroused the sailors' chauvinist sympathies because he was one of them, a Russian who understood the simple people and came from the Volga, as opposed to the internationalist "Jewish Bolsheviks," Trotsky and Zinoviev.[116]

In 1922 Nikolai Valentinov, who happened to be in a village not far from Moscow, heard the same formulation from a peasant: "Lenin is a Russian man, he respects the peasants and does not allow them to be robbed, driven into village communes, whereas that other ruler—Trotsky—is a Jew; he does not know their work and life, and does not value them and does not care to know them."[117] Valentinov believed that Lenin had earned his favorable reputation among the peasantry through the New Economic Policy, adopted in 1921, which brought about a sudden rise in the standard of living. Valentinov recalled that the custodian of his apartment house expressed sorrow when Lenin died, explaining that Lenin had permitted trade and had brought back white bread, potatoes, and sugar. "If Lenin had not done this, we would to this day be standing hungry in queues."[118] Once again, as with the land decree, Lenin had given the peasants what they wanted.

The New Economic Policy had been officially launched by the Tenth Party Congress of March 1921, held during the Kronstadt rebellion. This congress marked a watershed in party history. Never had Lenin's personal authority been more powerful, and never since 1918 had opposition to him been more vocal. A faction known as the Workers' Opposition sought greater autonomy for workers and trade union leaders. Anticentralist delegates unleashed a wave of protest against Lenin's insistent demand for centralism and discipline in party organization. The New Economic Policy was designed as a conscious attempt to conciliate an increasingly discontented peasantry that had resorted to open rebellion by the winter of

1920–21. But there was no compromise with the Workers' Opposition or those party members who chafed under the Central Committee's dictatorship. On the contrary, Lenin forced through the congress a resolution on party unity, banning factions from presenting organized policy positions.[119]

Lenin had achieved a formal sanction of his growing dominance of the party. His leadership was to guide the party through the projected long period of the New Economic Policy. As head of the hierarchical party organization, he retained a firm grasp on the link that still gave him control of the chain of Soviet history. To his supporters he represented an assurance that Russia would blaze a path to socialism.

THE DEMONOLOGY of Soviet agitation and propaganda developed more quickly than did its hagiography and was to have a long and complex history. The double images of good and evil, monsters and heroes, were to reinforce each other and intensify (although not in pictorial form) after the civil war, when the complement of designated enemies grew larger and larger and drew closer and closer to the sacred party center. The war was fought against class enemies, Mensheviks, Socialist Revolutionaries, foreign interventionists, White armies, but it would not be long before enemies were to include party factionalists, trade union spokesmen, and the rebellious sailors of Kronstadt. Finally, after Lenin's death, they were to be joined by members of the Politburo—first Trotsky and then, one by one, Lenin's oldest lieutenants, as the grisly purge of the 1930s was set in motion. As the line separating good from evil, friend from enemy, grew thinner, as the enemies' purported claims grew greater and greater, so were they depicted in terms and images that were increasingly monstrous.

Concomitant with the growing proximity of the circles of hell was the increasing perfection of the heavenly host—and above all of Lenin. His progressive deification by the party developed in the context of party mythology. Neither the demonology nor the hagiography was fully standardized until Stalin was in firm control of Soviet Russia, but the process had begun during the civil war and continued shortly after with the creation of mythical heroes of revolutionary Russia, the workers, soldiers, and poor peasants, and the idealized personification of the party in the person of its founder

and leader. Lenin's prestige, authority, and heroic stature made him   **111**
irreplaceable in the structure of Soviet politics and Communist
Party mythology.

Then in 1922 he fell ill, and an expanded propaganda apparatus
moved to perpetuate his authority by establishing the first institutions of the Lenin cult.

4 Illness and Immortality

In the early spring of 1922 Lenin was plagued—as he had been for some time—by insomnia and frightful headaches. Two distinguished German physicians journeyed to Moscow to diagnose the case. (Lenin was suspicious of Russian doctors when it came to his own health and that of his friends.) One, Dr. Felix Klemperer, suggested the symptoms might indicate lead poisoning caused by the bullets remaining in Lenin's body since the attempt on his life of August 30, 1918. His colleague disagreed with him; nonetheless, on April 23 one of the two bullets was surgically removed. The diagnosis of lead poisoning and the subsequent surgery were quite possibly measures intended above all to relieve Lenin's anxiety and impatience to return to work.[1]

Lenin spent that night in a hospital. The doctors wrote in the hospital records: "Regarding the nervous system—there is a general nervousness, occasional insomnia, headaches. The specialists have found a neurasthenia, the result of overwork."[2] On May 26 of that year, Lenin suffered a stroke that left him partially paralyzed and unable to speak properly. At first the doctors speculated that he was suffering from a stomach ailment, caused by some bad fish he had eaten the night before, but no one else who had eaten the fish was sick, and the paralysis and speech loss indicated the worst. By the end of September he was still unwell, but he refused to stay away from work. He resumed his regular duties in Moscow on October 2 and immediately began working at a full pace.[3] In mid- and late December Lenin suffered a series of strokes; by the end of the month his condition was very poor. He was never to recover sufficiently to return to work. He spent the last year of his life on a beautiful estate in the village of Gorki, some thirty kilometers from Moscow. He wrote several articles in January,[4] publishing two that month. They were drafted with a great deal of perseverance and suffering. He could not control a pen, but was unused to dictation and found it frustrating to see the stenographer waiting for him to complete a thought. He occasionally resorted to dictating over the telephone to a stenographer who sat in an adjoining room wearing earphones.[5] He was permitted to dictate only for a short time every day. The mental exertion taxed him greatly. His headaches were terrible, and cold compresses were constantly kept on his head.

On March 9, 1923, Lenin suffered a major stroke. His right side was totally paralyzed and he lost the power of speech. Completely incapacitated for a long time, he remained in Gorki, attended by his wife and his younger sister Maria Ilinichna Ulianova. Lenin had advanced arteriosclerosis, and the chance of recovery was remote.[6] He struggled. With painful efforts he made some progress in his speech, and by September he could walk with a cane. But his condition remained poor.

After the stroke of March 1923, Lenin's comrades in the Politburo were to heap extravagant praises on the dying leader, but before it they treated him shabbily, in his view. On December 24, 1922, his doctors, along with Stalin, Kamenev, and Bukharin, imposed a regimen on Lenin: "Vladimir Ilich may dictate every day for 5 to 10 minutes, but this cannot have the character of correspondence and Vladimir Ilich may not expect to receive any answers. It is forbidden for him to receive any [political] visitors. Neither friends nor those around him are allowed to tell Vladimir Ilich any political news."[7] Lenin's secretary recalled that "Vladimir Ilich became convinced that it is not the doctors who give guidance to the Central Committee, but the Central Committee which has instructed the doctors."[8]

In particular Lenin had both political and personal grievances against Stalin.[9] Stalin took a great personal interest in Lenin's illness and read medical literature on the subject. At the end of 1922 he decided that Lenin's illness was incurable and told some of his colleagues that "Lenin is finished" (*Leninu kaput*). These words reached the ears of Lenin's sister Anna, who found them disgraceful. The pronouncement also reached Lenin himself. "I have not died yet," he is reported to have said, "but they, with Stalin at their head, have buried me."[10]

On the eve of Lenin's operation in April 1922, the party press made public Lenin's indisposition. An article in *Bednota* quoted Commissar of Health Semashko, who said that fatigue had made Lenin feel unwell in recent months. His colleagues had tried to make him rest, said Semashko, but he would not stop working. "Not one important decree was issued without him." Even though his job required him to work extraordinarily hard, it could not endanger his health because his body "has already endured one test which, I think, hardly anyone else could have endured," the gunshot wounds of 1918. Semashko then revealed the belated news that the bullets had been dipped in curare, a poison that Indians smear on their arrows. Now one could understand why, after the shooting, "Vladimir Ilich was grinding his teeth in pain . . . If Vladimir Ilich endured this poisoning, he has a constitution which need not worry us." Semashko also indicated that the public would be apprised of Lenin's physical condition, since the masses have a "legal right" to be informed.[11]

In fact, the public was systematically misinformed about the state of Lenin's health. His personal authority was so central to the regime's public image that to weaken it by revealing Lenin's illness was undoubtedly considered risky. Until March 14, 1923, when the government issued a communiqué announcing the sudden worsening of Lenin's condition after his paralytic stroke of March 9, the gravity of the situation was a well-kept secret. Nikolai Valentinov, who worked in the Supreme Council of the National Economy, later recalled that neither he nor most of his colleagues knew about Lenin's illness. In 1922 Valentinov wrote to Lenin asking for an appointment. He received no response for a very long time and assumed that his letter had never reached the busy Lenin. At the end of December he was asked to call on Lenin's sister Maria at the editorial board of *Pravda*. She explained to Valentinov that Lenin had received his letter, wanted to thank him for it, and would be happy to see him as soon as he felt better. "Is Vladimir Ilich sick?" asked Valentinov. "What is the matter with him?" Maria Ilinichna was not a liar, asserts the author. "She could not tell me, of course, that Lenin had suffered a second paralytic stroke. The nature of his illness was *painstakingly hidden*." Lenin's sister explained nothing, yet

did not deny that her brother was ill. She blushed, lowered her eyes,
and answered, "At the moment Vladimir Ilich feels much better."[12]

Lenin himself apparently was aware of the secrecy surrounding his illness. When he learned that, after his stroke of May 1922, the government had issued a bulletin stating he had a stomach ailment, he remarked: "I thought the best diplomats were at the Hague, but it seems they are in Moscow—they are the doctors who have composed this bulletin about my health."[13]

The manner in which Lenin's illness was presented to the people reveals the process by which the government and party tried to maintain their symbol of strength. What follows is a narrative describing the progress of Lenin's illness which I have drawn solely from *Pravda* and *Izvestiia* from mid-1922 until the end of 1923. It shows how the state of Lenin's health would have been perceived by the public whose source of information was the central press.

Lenin's Illness: The Official Scenario

In September 1918 the life of Vladimir Ilich had been in grave danger following an assassination attempt by a Socialist Revolutionary, but he had quickly recovered from his wounds. In late April 1922, one of the bullets that had remained in Lenin's body was successfully removed by a team of distinguished doctors.[14]

About one month later the chairman of the Council of People's Commissars was stricken with gastroenteritis, a stomach ailment. He was also suffering from overwork, which caused a slight obstruction in his circulatory system. The doctors said he needed some rest, but was on his way to a complete recovery.[15] Within a fortnight Lenin was up and around and feeling fine.[16] By the end of July he was no longer convalescing. He was simply "on vacation."[17]

At the end of September Vladimir Ilich was completely well and ready to resume his duties,[18] and a few weeks later he was busily working at his desk in the Kremlin.[19] That the leader's good health continued through January 1923 is demonstrated by the fact that he published two new articles during that month.[20] He continued to be well until mid-March, when exhaustion, the symptoms of which had been apparent for some months, resulted in a considerable worsening of his condition. He suffered some obstruction in his blood circulation, causing "a certain weakening of the motor functions of

116   the right arm and right leg." His speech also displayed "some disorder."[21] Lenin's difficulty in moving his right limbs continued, but his
speech began to improve rather quickly, as did his general physical
condition.[22] Within a couple of days the arm and leg showed signs
of improvement.[23] A few more days and the movement of the limbs
was still better, and his general condition was deemed good.[24]

Lenin's was a disease of the blood vessels, an illness from which
almost complete recovery could be generally expected. The convalescence, however, would be a long one.[25] At the end of March
Lenin occasionally suffered an increase in his temperature and pulse
rate, which would tire him, but in general he was improving. In the
beginning of April he developed a catarrh in the left lung, but it diminished very rapidly.[26] Within less than two weeks it was almost
gone, and once again Lenin's condition was satisfactory.[27]

Toward the end of April Lenin was once more gravely ill; on his
fifty-third birthday, the editorial board of *Pravda* published a birthday greeting that concluded: "Our thoughts, our feelings, our hearts,
are with him at his bedside where he is now battling a grave, tortur-
ous ailment."[28] A few days later Lenin's temperature was up again,
due to the recurrence of a catarrh in the left lung.[29] At the same
time, however, his speech and the movement on his right side
showed signs of improvement.[30] Again the lung problem was short-
lived.[31] By the end of the month Vladimir Ilich must have been
somewhat better; in his own hand, shaky but legible, he wrote a
brief note about the agricultural exhibition to be held in Moscow in
a few months' time.[32]

During the summer of 1923 it was not clear just how ill Lenin
was. Presumably he was still too sick to return to work, because a
return was never mentioned in the press. Finally, at the end of the
summer, it seemed that Ilich was overcoming his grave illness.[33] He
looked fresher and healthier, and his faculties of speech and movement were even more improved than the doctors had expected.[34]
Within a month or so he was able to walk by himself and was working hard on the full restoration of his speech.[35] Some time later,
Commissar of Health Semashko announced at a Communist Party
gathering in Odessa:

> The substantial improvement in the health of Ilich, which started at
> the beginning of August, has made great strides. The health of Com.
> Lenin is systematically getting better every day. The right leg is al-

most completely healed. Com. Lenin walks and even climbs up the stairs to the second floor without assistance. His speech has improved so much that Com. Lenin speaks almost freely. He feels well, he jokes, is interested in public affairs—the All-Union Agricultural Exhibition, and the international peasant conference.[36]

On December 13, A.M. Lezhava addressed a gathering of railroad workers in Briansk. Someone called out to him: "We want to know about Ilich's health!" Lezhava answered that Ilich's health was improving and that it would not be long before he would "if not take the helm of government, then have the capability to give us directives and counsel."[37] By the end of 1923, then, it seemed quite clear that Vladimir Ilich was well on the road to recovery.

IN 1922, in order to strengthen the impression that Lenin was in good health, the central press published special supplements with photographs of him. On September 24 *Pravda* printed a supplement entitled "Com. Lenin on Vacation." Twelve photographs show him looking a bit tired and old, but relaxed and friendly. One photograph shows him petting a cat. In another he is strolling, hands in pockets, along a little country road. Most of the snapshots show him in the company of family and colleagues—Krupskaia, Kamenev, Stalin. Accompanying the photographs is a collection of short articles by Politburo members indicating Lenin's renewed vigor. Stalin, for example, reported that during his recent visit Lenin showed no sign of fatigue and was once more "our old Lenin gazing shrewdly at his visitor, screwing up one eye."

Less than a month later, *Pravda* hailed the fifth anniversary of the October revolution with another supplement, "October: Five Years." It also included six photographs of Lenin. One of these shows him at rest, reading in a lounge chair (the only widely distributed photograph of Lenin wearing spectacles). Most of them, however, demonstrated that the head of state had resumed his role in the government. "At his post with renewed strength," reads the caption of a picture of the leader sitting upright at his desk wearing a suit and tie. Two others show him busily working, sitting behind a pile of newspapers. The caption: "Once again at work in his office." Another shows the leader chairing a large gathering and says: "Once again in the ranks of the old guard (sovnarkom)."[38]

When the sudden worsening of Lenin's condition was made pub-

118   lic in March 1923, Valentinov recalled that the news took everyone by surprise, since "almost everybody, especially those who had recently read his articles,[39] was convinced that he was governing the country as before." It seemed to Valentinov that Lenin's illness was the main topic of conversation in every house in Moscow. Immediately rumors started that Lenin was dead or dying, that he had asked for poison, that he was suffering from advanced syphilis. According to Valentinov's immediate superior in the council, M. A. Savelev, the rumor that Lenin had syphilis was so widespread that the Politburo felt it had to do more than simply deny it. The Central Committee appointed a secret commission to investigate the matter. The commission carefully studied Lenin's medical record and concluded that he did not have hereditary syphilis (that he might have contracted the other form was not considered).[40]

The party leaders were apprehensive about informing the public of Lenin's physical deterioration; they feared consequences far worse than malicious gossip. Trotsky articulated their anxieties in a speech he made at the Seventh All-Ukrainian Party Conference on April 5, 1923:

> When Lenin's condition worsened at the beginning of March, and the Politburo of the CC met to exchange views on how to inform the party, how to inform the country about the deterioration of Comrade Lenin's condition, I think, comrades, you can imagine the mood in which this meeting of the Politburo took place ... We had to think not only of the health of Comrade Lenin. True, at first we were preoccupied during those moments with his pulse, his heart, his temperature. But we also thought about the reaction ... of the political pulse of the working class and our Party.
> ... And then we had to announce the worsening of his condition. We asked ourselves with genuine alarm how those outside the party would receive the news—the peasant, the Red army man. *For in our government apparatus the peasant believes above all in Lenin ...* Would not the peasant expect—some of us wondered—that Lenin's policy would change if he would be absent from work a long time? How would the party react? The working mass? The country?[41]

Lenin's serious illness was made public because there was no longer any hope of maintaining a myth about his "iron disposition." There could be no new photographs of the leader back at work or even on vacation, and he would produce no new articles. Lenin had ceased active political leadership in 1922, with Alexei Rykov assuming the job of chairman of the Council of People's Commissars. But who could replace Lenin as the popular symbol of authority, the personification of the party, the "brain and heart of the proletariat" whose genius was to guide his country to socialism? So much appeared to depend on Lenin's personal power that his heirs had to keep that power alive as he lay dying. Lenin's illness prompted them to immortalize him as a political symbol and to maintain his constant political presence through the institutions of a cult.

The cult emerged rather quickly in 1923, but piecemeal, with no single central management. Unlike the limited agitational campaign of 1918 that encouraged popular portrayals of Lenin in the phantasmagoric language of the narod, the 1923 cult elements were deliberate creations of party organizations. Spontaneous adulation of Lenin would surface again after his death as it had after his wounding. But it would largely follow the acceptable forms demonstrated in the central press and circumscribed by the boundaries drawn by party officials. The vast campaign of agitation that engulfed Soviet Russia after Lenin's death would indicate that some party and government leaders, along with their agitprop agencies, were deliberately preparing for Lenin's death and the perpetuation of his authority. Others, not so farsighted, might simply have been seeking ways to enable the regime to survive his illness. In 1923 Lenin could no longer lead the government he had helped to create. It was functioning without him. But no illness could prevent him from continuing to serve as the author of policy and the idealized exemplar for the party and people—if the publicized Lenin were invested with permanence. The most important vehicle for his continuing presence in Soviet political life was the one through which he had attempted to wield power before 1917, when he was as far from ruling Russia as he was when languishing in Gorki in 1923. That vehicle was his writings, which at this time came to be known collectively as Leninism.

Leninism

Much of the material published about Lenin during the period of his active rule lauded him as a great revolutionary, as a man of action. He was viewed as a master tactician and strategist. Marx was

120 the great theoretician of the revolution, but Lenin was an agent of history. His genius was reflected in what he *did*—always busy, always fighting on revolutionary "fronts," always working. When he fell ill he was still praised as a revolutionary, but there was a palpable shift in emphasis. All the strength of the "living" Lenin was now depicted as residing in his teachings and writings.

The term "Leninism" was in public use at least from January 3, 1923, when Vladimir Sorin, head of the agitation and propaganda department of the Moscow Party Committee, published an article in *Pravda* entitled, "Marxism, Tactics, Lenin." He argued that too little was being done in the "propaganda of 'Leninism.'" He also introduced the idea that the knowledge of Leninism was indispensable to the understanding of Marxism. We must study Lenin, he said— really study, "pencil in hand." Marxism before Lenin was not truly Marxism. "Marx-Engels plus Lenin"—that is the formula of Communism or Marxism. Four months later, *Pravda* printed its first article discussing the relationship between Marxism and Leninism.[42] "The theory of Marx plus the practice of proletarian revolution— this is Leninism," wrote N. Babakhan. We must seriously study Leninism, he said, so that we can derive lessons in tactics for the revolutionary struggle against capitalism. The nineteenth century saw the rule of theory; but in the twentieth century, Marxist practice prevails. Theoretical Marxism is embodied in Leninism; Leninism is inconceivable without Marxism. Those so-called pure Marxists who reject Lenin are dogmatists and "dried-up mummies." "We are not only Marxists," wrote Babakhan, "but are mainly Leninists."

This article provoked a public debate about the "true" nature of Leninism. A writer who called himself "Materialist" was outraged by Babakhan's distinction between Marxism and Leninism. Not one word in all of Lenin's writings could be considered a revision of Marxism, he wrote indignantly. Babakhan, in drawing this false distinction, can only imply that our own Lenin is a revisionist. Lenin's teaching is pure Marxism. Lenin's is the only possible path for a Marxist to take. No revolutionary can "take a single step" without the study of Lenin. And, "as *Marxists*, we will study Lenin, every line of his works," in order to become better Marxists. Let us make Marxism our sixth sense, he concluded, "and then we will be able to bear the name, 'student of Lenin.'"[43]

Until Lenin's illness his topical articles were regularly published in the central press. After the stroke of March 1923 he was to write no more, but the press kept up his political visibility by publishing his past articles and analyzing them as if they were of current import. For example, on the very day *Izvestiia* published the government bulletin on Lenin's grave illness, it also printed an article celebrating the thirtieth anniversary of Lenin's "literary-political activity," beginning with a newly discovered piece Ulianov wrote in 1893.[44]

To emphasize its power, the collected body of Lenin's writings was now described in military terms. In the beginning of April 1923, an article in *Pravda* urged the forthcoming Twelfth Party Congress to consider "the strengthening and utilization of that sharp instrument for the battle and the victory of the working class—the teaching of *Leninism*."[45] Mikhail Pavlovich insisted that the Social Democratic "rout" of populism in the 1890s had been achieved by the "heavy Marxist artillery" of Lenin's writings.[46] Several months later, in an article commemorating the fifth anniversary of the 1918 assassination attempt, Zinoviev wrote: "Leninism is an unequalled weapon in the hands of the proletariat; with [Leninism] it will be invincible."[47] Lenin was ill, but his writings had force.

Just as praise of Lenin had become an accepted convention of discourse for expressing loyalty to Communist power, so in 1923 the avowal of fealty to Leninism came to serve the same function of asserting solidarity with the party line. "Youth—take not one step away from Leninism," trumpeted a journal of the Communist Youth Organization. Only the works of Comrade Lenin "show the correct path to tread."[48] By 1923 expressed political positions had to find legitimacy in Leninism; no thought could be both right and inconsistent with Leninism. This phenomenon was to become an integral part of party life and a salient feature of the Lenin cult. Devotion to Leninism came to mean loyalty to the government and party leadership. At the Twelfth Party Congress, a Comrade Ivanov criticized some statements made by the Democratic Centralist, V. V. Osinsky: I haven't read much of Marx's *Capital,* he said, but I am a Bolshevik. Remember, he cautioned, "we take all criticism very seriously, especially criticism of that which has gone down in history under the name of Leninism."[49]

The congress met in April 1923. With the exception of the sixth, held in 1917 when Lenin was in hiding, it was the first to be held in his absence. The tone of the congress was deeply colored by the emerging cult of Lenin. After 1917 there had often been official greetings to Lenin as leader, teacher, beacon, helmsman, or even architect of the party. Now the greetings were more elaborate: "Long live Vladimir Ilich Lenin, our world leader and a friend to children!"[50] During his active rule Lenin was regularly criticized at party congresses, but with 1923 this ended.

Kamenev opened the Twelfth Party Congress with praises of Lenin, wishes for his speedy recovery, and the pledge that his *writings* would replace him as the party's guide.[51] The congress was in session on April 23, the day after Lenin's fifty-third birthday, and on that day Kamenev asserted that "Lenin's teaching has been our touchstone every time this or that problem, this or that difficult question confronted us. Inwardly, each of us asked himself: and how would Vladimir Ilich have answered this?" We hope, he continued, that our decisions at this Congress are those that Vladimir Ilich would have made, for we have a new responsibility toward our leader. We must show him, when he rises from his sickbed (and we fervently believe he will), that his teachings provide a guideline for all of our actions and all of our decisions.[52] Kamenev had set the tone for the congress, and the other leaders followed suit. Zinoviev delivered the keynote address. This speech had always been Lenin's prerogative, and Zinoviev began by rhapsodizing about the thirst with which the party had listened to Lenin's keynote speeches, which he likened to that "of a thirsty man who on a hot summer's day falls upon a deep clear spring to drink his fill."[53]

The reverential attitude toward Leninism exhibited at the Twelfth Party Congress marks a very important change in party politics. Until 1923 effusive praise of Lenin had been largely reserved for mass agitation. In party congresses ritualized epithets had hailed the leader, but that was all. The Twelfth Congress' solemn confirmation of Leninism as the sole repository of truth was a victory for the Politburo and Central Committee members who tenaciously sought to maintain, despite Lenin's incapacitation, control of the party. Within a short time the party's leaders would compete with each other for the mantle of the truest interpreter of Lenin's legacy. But at the Twelfth Congress the competition among them was cloaked in a unified public reverence for Lenin and his ideas. Lenin was dying, and his eventual successors sought to use his authority to bolster their own legitimacy. They would rule the party without him—but in his name. The party thus sought to enshrine and immortalize that part of Lenin that could not die, his writings. Part of this process was the establishment, in 1923, of an institute to serve as the collector and guardian of Lenin's writings.

The Lenin Institute

On January 3, 1923, in the same *Pravda* article in which he argued for a systematic study of Leninism, Vladimir Sorin also suggested establishing a Lenin Institute in Moscow whose purpose would be to gather all literature written about Lenin, to keep an archive of Lenin's writings, to direct the publication of his works, and to serve as a repository where scholars could study the works of Lenin. Thus both Leninism and the Lenin Institute appear to have originated with the Moscow Party Committee Agitprop. As its head, Sorin knew his job and recognized the importance of institutionalizing Lenin as a political symbol.

In early April 1923 the tenth conference of the Moscow party organization unanimously resolved to establish a Lenin Institute in Moscow to mark the occasion of the twenty-fifth anniversary of the Russian Communist Party.[54] Kamenev, chairman of the Moscow Soviet, was to be its head. The Institute did not formally open until 1924, but it began its preparatory work in the summer and fall of 1923.[55] On July 8, 1923, Stalin, as secretary of the Central Committee, and Kamenev, as head of the Lenin Institute, published an appeal in *Pravda*. They asked all citizens who happened to own letters, memoranda, or other material written by Lenin to turn them over to the Institute. The authors assured those readers who did not want to lose possession of their documents that the Institute would copy and return them. People could even send documents sealed, with instructions to have the papers examined on a date of their choice. At the same time, the Central Committee asked the secretaries of every party committee to appoint an individual whose sole function would be to search the committee's archives for documents bearing any trace of Lenin. Copies were to be made, and the originals sent to Moscow. Party members were reminded that "every scrap of paper" bearing an inscription or mark by Lenin could provide an important contribution to an understanding of the great man. This point was

124   reiterated some six weeks later in an article by A. Arosev, the man in charge of Lenin manuscripts at the Institute: "any bit of paper typed on a typewriter," if it carried the signature of V. I. Lenin, should be sent in to the Institute.[56]

By mid-August the Institute had received a large number of relevant documents,[57] but was receiving less than full cooperation from its colleagues in the Institute of Party History (Istpart). A number of provincial offices of that agency were requesting provincial administrators to send Leniniana to Istpart offices rather than to the Lenin Institute in Moscow. The Institute requested that this process be stopped and that materials be sent directly to Moscow.[58] By the end of August, the Institute announced its intention to expand. It had begun preparations for the organization of a Lenin museum to be housed in the same building as the other sections of the establishment. This museum was to include a large number of photographs and films. The Lenin Institute also sought to acquire artistic portrayals of Lenin—drawings, paintings, engravings, and busts.[59] It also planned to display in the museum original manuscripts in Lenin's hand.

Despite its proclaimed importance, the establishment of the Lenin Institute was hampered by financial strains.[60] In early September almost all of its workers were volunteers. But this problem was soon remedied. The Lenin Institute was transferred from the jurisdiction of the Moscow Soviet to that of the Central Committee of the Communist Party. Kamenev remained as the director of the Institute and a council was established, which initially included Stalin, Zinoviev, Bukharin, Arosev, and Krupskaia.[61] The day after *Pravda* published the names of the council members, it printed an article lauding the Institute's transfer to the Central Committee. Its explanation was that obtaining Leniniana was quite difficult and that the Institute would be much strengthened by having the authority of the Central Committee behind it.[62] One can only speculate why the transfer occurred. Perhaps Kamenev requested it because he felt the Institute lacked sufficient funds and prestige. But it is also conceivable that Stalin, who by this time had already built up a great deal of power, invited Kamenev to bring the Lenin Institute under the Central Committee's jurisdiction. The general secretary of the party had known for a long time that Lenin's condition was hopeless; he may have thought it useful to control the center of the developing Lenin cult.

Whatever the reason for the organizational change, by the fall of 1923 the Lenin Institute reported that its work was progressing satisfactorily. Its publications department began compiling a collection of documents entitled "Toward a History of the RKP Program." It was also publishing a collection of speeches about Lenin by Bukharin, Lunacharsky, Semashko, and others. Most important, it was preparing an edition of the complete works of Vladimir Ilich Lenin.[63]

Work on the museum was also coming along. One room, its walls covered with photographs of Lenin, was already almost completed. Many of these photographs, showing him as a child and as a young man, are now familiar to every Soviet citizen. But in 1923 they were rare. Most of the photographs of the leader distributed up to that point had been taken after 1917. Why should it have been otherwise? It is perfectly normal to publicize the head of state and make him visible and familiar to the people by releasing photographs. But Lenin was dying, and no new photographs of him would be taken. The photographs from Lenin's past were displayed to help piece together the entire life of the cult figure.

The museum contained nearly three hundred items.[64] In addition to photographs, these included posters portraying Lenin, some of his original manuscripts, photographs of original manuscripts, portraits, craftwork he inspired, and a large number of gifts presented to him. A number of these gifts, mostly bric-a-brac and weapons, were prominently displayed in a glass showcase in the middle of the room. The showcase also included the memorabilia from Lenin's ceremonial unveiling of the commemorative bas-relief at the Kremlin in 1918. Recall that Lenin had remarked at the time that the scissors he used to unveil the bas-relief should be put in a museum.[65] And they were—in the Lenin museum.

It is interesting that gifts to Lenin were included in a museum that ostensibly was established in order to educate the people about their great leader. If these gifts were of artistic merit, their inclusion would be understandable, but clearly this was not the case. They were included for a political reason, as material demonstrations of popular love for Lenin. Lenin did receive many gifts during his ill-

126   ness and even before it. Most of them came from organizations—
factories, local party committees, military units, and schools.[66] Often
they were gifts of food or clothing.

The Lenin Institute was to help coordinate party propaganda
about Lenin. In 1923 he also was the center of a limited agitational
campaign designed to aid the *smychka*, the union of workers and
peasants on which the New Economic Policy was predicated, at a
time when the economy was suffering. This campaign took the form
of a huge agricultural and trade exhibition held in Moscow in the
fall of 1923. Hundreds of thousands of peasants were expected in
Moscow for the exhibition, and its organizers prepared a deliberate agitational creation designed to appeal to them: the first Lenin
Corner.

The Lenin Corner

Four months before the exhibition opened, the press put Lenin's
imprint on it by publishing a reproduction of a well-wishing note
written by Lenin in his own hand, shaky but legible.[67] Its publication just six weeks after Lenin's major stroke is explained by the fact
that the exhibition was to have taken place the previous year; Lenin
wrote the note in November 1922.[68] Doubtless *Izvestiia* reproduced
the note to show that Lenin was indeed capable of writing; it was
also an attempt to provide a link between Lenin and the exhibition.

The All-Russian Agricultural and Domestic-Industrial Exhibition
opened on August 19, 1923. Lenin was lying mortally ill in Gorki,
but his presence at the exhibition must have been felt despite his
physical absence. For one thing, he was hard to miss:

> On the main floor of the exhibition, above beautifully arranged
> palms and a sea of harmoniously collected flowers, there looms the
> portrait of a *bogatyr* [a heroic warrior of Russian legends] woven
> from thousands of living plants. This is Comrade Lenin. Yes, this is
> he, Ilich with his penetrating serene gaze and his ironic smile faintly
> playing on his lips.[69]

This seems to be the first time Lenin was portrayed in an unusual
medium, and the first attempt to publicize Lenin's image through
entertainment. Reportedly the "portrait" was a great success with
both workers and peasants.

The main information center for visiting peasants was the Central Peasants' House, used for recreation, party propaganda, and new farming information.[70] In the Central Peasants' House a Central Executive Committee commission had organized a "Lenin Corner"—a display of Leniniana filling several rooms. A tour guide escorted visitors around the Lenin exhibit and answered questions as they gazed upon memorabilia that traced the story of his life.[71] Some thirty-five paintings of Lenin and of revolutionary scenes were displayed in the Lenin Corner. The photographs numbered over two hundred; many of them were of documents, articles, and other papers.[72] A special biography of Lenin was written for the occasion.[73] Special postcards with portraits of Lenin from various periods of his life were issued for distribution in the Corner.[74]

The Lenin Corner was directed toward the peasant and was undoubtedly derived from the *krasnyi ugolok,* the icon corner of the Russian home. First of all, its name—*Leninskii ugolok*—was obviously calculated to evoke an attitude of reverence. This seems to have been a deliberate attempt to use a religious form to arouse political allegiance in the common people. Peasants might be won over if the state were identified with Lenin within a positive, familiar framework. *Izvestiia* reported—on the fifth anniversary of the 1918 shooting of Lenin—that the Lenin Corner was so popular with peasant visitors that the rooms smelled of hay and worn leather.[75] Those in charge of the exhibition were most eager for the idea of the Lenin Corner to be put to good use, and in the press urged others to do so. The exhibition must generate a popular enthusiasm for a country that has been entrusted to workers, wrote one author.[76] Another writer stressed the successful agitational role played by photographs and other forms of artistic representation, especially the paintings and drawings, which made up a large part of the Lenin Corner: "This exhibit has definitely confirmed the opinion of those party circles who claim that realist-artists can serve the new Soviet Russia in the new phase of economic construction . . . The entire life of Lenin . . . will pass before the peasants and workers, i.e., before those visitors for whom the exhibition as a whole and the Lenin Corner in particular were organized."[77] The ultimate success of the Lenin Corner could be gauged only later, when the leader remained a living memory, more familiar and ubiquitous than he had ever been during his lifetime.

Lenin's mythical persona had taken varied forms in the Leniniana of his years as leader of Soviet Russia. The period of Lenin's illness was a time for testing politically acceptable public depictions of Lenin for the purposes of agitation and propaganda. This process was particularly evident in popular biographies of Lenin, which were not yet standardized and contained a variety of both deliberate and accidental distortions.

In 1922 Georgy Shidlovsky wrote that "in the very lifetime of comrade Lenin there is already being woven a web of myth about his biography." He complained that in three biographies of Lenin, all from the same district library, there were three completely different descriptions of the class origin of Lenin's father. The authors of these biographies apparently felt free simply to make up whatever legends they wished.[78] These legends were not arbitrary excesses; they were written to suit the political purposes of the writers.

In fact, it was important to determine Ilia Ulianov's class origin because Lenin's background presented a political problem: his Soviet biographers found it altogether too comfortable for their tastes. His paternal grandfather had indeed been poor. This deprivation somewhere in Lenin's background was inordinately stressed to fit him more closely into the mold of the ideal revolutionary hero.

One popular biography of Lenin, written in 1922 expressly for children, so distorted the facts of Lenin's life that his older sister, Anna Elizarova, was moved to write a scathing indictment of it.[79] She angrily corrected the many inaccuracies that, she correctly perceived, had been included for political ends. It was *not* true that the director of the Simbirsk gimnazium, Kerensky, found it difficult to award Vladimir Ilich a gold medal because of Alexander Ilich's execution. Kerensky, on the contrary, not only gave Vladimir a gold medal, but included as well a letter of reference that was very favorable, "even, in places, violating the truth."[80] It was *not* true that Vladimir Ilich disliked Kerensky's son, Alexander. This son was in the lower grades when Vladimir was graduating, and Vladimir had no reason to be interested in the younger boy. "This whole legend has been adduced in order to say that Kerensky 'already was disliked by Lenin thirty years ago.'" It was *not* true that Vladimir

Ilich read Marx with his brother Alexander. The latter read *Capital*   **129**
when he was twenty, but Vladimir was sixteen then and read *no*
Marxist books.

Lenin's sister saw a cult in the making and did not like it. She felt
it was legitimate to write about Lenin as a political figure, but she
could not understand the necessity for so distorting his personal life.
She was not above noticing the humor of this attempt to glorify
Lenin. She asked her readers to consider the realistic implication of
the assertion that "Vladimir Ilich . . . writes a great number of pamphlets and books (and books!!) on every state undertaking!!"

During Lenin's illness, writers said things about Lenin that they
may have felt were perfectly appropriate and that were accepted at
the time, but by later tastes seem daring or strange. Lenin was the
subject of much adulatory writing during this period, and though it
appears to have been more strictly supervised than were the paeans
of the civil war period, it reflected the writers' personalities more
than would the writings on Lenin that followed his death.

An example of this pattern of cult development is the representation of Lenin's relationship to children. Today it is "well known"
that Lenin loved children, and he appears in paintings romping
through fields with youngsters. In 1922 and 1923 views on the subject were not uniform. Lunacharsky wrote that Lenin loved children, but as a distraction; he could play with both children and cats
"for hours on end."[81] Mikhail Koltsov also wrote that Lenin loved
children and cats.[82] In an article published in *Izvestiia* on the same
day as the official announcement following Lenin's stroke of March
9, 1923, Commissar of Health Semashko wrote that Lenin, like all
great men, loved children. In fact, Lenin had a magic way with children, and Semashko's own children "worshiped" him.[83] But Lepeshinsky said in, of all places, a collection of articles and poems about
Lenin put out by the Communist Youth Organization (Komsomol):

> By the way, if I am not mistaken, Vladimir Ilich is not particularly
> fond of small children, i.e., he always loved the sum of the mysteri-
> ous potential possibilities of the future structure of life, but actual
> Mitkas, Vankas and Mishkas did not evoke in him a positive reac-
> tion. It seems to me, if he were brought to a school of frisky eight-
> year-old boys, he would not know what to do with them, and with
> hungry eyes would start searching for his cap. As much as he was

always drawn to playing with a beautiful, funny cat (cats are his
weakness), so he has not the slightest appetite for messing with two-
legged "snivelers" (excuse the inelegant expression).[84]

Lepeshinsky went on to describe how Lenin had found it irritating
to take care of Lepeshinsky's daughter because she teased him about
being bald.[85] Such a statement would never have been included in a
later Communist Party anthology.

Indeed, during this period, some very straightforward descriptions of Lenin appeared in party publications. A most striking piece
included in the Komsomol anthology was an excerpt from B.
Gorev's *From Thomas More to Lenin,* a book published in five editions between 1922 and 1924. Gorev discussed Lenin's features as a
revolutionary leader and provided quite a fair assessment of Lenin's
skills. He spoke of Lenin's organizational abilities and keen sense of
history. And, Gorev wrote, Lenin has the talent, necessary in a
leader of a party and of the masses, of "social hypnotism, i.e., the
ability to use the oral and written word to influence the reason and
will of the mass, so that it will succumb to the will of the supreme
leader." Lenin "combines in himself a keen revolutionary enthusiasm and even fanaticism with cold political deliberation, following
the principle, 'the ends justify the means.' "[86] A rather accurate assessment, but not flattering.

The Komsomol volume also included articles specially edited to
make Lenin a more positive figure whom young people should
emulate. Lunacharsky's 1919 memoir on Lenin was reprinted in
1923 and included in the anthology for Communist youth with this
sentence missing: "I cannot say from personal experience that Lenin
is hard-working; I somehow have never seen him immersed in a
book or bent over a desk."[87] Lenin was an especially important
model for children, with his studiousness a significant part of his
cult image.

LENIN'S immortality preceded his death. In the summer and fall of
1923 he was learning to talk again, painfully and slowly. All he saw
of Russia was the lovely country of the Gorki estate, which he tra-
versed in a rattan wheelchair. But Russia knew him as the powerful
personification of the Communist Party. The absence of the living
Lenin had encouraged the beginning of his cult. His writings had an

institutional guardian in the Lenin Institute; the Lenin Corner of the
agricultural exhibition had provided a model for later replication
and had depicted in photographs the idealized *vita* of the leader.
The spontaneous outpourings of adulation for Lenin inspired by the
1918 shooting had given way to party manipulation of his image for
its political ends. In the power struggle that began in 1923, "cutting
up the skin of the bear before he has died," to cite a Russian proverb, Lenin's successors each tried to present themselves as true Leninists. The party and government also strove to retain the political
stability and authority that they believed Lenin to have provided.
They themselves had contributed to Lenin's public image as the
personification of the regime, and they now sought to prevent that
equation from undermining their own success at ruling Russia in his
absence. They invoked Lenin's writings and the symbolic import of
his idealized image and his name.

Schools, factories, mines, collective farms, and villages were
named after Lenin, both to honor him as leader and to inspire the
local communities. Lenin's name was to provide the newly christened enterprise with the resolve to be strong like Lenin. We are no
longer Simonovka, a resident of a newly renamed village is alleged
to have said; we are Leninka, so we must be strong.[88] It is like being
the chosen people: the privilege is great, but so is the responsibility.
"Remember that you bear the name of Lenin," warned the inscription on the door of the Lenin Military School of Physical Culture.[89]

The mythical Lenin was a dynamo of power and energy. In his
last year, paeans sometimes linked him with the power source he
sought to bring to Russia—electricity—just as saints of the church
had been connected with water sources they miraculously found. In
November 1923 a newly electrified commune called its electric bulbs
"little Ilich lamps" and thanked Lenin for having granted them electricity.[90]

Lenin's martyrdom of 1918 was officially confirmed on the fifth
anniversary of the assassination attempt. The event was commemorated as an act that had forged Lenin's emotional bond with his
people. In August 1923 Zinoviev wrote: "As a mother loves her son
even more intensely after some grave danger has befallen him, so
our country—and the workers of the entire world—came to love
Vladimir Ilich even more . . . wholeheartedly after that danger that
threatened him in the first days of September 1918."[91] An article in

132   *Pravda* on the anniversary of the shooting reiterated the dichotomy
Lev Sosnovsky made in 1918 between Lenin the immortal and Ilich
the man, describing "V. I. Ulianov (Lenin)—the awesome head of
the victorious republic, and Ilich—the simple, close, older
brother."[92]

On the sixth anniversary of the revolution Lenin was described as
a total abstraction, all-encompassing and eternal:

> Lenin is not only the name of a beloved leader; it is a program and
> a tactic . . . and a philosophical world view . . .
>
> Lenin is the hatred, the ardent hatred of oppression and the ex-
> ploitation of man by man . . .
>
> Lenin is the rule of pure reason without the recognition of any
> mystery.
>
> Lenin . . . is the rejection of all compromises, of all half-
> measures . . .
>
> Lenin is a limitless enthusiasm for science and technology . . . a
> symbol of electrification . . . the inevitable triumph of . . . the all-
> powerful machine over dead nature . . . All problems find a solution
> in this name . . .
>
> If it is true that beauty consists in contrasts, then Lenin has the
> greatest beauty in the world, because he is the incarnation of a
> seeming contradiction, because Lenin—is the dynamic and the dia-
> lectic of the proletariat . . .
>
> Lenin is the suffering for an idea; it is bleeding for the proletariat;
> it is a struggle under the most intolerable conditions, without bread,
> without water, without light . . . a fight against a whole world of en-
> emies armed to the teeth . . .
>
> Lenin is a symbol of destruction to the very foundations . . . but
> . . . also a symbol of the restoration of agriculture . . .
>
> Lenin . . . is the one Communist Party of the Red Globe.
> Long live Comrade Lenin![93]

The immortal Lenin was ready to replace the weakened Ilich.

But the man was not ready to die. He fought tenaciously to overcome his paralysis and aphasia, but the progress was painfully slow.
By January 1924 he could barely manage more than words of one
syllable. Krupskaia often eased his anguish by reading aloud to her
husband. On January 19, 1924, she read him "Love of Life," a story
by Jack London. It tells of a gold prospector struggling to survive in
the Canadian wilderness. He has a sprained ankle, his partner has

abandoned him, and he has no food; he painfully limps across the frozen wasteland toward the safety of a ship. Half-crazed by hunger and pain he nonetheless moves nearer his goal. Toward the end of his ordeal a sick and starving wolf appears and slowly follows him, waiting for him to die. The man can see, only a few miles away, the Arctic Ocean and the ship, but he can barely move and finally falls into the snow. The wolf, weak as it is, attacks him, but the dying man overpowers the wolf, drinks his blood, and then falls unconscious. Some men from the ship spy him, rescue him, and he survives.[94] Lenin liked the story very much.[95] Although during his protracted illness Lenin was depressed and given to weeping spells,[96] in general he was as resilient as the hero of the London tale. He was determined to win his struggle with death.

The same day Krupskaia read Lenin the story, January 19, Mikhail Kalinin, chairman of the Central Executive Committee of the Congress of Soviets, opened the Eleventh Congress of Soviets in Moscow. Vladimir Ilich is fighting an illness, he said, but "rays of hope are already visible—the end of his long grave battle with this disease." A voice from the audience then shouted, "Long live the leader of the world proletariat, comrade Lenin!" This was followed with cries of "hurrah!"[97]

Two days later, January 21, Lenin suffered a massive stroke. Late in the afternoon he had convulsions; his temperature rose precipitously and he lost consciousness. At 6:50 in the evening he died.

5 The Nation Mourns

Lenin's death came as a shock to almost everyone, even to those who ought to have expected it most. Tuesday, January 22, 1924, was the nineteenth anniversary of Bloody Sunday, the 1905 massacre of workers by imperial troops. News of Lenin's death did not appear in that morning's newspapers, and so when Kalinin asked the delegates to the Eleventh Congress of Soviets assembled in the Bolshoi Theater to rise, many assumed they were about to hear a commemorative tribute to the victims of Bloody Sunday. The orchestra started to play a funeral march, but stopped abruptly. "Comrades," began Kalinin, "I must tell you some terrible news. The health of Vladimir Ilich . . ." A few screams were heard from various parts of the hall. The health of Vladimir Ilich had been improving of late, continued Kalinin, but yesterday he had a stroke and died. The delegates exploded into sobs and wails.[1] "The emotional Slav temperament reacted immediately," *The New York Times* reported. "For one appalling moment a dreadful outbreak of mass hysteria seemed certain." But with his commanding voice, A. S. Enukidze, deputy chairman of the Central Executive Committee, demanded quiet, and Kalinin was permitted to continue.[2]

On behalf of the presidium of the congress, Kalinin proposed that January 21 be proclaimed a day of mourning. The resolution was passed by a unanimous sob.[3] Kalinin broke down completely before he could make any announcements about the forthcoming funeral, and Zinoviev, Kamenev, and other members of the presidium "laid their heads on the table and cried like children." The delegates were told that members of the presidium and a number of others would go to Gorki by special train the next morning to bring Lenin's body to Moscow to lie in state until the funeral the following Saturday.[4] The orchestra played a funeral march and the meeting ended.

Once released, news of Lenin's death traveled quickly across Russia by telegraph. In some cities the people were called to hear the news by means of a curious revision of an old custom. Formerly, church bells chimed to bring people out for important news. The postrevolutionary version substituted factory sirens. In Moscow, special flysheet editions of *Pravda, Izvestiia,* and *Rabochaia Moskva* with the official announcement of Lenin's death were distributed on street corners and posted on the walls of party and government offices. By mid-afternoon it was dark and bitterly cold, but people in the streets gathered in small clusters around those with copies of the announcement of Lenin's death. The false optimism of the press coverage of his illness had left the populace totally unprepared for the event.

Lenin's death appeared to precipitate the gravest political crisis the Bolshevik regime had had to face since the close of the civil war. Lenin had been its main source of legitimacy even during his illness, when party leaders invoked his spirit to authorize policy. Now they were on their own. "Literally millions have asked themselves, how will we manage without him tomorrow?" wrote Kalinin.[5] Turmoil, surely, and possibly civil war might follow. What if the peasantry should revolt out of fear that the New Economic Policy would be abolished? What if trade unions and opposition groups in the party should make a bid for power now that Lenin was gone? There was also reason to fear that Lenin's death would weaken Soviet Russia in the eyes of the Western powers, many of whom now expected the imminent collapse of the Soviet system.[6]

Lenin's heirs responded to the crisis with a massive campaign to mobilize the population, using his death to launch a cult of his memory that was to engage the largest possible number of Soviet citizens. The funeral rites were to provide a format for the Lenin cult rituals of the 1920s. They were designed to ensure political stability, inspiring in the populace loyalty to the regime that would continue to rule Russia in Lenin's name.

The country immediately plunged into deep mourning. For an entire week the press devoted itself totally to Lenin's story. Theaters

136   and other places of amusement closed for a week. All work places
were closed, except shops selling red and black mourning cloth and
portraits of Lenin. These portraits suddenly appeared draped in red
and black crepe in countless windows. Every factory, every school,
every conceivable organization held meetings packed with mourners ready to pledge their money and time to honoring Lenin's memory and fulfilling his legacy.

On January 22, 1924, at 3:30 in the morning, the Central Executive
Committee established a commission to organize Lenin's funeral.
That its first concern was political stability is evident in the selection
of Feliks Dzerzhinsky, head of the Cheka, as its chairman.[7] Most of
its real work, however, was carried out by V. D. Bonch-Bruevich,
whose long-time study of sectarianism had doubtless given him the
understanding of Russian religious enthusiasm that shaped the simple yet dramatic funeral rites he helped to design.[8]

The Funeral Commission set up its offices in the Moscow Trade
Union House. Built in 1784, this elegant edifice had a large and ornate Hall of Columns, which was selected for the lying-in-state.[9]
The hall's tall white columns were entwined with wide ribbons of
black and red. From its high ceiling were hung black banners of
mourning. Red ribbons emblazoned with slogans flickered and
swayed like tongues of flame. The chandeliers were draped in black
crepe, and the hundreds of bulbs gleaming through the black gave
off an eerie, melancholy glow. A red carpet ran from the entrance of
the building through the hall.[10]

On Tuesday, January 22, the entire Central Committee and other
members of the party and government went to Gorki to pay their
respects to the dead leader. During that evening and night the first,
self-appointed honor guard stood by Lenin's body. Friends and colleagues took turns standing at attention near his remains. The party
and government delegations stayed the night—talking, reminiscing,
waiting for dawn.[11]

Many peasants, some even from far-off villages, came to pay
homage to Lenin in Gorki. It was a freezing, snowy day, and the
peasants arrived with snow covering their sheepskin coats. Many
kneeled down to pray beside the body; no one bothered them. Many
bowed to the body, some making low genuflections, their heads
touching the floor. Then, as they were leaving the room, they
stopped and again bowed low, facing Lenin. They had come, hun-

dreds of them, after hearing news of his death by word of mouth. "Remember that he, our Ilich, suffered for the peasantry," said an old man, "and see, his death was a deserving (*pravednaia*) one, an easy one ... no suffering ... he sat down ... said, 'I'll have something to drink' ... and within an hour he was dead."[12]

At 6:00 the next morning, the train bearing mourners (including a large delegation from the Eleventh Congress of Soviets) left Moscow for Gorki. Forty-five minutes later it arrived at its destination. It was still dark, but a large crowd waited outside the villa for the body to be brought out. It lay upstairs in Lenin's sickroom, on a sheet-draped table surrounded by flowers and fir branches. At 10:00 Lenin was placed in a coffin lined with red cloth, with a small red pillow under his head. The coffin was carried downstairs where it was covered by a glass lid. Then it was borne—in silence—by Steklov, Bubnov, Krasin, Bukharin, Zinoviev, and Kamenev—to the Gerasimovka railroad station.[13] Lenin's widow and sisters walked alongside the coffin. It took an hour for the procession to reach the little train station. There, the pallbearers and mourners carried the coffin onto the train and boarded. The locomotive, draped in red and black mourning, slowly chugged away, leaving behind a mass of people, their heads bared despite the bitter cold.

Moscow had been preparing for the arrival of the body since the earliest hours of the morning. The route to be taken by the procession to the Trade Union House was lined with troops. Behind them and above were the spectators and mourners—on the streets, in alleys, on rooftops, on balconies, and leaning out of open windows. One American observer remarked that on that day "Moscow became an armed camp ... I sleighed to the railway station through streets lined on both sides with solid ranks of infantry."[14] The temperature hovered around forty degrees below zero on that January day. To keep warm, the soldiers and the people behind them piled up logs and made bonfires, so the procession route was marked by intermittent columns of smoke and glimpses of orange flame.

The funeral train was due to arrive at the Pavletsky train station at 1:00 in the afternoon. As that hour approached, a large crowd gathered at the station. In it were many members of the party, the government, and the Comintern who had not gone to Gorki, joined by delegations of workers and representatives of various organizations. The train pulled into the station on schedule as a band

138   struck up a funeral march. The first car came to a halt just across from a Communist Party banner, entwined with crepe and lowered as a sign of mourning. All heads were bared despite the cold, which was extraordinary even for Moscow.[15] The members of the government and party and other mourners descended from the train. Funeral wreaths, many of fir branches, were brought out of the first car. Then the coffin, covered with red cloth and laden with flowers, was carried out by Kalinin, Bukharin, Tomsky, Kamenev, Stalin, Rudzutak, Zinoviev, and Rykov.[16]

The procession formed and slowly began to make its way along the five-mile route to the Trade Union House. First came those bearing wreaths, followed by others carrying banners draped in mourning. Then a marching band. Lenin's coffin followed and behind it walked his widow, his sisters, and other members of his family. After them came a long procession. Lenin's coffin and family were followed by honor guards, and then by members of the party, members of the Central Control Commission, the Moscow Control Commission, the Executive Committee of Comintern, the Central Executive Committee of the Soviet Union, the Council of People's Commissars of the nation and of the Russian republic, the military leadership, and finally numerous delegations from factories. A military escort brought up the rear.[17] Funeral music was played by the band at various times during the procession. Muscovites stood along the entire route, some holding portraits of the dead leader, others displaying posters with slogans that were to become familiar: "Lenin has died, but his cause lives on" and "Ilich is alive in the hearts of workers." At the Moskvoretsky bridge, airplanes flew overhead, dropping leaflets bearing messages of mourning.[18]

An honor guard two rows deep met the cortege when it arrived at the Trade Union House. To the strains of a funeral march, the coffin was carried into the Hall of Columns. Lenin was placed on a raised platform draped in red and surrounded with potted palms and sepulchral lilies. His feet were covered with the gold-embroidered banner of the Central Committee of the party, his body draped in the banner of the Central Committee of the national organization of trade unions. On his breast was pinned the Order of the Red Banner, which he had never worn while he was alive. A white pillow supported his bare head.

As soon as the coffin reached the catafalque, another honor guard—consisting of members of the Central Committee, the presidium of the Central Executive Committee, the Council of People's Commissars, and other dignitaries—formed around it. The guard was replaced every ten minutes. For these first few hours of the lying-in-state only the privileged and family and friends were allowed to pay their respects. One could not enter the Trade Union House without a permit.[19] At 7:00 that evening, the doors were opened to all.

Lying in State

A lying-in-state before burial is a tradition common to many societies. But in Russia before Peter the Great, tsars and grand princes were buried as soon as possible after their deaths—often the same or next day. Funeral masses, however, were said for them for forty days.[20] Peter the Great was the first Russian monarch to have obsequies of a European style. Peter himself had introduced to Russia the funeral ceremony then current elsewhere. The imperial lying-in-state was a magnificent ceremony. The emperor's body was surrounded by tropical plants and wreaths, many of them made of precious metals. Elaborately uniformed honor guards stood by the body as the common folk filed by to pay their respects. This was a moment of greatest intimacy between tsar and people; the lowliest peasant could gaze upon the little father and kiss his hand. At that one instant the living peasant was more powerful than the dead ruler.

Lenin's lying-in-state was much more subdued than those of his imperial predecessors. No church bells pealed, no honor guards with elegant uniforms and jeweled swords stood by his body. But the ceremony did bear some resemblance to those of the past. Palm branches (originally symbolic of Christ's martyrdom) filled the Hall of Columns, and so many wreaths, thousands of them, were sent to the Trade Union House by schools, factories, and other organizations that they were systematically transferred to a large hall in the Kremlin.[21] The central press encouraged its readers to send wreaths by publishing daily the names of the donating organizations and individuals.

Mourners did not kiss Lenin's hand, but the lying-in-state nonetheless was designed to generate an emotional bonding between the people and the dead leader. Estimates vary, but probably well over half a million people filed by the bier between January 23 and 26.[22] To see Lenin they had to wait outside for hours in severe cold. Bonfires burned next to the long queues. Day and night a steady stream of people flowed by. At first mourners passed the catafalque in single file, but this could not accommodate them quickly enough, so they were admitted three at a time every minute.

The entrance to the building was draped with banners. The visitors walked silently down the long corridor, then turned into the Hall of Columns. The platform on which the body lay was in the middle of the large hall. Krupskaia attended her dead husband much of the time. At the sides and end of the coffin the honor guard stood perfectly still and stared straight ahead. "Never have I seen men so completely still. Not a muscle in their eyelids flickered, and they hardly seemed to breathe," wrote *The New York Times* correspondent, Walter Duranty.[23] At first the honor guard consisted of eight men and was replaced every ten minutes. So many wanted to serve, though, that it was doubled to sixteen and later trebled to twenty-four. Even this could not accommodate all who wanted to be included, so the guard was changed every five minutes and then, in the last hours, every three minutes.[24]

The atmosphere in the Hall of Columns produced heightened emotions. Occasionally an orchestra in the hall would play Chopin's Funeral March or some other solemn air. But it was the smell of lilies, the color of the banners, the lights, the strange immobility of the honor guard, the waxen face of the corpse, which led to the aura of unreality, the more so since most of the mourners entered this room of color and muted light, of death, sweet flowers, and mournful music, after having stood for hours in the dark and cold. In Moscow there were few hours of sunlight in January. The effect was overwhelming. Hundreds fainted and were carried away on stretchers stacked in the hall for this purpose.[25]

Why did hundreds of thousands of people wait for hours in freezing temperatures, often in driving snow, to get a glimpse of Lenin's body? One Western observer called the enormous lines of mourners a "post-mortem vote of confidence," a demonstration of loyalty to the regime.[26] To a certain extent this vote was organized from above. Day after day the press described the lying-in-state, and institution after institution sent delegations to file by the bier. Valentinov, who attended the lying-in-state, saw in the event a demonstration of the Russian attitude toward death and of genuine popular devotion to Lenin:

> During three days, hundreds of thousands of people went in an endless stream to the coffin "to bid farewell to Lenin." They went both day and night. There was a cold, a frost that was unbearable. People were freezing, they caught colds, yet they somehow waited for hours for their turn on line to see the coffin. It seems to me that the Russian people has a far greater special mystical curiosity than other people, some kind of pull to look upon a corpse, a deceased person, especially if the deceased was above the common rank. In the pilgrimage to Lenin's coffin there was this curiosity, but undoubtedly there was another impulse as well: to testify before the deceased to one's respect, love or gratitude toward him.

"An enormous proportion of the population," he attested, "reacted to Lenin's death with unmistakable grief."[27]

The journalism of the time emphasized the people's sorrow. Published eulogies focused on the enormity of the sadness felt by Lenin's mourners. Never before has a person been so deeply mourned, Kalinin wrote. Lenin's death was a personal tragedy felt with pain by every individual. Never before had mankind suffered the loss of an individual to such an extent.[28] This sentiment was echoed by Zinoviev: Lenin's death was a stone on the heart, "inhumanly heavy. No one has ever suffered such terrible moments."[29] When workers spoke at meetings during mourning week, they too emphasized the depth of their sorrow: "Our grief . . . is . . . boundless. Words are insufficient to express our grief."[30] Article after article emphasized the people's grief by observing that many wept openly, vainly struggling to hold back their tears. The women did not struggle so much; their weeping and wailing seems to have provided background sound in every meeting at which they were present.[31] The more dramatic scenes involve strong men whose enormous grief broke through their self-control. Zinoviev described the Finnish revolutionary who was Lenin's bodyguard after the July uprising. "At the time of great danger, he never flinched a muscle in his face. Now he is deathly pale. And he carefully hides his tears."[32] Grown men are pictured racked with sobs, like children.[33]

142   The grief Lenin's death induced might have been only partly
connected with him. The lying-in-state in Moscow and the memorial ceremonies in other cities doubtless functioned as cathartic experiences for a populace that had suffered almost a decade of war,
revolution, civil war, famine, and epidemics. Lenin's death was the
first nationwide ritualized ceremony of mass mourning following
those traumatic years. It resulted in a general hysterical frenzy both
aroused by and channeled into the lying-in-state and mourning
meetings held all over the country. The cult of Lenin, established
across the country in 1924, was to perpetuate grief at Lenin's passing
and in this lay part of its success, for it evoked real feelings derived
from the difficult lives led by Soviet citizens in those years of great
privation.

But the widespread sorrow expressed after Lenin died also testi-
fied to a genuine popular attachment to the leader. How much of
this had come spontaneously from the traditional Russian attachment to rulers, how much from Lenin's personal success in winning
the devotion of the Russian people through his choice of policy and
effective leadership, and how much from the emerging cult of Lenin
that since 1918 had made him an increasingly important and dramatic focus of attention, is impossible to determine. But one thing
became certain: the image of Lenin would be utilized for the political ends of the regime that now had to continue without him.

In the name of Lenin, the leadership mobilized the nation in support of the regime. Lenin's death, which might have weakened the
party, was instead used to prevent political instability. Agitation was
the first priority. The Funeral Commission created an Agitation
Commission to supervise the hurried production and distribution of
posters, leaflets, bulletins, and flysheets.[34] It published enormous
editions of books containing photographs of Lenin and narratives of
his life and work. As early as the morning of January 24, the Agitation Commission sent out hundreds of thousands of posters, brochures, and flyers to cities in various parts of the Soviet Union.[35]
Much Leniniana was prepared especially for distribution on the funeral day. Tens of thousands of posters and short biographies were
made ready for free distribution. Half a million Lenin medallions
were made for those participating in the funeral processions.[36]
Medals, badges, posters, biographies—the cities of Russia were inundated with his name and face.

But traditional methods of agitation would not suffice: the political situation was too uncertain. Some means had to be found to assert control directly over the population. In Moscow Lenin's body served to rally the people. In other cities (and in Moscow, too) mourning meetings were held to honor the dead leader. These meetings were the main medium through which citizens were able—and indeed may have been required—to express their sorrow and demonstrate their solidarity. The party press stressed the importance of these gatherings by reporting them in great detail. In so doing the newspapers also indicated to the uninitiated just how these meetings were to proceed.

The most widely reported were workers' meetings in factories. There were so many of these that little work was done in many factories during mourning week. By urging the populace to take time off from work to attend these meetings, the government was asserting its priorities. Everyone knew how important work was, but Lenin was more important.

The First Cult Ritual

Mourning meetings generally began with statements by workers. "Words are insufficient to express our grief," exclaimed a worker at a meeting of Petrograd metalworkers.[37] The speech continued:

> Eternal memory to the great, unforgettable leader and teacher.
> Long live his first-born—the Russian Communist Party!
> Long live the Leninist parties of the whole world!
> Long live the world-wide bolshevik revolution, ignited by our great leader![38]

At times the tone taken at these meetings was defensive. The mourners wanted to express sorrow, but feared others would view them as weak. "Our loss is great but we are not weeping; we shed no tears; we are not slobbering *meshchane* [members of the petty bourgeoisie]." They were revolutionaries, they warned, and as revolutionaries swore to carry out Lenin's legacy.[39]

Some messages reflected the particular character of the organizations sending them. An association of artists and performers, for example, followed up its mourning meeting by sending to the Petrograd Soviet a telegram: "We, the workers in the Petrograd state

144   theaters and circuses, united in the common grief afflicting all workers, promise to devote all of our strength to the goal of making theater and art in Petrograd the true comrade and helper of the working class."[40] Students met at the universities, and virtually every school held a meeting of some sort to pay homage to the dead leader. At one such meeting it was resolved that the students had made a sworn promise to use all the knowledge acquired at school to further the interests of the working class.[41]

The didactic nature of these mourning meetings was especially pronounced in children's meetings. Sentiments of the Pioneers, the Communist children's organization, were exemplified by a group associated with an orphanage in Petrograd:

> We, the young pioneer detachment named for Grandfather Ilich ... swear on the remains of our dear Ilich that we will prepare ourselves for the difficult and arduous work that awaits us in the future.
> We will work for the benefit of the working class as tirelessly as did Grandpa Ilich ...
> Sleep peacefully, dear grandpa! You know that the young pioneers are getting ready to fulfill your legacy.[42]

In the military the tone was decidedly vengeful. A meeting of the twentieth army division, for example, swore to close ranks around the Russian Communist Party and to support Soviet power. To its enemies the division said: "The meeting sends curses to the SR party, whom it considers guilty for the premature death of Vladimir Ilich."[43] This angry tone is echoed in "Damnation to the Traitors": "The entire assembly of the laborers and white collar workers of the Romodovana cooperative curse the people who betray the interest of the working classes, at whose hand Lenin was killed. Let the swine know that they killed the body of Lenin, but not his holy legacy."[44] Everyone involved in informing the public about Lenin's death made it quite clear that Lenin had died a natural death.[45] But accusing Lenin's political enemies of bringing about his death was an effective means of asserting political solidarity and control. The people were to be roused into loyalty through rage at the "enemies of the state."

Baseless accusations, although not representative of the mourning statements, are symptomatic of a behavior pattern that was to become pronounced later: making patently irrational declarations in order to prove loyalty. A publicly stated untruth can be taken as a measure of one's willingness to distort truth in the interests of a cause. It is particularly helpful if the distortion increases the evident monstrosity of named ememies. This kind of behavior fitted a tactic that was already extant in the early days of the revolution: to blame one's enemies for anything bad that occurred.

With declarations of grief,[46] warnings, and threats came pledges, promises, and resolutions. The most common were pledges of money for the building of a monument to Lenin, either in the city or in the particular place of the meeting. In Kronstadt, for example, the sailors proclaimed their intention to finance a monument. The primary task of a special commemorative committee in the Baltic fleet was to collect money to pay for a bust of Lenin for the fleet's "hall of the revolution," where on occasion Lenin had addressed them.[47] At a meeting of students of Petrograd's vocational schools, it was resolved that a collection should be taken up for a monument. It was decided as well that a Lenin museum and library bearing his name should be constructed in each school.[48] Everyone seemed to be collecting money for Lenin—for wreaths, for monuments, for busts. The directors of all the theaters in Petrograd resolved that busts of Lenin were to be displayed in their halls.[49] Schools organized collections for special scholarships in Lenin's name. Sometimes in the rush to collect money there was no time to think of what should be done with the proceeds. The Moscow printers' union established a Lenin fund, but the article announcing the event acknowledged that no decision had been made regarding the fund's use.[50]

Petrogradskaia pravda noted that many workers' organizations expressed a desire to have a monument to Lenin built in Petrograd. To this end collections were taken in many factories. To facilitate the collection of these monies, the newspaper itself opened a special bank account for the Lenin monument and informed its readers that they might contribute directly to it.[51] Every day during mourning week *Petrogradskaia pravda* reported just how much money had been sent to its offices for the Lenin account. This was done in a special column of the newspaper entitled "For the Monument to Ilich." The money poured in. On January 25 alone, over one and a quarter million rubles were sent to the newspaper's offices and transferred to the bank.[52] Some workers offered a certain percentage of their monthly salary to the collection for the monument.[53]

Many workers pledged time rather than outright cash for the building of the Lenin monument and similar projects. Some pledged to work on Sunday, donating the proceeds of their labor to the construction of a Petrograd Lenin memorial.[54] At one Petrograd factory, the "Bolshevik," the workers resolved to work one extra day for the Lenin memorial plus another extra day for the enlargement of the factory's Lenin club. They also determined to place a marble plaque in their cannon shop, where Lenin had given a speech in 1917.[55] This vast money-raising for city monuments went on in smaller towns as well. Many workers in Ivanovo-Voznesensk pledged a Sunday of work to finance a monument in their city; in Kharkov as well it was decided that a memorial statue would be built solely at the expense of the workers.[56]

A newspaper article describing several workers' meetings asserted that "collections for memorials began spontaneously."[57] As with other public manifestations of mourning for Lenin, it is impossible to separate the spontaneous elements from the directed ones. Mourning meetings were the first Lenin cult rituals enacted on a mass scale. They were also the first political rituals of any kind to mobilize on such a vast scale Russian workers, students, and other Soviet citizens who were not party members. Since 1918 the anniversary of the October revolution had been celebrated annually, but those festivities had been far more limited in scope and emotional intensity than were the mourning meetings. The immediate aftermath of Lenin's death was thus an important moment, not only in the development of the Lenin cult but also in the history of Communist ritual. It marked a large step in the regime's political mobilization of the populace. Throughout Russia attendance at mourning meetings was a political obligation and, for many, it was doubtless their first direct participation in political activity.

Contemporary Soviet press accounts of mourning meetings convey the impression that they took place in an atmosphere of high emotion. The format was immediately standardized, with variations that reflected the particular calling of the institution at which the meeting was held. For example, several groups of young sailors in the Baltic fleet resolved that new sailors take their enlistment oaths not on the traditional date of May Day, but on the day of Lenin's funeral.[58] The printers of Petrograd resolved to publish Lenin's

complete works in cheap editions for workers and peasants and to
finance the printing through voluntary donations of labor.[59]

At mourning meetings sentiments of enthusiasm for Lenin and
sorrow at his passing were aroused not only by pledges but by
music, which was a standard part of these memorial gatherings. At
some, there was a band; at others, only one or two instruments. The
people were often ushered into their meeting place to the strains of
Chopin's Funeral March.[60] Typically the gathering sang two songs
commonly included in all political ceremonies, the popular revolutionary hymn "Vy zhertvoiu pali" (You Have Fallen Victims)[61] and
the "Internationale." At the end came a funeral march or another
hymn. Singing was critical to a meeting's success, since it must have
been boring to listen for hours on end to speeches about the glories
of Ilich. But like making proposals (which was shouting) and making pledges (which was also shouting), singing was engaging and
rousing.

"Into the Ranks of the RKP!"

Perhaps the most stirring moments in commemorative meetings
were the mass pledges to join the Communist Party in Lenin's name.
This was done extensively and appears to have had a standard format. At a meeting of the Lenin club at the "Bolshevik" factory,
workers stood up, one after another saying a few words about Lenin
and asking to be accepted into the Communist Party.[62] With its
singing and vows, the mourning meeting was similar to an evangeli-
cal revival where initiates come forward and seek admission to
the ranks of the faithful. The press almost invariably headlined accounts of pledges with hortatory titles like "Under the Banner of the
RKP—Under the Leninist Banner!"[63]

Contemporary newspaper articles described meetings in which
people declared their intentions to join the party, not spontaneously
but as a response to a speaker's urgent request to do so. At a memorial meeting of working women, a Petrograd party leader, Comrade
Gordon, urged the assembled women to enter the ranks of the Communist Party. This "would be the best wreath on the coffin of the
deceased leader." The women parroted Gordon's imagery in their
resolution: "We know that the best flowering wreath on your coffin

148   will be our entrance into the RKP, and we swear to be worthy pupils of our great leader."[64] The phrase "the best wreath for Ilich" was used time and again in the meetings covered by the press.[65]

At one workers' meeting, a worker explained why people should join the party. Lenin's death was a great loss, he said. To fill this void they must fill the ranks of the party by the thousands. "We must replace the leader with our collective spirit."[66] Just as collective leadership was to take the place of the former head of the government, so thousands of people were to take Lenin's place within the party. This sentiment was echoed in many speeches and slogans. The imagery used during the period of mourning made the relationship between Lenin and the masses an intimate one in an almost mystical sense. "In all of us there lives a small part of Lenin," wrote Trotsky on the day after the leader's death, "and this is the best part of each one of us."[67] In an official statement on Lenin's death written by the Central Committee and distributed in millions of copies in newspapers, journals, and collections, Lenin was portrayed as being in everyone:

> Lenin lives in the soul of every member of our party. Every member of our party is a particle of Lenin. Our entire communist family is a collective embodiment of Lenin.
> Lenin lives in the heart of every honest worker.
> Lenin lives in the heart of every poor peasant.[68]

The collective, in these terms, is more than simply an ideal: it is Lenin. Lenin lives in the hearts of all worthy people, but every member of the party *is* Lenin. This is a religious concept of communion, like being one with Christ.

The pressure to join the party was as great among the youth as it was for adults. The Komsomol urged young people to join its ranks or those of the Pioneers.[69] In bold-face letters *Petrogradskaia pravda* printed the appeal: "Millions of young Leninists are the greatest monument to Ilich. The pioneers will never be false to Ilich's legacy."[70] Students at institutions of higher learning were also called upon to enter the party as the best fulfillment of Lenin's legacy.[71] And the Komsomol raised a banner bearing the following slogan at a vast funeral demonstration held in Leningrad on the day of the funeral: "Ilich is dead; the young have but one conclusion to draw: into the ranks of the RKP!"[72]

These pledges to join the party may have demonstrated a genuine   **149**
proletarian enthusiasm for Lenin's legacy, but as a whole they must
be understood as the first, pivotal stage of a vast planned campaign
to increase the party's working-class membership—a campaign expanded after Lenin's death and named the Lenin Enrollment (*Leninskii prizyv*).[73] The dynamic behind this drive derived from the period following the return to peace, which was marked by a trend
toward the deproletarianization of the Communist Party's membership.[74] This trend seemed irreversible without a recruitment drive
among blue-collar workers.[75] Loyal proletarian party workers became even more necessary for the party's retention of socialist legitimacy during the period of the New Economic Policy than they had
been during War Communism. On January 18, 1924, the Thirteenth
Party Conference adopted a resolution authorizing a recruitment
drive to increase the party by 100,000 new members, all from the
proletariat. At the same time, admission was closed to all nonprole-
tarian elements.

The Thirteenth Party Conference, held just days before Lenin's
death, was the gathering where, for the first time, Trotsky was
openly identified with the opposition, which was denounced as representing a "petty-bourgeois deviation."[76] Trotsky did not stay in
Moscow to watch his power begin to crumble. He left for Sukhum
on the Black Sea, to regain his health and compose his shattered
nerves, which was why he was not in Moscow at the time of Lenin's
death.[77] In this context, the recruitment drive was a political move
on the part of Stalin and his allies. The prospect of 100,000 new
members—unsophisticated and easily manipulated—was most appealing to the general secretary, who doubtless anticipated their inclusion in his power base.

Lenin had always advocated a large proletarian element within
the party, but it had to be composed of workers with an advanced
consciousness. Lenin's maxim had been that quality, not quantity,
was crucial for the party's membership. Thus Lenin would have
been decidedly against a mass recruitment of workers. It is ironic,
then, that ten days after Lenin's death the Central Committee
named the recruitment drive the Lenin Enrollment and called for a
three-month campaign to gain members from the working class.[78]
This was the "first large-scale recruitment to the party planned and
organized for a conscious and specific purpose," E. H. Carr writes.

150   "The Lenin enrolment was undertaken under the pervading influence of the struggle with the opposition."[79]

The drive was announced on January 18 and, though it was officially launched after Lenin's funeral, the campaign actually began right after his death. The mourning meetings served as convenient forms for the message, "Into the ranks of the RKP!" The press helped out with its agitational coverage. From the very first days of mourning, the proletariat was urged to join the party in Lenin's name. Those who commemorated Lenin's death in the "best possible way" were those who pledged themselves to the party. The campaign had begun. The leadership capitalized on the nation's mood of genuine grief and anxiety, assuring the workers that this was the way Ilich would have wanted them to display their love for him. It was a lie, but an effective one.

The Name of Lenin

In Petrograd, workers and students at memorial meetings requested that Lenin's remains be buried in that city.[80] Some groups even *demanded* that he be interred in Petrograd.[81] Others, such as the workers at a Petrograd leather factory, addressed a request to the Congress of Soviets and the All-Russian Party Conference that Lenin be buried in "Red Petrograd." The workers' resolution explained why Lenin should be interred there. All of Vladimir Ilich's underground work and his seizure of power was achieved in Petrograd. There, they said, he led the strike of textile workers in 1896; there he supported the workers' Soviet in 1905; there he gave the people the slogan "All power to the Soviets" in 1917 and realized that slogan as the leader of the Petrograd workers.

The leadership was quick to respond. Grigory Evdokimov, deputy chairman of the Petrograd Soviet, addressed this question at its memorial meeting as he read a list of proposals by the presidium regarding ceremonies mourning Lenin's death. Evdokimov read the proposal that a delegation of one thousand people be sent to attend the funeral in Moscow on behalf of Petrograd. "Let's have the funeral in Petrograd," said a voice from the audience. Evdokimov replied that several factories had already passed resolutions asserting that Lenin must be buried in Petrograd. But Moscow is the nation's capital, he continued, and Lenin, as chairman of the Council of

People's Commissars, must be buried in the capital. Both the government leadership and the Central Committee of the party had already decided that the funeral would be in Moscow.[82] The resolution calling for a Petrograd delegation to be sent to the funeral was approved.

It was out of the question for Lenin's remains to be interred in Petrograd. There was another way the city could honor Lenin's memory and itself be honored in return. The workers at some factories, Evdokimov said, indicated that Petrograd should be renamed Leningrad. Evdokimov then read a letter from Zinoviev in which he, the head of the Petrograd Soviet, suggested the same thing. This was met with hearty applause.[83] Obviously, if Zinoviev himself was requesting this measure, it would be accepted. When the Second All-Union Congress of Soviets met to pay tribute to Lenin on January 26, 1924, it resolved among other things to rename Petrograd.[84]

The newspaper *Krasnaia gazeta* asserted that the workers were not satisfied with renaming Petrograd "Leningrad." They wanted their city to be named after their leader in a more direct way—simply "Lenin."[85] Suggestions were also made to change the name of Peterhof to Leninsk.[86] Naming things after Lenin was not new. Factories, clubs, and even towns had named themselves after him during his lifetime. But Lenin was not the only one to have been so honored. Already there was a town called "Trotsk." By 1924, the number of factories and buildings named after dignitaries, living and dead, was large.[87]

It is not at all surprising, then, that Lenin's death should have unleashed a flood of proposals, requests, demands, and declarations from a variety of institutions wishing to take the name of Lenin. These renamings often took place at the Lenin memorial meetings. Some had specific justifications: the railroad workers of the Riazano-Uralsky railroad proposed to name the Pavletsky Railroad Station and the road leading to it the Lenin Station and the Lenin Road. The explanation given was that it was there that Lenin made his last journey.[88] But most of the proposed rechristenings had no special justifications; various groups wanted to demonstrate their loyalty and their respect for Lenin's memory. The Central Committee of the Komsomol announced that the Pioneers were to bear Lenin's name. This name would serve as a watchword: "The 'Spartak' Pioneers of the Soviet Republic must now be worthy of that great name which is written on their banner."[89]

Lenin's name—like his body, his portrait, and his writings—continued to emanate power after his death. An institution bearing this name identified itself as having power and status. It also showed that it was loyal and trustworthy, willing to shoulder the responsibility of bearing the name of Lenin.

On the Eve

The most important official mourning meeting took place on the eve of the funeral. The gathering was the Second All-Union Congress of Soviets, and all the prominent Bolshevik leaders were there, except Trotsky. Kalinin, president of the congress, was the first to speak. His speech was appropriate, if a bit dull. He spoke of how great a loss Lenin's passing was and called for unity and solidarity to keep the nation strong.[90] Then Krupskaia spoke. The speech—short, unpretentious, stoical—came from the one person who might have been allowed emotional license. She spoke of Lenin's love for the workers, his devotion to Marxist theory, and his personal simplicity.

The speech Stalin made that evening was his legendary "oath speech." Coming after Kalinin's, Krupskaia's, and Zinoviev's, his words had a catechistic format. Stalin described the important aspects of the political edifice Lenin had created and the basic tenets in which he had believed. Stalin then described his country as an unshakable "huge rock" in the "ocean of bourgeois states." Its strength came from the unflagging support and sympathy of the workers and peasants of the entire world. He enumerated the several virtues of Soviet power, following each—the party, the dictatorship of the proletariat, the union of workers and peasants, the union of republics and the Communist International—with a vow: "Departing from us, comrade Lenin directed us to guard the unity of our party as the apple of our eye. We swear to you, comrade Lenin, that we will also fulfill this commandment with honor." Stalin ended his speech with the following:

> You have seen during these days the pilgrimage of tens and hundreds of thousands of working people to comrade Lenin's coffin. Before long you will see the pilgrimage of the representatives of millions of working people to the tomb of comrade Lenin. Do not

doubt that after the representatives of millions there will then come the representatives of tens and hundreds of millions from all the ends of the earth in order to testify that Lenin was the leader, not only of the Russian proletariat, not only of the European workers, not only of the colonial East, but of the entire working world of our globe.

Departing from us, comrade Lenin directed us to be faithful to the principles of the communist international. We swear to you, comrade Lenin, that we will not spare our lives in order to strengthen the union of the working people of the entire world—the communist international!

Western scholarship has made much of this speech. It is often cited as proof of the contention that Stalin was the architect of, and moving force behind, the Lenin cult.[91] After all, if a cult demands a rhetoric of a religious sort, this speech must be a keynote of the cult.

There is no doubt that Stalin played an important role in the development of the cult of Lenin. But the oath speech itself was neither particularly remarkable nor especially important at the time of its delivery.[92] In the published eulogistic literature of the time, there is no other major speech similar to it.[93] But the speech had definite antecedents in the contemporary literature; it was part of a genre. The propriety of making vows on Lenin's memory—and making these vows in ritualistic succession—is evident in eulogies and accounts of workers' meetings reported in the press.[94] At many mourning meetings, oaths were taken to fulfill Lenin's legacy— oaths as solemn, though not as pretentious, as those of Stalin. "We swear we will not deviate one step from the Leninist union of workers and peasants," a meeting of working women in Petrograd resolved. At this meeting the women stood up and, one by one, swore they would always be true to Lenin's legacy. Like Stalin, the women also swore to Lenin directly: "We swear to you, great helmsman of the revolution, to continue on your path to world revolution and communism."[95]

Not only was solemn oath taking before Lenin part of a widespread practice at this time, but so too was the use of religious phrases of the sort Stalin included in his speech. On the day of the funeral, when *Pravda* summarized the speeches made at the memorial meeting of the Congress of Soviets, the summary of Stalin's speech completely stripped away the religious tone of his oration. It simply stated that Stalin spoke of the basic precepts of Lenin and of the readiness of the Central Committee to honor them. The summary then enumerated the stated features of Lenin's legacy.[96] Stalin's words also received the shortest summary of all the speeches made that evening. The speech became significant later, when it was reprinted in Stalin's works and when Western scholars seized upon it as a manifestation of the deep religious and Eastern cast of Stalin's mind. Of course, it also became important because Stalin became important. But no one remarked on it at the time of its delivery, in any published works, and it was not included in the thousands of pamphlets distributed on and just after the funeral day.

There was, however, a much more powerful speech delivered at that meeting, a speech that bore directly on the cult of Lenin. It was made by Zinoviev, who spoke just before Stalin. Zinoviev's lengthy message was strong. The way the Russian people had responded to Lenin's death demonstrated how Lenin had inspired the loyalty of the people. The collective leadership must keep Lenin's power alive. This was Zinoviev's meaning, not his words, for his technique was more subtle. He declared that the events of the past week, the sight of endless queues of mourners in Moscow, revealed the extent of Lenin's historical significance. That crowd was a wonder. "Have you ever before seen such a beautiful, united mass of people, a living giant wave of hundreds of thousands of proletarians who organize themselves on the streets, who day and night stand and wait in this winter storm for their turn to pay their respects to the remains of the leader?" Meaning: the crowd was indeed a post-mortem vote of confidence. Zinoviev said that in these few days it seemed as if the populace were reliving the great October revolution. The huge crowds are the crowds of October. Meaning: this is a show of tremendous political support, of fervent loyalty.

Zinoviev then read two letters written by workers. The first addressed the dead leader directly.

> To our father. Our dear father! You have left your children forever, but your voice, your words will never die in our proletarian hearts.
>
> Many thousands of us go to bid farewell to our dear leader; we weep at your coffin . . .
>
> Our father has dealt us a terrible blow with his death. Reading the

newspapers we had thought that he would return to us soon, and we
waited for him every minute. But a vicious illness took away from us
our unforgettable father—the father of the whole world.

Zinoviev implied that the letter proved Lenin had been a beloved
ruler, one who—like the tsar—bore the epithet of father to his children. The depth of such a relationship is invaluable, he said, and
should be intensified by all possible means.

With the next letter, Zinoviev showed the congress that Lenin had
entered the world of the Russian spirit. The letter, written by a
miner, begins in a traditional folk idiom—"the sun has grown dim;
the star has disappeared"—and reads like a folk tale. It begins during the first world war, with the tsar's troops praying to heaven in
vain.

> And here through woods and through meadows, where horrible
> bombs exploded every minute, amidst the corpses and the moaning
> of the wounded, there surged past—Lenin.
>
> Lenin came from abroad.
>
> "It is difficult for you, I know," said he. "Listen to me. Follow
> me." His call was the call of a leader. This call penetrated deeply
> into every soldier's bloodstained heart. They followed him. They did
> not hesitate to give their lives for Lenin's slogans. They died with
> joy; no one grieved for himself.
>
> That which he promised came to pass. Red poppies bloomed.
> Black grief was replaced by joy. Hunger and devastation were left
> behind; there was plenty of bread to eat.
>
> It was impossible not to believe in Lenin. We believed in such a
> one. We said to him: "Call us, lead us, we will follow, you will not
> deceive us! . . ."
>
> He became ill. We took care of him constantly. Lenin, live! It is
> only you who understands us, no one else. Us, muzhiki . . .
>
> And today each of us carries a black spot in his heart. The star has
> disappeared . . . The sun has grown dim.
>
> The great Lenin is no longer among us.

In reading this story Zinoviev was telling the congress that Lenin
had become, for the narod, a leader of enormous stature, a prophet,
and a savior. In his speech Zinoviev himself called Lenin a prophet
who had given his life for the revolution and had almost lost it in
1917 and again in 1918. In a deliberate attempt to raise Lenin above
the rest of humanity, he echoed the passage in Gorky's 1920 edito-

rial about Lenin in which the writer said that, in a religious era, Lenin would have been considered a saint. He closed by reiterating a precept Kamenev had articulated at the Twelfth Party Congress the previous year. When each of us will be faced with making a responsible decision, let us ask ourselves: "What would comrade Lenin have done in my place?"

After Zinoviev, Stalin spoke, and after Stalin came Bukharin. His speech was adulatory and unimaginative. Bukharin described Lenin as a colossus but at the same time a comrade who approached the worker and peasant as a friend. A "herald, a prophet, a leader," Lenin was the brilliant master of revolutionary tactics. He was the helmsman who had safely guided the ship of state past dangerous reefs and shoals. There were many more speakers after Bukharin. The German Communist, Clara Zetkin, said that Lenin gave his life's blood, "drop by drop," for the sake of the proletariat.[97] This speech, like many delivered that evening, was followed by the playing of a funeral march. Besides the important speakers, there were others. A representative of the people of Turkestan, predictably, called Lenin the liberator of the East. A worker uttered a series of platitudes. But the speech of the peasant, Kraiushkin, was original. He spoke of Lenin's immortality, saying that the leader would "direct us from his grave." He referred to Lenin as his "father" and then, peasant-style, told a parable about a dying father who gave his sons a wreath and bade them to break it. It would not yield unless it was untied, and then it broke apart. The obvious moral was that the country would be strong if united. The peasant ended his speech on a delightfully inappropriate note: "Eternal memory to dear Ilich, and to us—good health."

The Second All-Union Congress adopted a number of resolutions concerning the commemoration of Lenin's death: (1) January 21 was made a national day of mourning. (2) The leader's coffin would be put into a vault constructed at the Kremlin wall and would be accessible to visitors. This resolution confirmed one passed by the presidium of the Central Executive Committee of the Soviet Union on January 25. That resolution was prefaced by an explanation, included in the final version passed by the congress, that the vault was being constructed as a response to the requests of numerous delegations so that those not able to get to Moscow for the funeral would be allowed a means to "bid farewell to their beloved leader." (3) The construction of statues of Lenin was ordered for Moscow, Kharkov, Tiflis, Minsk, Tashkent, and Leningrad. "The image of our great leader must be immortalized for all future generations and should serve as a permanent reminder and a call to the struggle for the ultimate victory of communism." (4) Petrograd was officially renamed Leningrad in honor of Lenin's revolutionary activity there. (5) A special Lenin fund was established for orphaned children. (6) The Lenin Institute was ordered to take "urgent measures" to publish the selected works of Lenin so that they would be available to workers and peasants in millions of copies and several languages. At the same time the Institute was charged with the task of quickly publishing the complete works of Lenin.[98] When the long meeting was ended, the entire congress filed by Lenin's bier in the Hall of Columns, which by this time was closed to the public.

Every major party dignitary had spoken at this memorial meeting with one notable exception, Trotsky. He was away from Moscow when Lenin died and did not return for the funeral. The best known and most respected Politburo member after Lenin, his failure to appear at the visible center of power just when Lenin's authority was being assumed by his successors was a disastrous political mistake and might be explained by Trotsky's depressed emotional state or a simple fear of wielding power. He had been ill in the winter of 1923–24 and was weakened as well by the intense Politburo infighting of those months. On January 18, 1924, he had left Moscow for Sukhum, a Black Sea resort. On January 21, the day of Lenin's death, Trotsky had not yet reached his destination. He was at the railway station in Tiflis when an aide brought him the decoded message from Stalin imparting the stunning news. Trotsky cabled the Kremlin asking whether he should return for the funeral. Later he recalled the answer:

> "The funeral will be on Saturday, you can't get back in time, and so we advise you to continue your treatment." Accordingly, I had no choice. As a matter of fact, the funeral did not take place until Sunday, and I could easily have reached Moscow by then. Incredible as it may appear, I was even deceived about the date of the funeral. The conspirators surmised correctly that I would never think of verifying it, and later on they could always find an explanation.[99]

158   The impossibility of reaching Moscow in time was certainly not the main reason why Trotsky chose to continue on to Sukhum rather than return to the capital. It had taken him three days to get from Moscow to Tiflis; the return journey might have taken somewhat longer in view of the crush of people headed for Moscow. But in his position as head of the armed forces, Trotsky could have requisitioned a train to speed him to Moscow if, for some reason, he feared a breakdown in the regular service. Or he could have ordered that the funeral be postponed for a day or two, to ensure his presence there. But Trotsky did nothing.

One can only conclude that Trotsky *chose* to remain far from Moscow. Although he blamed Stalin for tricking him, he never provided any plausible explanation for his absence. But he does make one thing very clear: at the time of Lenin's death, he was in a state of extreme depression. When the Tiflis party leadership requested him to write a piece on Lenin's death so that his thoughts might be cabled to Moscow, he did not want to do it. "I knew only one urgent desire—and that was to be alone. I could not stretch my hand to lift my pen."[100] He finally realized that he was obliged to write a few pages, and the train's departure from Tiflis was delayed for half an hour while he penned the heartfelt piece, "Lenin is no more" (*Lenina net*), published in *Pravda* and *Izvestiia* on January 24, the day they resumed regular publication. At Sukhum, his depression continued: "I spent long days lying on the balcony facing the sea. Although it was January the sun was warm and bright. Between the balcony and the glittering sea there were huge palms. With the constant sensation of running a temperature were mingled thoughts of Lenin's death."[101]

Lev Trotsky was surely Soviet Russia's most celebrated living leader; his name was coupled with Lenin's "in every-day speech, in articles, poems, and folk-ditties."[102] But he lacked the will even to pay homage to Lenin by attending whatever memorial demonstration was held in Sukhum on the day of Lenin's funeral. He heard the salute of artillery salvos from "somewhere below" as he lay motionless on his balcony.[103] Trotsky's friends and colleagues awaited his arrival in Moscow daily. His wife wrote of a letter she and her husband received from their son. He was in Moscow and was, himself, ill with a cold and running a fever of 104. Yet he went "in his not very warm coat to the Hall of Columns to pay his last respects, and waited, waited, with impatience for our arrival. One could feel in his letter," she continued, "bitter bewilderment and diffident reproach."[104] This reaction was justified on more than one count. With thousands enduring severe discomfort in order to pay their respects to the dead leader, Trotsky's absence may well have been viewed as a sign of disrespect. Many people traveled to Moscow from farther than Tiflis to attend the funeral.

Trotsky's absence surprised Western observers, among them *The New York Times*'s Walter Duranty, who vividly described the expectations of Trotsky's arrival:

> For the last three days there had been a report that he was returning from the Caucasus where he was ill. More than once crowds assembled to greet him at the station, and official photographers were sent to wait chilly hours before the Hall of Columns to film his entry. To the last many believed he would come. A dozen times came a cry from the throng around the mausoleum, "There's Trotsky," or "Trotsky's here," as anyone in a military greatcoat faintly resembling Trotsky passed before us.[105]

Trotsky's refusal to return to Moscow was a mistake for political reasons. The week of mourning meetings and funerary proceedings was a crucial time, something that ought to have been foreseen by any person of political sensibility. Suddenly the men who had been governing the country in Lenin's name for more than a year became visible to the populace. This was the time to display a strong, unified government to an anxious citizenry.

This is precisely why Lenin's death unleashed such a great flood of Leniniana and marked a tremendous upsurge in the importance and scope of the Lenin cult. The cult developed its organized institutions during mourning week. At the same time, the "new" leadership made speeches, carried Lenin's coffin, stood at attention in the honor guard, carried the coffin again, and made more speeches. But Trotsky, who was so widely renowned, was not there: "My God," wrote the French correspondent Rollin, "what an opportunity to miss! Achilles sulking in his tent . . . If he had come to Moscow . . . he would have stolen the whole show."[106]

With Trotsky gone, Zinoviev played the (doubtless, heartfelt) role

160 of chief mourner, although later Stalinist history put Stalin in that role.[107] Nor did Stalin or anyone else deceive Trotsky about the funeral date. The funeral *was* originally scheduled for January 26, but was later postponed to the next day both to accommodate the many travelers who needed more time to reach Moscow and to allow for the hurried construction of a temporary crypt by the Kremlin wall.

The Funeral

Zinoviev later made the exaggerated claim that "the common people, inspired by the ideas of Lenin, improvised this funeral together with us."[108] Although the funeral procession was enormous, it was in no way spontaneous. The funeral had been carefully planned by Bonch-Bruevich and the rest of the Funeral Commission. Every one of the numerous delegations in the procession knew exactly when and where it was to meet and what route it was to take.[109]

Throughout the night of January 26–27, Lenin's family, comrades, and other important personages stayed by the coffin in the Hall of Columns. The honor guard changed more and more frequently as the night passed, to give as many people as possible the opportunity of serving. By 7:30 in the morning the hall was almost cleared of the vast numbers of banners and wreaths that had kept accumulating around the bier. Party and government officials had begun to gather in the Hall of Columns. At the sides of the hall, benches were set up for visiting diplomats and journalists.

At 8:00, the ceremonies began. A special honor guard was formed, consisting of Zinoviev, Stalin, Kalinin, Kamenev, and four workers. This was replaced by a second group of Bukharin, Rykov, Molotov, Tomsky, and four more workers. The orchestra of the Bolshoi Theater arrived and filled the hall with the sounds of Chopin's funeral march. A third honor guard took over: Dzerzhinsky, Chicherin, Petrovsky, and Sokolnikov. By 8:40, the Hall of Columns was filled to capacity with party and government dignitaries, workers' delegations, and other invited mourners. The orchestra played funereal music by Wagner and Mozart. The honor guard changed again: Kuibyshev, Ordzhonikidze, Piatakov, and Enukidze. The orchestra stopped playing and the entire gathering sang "You Have Fallen Victims," the revolutionary hymn. Lenin's widow, his two sisters, and his brother took their places by the coffin. The orchestra played the "Internationale" and everyone sang.

Four at a time, the mourners slowly moved out of the Hall of Columns. Only Lenin's family and closest colleagues stayed by the coffin. At 9:00 the military command was given: "Smirno!" (Attention). The orchestra played a funeral march and banners were lowered. Stalin, Zinoviev, and six workers carried the lidded coffin out of the Trade Union House. The two Politburo members were replaced as pallbearers by Kalinin and Kamenev. The banners of the Comintern and of the Central Committee of the party, suspended on poles, were held over the coffin, which was draped with red cloth. The coffin was followed by Lenin's family, then by the Executive Committee of the Comintern, the Central Committee of the party, and members of the government.

Red Square had been cleared of pedestrians at 6:00 that morning. Within the hour, delegations began pouring into the square. Many carried large banners bearing slogans. The Leningrad delegation's read: "All around us, everywhere, Lenin is completely with us."[110] At 9:30 the first sounds of a funeral march were heard, and several minutes later the pallbearers placed the coffin onto a specially built wooden rostrum in Red Square. Then came the reading of the funeral oration. The speaker was Grigory Evdokimov, deputy chairman of the Leningrad Soviet, reportedly chosen because his was said to be the loudest voice in Russia.[111]

> We are burying Lenin. The world's greatest genius has left us. This giant of thought, of will, of work has died. Hundreds of millions of workers, peasants, and colonial slaves mourn the death of the mighty leader ... From all the ends of the earth there surge waves of lamentation, mourning and grief. His enemies ... are forced to lower their bright banners. Everyone has understood that the bright star of mankind has been eclipsed. From his grave Lenin stands before the world in his full gigantic stature ...
>
> Lenin was the leader of the mass of mankind. He had the keys to the souls of all the most backward workers and peasants. Penetrating their very hearts, he awakened their consciousness, their class instinct ...
>
> We have lost in Lenin the chief captain of our vessel. This loss is irreplaceable, because in the whole world there has never been such a lucid intellect, such a mighty effort, such an inflexible will as that

of Lenin . . . Hundreds of thousands of disciples of Vladimir Ilich firmly hold up his great banner. Millions rally around them. And even with his very physical death Lenin gives his order: "Workers of the world, unite!" . . .

The oration was followed by the playing of the "Internationale."

Then, for six hours, thousands upon thousands of mourners filed slowly by the bier. The workers were organized in columns, and as each column passed by the coffin, the heads of that column lowered their banners and flags. Orchestras played funereal music and hymns. Occasionally sobbing was heard, but mostly there was silence. It was too cold for speech. It was so cold, 35 degrees below zero, that special instructions were issued forbidding children from participating in the procession.[112]

People stood by bonfires for hours, waiting their turn to enter Red Square. A living mass of people enveloped in a gray mist—from the smoke and the breath of hundreds of thousands—covered the square. The icy fog hung over the square "like a smoke sacrifice," wrote Duranty.[113] As they walked, some mourners carried portraits of Lenin, held high like icons in religious processions. Others chanted slogans about Lenin in slow measured tones: "Le-nin's grave is the cra-dle of free-dom of all hu-man-i-ty."[114]

At 3:55 the banners of the Central Committee and the Comintern were removed from the coffin. Stalin, Zinoviev, Kamenev, Molotov, Bukharin, Tomsky, Rudzutak, and Dzerzhinsky then lifted the coffin, and at precisely 4:00 they lowered it into the prepared vault. At that moment all of Russia commemorated the passing of Lenin. Everything that could make noise—factory sirens, steamship whistles, train whistles—sounded for three minutes. The noise was deafening. Rifle shots resounded, and cannon were fired, one salvo every minute. At 4:00 exactly, all radio broadcasts, all telegraph lines, transmitted one message: "Stand up, comrades, Ilich is being lowered into his grave!" Everything stopped everywhere in Russia for five minutes. Trains stopped, ships stopped—the entire country paid a dramatic homage to its leader.

In Moscow those present at the funeral bared their heads. No words were spoken as the coffin was lowered into its crypt to the thunder of cannon and the wail of factory sirens. At 4:06, the radio stations and telegraph operators across Russia transmitted a new message: "Lenin has died—but Leninism lives!"[115] In Red Square hundreds of thousands of people stood at attention and sang the Bolshevik funeral hymn. It was over.[116]

ALMOST every city and every town in Russia marked Lenin's funeral day with a commemoration of some kind. In Kiev, a mourning procession of 100,000 was organized. In Viatka, thousands of residents flooded Bolshevik Square, despite the fact that the demonstration planned in that city had been canceled due to an unusually severe cold wave.[117] Kharkov, Rostov, Kostroma—each held ceremonies, with speeches and large crowds. These ceremonies were an expression of sympathy, but also a political statement. Provincial Russia showed the central government in Moscow that it was staunchly loyal.

In Russia's second city, the newly named Leningrad, 750,000 people participated in the mourning demonstration.[118] Columns of mourners poured into the Place of the Victims of the Revolution where 53 bonfires blazed—one for each year of Lenin's life. At 4:00 the salute came from the Peter and Paul Fortress and from the sirens of battleships as well as factories. The executive committee of the Petrograd party organization, in charge of this demonstration, made a tremendous effort to urge its population to take part. On January 25, 26, and 27 the press carried hortatory messages, ordering people to join the demonstration: "EVERYONE, UNITED, ONTO THE STREETS—INTO THE RANKS OF THE MOURNING DEMONSTRATION!"[119] Every neighborhood was organized, and everyone knew when and where to meet. Gordon, the chairman of the commission in charge of the demonstration, plainly announced that all workers, office workers, students, soldiers, and sailors were to take part in the event.[120] Medical stations were set up to take care of frost-bite victims, and all troops carried first-aid kits for the same reason.[121]

The processions, the noise making, the five-minute work stoppage—all of the elements that marked the day of Lenin's funeral were also important moments in the extension of Lenin's cult. The entire nation was united in commemorating its dead leader. Lenin was being used as a bond to hold the country together—in death no less than in life. The solidarity expressed by the millions of people who stood at attention on the afternoon of January 27 throughout all of Russia was undoubtedly the most remarkable feature of the funeral day.

164   The other striking aspect of Lenin's funeral, of its final moments
in particular, was its strange lack of ritual ceremony in connection
with the body.[122] Salutes were given, banners lowered, heads were
bared. But that was all. In a traditional Orthodox funeral, prayers
are said, of course, and at the very end of the ceremony the priest
sprinkles the coffin with earth, ashes, and oil. A requiem is chanted
as the body is lowered into its final resting place.[123] At the final moment of Lenin's funeral, absolutely nothing was said. No earth was
sprinkled on his coffin. No last rites of any kind were performed on
the body of the deceased leader. There would be time—more time
than anyone might have imagined—to engage in rites surrounding
the body of Vladimir Ilich Ulianov.

1. Lenin's first official portrait as head of state.
January 1918.

2. Lenin in the Kremlin
courtyard shortly after the
attempt on his life.
Autumn 1918.

3. Lenin stands at the Kremlin Wall between a portrait of himself
and one of Marx (not visible). May Day, 1919.

4. "Com. Lenin cleans away the earth's dirt."
Kazan, 1920.

5. "A specter is haunting Europe, the specter of communism."
Baku, 1920.

6. Poster commemorating the fifth anniversary of the October revolution. Moscow, 1922.

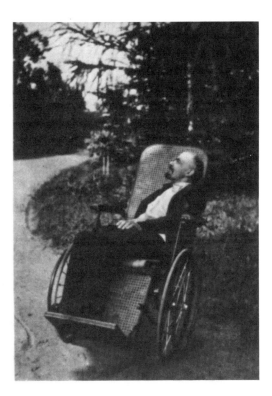

7. Lenin in Gorki.
Summer 1923.

8. Lenin's portrait made from living plants.
August 1923, Moscow.

9. Lenin dead in Gorki.

10. People waiting to view Lenin's body at his lying-in-state.

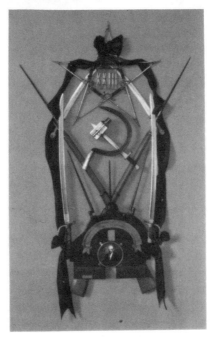

11. Samples of the numerous wreaths sent to Lenin's lying-in-state.

top left   From schoolchildren, a red paper wreath with green paper leaves, each of which carries a signed message from a pupil.

top right   "Farewell, friend. M. Gorky."

below   From the 23rd Kharkov Infantry Division, a wreath fashioned out of weapons, with an oil portrait of Lenin.

12. Lenin's funeral.

1870 1924

В. И. Ульянов-Ленин

13. A mourning poster conveying the message that Lenin's death
has united workers and peasants.

14. A mourning poster showing the stages of Lenin's life in a format resembling Christian iconography. The banner at top left reads: "Ilich died—Lenin lives."

15. Lenin's first crypt, constructed during mourning week.

16. The wooden mausoleum.

17. The granite mausoleum. Watercolor by its architect, A. V. Shchusev.

8. Lenin in his sarcophagus, 1930.

The cult of Lenin fades

19a. "Long Live Leninism!" A 1928 poster showing a remote Lenin as background to a happy populace.

19b. Stalin talks to Lenin, 1930s.

The recent Lenin cult

20a. The Lenin Library, Moscow. May Day, 1978.

20b. Ulianovsk Pioneers salute
Grandpa Ilich on his 108th birthday.

20c. Papier-mâché plaque, 1965.

20d. Pioneers gaze upon
Volodia Ulianov.

20e. "CPSU. Even now Lenin
is more alive than all
the living."

6 The Body and the Shrine

A regime that derives its legitimacy from a single ruler risks instability upon his death. But if after death that ruler becomes the object of a cult predicated on his continuing living power, then that cult can serve as a stabilizing force. This is precisely what happened with Lenin. The cult established nationwide upon his death was based on one theme: Lenin lives! Lenin's death was not to interfere with his continuing leadership of Soviet Russia. In the words of the All-Russian Soviet of Trade Unions, "Healthy or sick, living or dead ... Lenin remains our eternal leader."[1]

A declaration of Lenin's immortality was a pledge of faith and loyalty to the party and government. This gesture was made over and over again during mourning week in many of the slogans, poems, and eulogies that filled the press. It was a political act in that it implied a desire to perpetuate the system of rule personified by Lenin. "He has not died and will never die!" read one slogan.[2] "He lives. He lives. He has not died. He will not die," was the opening line of a poem published shortly after Lenin's death.[3] Another elegaic poem denied that any death could kill Ilich.[4] Some responses to Lenin's death were more expansive, explaining how or why Lenin continued to live: "Lenin has died, but Leninism, which has become rooted in me, in all the working class, lives! It lives, comrades! For us Lenin has not died."[5] Many statements stressed the immortality of Lenin's cause. The headline in *Izvestiia*'s first regular issue published after Lenin's death read: "That which was mortal in Lenin has died, but his cause and his legacy will abide forever."[6]

166   There were also slogans and statements suggesting that Lenin was eternal and omnipresent, a true spiritual entity. One eulogy described Lenin as a life force that cannot be killed: "Lenin and death—these concepts are mutually exclusive of each other ... Lenin—like nature and the world surrounding us—lives outside of our subjective ideas."[7] The last phrase mixes Marxism and mysticism: Lenin, an omnipresent spirit, is part of the objective world as an immortal life force. The first theme, that Lenin and death cannot coexist, is also stressed in Vladimir Maiakovsky's poem, "Komsomolskaia."

> 'Lenin' and 'Death'—
> > these words are enemies.
> 'Lenin' and 'Life'—
> > are comrades ...
> Lenin—
> > lived.
> Lenin—
> > lives.
> Lenin—
> > will live.[8]

Some eulogies spoke of the special relationship between Lenin and the people.

> ... Lenin has not died.
> Lenin lives.
> Lenin has ceased to be an individual—Lenin belongs to the millions.
> Lenin—has for a long time already been the revolution itself, ... the great wisdom of proletarian tactics, the great will of the proletariat, will and confidence in history ...
> Lenin has not died. Lenin lives. There is not a corner in the world where there are working people, oppressed [people], exploited [people], where Lenin is absent.[9]

This assertion of Lenin's replacement by the collective was a common theme in 1924. Emelian Iaroslavsky's widely distributed biography of Lenin made this point with special emphasis: "Yes, Lenin has died ... but if we wholeheartedly work for his cause, *we will be able to replace him with our collective strength, collective work, collective will.*"[10] The concept of Lenin's purported collective immortality echoed the deification of collective humanity celebrated twenty years earlier by the Bolshevik god-builders. It also resembled the Christian tenet that after the ascension Christ's spirit became available to groups of the faithful.

Lenin as Christ was a palpable image in some of the eulogies evoked by his death. Curiously, it was especially evident in the writings of journalists of Jewish origin, perhaps indicating their cultural distance from the Russian narod and their self-conscious attempts to concoct formulas that would move Orthodox readers. The most striking example was provided by the Jewish-born journalist, Lev Sosnovsky. The day of Lenin's funeral he published a eulogy in which he reiterated the duality of Ilich the man and Lenin the immortal that he had earlier formulated after the 1918 assassination attempt. This wonderful being has two persons, he wrote, Lenin who is eternal and Ilich the man. Ilich was characterized by his simplicity, accessibility, thoughtfulness, wisdom, and fairness. He was "a person of rare morality, purity, modesty and self-restraint in his private life (in the old days people would have said: a person [living] a saintly life)." Lenin was a pervasive, immortal spirit. "Lenin lives . . . Lenin beats in [our] hearts and will beat [there] until the demons of capitalism and exploitation will be chased into hell." "But," continued Sosnovsky, "if Lenin has not died and will not die, why such grief and sorrow?" Why did hundreds of thousands of workers stand in line in the cold to pass by the coffin in the Hall of Columns? "They bid farewell to Ilich. Yes, most unfortunately, Ilich has left us. The living person, so familiar, so close, so dear and beloved."[11] This dualism imitates Christ and also the medieval Russian tsar in his ideal form, humble in his human persona, awesome and immortal in the majesty of his office. Whatever else Sosnovsky may have had in mind, his many years as an agitator and journalist of publications geared toward the peasant reader doubtless prompted him to expect that the Ilich-Lenin formulation would find resonance in the political or religious consciousness of his readers.[12]

Similarly, on the funeral day, *Pravda's* lead editorial depicted Lenin as both mortal and immortal. Its author, Peter Stuchka, chairman of the USSR Supreme Court, added that Lenin was an active agent in his immortality, that Ilich created his own immortal persona as his replacement and fell ill so as to allow the nation to get used to his absence. After the 1918 shooting, Ilich had to recover, for

168   Soviet Russia could not survive his loss. But he knew he would soon
leave his party orphaned:

> But Ilich foresaw even this: he not only circumvented the Entente,
> he even outwitted nature. He gave us a breathing space to accustom
> us to the thought of how to live without him. And when *Ilich* was no
> more, we still had *Lenin*. This metamorphosis went on before our
> eyes imperceptibly. For a long time he combined Ilich and Lenin . . .
> At that time when all of Russia knew its Ilich to the remotest corner,
> already the portrait of Lenin marched together with the mother of
> god in Italy's dark villages.[13]

Stuchka self-consciously described Lenin as a religious leader, comparable to but more successful than Mohammed, Christ, and Buddha. What those three had accomplished over centuries in limited
areas of the globe Lenin had achieved during his lifetime throughout the world—the salvation of all oppressed people.[14]

Izvestiia's lead editorial also portrayed Lenin in religious terms.
Iury Steklov, the newspaper's editor (like Sosnovsky, of Jewish origin), said that Lenin's name had entered the revolutionary *sviatsy*
(church calendar). He also wrote of Lenin's grave: "This grave will
become the place of a world pilgrimage . . . the mausoleum with his
remains will be a place of pilgrimage for all the oppressed [people]
. . . of the world."[15] A pilgrimage is a religious journey to a sacred
place, to a shrine. If Lenin's grave is a place of pilgrimage, then it is
holy. In his widely circulated article on Lenin's death and funeral,
Zinoviev (also a Jew) likewise referred to Lenin's grave as a site of
pilgrimage: "Decades and centuries will go by; this grave will become closer and dearer to tens and hundreds of millions of people,
to all mankind. To this place there will begin a pilgrimage not only
from all ends of our Union of Republics, comprising one-sixth of all
land, but from China, India, America, from the entire world."[16]
Within six months Lenin's embalmed body was enshrined in a
wooden mausoleum to which pilgrims began coming in a steady
stream.

From the moment of his death, the remains of the leader were invested with life and power: "And he is pale-yellow, calm, great even
in his coffin; even in silence he continues to do that with which he
was busy his entire life: he organizes, rallies, calls people to the
struggle again and again."[17] Lenin's body was to become the focal

point for the cult that followed his death. Leninism would commu- **169**
nicate his political vision to future generations, Lenin Corners
would serve as local shrines for the veneration of his memory, but
the body made him simultaneously a proven saint with visibly incorruptible remains and an immortal.

The Autopsy Report

Before Lenin's body was taken from Gorki to Moscow, it underwent
a complete autopsy. The operation was performed by a large team
of physicians supervised by Dr. A. I. Abrikosov.[18] The autopsy
lasted four hours and forty minutes and was carried out in the villa
where the body was kept until the morning of January 23. Approximately halfway through the process Lenin's brain was opened, and
the direct cause of death was ascertained. He had suffered a brain
hemorrhage. Due to severe sclerosis of the arteries leading to the
brain, the blood vessels of that organ had been seriously impaired.
The sclerosis meant that fatty deposits in the arteries had calcified
and prevented a normal flow of blood, and with it a necessary
amount of oxygen, from reaching the brain. The cerebral blood vessels were in an extraordinarily weakened state, and when Lenin suffered a stroke on January 21, 1924, a large amount of blood rushed
into his brain, much more blood than the sclerotic arteries had been
transmitting. This pressure was too great for the brain's damaged
vessels, and the walls of those vessels broke down, flooding the brain
with blood. The blood vessels immediately destroyed were in that
section of the brain controlling the respiratory function, and for that
reason Lenin's breathing stopped.[19]

A brief mention of the direct cause of death was the only autopsy
result included in the medical bulletin circulated in Moscow not
long after the operation. Nothing more detailed was published until
three days after the autopsy had been performed.[20] The most striking feature of the official autopsy report published in all newspapers
on January 25 is the great detail in which Lenin's corpse was described. In the report, the doctors discussed Lenin's brain, noting that
symptoms from which Lenin suffered during his protracted illness—
paralysis and aphasia—were explained by the extreme sclerotic
condition of his cerebral arteries. The report also detailed the condition of his skin, including scars and lesions, described his heart,

170 with exact measurements, and provided information on his stomach, kidneys, and other organs.

In his newspaper story, Walter Duranty observed that the sanguine Russian reaction to this report was yet another proof of the difference between East and West: "To a Western country, such detail as the publication of the extraordinarily minute report of the autopsy may seem rather horrible, but the Russians have a different outlook, and the fact is, the dead leader was the object of such interest that the public wants to know everything."[21] If Valentinov and his friends were at all representative of the contemporary nonparty Moscow intelligentsia, the autopsy report evoked a good deal of surprise and shock. "It seems to me, " Valentinov wrote, "at no time before this and nowhere in the world were dead leaders, tsars, kings, etc., presented in such a way, naked, down to the tiniest anatomical detail. There were no anatomical secrets kept; everything was revealed."[22] Valentinov's associate, E. L. Smirnov, felt that the report was an expression of the Bolsheviks' crude materialistic conception of human nature. Another colleague added: Lenin was known as a revolutionary, a leader, a dictator, if you will. One could sympathize with him or not. But he was a person, a soul (*psikhika*). Yet the report conveyed the message: "Lenin is only *matter*, nothing more than a combination of a cranial hemisphere, intestines, an abdominal cavity, a heart, kidneys, a spleen, with such and such characteristics. In this there is something quite shocking."[23] Valentinov points out that his Communist friends were impressed not as much by the detailed character of the autopsy report as by one piece of information it contained. The weight of Lenin's brain was 1340 grams. One of Valentinov's Communist colleagues who seemed genuinely grieved at Lenin's passing, assured him that Lenin's genius was directly connected with the large size of his brain.[24]

The autopsy report and published pieces on the post-mortem by Commissar of Health Semashko and by Lenin's doctors all emphasize the fact that the sclerosis of Lenin's brain arteries was most severe. Even Krupskaia wrote that "the autopsy revealed a colossal sclerosis."[25] According to the doctors, his arteries were so calcified they sounded like bone when tapped with a metal instrument during the operation.[26] The contemporary press observed that some arteries were so clogged that they evidently had let no blood enter the brain at all; the apertures were not even wide enough to permit a hair to pass through. Medical reports all emphasized the extreme sclerotic condition of Lenin's cerebral arteries, which presumably conformed to the truth, but at the same time relieved the doctors of blame for having failed to save his life. Semashko asserted that nothing could have been done to save Lenin; the blood vessels and arteries were totally ruined, and "*with such blood vessels it is impossible to live.*"[27] One of Lenin's physicians, Dr. Otfried Foerster, added that the illness "developed according to inner laws, independent of external factors, with merciless inevitability."[28] Trotsky used the same metaphor in his eulogy: "Obscure laws by which the work of the blood vessels is governed have ended this life."[29] Besides vindicating the doctors, the inexorable laws with their inevitable end had a familiar Marxist ring to them and were somehow fitting for a fatal disease of the leader of the Communist Party.

Another reason the severity of Lenin's illness was emphasized was to set him apart from other men. Lenin and death were described in the press as locked in a heroic struggle—this became part of the Lenin myth. Lenin had been determined to conquer his illness by the strength of his will, wrote a Petrograd journalist. And he would have attained this goal had he not suffered a fierce attack that carried him off to his grave.[30] Lenin lost the fight because his enemy, Death, was heavily armed and Lenin was vulnerable. His blood vessels had been so terribly weakened by the lack of blood to nourish them that Death had only to strike one fierce blow—the stroke of January 21—and even Lenin's genius could not stave it off. The press report strongly implied that another person would have lost much sooner to such a formidable enemy. Semashko pointed out that a significant portion of Lenin's brain had been destroyed, yet he had been able to read newspapers, take interest in politics, and go out hunting. The doctors who performed the autopsy marveled at this too. Other patients, they said, would have been totally incapable of any kind of mental exertion, given a similar sclerotic condition. The strength of Vladimir Ilich's intellect was thus shown to have been remarkable.[31] "Only Ilich was capable of thus doing battle with death and of retaining in the remainder of his brain all of his clarity of thought, his energy, his interests."[32] In fact, the 1923 press accounts of Lenin reading newspapers and hunting had been grossly exaggerated. His vocabulary had been limited to a few words, he had been unable to read, and hunting had consisted of being

172   wheeled outside the villa in his wheelchair and from there moved into some other vehicle. The autopsy *proved* that the reports of his activities during 1923 had been false—or that Lenin was possessed of miraculous powers.

While marveling at Lenin's fortitude, Semashko took it upon himself to explain why the leader had been stricken by this particular disease. The primary factor was hereditary. Vladimir Ilich's father died prematurely of arteriosclerosis (he was fifty-four). Lenin's mother also suffered from sclerosis although she lived to be old.[33] But, asserted Semashko, a much more significant role was played by acquired rather than inherited characteristics. The sclerosis struck Lenin's brain, the organ that he had taxed most during his life with work and agitation. This disease tends to affect the most vulnerable part of one's body. (Semashko even provided his readers with the Latin term for this, *locus minoris resistentiae*.) Thus, concluded the Commissar of Health, Lenin's autopsy showed that his "superhuman mental activity, life of constant agitation and ceaseless anxiety brought our leader to untimely death."[34]

To state that acquired characteristics are more important than inherited ones as a cause of disease is, more or less, to take a Marxist position. But there is a more significant implication; Lenin sacrificed his life for the people and the revolution. This sentiment is present both in medical writing and in various paeans to the dead leader. Dr. V. N. Rozanov, the physician who treated Lenin after the attempt on his life in 1918, wrote: "Undoubtedly, Vladimir Ilich's death was exclusively produced by the fact that he gave absolutely all of his strength to the service of the interests of the working people."[35] Semashko, in the same tone, concluded his article on the cause of Lenin's death by saying that it came about *"because he did not save his strength, he worked his entire life, he rushed, he never knew what it was to rest from his labors.* He persisted for the great cause of the liberation of working people."[36]

It is true that Lenin worked hard and steadily even when unwell—but he also knew how to rest. He was very self-protective in that regard, taking time to rest, particularly to go hunting, even during the difficult civil war period when his constant presence was most needed.[37] The assertion that Lenin never rested became part of the cult mythology and demonstrates the need to prove Lenin's total devotion to his people as well as his unceasing powers of protection. (This image of the ever-watchful, eternal guardian of the people also characterized Stalin's cult image.)

The medical reports that said Lenin died for the revolution were depicting him as a saintly prince whose dedication to his people robbed him of a long life. He died as a consequence of fulfilling his duties as ruler of Russia. During the days of mourning the press emphasized this sacrifice, calling him a "great sufferer."[38] But the most evocative symbol of Lenin's sanctity and immortality was the preserved body exhibited in the mausoleum. It perpetuated the popular devotion to him exhibited at his lying-in-state and turned him into a holy relic whose powers continue beyond physical death. This canonization of Lenin was partly inspired by the hundreds of thousands of people who endured hours of bitter cold in order to venerate his remains. In this they resembled the faithful who, in old Russia, flocked to the gravesides of men and women they considered holy. But just as only church officials had the power to canonize, so with Lenin not these pilgrims but the Funeral Commission enshrined the body of the leader.

The Decision To Embalm

There is no direct evidence on how the commission reached the decision to preserve the corpse. In its official report it claimed to have responded to thousands of letters and telegrams from the public, expressing the wish to be able to see their deceased leader.[39] A few such letters appeared in the press before Lenin's funeral. On January 25, 1925, the Moscow daily *Rabochaia Moskva* published three under the headline, "Lenin's Body Must Be Preserved!" One letter said: "Under no circumstances can we give to the earth such a great and intensely beloved leader as Ilich. We suggest his remains be embalmed and left under glass for hundreds of years . . . Let him be with us always." Another letter pointed out that future generations would need to see the body of the man who had brought about the world revolution. The letters all ask for the same thing, that Lenin be preserved and exhibited under glass. It would appear their authors had been coached, but by whom? Valentinov indicates that the idea of preserving Lenin's body had been discussed among Polit-

174   buro members several months before Lenin's death. This would allow time for the idea's supporters to spread the word to selected comrades and mobilize popular backing for it.

The meeting of Stalin, Kalinin, Bukharin, Trotsky, Kamenev, and Rykov took place in the late fall of 1923.[40] It was not a full Politburo meeting; Zinoviev and Tomsky were absent. Stalin informed the group that because of a worsening of Lenin's condition, a fatal outcome could be expected. Responding to Stalin, Kalinin declared that the impending death of Lenin raised the question of how the party would organize his funeral. This terrible event must not take them unawares, he said. "If we bury Vladimir Ilich, the funeral must be the grandest the world has ever known."

Stalin fully supported Kalinin. It was most important that everything be arranged ahead of time so the leadership would not be caught unprepared in a time of intense grief. This question of Lenin's burial, continued Stalin, was a source of great concern to "certain of our comrades in the provinces":

> They say that Lenin is a *Russian* and *ought to be buried in accordance* with this fact. For example, they are categorically opposed to the cremation, the incineration of Lenin's body. In their opinion, cremation does not at all conform to the Russian conception of love and veneration of the deceased. It could even appear to be an insult to his memory. In cremation, annihilation, the scattering of the remains, Russian thought has always seen a last judgment upon those who had to suffer execution. Certain comrades believe that contemporary science offers the possibility, by means of embalming, to preserve the body of the deceased for a long time, in any case for a long enough time to permit our consciousness to get used to the idea that Lenin is no longer among us.

Trotsky was outraged:

> It was only when comrade Stalin finished his speech that it dawned on me in which direction these originally incomprehensible arguments and instructions—that Lenin is a Russian person and must be buried in the Russian manner—were going. The Russian manner, in accordance with the canons of the Russian Orthodox church, that makes relics out of its saints. Apparently we, the party of revolutionary Marxism, are advised to behave in the same way—to preserve the body of Lenin. Earlier there were the relics of Sergius of Radonezh and Serafim of Sarov; now they want to replace these

with the relics of Vladimir Ilich. I would very much like to know who these comrades are who, according to the words of Stalin, propose that with the help of modern science the remains of Lenin should be embalmed, transformed into a relic. I would tell them that they have absolutely nothing to do with the science of Marxism.

Bukharin agreed with Trotsky and was just as indignant. He felt that the mummification of Lenin's remains would be an affront to his memory; it diverged so completely from Lenin's world view that it should not even be discussed further. He added:

I notice that there is a strange spirit moving somewhere in the party ... They want to exalt physical remains ... They are talking, for example, of the transfer of Marx's remains from England to us in Moscow. I have even heard that these remains, buried by the Kremlin wall, would somehow add "sanctity" and significance to the entire place, to all those buried in the fraternal cemetery. The devil knows what this all is!

Kamenev also spoke out vehemently against the proposed embalming, denouncing it as the very kind of "popery" that Lenin himself had fulminated against.

Stalin appeared unmoved by the protests of Trotsky, Bukharin, and Kamenev, and refused to name the "comrades from the provinces" who had suggested that Lenin's remains be embalmed. Meanwhile Kalinin, who was of peasant origin and the party's link to the peasantry, continued to insist that Lenin could not be buried like an ordinary mortal. Rykov was inclined toward Stalin and Kalinin. He did not directly speak out for embalming, but indicated that Lenin must be buried in some special manner.

When Lenin died, the question of his cremation could be only theoretical, since there was at the time no crematorium in Russia. This very fact indicates that Stalin was correct when he warned that the reduction of the body to ashes might shock the Russian people. "Cremation has always been abhorrent to Christian feeling, and though it was contended that the fate of the immortal soul was not affected by the mode of the disposal of the body, there can be little doubt that the real cause of the revolt against the funeral pyre is to be found in the doctrine of the resurrection of the flesh."[41] The resurrection of the body is a most important aspect of Christian eschatology. Eternal life must be life in a body: "The body will rise again, all of the body, the identical body, the entire body."[42]

176   Immediately after Lenin's death, plans were evidently made to bury him at the end of that week, for on Tuesday, January 22, Dr. Abrikosov, who had performed the autopsy, embalmed the body with the express purpose of preserving it for six days—until the funeral.[43] Within a few days, according to Bonch-Bruevich, a decision was made to embalm the body for forty days.[44] This is a traditional number in the Russian Orthodox church; prayers for the dead are said for forty days.[45] The USSR Central Executive Committee (CEC) announced the decision in a resolution that left vague the number of days intended for Lenin's continuing wake. It implied that burial was to be temporarily delayed:

> Responding to the wishes of numerous delegations and appeals to the USSR CEC, and with the goal of enabling all those who would wish to, but will not be able to come to Moscow in time for the funeral, to bid farewell to their beloved leader, the presidium of the CEC of the Union resolves:
>
> 1. To preserve the coffin with Lenin's body in a crypt, which will be accessible to visitors.
>
> 2. To construct this crypt at the Kremlin wall in Red Square among the fraternal graves of those who fought in the October revolution.[46]

Abrikosov was placed in charge of the body. He feared that the autopsy he had performed might have hindered the possibility of a successful preservation. But he nonetheless expressed the hope that Lenin's body would remain unchanged for a long time, "three or four years at least," if the temperature of the crypt were kept at around zero, the humidity very low, and if the coffin were completely airtight.[47] Consequently, on January 26, the Soviet press reported that the temperature inside the crypt would be kept at zero "for the better preservation of the body."[48] On Lenin's funeral day Steklov rhapsodized about the prospect that Lenin's body might be preserved:

> No, he will not go! He will stay with us even physically, at least for a while. Oh, how well we understand the workers' earnest desire to preserve Lenin's body forever, so that all future generations might see him . . . Unfortunately, until now, science has not found a way of preserving human remains forever. But we know that all possible measures will be taken to preserve Lenin's body from decay as long

as possible, and to enable all those who so wish, to venerate his remains.

Steklov was eager to reassure those who mistakenly and "sorrowfully think that they will not be able to see his face."[49] And two days later he wrote of Lenin: "The whole populace hopes that his remains can be preserved forever, so that they might be able to gaze on him."[50]

Despite this publicity, as late as the day after the funeral Krupskaia was apparently unaware of the planned preservation of her husband's remains. She wrote to I. A. Armand on January 28: "Right now they have not closed up his grave yet, and it will still be possible to look upon Ilich."[51] Obviously, explains her biographer Robert McNeal, she assumed that Lenin would soon receive a decent burial.[52] But about that time the decision was made to exhibit Lenin's body not for forty days, but for as long a time as possible.

It appears likely that Krupskaia learned of the decision to preserve the body indefinitely on January 29. The following day she published in *Pravda* a "veiled protest."[53]

COMRADES WORKERS AND PEASANTS!
I have a great request to make of you: do not allow your grief for Ilich to express itself in the external veneration of his person. Do not build memorials to him, palaces named after him, [do not hold] magnificent celebrations in his memory, etc. All of this meant so little to him in his lifetime; he found it all so trying. Remember how much poverty and disorder we still have in our country. If you want to honor the name of Vladimir Ilich—build day care centers, kindergartens, homes, schools . . . etc., and most importantly—try in all things to fulfill his legacy.[54]

Bonch-Bruevich also mentions that "Nadezhda Konstantinovna, with whom I spoke intimately on the subject, was against the mummification of Vladimir Ilich."[55] Although Krupskaia did not succeed in altering the plans to preserve Lenin's body, she continued to protest silently by never visiting the mausoleum or standing on its tribunal at revolutionary celebrations. And she never mentioned the body in the mausoleum in her published works on Lenin.[56]

Lenin's sisters, Anna and Maria Ilinichna, and his brother Dmitry Ilich were also opposed to the embalming. So was Bonch-Bruevich, the member of the Funeral Commission who was in charge of building the crypt, being convinced that the deceased would have been totally opposed to this treatment of his (or anyone else's) body. Lenin, he said, had been in favor of a simple burial or cremation, often remarking that a crematorium ought to be constructed in Russia.[57] It is perhaps for this reason that Commissar of Health Semashko insisted on Lenin's cremation. On the day before the funeral he was quoted as saying that Lenin must be cremated and that his body should be preserved until a crematorium was built, adding that it was "timely and necessary to introduce cremation into Russia in general."[58] But, according to Bonch-Bruevich, the idea of embalming Lenin's body and putting it on permanent display "took hold of everyone, was approved of by everyone."[59]

Bonch-Bruevich was mistaken in thinking that, besides Lenin's family, he alone opposed the embalming. In the autumn 1923 Politburo meeting, Trotsky, Kamenev, and Bukharin had spoken out against mummification. After Lenin's death, none of these men came forward with public protests against the planned embalming. Bukharin, however, found a way to express his negative views on this treatment of Lenin's body. He was editor of *Pravda*, and that newspaper consistently played down the story of Lenin's body and the Lenin mausoleum. Far fewer articles on the subject were published in *Pravda* than in *Izvestiia*, and those that were printed tended to be smaller than those in *Izvestiia* and placed further back in the newspaper. But on January 30 all three major newspapers carried Zinoviev's long article on mourning week in which he spoke out in favor of the plans for Lenin's body: "How good it is that it has been decided that Lenin be put into a crypt! How good that it was thought of in time! To bury Ilich's body in the ground—this would be simply unbearable."[60]

The means by which the party leaders made the decision to preserve Lenin has never been revealed; nor have Soviet authorities published the minutes of any deliberations that explain why Lenin was fated to meet this (to date) unique end. The only publicly stated reason appeared in the press in mid-June 1924, when the embalming of Lenin was nearly complete:

> On the first night after the death of Vladimir Ilich, his body was submitted to an embalming and an autopsy, the results of which were immediately thereafter published in the press.

The embalming was performed by A. I. Abrikosov, professor at
Moscow University; he was charged with the task of preserving the
body of V. I. for a short time, until it would be committed to the
earth . . .

We all remember the days when hundreds of thousands of people
stood for hours in 28 degrees of frost, attempting to see and engrave
in their memories the physical features of [their] beloved leader.

During three days and nights access to the Trade Union House
was continuous, and this period of time turned out to be not big
enough for a significant proportion of Moscow's population.

For this reason, the government made the decision to not commit
Vladimir Ilich's body to the earth, but to put it in a mausoleum and
to allow those who wished to, to visit it.[61]

Certainly the overwhelming popular response to Lenin's lying-in-
state must have played a significant role in prompting the decision
to preserve and display Lenin's corpse. As a relic, he was to continue
to legitimize Soviet power and mobilize the population. Bonch-
Bruevich resigned himself to the idea because of its political benefits. " 'Well,' I thought . . . 'Let him after death, as in life, serve the
proletarian cause, the cause of the working class.' "[62] This political
consideration was of primary importance in encouraging the actual
implementation of the idea to turn Lenin's grave into a shrine. Yet
what gave rise to the idea in the first place? There is no single answer
to this difficult question, but the context in which the idea arose
points to four probable sources: the discovery of the tomb of the
Egyptian pharaoh, Tutankhamen, fifteen months before Lenin's
death; Russian Orthodox popular tradition, which held that incorruptible remains were a proof of sanctity; the influence among the
Bolshevik intelligentsia of Fedorov's philosophy, which sought
human salvation in the physical resurrection of the flesh; and the
Bolshevik god-building movement, which had looked to Bolshevism
for a new religion and one of whose main proponents, Leonid Krasin, was in charge of the embalming.

Although there is no direct evidence of a link between the tombs
of Lenin and Tutankhamen, the discovery of the pharaoh's unplun-
dered grave in Luxor in 1922 received worldwide publicity. At the
time it would have been unseemly to publicize in the Soviet press
the unearthed treasures of a slaveowning society, but the news undoubtedly reached the Soviet Union through the Western press.

Throughout 1923 European and American newspapers described every significant new discovery as the slow process of sorting the fabulous treasures proceeded. Tourists flocked to Luxor. Royalty was invited to witness important stages in the excavations.[63] Businessmen from all over the world scrambled to produce fabrics and sandals whose designs were taken from items found in the tomb.[64] When Lord Carnarvon, director of the excavation, died of pneumonia in the spring of 1923, the Western press published stories about the "curse" of the pharaoh's mummy.[65]

Although the bandages binding the mummy were not unraveled until after Lenin's body had been embalmed, the archeologists' intention to examine the mummy had been announced and the press had stories about the anticipated event. The strange power of a body preserved for three thousand years impressed many, doubtless including some Soviet readers of the Western press. The discovery of the tomb of Tutankhamen thus may have had some influence on the decision to preserve Lenin's body and build for it an imposing mausoleum. In an oblique reference to Egypt, Iury Steklov compared Lenin's funeral to those of "the founders of great states in ancient times," whose slaves were buried together with them. The royal bodies were hidden in elaborate mazes, he explained, lest the "oppressed masses" desecrate their graves.[66] And when the mausoleum and Lenin's embalmed remains were opened to the public on August 1, 1924, one of the embalmers in a press interview deliberately compared their achievement with those of their ancient Egyptian counterparts.

It is impossible to gauge the extent of the Egyptian influence on the final disposition of Lenin's remains. But the role played by Russian religious tradition is much clearer. Stalin's suggestion, in 1923, that Lenin should be buried in a "Russian" manner undoubtedly referred to the public display of holy relics in the Orthodox church, as Trotsky angrily observed. Stalin had studied for the priesthood in the theological seminary of Tiflis, and the influence of his early training was evident in his introduction of the idea of preserving Lenin's corpse. But although Stalin expressed support of the idea to his fellow Politburo members, he said that it originated with certain provincial comrades whom he would not name. Their identities were never revealed, but Konstantin Melnikov, the architect who designed the sarcophagus for the body, later said that the "general

idea" of permanently preserving and displaying Lenin's body originated with Leonid Krasin.[67]

A man of energy, talent, and imagination, Krasin was an engineer by training, a diplomat, and, at the time of Lenin's death, Commissar of Foreign Trade. He had the sense of adventure it took to devise such a bold scheme. He also had personal reasons for wishing to keep Lenin's body intact. Earlier in the century he had been an outspoken god-builder.[68] Along with Gorky, Lunacharsky, and Bogdanov, he had sought within Bolshevism a spiritual regeneration, a celebration of the deification of man. For him, as well as for Lunacharsky, who supervised the design plans for Lenin's permanent mausoleum, the cult of Lenin may well have been a channel for expressing these earlier religious strivings. Their immortalization of Lenin was a true deification of man. It was also reflective of the general early twentieth-century apocalyptic mood that had stirred the Russian intelligentsia and had inspired the god-builders to celebrate the anticipated revolution as the true Second Coming.

Krasin had been won over by Bogdanov's faith in physical immortality and may have been influenced as well by Fedorov, the respected philosopher who combined a faith in Christ with faith in human community and in the miracle-working powers of technology. Krasin shared these philosophers' faith in the future possibility of physical resurrection. In 1931 Olminsky wrote that Krasin had been a follower of Bogdanov and had returned to the fold only in 1918. In 1921, Olminsky continued, Krasin publicly preached his belief in the resurrection of the dead. It was at the funeral of L. Ia. Karpov that Krasin said:

> I am certain that the time will come when science will become all-powerful, that it will be able to recreate a deceased organism. I am certain that the time will come when one will be able to use the elements of a person's life to recreate the physical person. And I am certain that when that time will come, when the liberation of mankind, using all the might of science and technology, the strength and capacity of which we cannot now imagine, will be able to resurrect great historical figures—and I am certain that when that time will come, among the great figures will be our comrade, Lev Iakovlevich.[69]

Three years later Krasin took charge of the preservation of Lenin's body. If Lev Iakovlevich was worthy of resurrection, was not Vladi-

182   mir Ilich? It is more than likely that Krasin believed Lenin should be preserved intact for his eventual resurrection.[70]

Krasin was suddenly brought into the Funeral Commission on January 29, 1924, and six days later was named a member of its executive troika. He immersed himself in the regulation of Lenin busts and monuments. But his most immediate task was the preservation of Lenin's body and the construction of a mausoleum.

The Attempts at Preservation

During mourning week, in three days and three nights, the Funeral Commission had supervised the construction of a temporary crypt for Lenin by the Kremlin wall. On February 3, the commission announced that measures would be taken to protect the crypt from fire and water seepage and that electric heaters had been installed to prevent the temperature from going too low and damaging the body—it had to be kept at constant zero. At the same time, minor changes were to be made on the outside of the crypt.[71] The next day Krasin began to supervise the construction of a refrigeration system to circulate cold air into the glass-lidded sarcophagus in which Lenin's body was to be placed.[72] By the beginning of March the cooling unit was under construction in the Senate tower of the Kremlin.[73]

Two weeks earlier Krasin had organized a competition for the design of Lenin's sarcophagus. Competitors were given a week's time to complete their drawings and models, and a cash prize was to be awarded to the best project. The specifications were as follows: Lenin's face was to be visible, so the sarcophagus had to have a glass cover; the glass should be light enough so that its weight could be supported by a thin frame; and, most important, the sarcophagus must be able to be hermetically sealed and fastened to the refrigeration unit.[74] It was also necessary that the design lend itself to construction with whatever materials the commission could requisition (in the end, the glass used for the sarcophagus had previously been the front window of a restaurant).[75] The sarcophagus designed by the architect K. S. Melnikov won the competition.

On March 14 Krasin made a report to the Funeral Commission and announced that the refrigeration unit with ducts to move the cold air into the coffin would be built in duplicate, so that the second unit could take over if the first should break down. He confirmed the commission's choice of Melnikov's sarcophagus design. Krasin indicated that he himself would be in charge of the mausoleum, the sarcophagus, and the preservation of the body.[76] His early training as an engineer gave him the requisite knowledge for the job, and he earnestly set to the practical aspects of the work at hand.[77] He ended his report with the statement that all of the necessary work could be expected to be completed within six weeks.

But just at the time that Krasin was running his sarcophagus competition, perfecting his refrigeration unit, and overseeing plans for a temporary, wooden mausoleum, unforeseen problems arose. By the end of February and the beginning of March, Lenin's body began to show definite signs of decay. In the words of the Funeral Commission report, "time did its work" (*vremia delalo svoe delo*).[78] Warmer weather had set in and the skin of the corpse had become discolored.[79]

This raises the question of how realistic in the first place had been Krasin's assumption that simple refrigeration could preserve Lenin's body intact. Surely he was not inspired by a belief that Lenin's body, like that of an Orthodox saint, would not decay? Apparently his plan to keep the body in a perfect state by means of refrigeration had a scientific justification. A human body can remain unchanged for a long time if it is properly embalmed, refrigerated, and kept in anoxic conditions to prevent mold from growing. But if the growth of mold does begin, it is almost impossible to arrest the decay of the entire body. The discoloration of Lenin's corpse was doubtless a sign that mold had set in.[80]

In view of this development, a medical committee was hurriedly formed on February 26 to "take all responsibility for looking after the state of the embalming of the body of Vladimir Ilich Lenin and simultaneously to take all necessary measures" for that purpose.[81] This committee consisted of Commissar Semashko, Professor V. N. Rozanov, and Professor Veisbrod; after a few days, Professors V. P. Vorobev and B. I. Zbarsky joined the medical committee. The experts examined the corpse and came to the conclusion that immediate steps had to be taken to ensure its preservation.[82]

This was the moment for decision. Burial seemed necessary, since

184   Lenin's body had proved unable to defy corruption. Surely the public could not be shown a decomposing body, a failed relic. The Funeral Commission discussed the matter many times and came to the conclusion that it would attempt to find some way to preserve Lenin's body indefinitely. The Funeral Commission included a group of scientists in its meetings held on March 5 and 12 to discuss the possibility of repairing the damage and preserving Lenin intact. The scientists were charged with the following task:

> Our problem is to determine those measures which can be taken to preserve the body of Vladimir Ilich for as long a time as possible. Our aim is to preserve the body in such a state that it can be viewed, and that the external appearance of the body and face should preserve the physical features of Vladimir Ilich in just the same way that he looked in the first days after his death.[83]

Their task was a challenging one. Successful prolonged embalming was a scientific feat of great rarity. The ancient Egyptians, of course, were known for their embalming skills, but their mummies, when unwrapped, are unsightly. The skin is brown and leathery and totally dessicated. The face is unrecognizable. Likewise, other preserved bodies, such as that of Jeremy Bentham at the University of London, bear an ugly leathery appearance. To the Soviet scientists was entrusted a task that had no precedent. They were to make Lenin's body capable of withstanding air and normal temperatures so that thousands of people could visit it, and the face and hands (the only visible portions) were to look as if Lenin had just died.

Some of the scientists at the March meetings pointed out the impossibility of preserving a body in the presence of oxygen without a drastic change in the color of the skin—which is what had already happened to the corpse. Others felt that unless the body were kept in liquid, there was no way to prevent the skin from drying out. Some of the assembled scientists warned that no matter what method would be used to preserve the body, the face would inevitably and rapidly decay beyond recognition. There was a general agreement that contemporary science had not provided a means for solving the problem at hand.[84]

The public was not informed of the onset of decomposition in Lenin's body at this time, but the Funeral Commission announced on March 25, 1924, that it would attempt to keep Lenin's body intact:

> After the death of V. I. Ulianov (Lenin), his body was subjected to an ordinary embalming, with the aim of preserving the body temporarily.
>
> At the present time, responding to the desires of the wide masses of the USSR and other nations to see the physical features of the deceased leader, the Commission of the Funeral of V. I. Ulianov (Lenin) has decided to take measures, available in current science, to preserve the body for as long a time as possible.[85]

This was the first official statement announcing the intention to preserve the body indefinitely. Once made public, the decision was irreversible, and success imperative. To reflect this commitment to the creation of a body that would appear to transcend mortality, the Funeral Commission was renamed the Commission for the Immortalization of the Memory of V. I. Ulianov (Lenin), three days after the publication of the statement.

On March 26, 1924, two scientists began the work of restoring Lenin's body and reembalming it. The man in charge of the venture was V. P. Vorobev, professor of anatomy at the Kharkov Medical Institute.[86] Vorobev was primarily known for his work on the nervous system of the heart.[87] His closest associate in this task was Boris Zbarsky, a biochemist. These two men were assisted by a team of scientists.[88] The reembalming was under the general supervision of Leonid Krasin and Professors Veisbrod and Rozanov.[89]

Vorobev and Zbarsky began their four-month labor under a great deal of pressure. The plans had been made public, and failure would have been most embarrassing. A successfully reembalmed corpse would complement and justify the glorification of the deceased leader. It would "prove" Lenin's divinity and secure for the party a "living" source of legitimation. "We saw how much attention the party paid to this effort," Zbarsky later wrote.[90] This work was to extol not only the greatness of Lenin, but the brilliance of Soviet science as well. If scientists of the Soviet Union could succeed at a task no others had accomplished, this would demonstrate the virtues of the Soviet system of government. "Anyone can perform a burial," wrote a group of students from Rostov-on-Don to the Funeral Commission, but to preserve a body for many years, "this only the communist party can accomplish."[91] This assumption is a common element of Soviet propaganda, then and now. If the Soviet Union proves itself superior in scientific endeavors, it is clearly the best system of government. Conversely, since Communism provides the best government, it must excel in science. Such reasoning reflects the tremendous reverence the new Soviet regime held for science. The two professors had to vindicate Lenin and Soviet science. And they had to do it quickly, for spring had come and the body was badly in need of restoration.

They worked continuously, round the clock. They experimented on cadavers provided by morgues and by pathology institutes.[92] They applied various chemicals to Lenin's body, but before doing this they used the treatment on another body and watched for its effect. Their chemical treatment of the body required uninterrupted observation; Vorobev and Zbarsky took turns keeping a close vigil on the body while the other rested. After a few days, Dzerzhinsky had trolley tracks and wires put in just outside the mausoleum, and a trolley car furnished with beds and cooking and washing facilities was parked there for their use.[93] The doctors' work proceeded, under heavy guard. Soldiers were posted outside the crypt and within it. Guards with bayonets patrolled the Kremlin walls above it, and mounted troops paraded around the mausoleum. This all suggested, reported Walter Duranty, "that Lenin dead is more carefully guarded than Lenin living."[94]

The scientists labored to create an embalming fluid that would prevent the dessication of the bodily tissue without producing a discoloration of the skin. Ultimately they claimed to have achieved this goal by treating the body with a chemical solution containing formalin, glycerine, alcohol, and other substances.[95] Its precise formula is still secret.

By mid-June the work appeared so promising that the Immortalization Commission published a statement explaining that the body of Lenin had shown symptoms of decay but that the reembalming was nearing successful completion.

> The original embalming had had as its goal the preservation of the body for a short period, but time took its toll.
>
> In certain portions of the body there appeared a pigmentation, a change in the color of the skin, which indicated the beginning of processes that could influence the further preservation of the body.

In view of this, the Commission of the USSR CEC on the Immortalization of the Memory of V. I. Ulianov-Lenin arranged a series of meetings with specialists . . . to consider the possibility of preserving the body of Vladimir Ilich unchanged for an extended period of time.

At these meetings the specialists concluded that an extended preservation of the body would necessitate a new special embalming, which was delegated to the Professor of Anatomy of the Kharkov Medical Institute, V. P. Vorobev.

The new embalming was begun on March 26, about which an official announcement was made at that time.[96]

This mode of emblaming: 1) imparts a uniform appearance to the tissue, changing its color and consistency so it is like that of normal skin; 2) introduces a substance to hinder autolysis [self-digestion of the tissues]; 3) replaces the liquid in the tissues with one that will not evaporate.

Two months have elapsed since the beginning of the embalming.[97] The most difficult stages of it have been accomplished, and at this time, the process [is] in its final stages.

The commission ended its announcement with an assurance that the public would be allowed to visit Lenin's body in the near future.[98] The commission's willingness to share with the public the initial decomposition of Lenin's body is remarkable and demonstrates that its members were in no way attempting to pass off the preservation of the corpse as miraculous. On the contrary, they were celebrating the expertise of Soviet science.

The reembalming was completed at the end of July 1924. For four days, from July 22 to 26, a team of experts carefully inspected the body and studied all the documents recording the progress of the embalming. They came to the conclusion that the work accomplished by Vorobev was scientifically sound, and that one could expect the body to remain for decades in a condition that would permit observation of it in a closed glass-covered coffin, as long as the humidity and temperature were kept at an appropriate level. A second team then joined the first one in examining the body. This group stated that Lenin looked as if he had just recently died.[99]

On July 26, 1924, the entire Immortalization Commission made a detailed inspection of the body.[100] The commission held a meeting in the Kremlin on the same day. Dzerzhinsky opened the proceed-

188   ings by introducing Vorobev, who presented a detailed report of the reembalming. He declared that his method had been entirely successful. The team of experts that had spent the previous four days studying the embalming followed with its report. The scientists were satisfied that the body would remain unchanged for a very long time, but said that it would require constant attention.[101] The second inspection team also reported its approval of Vorobev's work. After hearing these reports, the Immortalization Commission resolved that Professors Vorobev and Zbarsky should attend to the observation and care of the body, under the general supervision of the Immortalization Commission.

Avel Enukidze, deputy chairman of the Central Executive Committee, then spoke of the significance of the preservation of Lenin's body. He protested the idea that the reembalming was done to popularize Lenin as a relic. The plain inference was that some people within the party still felt uncomfortable about making Lenin look like an Orthodox saint. Enukidze apparently felt it necessary to defend strongly the unusual disposition of Lenin's remains.

> Not only this commission, but all of our party and the Second Congress of Soviets that met in January, attach enormous importance to the preservation of Vladimir Ilich's body. It is obvious that neither we nor our comrades wanted to make out of the remains of Vladimir Ilich any kind of "relic" (*moshchi*), by means of which we would have been able to popularize or preserve the memory of Vladimir Ilich. With his brilliant writings and revolutionary activities, which he left as a legacy to the entire world revolutionary movement, he immortalized himself enough.
>
> I can boldly declare that in the history of the world, there has never before been a person who, during his lifetime, was so immensely popular, and was the object of such love on the part of the broadest masses of workers and peasants of the whole world . . . We wanted to preserve the body of Vladimir Ilich, not in order simply to popularize his name, but we attached and [now] attach enormous importance to the preservation of the physical features of this wonderful leader, for the generation that is growing up, and for future generations, and also for those hundreds of thousands and maybe even millions of people who will be supremely happy to see the physical features of this person. For this reason, you must understand that anxiety which we suffered during the first period

of the work on the preservation of Vladimir Ilich's body. There were many hesitations and doubts among the members of the commission, and among those specialists whom we had called in for this work.

Four months ago, when at one of our meetings we were unable to achieve a firm conviction that we would be able to preserve the physical features of Vladimir Ilich for an extended period of time, and to a great enough degree [of resemblance], we all clearly understood that Prof. Vorobev took upon himself, I should say, a very bold task. And today, after exactly four months, as Prof. Vorobev promised us, the results of the work done by him, according to the judgment of authoritative experts, have given us the assurance that *this work has been concluded completely satisfactorily.*[102]

With that Enukidze assured Vorobev that he and his associates would receive honors for their work, which they did.[103]

The Lenin Crypt

On January 22, 1924, the Funeral Commission had charged V. D. Bonch-Bruevich with the supervision of the construction of Lenin's grave. On that day he selected the site for the crypt near the Kremlin wall, close to the fraternal grave and to Sverdlov's. At this spot there once stood a rostrum from which Lenin had addressed his Moscow followers.

The next morning Bonch-Bruevich held a meeting of architects to discuss the design of Lenin's crypt. He opened the meeting by telling them where the crypt would be situated. He was met with silence. It was finally broken by the architect A. V. Shchusev: "Vladimir Ilich is eternal . . . How shall we honor his memory? How will we mark his grave? In architecture the cube is eternal. Everything proceeds from the cube, the entire range of architectural creation. Let the mausoleum, which we will erect as a monument to Vladimir Ilich, derive from a cube." Shchusev quickly sketched for the gathering an edifice based on three cubes. In Bonch-Bruevich's rhapsodic recollection, the assembly listened attentively to Shchusev's speech. "Everyone felt the sublime truth in the words of this thoughtful architect, and everyone agreed with him."[104]

It is understandable that any burial vault ought to express the

190   concept of time. But why the cube? Cubism was an important artistic movement of the period. One of its most important exponents, Kazimir Malevich, who also thought that the mausoleum ought to be in the shape of a cube, wrote some thoughts on the subject a few days after Lenin died: "The point of view that Lenin's death is not death, that he is alive and eternal, is symbolized in a new object, taking as its form the cube. The cube is no longer a geometric body. It is a new object with which we try to portray eternity, to create a new set of circumstances, with which we can maintain Lenin's eternal life, defeating death."[105] Malevich proposed a full Lenin cult, with music and poetry devoted to Lenin and with local Lenin corners. He suggested that every Leninist should have a cube at home, "as a reminder of the eternal, constant lesson of Leninism." Like the pyramid in Egypt, the cube would form the basis of the Lenin cult. And the body should be housed in a structure in which there is an entry into a cube, "as into eternity."[106] Shchusev, who was awarded the honor of designing and constructing a crypt for Lenin, produced a design of three cubes arranged horizontally and connected by corridors.[107] The central cube, which was to house the body, was topped by platforms in three tiers, forming a pyramid. The top tier was crowned with a tall narrow colonnade, supported by buttresses.

Since it had to be completed in three days and nights, work began immediately and went on around the clock. Scores of workers labored in two-hour shifts; the cold made longer exposure impossible.[108] The job proved extraordinarily difficult. The cold was so extreme that bonfires could not soften the frozen ground. Worse, when some drilling was done, the workers hit the foundations of an ancient wall that their drill could not pierce. They had to blast it out with dynamite. Some sixty charges were needed to break up the ground. Still the foundation was not ready until the morning before the funeral.

The crypt itself was built elsewhere while the blasting was going on, and it was fitted onto the foundation on the morning of January 26. Because there was so little time, the colonnade on top of the middle cube was not built, the dimensions of the crypt were smaller than had originally been planned, and only one entrance was constructed instead of the two Shchusev had envisioned.[109] The edifice was completed on the day of the funeral. Early that morning,

Bonch-Bruevich received a draft of the inscription for the facade of the crypt. It read:

1924

USSR

TO VLADIMIR ILICH

LENIN

Bonch-Bruevich crossed all this out and wrote, simply, LENIN.[110]

The completed wooden crypt was squat and ugly. Its three cubes with the three-tiered top on the central one were painted gray to make the wood resemble stone. Its edges were painted black as a sign of mourning. The inscription LENIN stood out on the facade in large black appliquéd letters. The interior walls of the crypt were lined with red fabric slashed here and there with black stripes. The ceiling above the platform on which the coffin rested was decorated with a hammer and sickle of black crepe.[111] The entire edifice and the space surrounding it were scattered with frozen wreaths of various sizes and shapes. After Lenin's funeral, work on the crypt continued to make it approximate the original specifications. At the same time, the public was told that a "monumental" crypt would be built in the spring.

The Wooden Mausoleum

Little more than a week after Lenin's funeral, Leonid Krasin initiated a lively press debate about the proposed crypt by publishing an article in *Izvestiia*, "The Architectural Immortalization of Lenin." Krasin emphasized the world significance of Lenin's grave, saying that it would surpass Mecca and Jerusalem. The crypt ought to be impressive but simple; it must not attempt to compete with the glorious architecture of the Kremlin. He suggested that on the crypt itself a rostrum be constructed, from which speeches could be addressed to large assemblies in Red Square. For this reason any large sculptures on the building would be inappropriate. As for the inscription, it should remain just as it was: LENIN. Krasin ended his piece by asserting that his aim in writing it was less to gain public acceptance of his scheme for the Lenin crypt than it was to provoke public discussion of the monument to Lenin at workers' and party gatherings and in the press.[112] What he sought, in other

192   words, was a *campaign* to mobilize the popular imagination around the celebration of Lenin's memory. Not only the proposed edifice but also its very conception was to inspire public enthusiasm.

It did. A number of artists and architects responded to Krasin's article with pieces of their own, representing a variety of opinions on such questions as whether Lenin's grave should also be the most important monument to him in Moscow, and whether the monument should be symbolic or representational.[113] At the same time, hundreds of suggestions about Lenin's monumental crypt were sent to the editorial offices of the Moscow press. One foreign service officer proposed that an enormous tower be built over Lenin's grave. This tower should be "something like the Eiffel, but even taller." The bottom of the tower should display a huge turbine, churning out the noise of a factory; on top of the tower a radio and telegraph station would send messages to the entire world, symbolized by a globe that should crown the whole edifice.[114] For the painter V. E. Tatlin the mausoleum was to be a "triumph of engineering" that would hold vast numbers of visitors. He also suggested that the mausoleum should have a huge auditorium and an information bureau with a radio station and (the ultimate sign of modernity) two to three hundred telephones.[115]

These and other proposals were prompted by Krasin's article, by an announcement, published a few days earlier, inviting all interested persons to participate in a competition for the design of the mausoleum,[116] and by the general popular engagement with Lenin that carried over from mourning week.

Among the many opinions about the Lenin mausoleum that found their way into the press in that heady atmosphere of nervous enthusiasm for Lenin so evident in the weeks following his funeral was an extraordinary piece in *Pravda*, protesting the Lenin cult and the planned mausoleum. The authors of this article, a group of nineteen members of the Communist Party and the Komsomol, referred to Krupskaia's open letter of January 30, 1924, in which she had asked that monuments not be raised in Lenin's memory. The article continued: "We must venerate not the corpse of Comrade Lenin, but his cause." The signators then proposed a number of measures for improving the Soviet Union (such as building homes and electric generators) as the proper way to honor Lenin.[117] It seems remarkable that a protest against the building of a mausoleum and the veneration of his body should have been published in the party organ. But Bukharin was its editor, and by publishing this protest he may well have seen an opportunity to express his own views. Predictably, nothing similar appeared in *Izvestiia*.[118]

This protest had absolutely no effect on the collection of grandiose schemes for Lenin's monument that continued to pour into the office of *Izvestiia*. But, for other reasons, the Funeral Commission ignored the results of its own announced competition and, on February 21, Krasin and his colleague Ilia Tsivtsivadze decided to accept one of Shchusev's designs for a wooden mausoleum, much more modest than most of the proposed stone or metal monuments, but incomparably more imposing than the unsightly crypt that was so hastily thrown together during the last week of January.[119] The reason for the decision to go ahead with a wooden mausoleum was simple: to design and build a proper architectural tribute to Lenin would doubtless be a lengthy procedure. In the meantime the leader's remains would need a proper, if temporary, resting place that could admit the viewing public. The extant structure of three cubes could accommodate neither visitors nor the technical apparatus deemed necessary for keeping the body intact.

The wooden mausoleum Shchusev envisioned was to be more than twice the size of the first structure, and much more elegant. It was to be one harmonious, unified edifice, not too large but giving the impression of height from its outer covering of vertical wooden beams. One central entrance, rather than two, was to lead into the tomb. One of the features of the projected new structure was Krasin's idea: the mausoleum was to be a major tribunal as well as a grave. Shchusev was asked to design speakers' platforms atop the mausoleum, with staircases leading up to them.

In the beginning of March, the Funeral Commission ratified Shchusev's plan.[120] Within a couple of weeks, construction of the mausoleum began and proceeded through April simultaneously with the reembalming of Lenin's body.[121] The edifice was almost complete by May 1, 1924. During the May Day celebration, banners were solemnly lowered before the mausoleum.[122] On May 10, before it was totally finished, one of its tribunals was used in a funeral ceremony after the suicide of Iu. Kh. Lutovinov, an early member of the Workers' Opposition; the leaders climbed the wooden stairs of the mausoleum and addressed a large crowd. Among those who spoke were two men who had opposed the preservation of the body—Bukharin and Trotsky.[123]

By the end of May, when the Thirteenth Party Congress met in Moscow, work on the mausoleum was finished. On May 23, the delegates to the congress gathered in Red Square and were addressed from the mausoleum's rostrum. They watched as some 10,000 young Pioneers paraded before it and swore a solemn oath to fulfill the precepts of Lenin.[124] The delegates were then invited to enter the mausoleum and view the embalmed remains of their dead leader.[125] This was the first time since Vorobev and Zbarsky had begun their labors that visitors were allowed to see Lenin's body. It was a special viewing, after which the mausoleum was closed again.

The mausoleum was reopened for one day on another special occasion—the Fifth Congress of the Comintern, which was held in Moscow in mid-June. On June 19, a session of the congress was held in Red Square. Kalinin stood on the rostrum of the mausoleum and extolled Lenin. There were five hundred delegates present and a crowd of 15,000 people.[126] The delegates descended into the mausoleum and filed past the body. At this time, the press took the opportunity to prepare its readers for their future shrine: "Vladimir Ilich lies exposed, as [he was] in the Trade Union House. In reverential silence, as though not wanting to disturb the peace of the sleeping leader, the delegates go by slowly, not taking their eyes off the physical features of the deceased."[127]

The Grand Opening

The public opening of the Lenin Mausoleum and the major debut of the reembalmed body was scheduled for August 1, 1924, at 6:00 in the evening. The Immortalization Commission announced this event in advance. At the same time, now that access to the tomb was to be regular, it published precise instructions regulating visitation to the Lenin Mausoleum. Visitors to the mausoleum were required to go in groups distributed according to districts. No one would be allowed to bring anything with him into the mausoleum; all briefcases, pocketbooks, canes, umbrellas, and so forth had to be checked with the guards.[128]

A solemn ceremony marked the opening of the Lenin Mausoleum. A procession of Communist Party members marched to Red

Square. It was met at the mausoleum by the members of the Immortalization Commission. The square was filled with thousands of spectators who watched as the banner of the Paris Commune, a gift from the French Communist Party, was carried into the mausoleum. The banner was placed in a special case on the wall of the tomb.[129] Then, for many hours, people moved through the mausoleum to gaze at the embalmed body.

They entered through the front entrance, under the huge black letters, LENIN. The outer beams of the building were of lacquered wood pierced with large, round nailheads. The mausoleum was surrounded by a paved courtyard in which flowers and bushes had been planted. Around the courtyard was an iron railing. Guards holding fixed bayonets were posted in the courtyard and at the entrance. The visitors entered the building and descended along a red-carpeted staircase to a corridor whose walls were lined with a red and black geometric design.[130] The corridor led to the small chamber containing the body. The walls of this room were also decorated in red and black, and the ceiling was red with a black hammer and sickle. The visitors walked around the room along a railed gallery constructed along its sides.

The body lay in a red-lined sarcophagus topped with glass. Lenin was dressed in a khaki tunic; on his breast was the Order of the Red Banner and the badge of the Central Executive Committee. His hands were crossed above his waist. The lower part of his body was covered with black and purple satin. At the head and foot of the coffin stood soldiers with fixed bayonets. Late into the night delegations of workers, soldiers, and other people passed through the mausoleum to see the preserved body of Lenin.

On August 3, Lenin's body was exhibited to foreign newsmen. "The body is in a perfect state of preservation," reported Walter Duranty. "Although the medical experts who embalmed the body say that neither wax nor any coloring material was used, the face appears normal in every way, there being no indication of pigmentation of the flesh, emaciation of the body or shrinkage of features. The embalmers have even contrived to impart a smile to the face."[131] Zbarsky compared his and Vorobev's work to the mummies of the Egyptian pharaohs. He told the newsmen that the Egyptians had been able to preserve only the bodies of their leaders and that the features of their faces were unrecognizable. Lenin, on the

196   other hand, looked simply asleep. Zbarsky added that the entire cost
of embalming the body of Lenin was only $7500, "in striking con-
trast to the fortunes which the Egyptians spent on the bodies of their
Pharaohs, nobles and high priests."[132] The professor said that the
commission of experts who examined the body expected that it
would remain unchanged for three or four decades, or even longer.
Zbarsky said that, in fact, if the temperature of the mausoleum
were kept constant, "Lenin's body should last forever." He and
Vorobev had achieved what the church might have called a miracle,
but it was actually a feat of science: "The Russian Church had
claimed that it was a miracle that its saints' bodies endured and were
incorruptible. But we have performed a feat unknown to modern
science . . . We worked four months and we used certain chemicals
known to science. There is nothing miraculous about it."[133]

Zbarsky apparently hoped that the embalming of Lenin would
demonstrate to the nation and the world the sophistication of Soviet science. But the Immortalization Commission and those party
and government leaders who had made the decision to preserve the
body expected it to do more than that. Lenin's embalmed corpse, exhibited in the heart of Moscow, was to provide a central and visible
symbol for the continuing cult of Lenin. It would be a constant reminder of Lenin's presence. The enshrined body was a symbolic
representation of the way that the cult's managers wished to have
Lenin officially regarded. He was awesome and yet accessible,
available to anyone who wished to brave the long queues that invariably formed before the mausoleum. He was a modern mixture
of saint, tsar, and revolutionary martyr.

Lenin's canonization was evident not only in the flesh, but also in
the biographies that described his life in terms of his prophecies and
political miracles, in iconographic posters, and the slogans and
paeans that asserted he had lived and died for the liberation of the
oppressed. Lenin dead was invested with the power to continue to
serve the people, to guide and protect them in perpetuity.

Foreign visitors to Moscow were often wonderstruck by the
strange cult of Lenin's body, particularly in the 1920s when there
was nothing else quite like it in the world. In 1928 Theodore Dreiser
wrote:

> I was told by many that his embalmed corpse—quite the same in
> looks to-day as the day he died—is enmeshed in superstition. So

long as he is there, so long as he does not change, Communism is
safe and the new Russia will prosper. But—whisper—if he fades or
is destroyed, ah, then comes the great, sad change—the end of his
kindly dream.

Mysticism? Thy name is Slav.[134]

Other Western observers frequetly interpreted the Lenin cult as a replacement for Russian Orthodoxy, at the time under increasing attack by the regime. Just after Lenin's funeral, Duranty of *The New
York Times* made just this connection:

Many foreigners here long familiar with the Slav character believe it
will be only a question of a short time before there will be "miracles," or at least temporary cures of hysterical disorder so common
in Russia, at Lenin's "shrine." They have begun to speculate on the
possible effects this may have on the peasant masses whose formal
religion has suffered heavy blows by Bolshevist hostility and se-
questration of church property and by the subsequent schism in the
Orthodox church, but whose superstitious instincts are stronger than
ever.[135]

In fact, no miracles were reported, and while Lenin became an official saint of the party, there is no evidence that his remains actually
inspired genuine popular worship. The Lenin cult was less an actual
substitute for religion than a party effort to fuse religious and political ritual to mobilize the population. It is likely that people were—
and still are—drawn to the Lenin Mausoleum not for spiritual reasons but out of a combined sense of political duty and fascination,
or even morbid curiosity. If nothing else, the body cult is a show. A
visit to the Lenin Mausoleum is memorable, with its solemn guards
hushing the visitors and hurrying them along, its gleaming walls of
polished gray and black marble slashed with a red zigzag, and the
figure of Lenin bathed in a pinkish light. Before the shrine was
erected, Agitprop had generated nothing even remotely so riveting.

The body has, from the first, been the subject of stories and
rumors, many of which claim that the figure in the mausoleum is
made of wax.[136] There is no way of knowing for certain whether or
not the displayed remains of Lenin are indeed his embalmed body.
As a rule, the Soviet system's supporters claim they are, and its detractors say the relic is a waxen doll—testimony to the political symbolism with which it is invested. In 1918 praise of Lenin
became a conventional rhetorical expression of political loyalty

to the Bolshevik regime. In 1924 that loyalty was expressed in the mystical assertion that "Lenin lives." The expressed belief that the body is "real" partly serves the same function. It is a gesture of faith in the system, for it is an acceptance of officially generated myth (which need not be false—some myths are true).

The popular myth that was in evidence after 1924 in folk stories inspired by Lenin's death held that Lenin had not died but still lived among his people. An Uzbek tale of 1925 described Lenin as wandering in the mountains searching for truth, and in 1926 a village correspondent from the northern Caucasus reported a local legend that "Lenin lives, but he secretly walks the earth and watches over Soviet power" and that another person had been buried in his place.[137] Another variation on this theme held that the living Lenin was but sleeping in the mausoleum. This was the assertion made in a poem published in Siberia in 1924:

> No! He has not died, Lenin has not died!
> No! Ilich has not died, he lives!
> Deathly shadows, fly away!
> We do not believe the cursed lie!
>
> He, having given up his immeasurable burden,
> He has not died, but merely sleeps:
> Our tired leader is resting
> Under his granite tombstone.[138]

A most striking story about Lenin's life in apparent death circulated in 1925 among the peasants of the Viatka countryside. It is called "Clever Lenin" (*Khitryi Lenin*). One day, it begins, Lenin was leafing through books and newspapers and in every one found writings about himself. "Why should we fear the Entente and America, when we have Vladimir Ilich, who goes by the name of Lenin?" Lenin worried about how his country would fare without him, so he sent for the finest Soviet doctor and explained that he wanted to appear to die but remain alive. "We will put you not in a grave," replied the doctor, "but in a spacious room, and we will cover you with glass so no one can poke you with his fingers."

And so, soon after, Lenin's death was announced. People wept and moaned: "What will become of us now? The British and French will attack us." But Kalinin consoled the people, urging them to stop weeping and start working. They put Lenin into a shed called a mausoleum and put a guard at the door. One day, two, a week, and then a month passed and Lenin grew tired of lying under the glass. One night he slipped out the back door of the mausoleum and went to the Kremlin, where the commissars met. He entered just after a meeting and asked two janitors, who had been listening through the door, what they had heard. "Did they mention Lenin?" he queried. "What a question. 'Look,' they say, 'Lenin died but we now have almost twice as many communists. Now let the Entente dare to make a peep.'" Lenin returned to the mausoleum and lay down under the glass feeling satisfied.

The next night he went to a factory. He asked the workers whether they were party members. "Before Lenin's death we did not belong to the party," they replied, "but now we are communists, we are Leninists." Lenin was very pleased. On the third night he journeyed to a remote village. In one hut a light was still burning. "Can one rest here a little?" asked Lenin. "Come on in," came the reply. Lenin entered and was astonished. No icons. Red posters and portraits everywhere. "Are you not Christians?" he queried. "We are citizens, Comrade, this is a reading room and here is the Lenin Corner." "And how does the peasant fare?" "Not very well, but things are improving." Lenin left the hut filled with joy, lay down in the mausoleum feeling reassured, and has been sleeping for many days now. He will probably awaken soon. What a joy that will be! Words cannot relate it, ink cannot describe it.[139]

"Clever Lenin" demonstrates that the Lenin cult institutions had already been incorporated into folklore and manifests dramatically the popular fantasy that Lenin was immortal. In this the Lenin tales resemble the famous legend widely current after the death in 1825 of Alexander I, which maintained that the emperor had not died but was wandering the Russian land in the guise of a hermit.[140]

The uniformity of fantasy surrounding the deaths of the two Russian rulers indicates that, although the deaths of Alexander and Lenin were separated by almost exactly a century, with major revolutions intervening, the Russian peasantry retained some consistency in its political attitudes. The emotional power as well as the structural form of the Lenin cult derived, in part, from "naive monarchism." The Lenin of officially generated myth—the Lenin of journalistic paeans—was like the just tsar of old, Ivan the Terrible or Peter the Great, kind and loving toward the people, terrible and wrathful toward their oppressors. The enduring success of the Lenin cult as a stabilizing and legitimizing force in Soviet political life was due, in some measure, to the extent to which its contours were shaped by traditional peasant culture.

But the power of the cult owes even more to its religious form and purpose. The Lenin body cult as a contrived religion began with atavistic popular behavior following his wounding and death, but it was primarily created by three men: Vladimir Dmitrievich Bonch-Bruevich, organizer of the funeral and student of Russian sectarianism; Leonid Krasin, who had made public his belief in physical immortality; and Anatoly Lunacharsky, Commissar of Enlightenment and the main exponent of god-building. More than a decade before Lenin's death Lunacharsky had expressed his belief that socialism would provide a new religion with a human god, a god that was all mankind. He claimed that the human community, the "universal connectedness" of life, would transcend death and achieve immortality.

In 1919 Lunacharsky obliquely reiterated his earlier commitment to god-building.[141] Although in 1923 he supported antireligious activities and wrote that the "belief in personal immortality" was a " 'peasant belief' no intelligent person could take seriously,"[142] it seems evident that he was still a god-builder. For the very next year Lunacharsky threw himself into the work of deifying Lenin. His eulogy on the day of the funeral was filled with the fervor and imagery of a religious zealot.

> After the passage of 100 years, the world will long since have known a new bright order. And people, looking back, will not have known an era more exalted, more holy, than the days of that Russian revolution which began the world revolution. And for this reason they will not have known a human figure who inspired more veneration, love and devotion than the figure, not only of a prophet, not only of a sage of the new communist world, but of its creator, its champion, its martyr (*muchenik*) . . . for Vladimir Ilich . . . totally destroyed his gigantic brain . . . by his excessive, superhuman, enormous work . . .
>
> We have seen Man, man with a capital letter . . . In him . . . are concentrated rays of light and heat.[143]

And in 1925 Lunacharsky bestowed on Lenin eternal life in the last verse of a poem called "Painting":

Look: in the fog like a beacon
There stands, firm and unchanged,
The ever living Predsovnarkom,
The guide of the world—Lenin.[144]

While Lenin's immortality was a common enough theme in the rhapsodic poetry inspired by his death, Lunacharsky's youthful enthusiasm for the deification of humanity would suggest that his poem was above all the work of an inspired god-builder who had, at long last, found a Bolshevik god. But Lunacharsky's real effort to immortalize Lenin as genius and creator came in the autumn of 1924 when he took charge of the arrangements to design a permanent mausoleum of stone that would enshrine the leader forever.

The Search for an Eternal Shrine

A permanent Lenin Mausoleum was to symbolize and facilitate an enduring cult of Lenin. Plans for its construction were begun even before 1924 was at an end. On November 13 of that year the Immortalization Commission heard its first report on the permanent mausoleum; the speakers were Krasin and Lunacharsky. Their report specified the necessary features of the edifice—a central hall for the sarcophagus, an underground chamber for the technical apparatus necessary for the continued preservation of the body, and enough large waiting rooms to prevent visitors from having to stand on long queues in inclement weather.[145] As every visitor to Moscow knows, this last feature was not included in the edifice finally constructed; only foreign tourists wishing to view the body are spared a wait of more than two hours and often much longer. The long lines of pilgrims that wind through the Alexander Garden and stretch into Red Square on every day the mausoleum is open, in all kinds of weather, are routinely described with pride in the Soviet press as proof of the continuing popular devotion to Lenin.

Another feature of the mausoleum not realized in the final construction was a series of frescoes on its interior walls depicting the main stages of the world revolution with emphasis on Lenin's role.[146] This plan corresponded to a genre of posters current at the time that mounted Lenin's portrait in the center of the page and surrounded it with revolutionary scenes or, more frequently, tableaux showing the happy and productive lives of Soviet people

202 brought about by his efforts. This propaganda method, which sought to link Lenin directly with social and economic improvements in the country at large, was in the end rejected in the stone mausoleum in favor of abstract designs on the model of those decorating the interior of the temporary wooden mausoleum.

On the basis of Krasin's and Lunacharsky's November report, the Immortalization Commission resolved that a first-round competition would invite ideas about the mausoleum's design not only from architects but from all artists "and even every thinking person."[147] It ended its resolutions with the instruction that a special committee would be formed simply to work out the details of the competition. Its head was to be Anatoly Lunacharsky.

The competition committee was formed on December 10, and a month later, January 9, 1925, the "first-round competition of projects for the construction of a monument to V. I. Lenin at Red Square in the city of Moscow" was formally opened. Contestants were informed that the monument would contain Lenin's remains, and would therefore need a central hall for the body and an underground space for the technical apparatus. Another underground chamber was to contain a museum for Lenin's books and manuscripts and a waiting room for up to two hundred people. Frescoes of the revolutionary movement were still envisioned at this stage, and the monument was to serve a tribunal function that necessitated a special place for an orator or orators. The mausoleum was to be in architectural harmony with the Kremlin wall and Red Square. The edifice needed to be at once simple, dynamic, and impressive. Along with the specifications of the form that the submitted designs should take, the commission announced that it would award cash prizes to the ten best entries, ranging from 400 to 1000 rubles.[148]

Lunacharsky planned a three-tiered competition. The first was to engage the country's artistic community and other members of the intelligentsia in the design of projects. The process of designing Lenin's tomb was itself to be part of the propaganda of Leninism. The nation's most creative minds were to apply themselves to the challenging and (it was hoped) uplifting task of finding the architectural structure that would best honor Lenin's memory. The top three designs were to be realized in the form of models that would be filmed and projected against a backdrop of Red Square.[149] Of these three, the most satisfactory design would be constructed in stone and would forever shelter Lenin's remains.

The competition was announced twice in 1925 and once in 1926, with all entries due in April 1926. In May of that year a special subcommittee of the Commissariat of Enlightenment met to review the designs and then made a full report to Commissar Lunacharsky. The propagandistic aspect of the design process was judged to have been successful; the contest had aroused a lively response from artists, architects, workers, peasants, and members of the working intelligentsia such as schoolteachers.

The competition entries numbered 117. They were ranged in three categories—rejects, doubtfuls, and those worth keeping for the next stage. Almost half the submitted projects (53) were rejected outright. These designs were often the products of untrained minds. A few projects were rejected immediately as "clearly absurd and fantastic or ideologically odious"—such as one design that pictured the mausoleum in the shape of a church. Many ideas had to be discarded simply because no known technology could implement them. One of these proposed a giant block that would house a tractor, a locomotive, and a flowing brook, all in constant motion. Another, entitled "Dawn of a New Life," took up all of Red Square and part of the Moscow River embankment; five enormous floodlights situated in different parts of the city were to illuminate the entire structure. A third proposed a statue of Lenin fifteen to twenty stories high, within which would be meeting halls for higher government institutions. In addition to these rejected projects were those that failed to meet the competition specifications, for example those that were merely monuments and made no provisions for the display of Lenin's body. Under the category of "doubtful" were 39 projects that merited further consideration but contained some major flaw. In this group were projects that could only be realized outside of Red Square as well as designs that met the formal requirements of the contest but demonstrated "vulgar taste." Twenty-five entries were designated "acceptable" and submitted to Lunacharsky for close study.[150]

The contestants sometimes included lengthy essays explaining the reasoning behind their designs. One G. Guranov submitted a project entitled "Proletarian Unity," in which the rostrum or tribune

204   took the form of a screw and two nuts, with slogans attached to the threads; the design included a grouped sculpture of Lenin meeting with representatives of the Third International. The designer appended an essay with his composition: "The life and work of Ilich are so multifaceted, that they reflect an entire epoch: leader and fighter, above all humanist and reformer in equal measure, turning life into legend, personality into myth." The monument, he continued, should reflect Lenin's commitment to industry as the source of Russia's future growth; "industry could be symbolized by a wheel, a lever, a screw."[151]

While a giant screw might seem grossly inappropriate as a monument to Lenin, in fact a similar concept was actually realized in Stalingrad where, on May Day 1925, a monument to Lenin was unveiled, depicting a statue of the leader atop a screw.[152] Moreover, the form of an upright screw was characteristic of many projected designs for the Lenin Mausoleum, which by and large were meant to be constructed in grandiose proportions. Obelisks and soaring towers were particularly prevalent in projects for mausoleum monuments planned in cities other than Moscow. Odessa, for example, ran a contest for the design of its own mausoleum (minus the body, of course). That projected structure was not hampered by the architectural constraints imposed by Red Square, and therefore the design entries tended to be flamboyant, fanciful, and huge.

In two years following Lenin's death, many major cities involved their artistic communities in plans for monuments to Lenin. The contest for the design of a Lenin Mausoleum in Moscow was part of this larger, nationwide effort to tap the creative energies of Soviet artists in the headlong pursuit of honoring Lenin's memory. There is reason to suspect that the well-publicized competitive process Lunacharsky set into motion in the winter of 1924–25 resembled the public debate over the first mausoleum in that it was intended chiefly, or even solely, as a *campaign* to politicize artists and architects by encouraging them to participate in the design of Lenin's monumental tomb. For, in the end, all 117 entries were rejected and, in 1929, a newly established government commission, charged with the construction of a permanent Lenin Mausoleum, simply invited A. V. Shchusev to recast the existing wooden mausoleum in stone.[153]

The decision doubtless reflected a judgment that the permanent display of Lenin's remains was both feasible and advisable. In 1924 Professor Zbarsky had told foreign newsmen that he expected Lenin's body to last forever. But this, he revealed two decades later, had been a lie. "I must say," he wrote in 1945, "that when we completed the job, we did not have complete confidence in it." He added that, when asked how long the embalming would remain effective, he routinely answered: "It is hard to predict, but certainly for two to three years."[154] By the summer of 1929 Lenin's embalmed body had survived for five years without visible deterioration. True, not all who saw it liked it. Nikolai Valentinov recalled his first visit to the Lenin Mausoleum in 1927 or 1928. He was filled with disgust by the "small lacquered doll with yellow whiskers" that bore no resemblance whatsoever to the Lenin he had known.[155]

The Lenin Mausoleum had been a site of mass pilgrimage for half a decade. In July of 1929, three months after the Sixteenth Party Conference ratified the First Five-Year Plan, construction on the new Lenin Mausoleum began.

A Final Resting Place

In the fall of 1930 Stalin laid Lenin to rest in a mausoleum of granite, porphyry, and labradorite. No agitational campaign or any press publicity marked the construction of the new mausoleum. Indeed, the timing of the event and the manner in which it was presented to the public made one thing clear: the permanent Lenin Mausoleum was intended primarily to be a triumph of Soviet engineering—one of the many feats of the Five-Year Plan—as well as a pedestal for Stalin.

Its construction took sixteen months and was supervised by a government commission headed by Stalin's close companion Klimenty Voroshilov, the Commissar of War. The actual work was done by a Moscow engineering trust called Mosstroi (Moscow Construction), directed by the engineer I. V. Pevzner.[156] The design of the new mausoleum imitated that of its wooden predecessor. Shchusev at first envisioned a two-tone color scheme of red and black, the colors of the Lenin cult. But he added gray granite. Gray, he explained, was the "workers' color."[157] The edifice was completed in October 1930, together with a major reconstruction of Red Square.

206   On November 1, 1930, *Pravda* carried the following small article nestled in the center of page five. Its opening paragraph:

> The Lenin Mausoleum is built. The work on its construction, unparalleled in complexity, lasted a year and four months. The most eminent foreign and Soviet architects, informed of the cubic capacity of the monument as a whole, of the incredible expanse of polished enormity, of the monolithic stones weighing many tons, estimated that the construction would take five years. The Lenin Mausoleum was built by Soviet workers in a year and four months.

The article went on to describe the various materials that went into the construction of the huge monument, including the porphyry letters over the entrance that spelled out LENIN. It gave credit to the mausoleum's architect and to the engineers who built it. But it made no mention of Lenin. On November 7, Stalin and his lieutenants stood atop that mausoleum and were greeted by cheering crowds. Voroshilov made the revolutionary celebration's formal address.[158] Four days later, a tiny announcement at the bottom of *Pravda*'s second page indicated that the stone mausoleum had opened on the previous day.

> November 10 at 3:45 the doors of the new mausoleum were opened. A detachment of students from the VTsIK [Central Executive Committee] school formed the honor guard. At exactly four o'clock the mausoleum was opened to the public.
>
> An enormous queue of people wishing to enter the mausoleum began to file into the mausoleum.[159]

The Lenin Mausoleum had been presented to Soviet Russia as nothing more than yet another accomplishment of the Five-Year Plan. The construction of the permanent mausoleum took place just when the Lenin cult was being transformed into a celebration of Stalin's Russia and Stalin himself. The stone edifice represented the demise of the Lenin cult. Under Stalin's rule the cult of Lenin grew as cold and lifeless as the stone mausoleum. It glorified the dead, not the living, Lenin. Stalin really had lain Lenin to rest, and not until the old man died did the immortal Lenin rise again.

7 Lenin's Life After Death

The Lenin cult as a pervasive feature of Soviet political practice emerged in full force in the weeks following his death. Almost at once it reached its most intense phase, which lasted for the better part of two years. The enormously complex process of cult creation took place on all levels of Soviet political and cultural life, and involved almost all institutions able to generate political activity. It thus served, for a short time, to provide Soviet politics with a unifying symbol that could and did inspire energetic loyalty during the potentially unstable interregnum that followed Lenin's death. Since the end of the civil war, party and government propagandists had deplored their reliance on negative agitation based on hatred of an enemy, and they sought some positive force on which to concentrate their efforts at political socialization of the populace.[1] Lenin's death provided that focus. In order to retain Lenin's power and the popular emotions of solidarity his death had unleashed, they followed mourning week with a massive campaign to establish a Lenin cult throughout the length and breadth of Russia.

At this, its earliest and most vigorous period, the nationwide Lenin cult was still only partially regulated, and reflected the widest possible range of motivations and moods. From the desperate need of Lenin's successors to establish a base for their legitimacy, to kindergarten teachers' assignments of poems on Lenin's death, from genuine outpourings of grief by the faithful to evident attempts to sell products—cigarette packets, cups, even cookies—by imprinting them with Lenin's portrait, the national obsession with Lenin that

208 collectively provided the emotional underpinning of the Lenin cult
tapped the real concerns of a vast and diverse group of politically
active individuals. The visual trappings of the cult also reflected an
entire spectrum of tastes, including the spare and graceful design of
the wooden Lenin Mausoleum constructed in Red Square in the
summer of 1924 and innumerable monuments of unimaginable vul-
garity.

The rush to honor Lenin's memory in the months after his death
was at once intensive and extensive, spontaneous and directed. It
followed the example set by the most powerful men in the land; it
conformed to the directives circulated by professional propagandists
and agitators; and it gave comprehensible shape to the political aspirations of countless people to whom politics had heretofore been
alien.

For Lenin's successors who helped inspire the formation of the
cult, and for the party and government propagandists who were its
architects, the ritualized veneration of Lenin was to serve several
functions. It was to evoke in the party and in the widest possible
sector of the populace a mood of loyalty toward the system and its
values. At best it would tap genuine popular sentiments and mobilize mass energy in a surge of political enthusiasm at a time—seven
years after the revolution—when such feeling had long since waned.
At the very least, the organized cult of Lenin was to be plainly a
display of power by those who wielded it, a demonstration of their
very ability to shape public political activity by fiat. The thousands
of men and women, both within the party and outside it, who participated in Lenin cult practices doubtless did so for a wide variety
of reasons. In 1924 the party eagerly supported their efforts to celebrate Lenin's memory. But not two years were to pass before the authorities came to value the cult's regulation as more important than
continued popular participation in its evolving design: by 1926 the
cult operated according to a reduced and standardized format.

Lenin's Heirs and the Cult

Lenin's death precipitated a succession crisis in a regime heavily dependent on the authority of its founder and leader, and lacking recognized provisions for his replacement by another individual. Rob-

ert C. Tucker has noted that part of the resolution to this problem was the general agreement articulated by Lenin's successors that Lenin's spirit and doctrine continue to lead Soviet Russia.[2] Tucker adds the evident truth that, while there might be a consensus that Leninism would determine all future policy, from a practical point of view such a determination could not be realized without "living interpreters of Leninism."[3] And, in fact, it was precisely as interpreters of Leninism that the aspirants to power, in the dramatic struggle that ensued before and continued long after Lenin's death, sought to validate their claims to rule Russia. In so doing, all of the contestants—Zinoviev, Stalin, Trotsky—as well as their supporters, contributed to the cult of Lenin.

It is likely that the ruling troika in the Politburo—Zinoviev, Kamenev, and Stalin—as well as Trotsky, their arch-opponent, acted consciously at this time to create a cult of Lenin. But that was undoubtedly a secondary consequence of the actions they took in response to the primary imperatives behind their public statements during Lenin's illness and in the months after his death. Those primary objectives were collectively to prevent civil war; to keep intact the power structure they dominated; and individually to assure for themselves that measure of power and influence they each sought to attain and maintain.

The first two aims were readily achieved: the government and party system established at the close of the civil war survived the loss of its founder with remarkable stability. No new civil war broke out, nor, in the short term, did any radical political change occur. There is no way to gauge the extent to which the popular enthusiasm for Lenin generated by his death—and sustained for more than a year after it by the Lenin cult—eased the succession crisis. What is clear, however, is that Lenin's heirs insistently maintained that some part, the most essential part, of Lenin was immortal and continued to guide Soviet Russia. Thus they located in their purported devotion to Lenin their mandate to rule. And at the same time, through the examples they set in their widely publicized speeches and articles, the Politburo leadership actively participated in the establishment of the full-blown Lenin cult.

Simultaneously, for the next three years, the same handful of men supported the Lenin cult through their chosen mode of political

210 battle. The protracted conflict between Trotsky and the troika in 1923–1925 and later between Stalin and his erstwhile partners, Zinoviev and Kamenev, is a story of great complexity and importance in the history of Soviet politics. That conflict began at the end of 1923 with an intense struggle between the party center, dominated by the troika, and Trotsky, who was linked with a wide-ranging opposition movement that sought to curb the dictatorial and bureaucratic direction in which party politics had been moving. The battlefields were the press, where accusations were hurled in both directions, the smoke-filled room, including Trotsky's bedroom (he was ill throughout much of the fall and winter of 1923) where Stalin and Kamenev fought with their ailing colleague over draft resolutions on a range of sensitive issues, and the public meeting hall. At stake was the determination of who would dominate party politics in Lenin's absence. The most sharply effective weapon wielded by both sides was Lenin—his directives, his writings, his spirit—which each contestant claimed to interpret correctly. This weapon was further honed when Zinoviev, in December 1923, opposed to the perfection of Leninism its demonic counterpart—Trotskyism.[4]

The party center won a decisive victory over Trotsky and the rank-and-file opposition at the Thirteenth Party Conference held in Moscow just days before Lenin died. The struggle for domination of the party intensified after his death and, in the hysterical atmosphere of mourning week and the succeeding months when the cult was at its height, Lenin became an even more powerful weapon. Every significant scholarly study of Soviet high politics in the mid-twenties has noted the extensive use of Lenin in the power struggle, particularly after his death.[5] All the contestants strove, in eulogizing Lenin, to make themselves credible as his heirs by emphasizing their past closeness to the dead leader and by demonstrating their current capacity to act in accordance with his spirit. Thus struggles over policy and personality now of necessity entailed increasingly elaborate defenses consisting of citations from Lenin. And they entailed more than that: each adversary put himself forward as Lenin's truest friend and most loyal spokesman.

Stalin's efforts are the most widely known because they were the most successful, although his effective use of Lenin's memory only partly explains his own subsequent spectacular accretion of power. On January 28, 1924, the day after Lenin's funeral (while Trotsky was languishing on the Black Sea shore), he delivered a speech at the Kremlin Military School that provided an affectionate and homely character sketch of the leader. In it Stalin presented himself as Lenin's modest and faithful follower, but at the same time introduced the hitherto unknown "fact" that his personal connection with Lenin had begun very early, in 1903, with a letter Lenin wrote him at the end of that year, a treasured document he now deeply regretted having burned.[6] Four months later he made his bid for the role of Leninism's interpreter in a lecture series at Sverdlov University, called "The Foundations of Leninism."[7]

Stalin may have claimed that his relationship to Lenin dated back to 1903 (his story was unverifiable), but Trotsky's first meeting with Lenin took place even a year earlier. He underlined this fact in a pamphlet, *On Lenin*, which was published in June 1924. It was a collection of reminiscences that began with a description of his first encounter with Lenin in London in the fall of 1902. Like Stalin, Trotsky was emphasizing his closeness to the leader but, unlike Stalin's, most of his memoir depicted his relations with Lenin as one of two equals, two talented, dedicated, and fallible human beings. Trotsky described himself literally in Lenin's shoes, which he wore to the opera one night, when his own were in bad repair. True, Lenin gave away the shoes because they pinched his feet (and Trotsky suffered in them as well, to Lenin's amusement). But the story was designed to underline the closeness between the two men. In the sections of the pamphlet dealing with 1917 and after, Trotsky made no effort to minimize his own indispensable role in the history of the revolution. He even indicated that the title of the new government, Council of People's Commissars, had been not Lenin's but his.[8]

Zinoviev, among others, attacked Trotsky's memoir, accusing its author of self-aggrandizement and insufficient respect for Lenin. Zinoviev's criticism was restricted to Trotsky's presumption in judging his own past mistake in 1918 at Brest-Litovsk, when he refused to sign the peace treaty with Germany, as little different from Lenin's mistaken decision in 1920 to march on Warsaw.[9] This criticism was Zinoviev's transparent attempt to weaken further Trotsky's rapidly deteriorating position in the party. The troika in this way actively shaped the growing Lenin cult by publicly defining the narrow boundaries within which Lenin could be described. And

212   once those parameters were drawn, Stalin and Zinoviev in particular sought to denigrate Trotsky by dwelling on his many past differences with Lenin. In 1924 it was necessary not only to *be* a Leninist, but to *have always been one* as well. After his death, the mere act of characterizing Lenin in print involved a unique political responsibility on the part of his successors. They were making him inviolable in order to make themselves unassailable—if they could correctly demonstrate their past connection to his person and their present association with his spirit.

Zinoviev, in early 1924 still the senior member of the ruling troika, made his own bid as the executor of Lenin's will. His articles about Lenin put special emphasis on Lenin and the Communist International, of which Zinoviev was the first head.[10] At the Thirteenth Party Congress of May 1924, the first held after Lenin's death, it was Zinoviev who delivered the keynote address. He attempted to validate his remarks beforehand in a preamble where he said that while it was no longer possible to make policy directly "according to Lenin," it would now be necessary to act "according to Leninism."[11] With that he proceeded to lay down a host of directives.

Although a discussion of how Politburo members used the rapidly escalating veneration of Lenin to bolster their own legitimacy to rule, and erode that of their adversaries, sheds light on the intricacies of political infighting in the mid-twenties, it does little to explain the formation of the wide-ranging Lenin cult that took root during those years. The Politburo's role in the formation of that cult was, in fact, less important than the role played by professional propagandists and agitators who, in 1924, consciously established the Lenin cult as a regular part of Soviet political practice. Zinoviev, Stalin, and Trotsky doubtless inspired or even directed their efforts from above. And certainly the power with which the self-appointed guardians of Leninism in the Politburo endowed their charge indicated that Lenin worship was to be taken with deadly seriousness. It was therefore the example and, presumably, the directive from above, as well as the groundswell of popular devotion to Lenin in the immediate aftermath of his death, that prompted all the existing agencies of propaganda and agitation to mobilize their resources toward the formation of a pervasive cult.

The Propaganda of Leninism

On February 9, 1924, the Agitation and Propaganda Department of the Communist Party Central Committee convened a meeting to discuss the "propaganda and teaching of Leninism." Present were representatives of the central agitprop agencies of the party, government, army, and trade unions, members of the Lenin Institute, and the entire Commissariat of Enlightenment. The result was a series of resolutions that established the organized cult of Lenin.

Lenin's death, they said, presents the agitators and propagandists of the party and all other organizations with one primary task—the propagation of his legacy. "It must be carried out both as a broadly based mass campaign and as permanent propaganda and political-enlightenment work." The stated primary goal of the campaign was "to show the broad mass of workers that Lenin's cause continues and will continue unchanged under the RKP and Soviet power." The campaign, furthermore, was to link itself to the "immediate concrete tasks" of the party and government—in particular, those of improving the rural economy and continuing the Lenin Enrollment that had been launched with feverish success in the immediate aftermath of Lenin's death.[12] The intense agitational work was to begin immediately, continue for several months, and then "flow into propaganda of a permanent, systematic character," which was to "saturate" all organized political activity—particularly within the party—with Leninism.[13]

It was deemed especially important to "penetrate" teachers with this propaganda.[14] All schools—for children, adolescents, and adults—were to undertake the teaching of Leninism. And they were to do it in a manner true to the spirit of Lenin's activity and writings. That is, the study of Leninism was not supposed to be "exclusively academic"; it was to be inspirational. The overall scheme of development for this important propaganda method included courses on Leninism, extracurricular study circles on the subject, and—particularly in adult education schools—the systematic inclusion of Lenin's views into social science courses. Education, especially political education, was to be saturated with Leninism.[15]

Straight away the Commissariat of Enlightenment declared that Leninism should provide the basis of *all* study: "We must use

Lenin's works extensively when studying every problem (independent of the 'topic' concerned) in order to formulate our view."[16] This principle was applied with enormous energy, with the help of the example set by Politburo dignitaries who cited Lenin to justify policy decisions on the widest possible variety of issues. The propaganda of Leninism was meant to be both permanent and pervasive. "In every endeavor the individual should remember that there is no sphere of work about which Ilich has not thought, about which he did not leave clear and comprehensible words and behests." It was up to party members to communicate those words and behests to the population at large.[17]

But how to find the appropriate words for each occasion? From the very start of the February 1924 campaign, propagandists in Glavpolitprosvet debated the question of how to train party cadres in the propaganda of Leninism. Some suggested an historical approach, a study of all of Lenin's major writings in the context of a more general survey of party history.[18] But the view that ultimately prevailed was that the propaganda of Leninism could best be carried out if special volumes for that purpose were published, handbooks with passages by Lenin on every subject, enabling every party member to fortify himself or herself with ready Leninist opinions for every situation. The central party organizations expected to take the responsibility for producing the plans, anthologies, bibliographies, and so forth, leaving to local party members the work of training agitators who were to engage in mass propaganda, in the establishment of Leninism study circles and courses.[19] These trained men and women were then to go out and bring Lenin to the people.

The task was not going to be easy. Economic problems compounded the obstacles posed by widespread illiteracy and political disorganization at the local level. It was perhaps possible to mobilize popular enthusiasm for Lenin, but the speedy and successful realization of party and government directives was severely hampered by the limited number of publications by Lenin available for purchase at the time of his death. When enthusiastic workers and party members, caught up in the spirit of the Lenin cult, tried to obtain copies of Lenin's writings, they often were frustrated by the poor production and distribution of those works, problems that plagued the publishing industry more generally. To make matters worse, newspapers and periodicals made a point of advertising the sale of

Lenin's collected works and then sent the respondents shoddy goods.

In March 1924 a group of Moscow factory workers published a complaint to this effect in *Rabochaia Moskva*. They told the following story:

> As soon as Gosizdat [State Publishing House] announced that the works of Ilich were available to subscribers, the guys in our [party] cell got into action.
> "Hey, it's for all of Ilich!"
> Seven people signed up.
> "It's expensive—4 *chervontsy* [40 rubles]."
> "It's a shame to criticize Gosizdat—they make good bindings."
> The arrangement—6 rubles apiece. Well, we sent off our *chervontsy* immediately. We wait. The package comes right away. It's four o'clock. The whole factory runs over to take a look. Alas, disappointment: they sent volumes 2, 5, 9, 10, and 11.
> "What the devil, why didn't they do it right?" Well, and instead of beautiful bindings—the devil knows what, but not bindings. Sugar sacks are better.
> Comrades at Gosizdat, come to your senses. Sell the works of Ilich not for 40 but for 25 rubles. Send them right, provide better bindings, sew them together more conscientiously—for these books are for our children for future decades.
> And then there will be more subscribers.[20]

Naturally publishers did not need workers to tell them to improve their production and distribution of Lenin's writings. They already knew that as of January 22, 1924, Lenin's works had top priority. Doubtless the authorities put pressure on Gosizdat and other publishers to take special care with Lenin's works, which were rushed into print upon his death. The Lenin Institute, headed by Kamenev, undertook the publication of Lenin's collected works (Kamenev himself edited them), and his writings were also published singly and in topical anthologies of all kinds. But will and necessity alone could not overcome economic and organizational problems overnight. While the presses scrambled to provide the requisite copies of Lenin's writings to their subscribers and to the countless Lenin Corners that mushroomed throughout the land, the mass of the population would have to rely on an institution dear to Lenin's heart, the library. The author of Bolshevism had done much of his real revolu-

216   tionary work—writing—in the libraries of Western Europe. After 1917, Krupskaia had devoted much of her career in the Commissariat of Enlightenment to the establishment of Soviet libraries. When Lenin died, that commissariat tried to mobilize those libraries to make Leninism available to the populace.

But how to *interest* the people in Leninism? The peasantry in particular neither understood nor cared for the political literature that was so heavily represented in the total output of the Soviet publishing industry.[21] And while Lenin's writings were generally favored over those of his colleagues, they nonetheless generated little interest among the common folk. The results of a 1920 questionnaire that asked members of the Red army Moscow garrison to name their favorite author placed Lenin thirteenth; the overall favorite was Tolstoy, followed by Pushkin, Gogol, and Marx. In a similar survey in 1923 Lenin had moved up to third place, with Tolstoy in second and the satirical poet, Demian Bednyi, in first. Lenin was gaining in popularity, but not consistently. A 1924 Red army survey asking soldiers to name their preferred books included Lenin's *State and Revolution* as the most popular of his books, in thirteenth place. In eleventh place was Cervantes' *Don Quixote*.[22] Of the political literature available in libraries and rural reading rooms at the time, the works favored by peasants, at any rate, were stories about revolutionary heroes. The author of a letter to the peasant newspaper *Krestianskaia gazeta* wrote that biographies of revolutionaries "acted on me more strongly than the suffering of the great martyr Saint George."[23] The life stories of revolutionary saints and heroes were the latter-day replacements for the saints' lives that had so moved the peasantry before 1917. And after January 1924 the *vitae* most readily available and widely publicized narrated the life of Lenin.[24]

If the enormously complex and difficult work of turning peasants into Leninists was to be even partially successful, it would have to be based on a thorough understanding of the peasantry and, in particular, of the peasantry's attitude toward Lenin. The first rule in planning the propaganda of Leninism in the countryside, wrote one Glavpolitprosvet worker, was to "approach the peasant cautiously; for the time being, learn more than you teach."[25]

The Commissariat of Enlightenment directed libraries to circulate questionnaires designed to elucidate popular responses to Lenin's writings. A sample survey that was reportedly "giving good results" only a short time after Lenin's death questioned the respondents about books they had read by and on Lenin. "Did you like the book or not?" "Did you understand everything written in the book?" "What didn't you understand? Write down the words you didn't understand." "What do you think Lenin meant to teach in this book?"[26]

Librarians were instructed to foster interest in Lenin's books. The most important advertisements were to be the Lenin Corners, which after Lenin's death were expected to be requisite features of every library. They were to display his works in a thematic arrangement and were to publicize his life, focusing on "the Lenin that the working masses knew and loved with their simple hearts, like a friend and older comrade." It was important, therefore, to emphasize the simple style of life he followed during his many years as a revolutionary, as well as "his personal qualities, his accessibility, his ability to understand every worker and peasant."[27] After the reading public was sufficiently motivated by an appreciation of Lenin's personal goodness and his concern for them (according to this reasoning), they would be ready and even eager to absorb his ideas.

If extraliterary means were thought necessary in order to arouse interest in Leninism among patrons of libraries, such methods were even more important to the success of the propaganda of Leninism in village reading rooms. These were small rural libraries that provided newspapers, a few books, and occasional informational programs for the local peasant population. They were woefully understaffed, as a rule, with pitiful collections and at best a semiliterate clientele. Generally, wrote Krupskaia in the spring of 1924, the cultural level in the countryside was so very low that "political education in the countryside is now the most urgent [task] from the viewpoint of the victory of communism." But, she continued, ordinary methods of agitation and propaganda could not be effective, because "newspapers [and] books do not reach the countryside, they are not geared toward the countryside, and are incomprehensible to peasants."[28]

So it was important that the propaganda of Leninism in the coun-

218   tryside be designed with special care, with the peasants' needs and limitations in mind. If the reading room hoped to "tell the village about Vladimir Ilich," it would have to move the peasants emotionally. Reading-room activities needed to demonstrate a commitment to rural life. Thus it would be helpful to consult with peasants themselves about how to go about the task of celebrating Lenin's memory. One peasant, for example, suggested that his village reading room display a portrait of Lenin decorated with ears of corn (presumably linking him to a good harvest). A political worker suggested that to keep Lenin's memory alive in the countryside every village reading room should undertake some project of practical benefit to the community, and do it in Lenin's honor, "so that later one will always be able to say: 'This was done when Vladimir Ilich died. It was done in his memory.' "[29]

Glavpolitprosvet also tried to locate and record all available folkloric creations about Lenin. In 1924 the Commissariat of Enlightenment published instructions to its political education workers, directing them to search towns, villages, and army units for local composers, folksingers, and storytellers, and to write down songs, tales, legends, poems, jingles, and riddles about Lenin in all extant variations.[30] In this way, Glavpolitprosvet hoped to acquire publishable propaganda material, to gain information that might help in designing the propaganda of Leninism in the villages, and at the same time to identify loyal supporters among otherwise unreachable, and often illiterate, individuals who were likely to wield some influence in their own communities.

Also active as recorders of popular feelings about Lenin were newspaper correspondents in villages, factories, and army units. In 1925 the Red army press published a volume of letters and articles written by these correspondents. The subject: the death of Lenin. A typical letter: "Our dear teacher, father and comrade! You have left us, but your words will never die in our hearts. For years you fought for us, you opened our eyes. You were the closest member of our family." Some peasant letters portrayed Lenin as a savior, "the great genius of mankind, such as is hardly born once in a thousand years. His whole life he suffered all kinds of deprivations . . . he won freedom for the poorest people, emancipating them from the power of capitalism." And again: "We peasants are firmly convinced that Lenin's work will be carried out to the end by his pupils, members

of the RKP . . . We ask that a book be published, fully comprehensible to peasants, about the life and work of dear Com. Lenin and
his legacy, so that this book could be our replacement for the Gospel."[31]

Professional agitators and propagandists who managed the cult of
Lenin placed an enormous premium on written evidence of popular
devotion to Lenin occasioned by his death. Officials in the political
administration of the Red army indicated their intention to study
carefully all written materials demonstrating soldiers' and peasants'
reactions to Lenin's death, and to make use of these materials "in all
agitational work."[32] And in the Red army that agitational work—on
Lenin and Leninism—was considerable.

The Red Army

Of all organizations in Soviet Russia that had the means to influence the peasantry, the Red army was by far the largest and most
powerful. When Lenin died, its political administrative department,
PUR, drew up immediate plans for an intensive campaign to propa-
gate his legacy.

On February 16, 1924, the head of PUR, Andrei Bubnov, and the
chief of its agitprop section issued a series of instructions explaining
these plans, which were to take effect at once. In the opinion of the
authors, the immediacy of the political work was crucial to its success, for their primary intention was to capitalize on the feelings of
solidarity Lenin's death had evoked "among the widest sections of
the working population." It was now necessary, they said, to channel the "aroused energies" of the masses into the fulfillment of
Lenin's legacy. This work was imperative because of the potential
political instability Lenin's death had engendered. PUR's eagerness
to manipulate mass emotions, and its belief that it had done so successfully in the past, was made patently obvious in the following revealing statement:

> The Red army is composed largely of peasant lads who did not fight
> in the civil war. They are now displaying the same cautious attitude
> evident in the villages, where the peasantry is somehow awaiting
> confirmation that Soviet power, even after the death of its leader,
> will continue the same politics of support for the peasant economy,
> the politics of strengthening the union of workers and peasants that

220   *Lenin* always advanced. At the same time, having been reared in a
       Soviet spirit through earlier [political] work, the Red army masses
       are profoundly upset by *Lenin*'s death. Their sympathy for Soviet
       power and the Communist Party has increased. It is imperative to
       take all this into account and make these sentiments the point of de-
       parture for our work among the nonparty masses.

Therefore Lenin's death necessitated mass agitation that would
"clarify" Lenin's role in the Communist Party and the Russian and
world revolutions, assure the populace that Lenin's politics would
be continued, and "strengthen the active sympathy of the peasant
masses" for the party and government. PUR officials calculated that
simple soldiers would be particularly moved by the story of Lenin's
personal suffering, and indicated that special care ought to be taken
to popularize "the history of his illness, the reasons for his death,
and his funeral (embalming, preservation in the crypt)."[33]

In her 1924 article on cultural work in the countryside, Krupskaia
stressed the importance of making full use of the Red army because
of its immediate ties with the village, since letters the soldiers
wrote—and demobilized soldiers themselves—went home.[34] In
planning their propaganda of Leninism, the management of PUR
kept this important fact in mind. The Red army, they wrote, was the
"champion of Soviet ideas in the village." Ideally every member of
that overwhelmingly peasant army should be moved to communicate the content of the agitational campaign to the countryside by
writing about it in letters to his family.[35] But surely this was not a
realistic expectation. The army needed some more reliable vehicle
for the transmission of political messages to the countryside. It did
have such a vehicle, a special booklet (*pamiatka*) presented to every
soldier upon the termination of his military service and sometimes
also given to soldiers on furlough.

Pamiatki were ideological handbooks designed to encourage the
demobilized soldier to retain and communicate to his fellow villagers the political education he had received during his years in service. Those published in the early twenties tended to be dry exposi-
tions of Marxist political and economic theory, and included
nothing of interest to peasant readers. It is more than likely that the
booklets promptly went up in smoke, their pages used as cigarette
rolling papers. Before Lenin died, pamiatki placed no special emphasis on his writings or biography.[36]

With his death Lenin became the central focus of this important agitational bridge between the army's political administration and the broadest mass of the peasantry. A representative pamiatka published in 1924 demonstrated a sophisticated effort to inspire demobilized soldiers with Lenin's memory and to turn them into a powerful tool for the politicization of the countryside. The pamiatka printed the Red army oath and, on the page directly opposite, included a funeral march to Ilich: "Today you have died at your glorious post,/ Taking millions with you/ . . . You died, ILICH, but the party lives on." Next came a portrait of Lenin and an article on his concern for the peasantry. The pamiatka continued with agitational articles lauding Soviet efforts on behalf of the peasantry, written in clear and simple prose and interspersed with hortatory slogans in large print, celebrating what ILICH did or said.[37] It was hoped that pamiatki would bring Lenin to the villages, but within the army the most pervasive agitational vehicles were the Lenin Corners established throughout the Red army in 1924 on the orders of PUR.[38]

Red Corners, rooms or parts of rooms displaying portraits and writings of revolutionary leaders, had existed in the Red army since 1921. After Lenin's death they were expanded in number and all renamed Lenin Corners. "Why are 'Red Corners' now called 'Lenin [Corners]'?" asks an agitational pamphlet of 1925. The answer: because Lenin is tightly linked to the Red army just as he is to the revolution and the construction of Soviet power, because when Lenin was no more, and a great sorrow swept the army, Red Corners were renamed after Lenin to honor his memory and to remind all soldiers of their solemn duties.[39]

In 1924 and 1925 old corners were revamped and new ones created according to detailed instructions published by the party and by PUR. The Lenin Corner had tables and benches where soldiers could read, separate tables for checkers and other games, some shelves with books, newspapers, and journals, and a small staff on hand to answer any questions the soldiers might have and to help them write letters. There was also a bulletin board with regularly updated reports on the health of members of the military unit. Most Lenin Corners had a gramophone and an accordion or other musical instruments. And, of course, there were drawings and photographs of Lenin and books by and about him. Some Lenin Corners displayed busts of the leader, others exhibited serialized photo-

222 graphs of his life, and a few even contrived to illuminate Lenin's portrait with concealed electric lamps.[40] These last were secular counterparts to the votive candles that burned before icons in Russian homes.

The Lenin Corner was quite clearly designed to be a social center that would make politics appealing by mixing it with play and with information of practical interest. The corner served the political function of saturating the army with Lenin's name, image, and ideas in order to strengthen the emotional bonding between the ruling party in Soviet Russia and the ruled. His presence was to be palpable to the soldiers when they were feeling relaxed, and, by gazing down at them from the walls as they played checkers and guitars, the immortalized Lenin was to penetrate their daily lives on a regular basis, providing a political dimension to social activity. By making the Lenin Corner partly recreational, its organizers were assuring themselves of an audience. Lenin would be "always with us" (in the words of a Lenin cult slogan that was to become widespread in the 1960s). Even when military units left their barracks to camp out in summer, Lenin was not left behind. In camp "Lenin Tents" were erected.[41] The Lenin Tent was designed to provide both entertainment and inspiration, frequently posting printed marching songs calculated to arouse courage and resolve:

> We may not sleep and do not sleep
> Because it is he who sleeps . . .
> In the dark night snakes are slithering,
> At nighttime wolves are howling.
> But [our] arm is strong, for it is commanded
> By Commander ILICH.[42]

Lenin Tents were obviously restricted to the army, but the 1924 campaign of agitation and propaganda directed the establishment of Lenin Corners in every conceivable institution—in schools, factories and other workplaces, in workers' clubs, libraries, and village reading rooms.

Lenin Corners

The widespread and hasty organization of Lenin Corners had begun during mourning week and thus willy-nilly reflected the standards and tastes of the workers, teachers, party members, or other individuals who happened to organize them. In February 1924, Glavpolitprosvet, as part of its effort to control the propaganda of Leninism, laid down guidelines according to which new Lenin Corners were to be set up and existing ones modified. It published a detailed description of the precise requirements for a satisfactory Lenin Corner, listing requisite photographs in proper order. It also provided slogans for each facet of Lenin's life celebrated in the display, which began with Lenin's precursors in the European and Russian revolutionary movements and ended with his funeral and the solemn incantation of his legacy (the unification and strengthening of the party, special attention to the needs of the peasantry, and so on).[43] Lenin Corners were to be centers of activity that would involve all party members in any given organization and thus serve to unify and standardize cell activity. And they were expected to mobilize popular loyalty around the memory of the leader by spreading his name "to every tiny village, every factory, every workshop."[44]

The organizers of Lenin Corners, and of the propaganda of Leninism more generally, expected their work to help attain many goals. Lenin should inspire children to study hard (as did little Volodia Ulianov) or workers to labor productively (as Lenin always did, particularly after 1917). This aspect of the Lenin cult—the linkage of Lenin's memory to immediate, practical tasks of the moment—would become a firmly entrenched feature of Soviet propaganda, especially when the cult assumed a reduced form in the latter part of the decade. And it was to revive with unprecedented intensity when a full-blown Lenin cult was resurrected after Stalin's death.

In 1924, some party officials maintained that Lenin Corners could also serve to improve the moral quality of the Russian spirit. Lenin was to be the omnipresent and eternal moral exemplar he had, in fact, hoped to become, a lever powerful enough to lift the trammeled Russian soul out of its age-old prison of selfishness and sloth. This concept was expressed in a pamphlet on the function of Lenin Corners in apartment buildings, which tells the following story. In May 1924, a large number of "undesirable" managers of cooperative apartment buildings in Moscow—former owners of the houses as well as new NEPmen spawned by the greater economic freedoms of the New Economic Policy—were purged and replaced with reli-

224 able party members and factory workers. But despite the purge, the residents retained selfish desires for the best rooms, feelings evoked by the bad managers (thus reads the pamphlet). How to combat those selfish instincts? Through the construction in all apartment buildings of Lenin Corners, which should be placed along the most heavily traveled corridor of each building and should be simple but eye-catching. And to make sure that residents continued to pay attention to them, their displayed illustrative material—portraits, busts, photographs—should be changed at least once or twice a month.[45] In this way Lenin's permanent but constantly changing presence would provide the moral inspiration necessary to stimulate spiritual growth.

In factories, Glavpolitprosvet expected Lenin Corners to be set up in workers' clubs, which it considered the loci for "the communist reeducation of the proletarian masses."[46] Not only the completed Lenin Corner but also the very process of its formation was to inspire enthusiasm in participating workers. In the same vein, party and government propagandists hoped that workers' clubs would engage the energies of their members in organizing lectures on Lenin, excursions to Lenin museums and to the mausoleum, and Lenin Evenings.

Lenin Evenings

Memorial Lenin Evenings had been an important part of mourning week throughout Russia. Programs of speeches, dramatic readings, poetry recitations, and musical offerings had provided forums for collective expressions of grief and solidarity. The agitation and propaganda campaign of 1924 sought to replicate those feelings at a later time by reproducing the programs.

A wave of Lenin Evenings was scheduled for February 21, 1924, to commemorate the passage of one month since Lenin's death. One workers' club reported to Glavpolitprosvet that every section of the club was involved in preparing the February 21 evening. The chorus was learning Lenin's favorite songs, the art group was planning decorations, the drama people were rehearsing a skit, "There in America" (about American workers' responses to Lenin's death), and even the sewing group was working on a tablecloth for the Lenin Corner.[47] The Moscow city Soviet of Trade Unions intended to make the February 21 evening a compulsory affair in workers' clubs and published a circular detailing exactly how it was to proceed, designing it to appeal above all to audience emotions. The commemorative evening was to include brief biographical lectures (preferably accompanied by slides), solo and choral musical performances, and skits. Workers were to take part in group dramatic readings of the following sort:

> All (clearly, staccato): Lenin—supreme leader,
> You have not died; you live.
> You have completely merged with immortal glory,
> Your thought,
> Your gigantic rush,
> Pours its lava into the millions
> To bear them into the decisive battle.
> Group 1:—to the sun . . .
> Group 2:—to happiness . . .
> Group 1:—And to life
> Group 2:—And to light.[48]

The songs for the evening were at once mournful and filled with resolve: "A funeral march crashes into our lives./ Do not grieve. Lenin is with us." The poems, like the songs, conformed to the same theme: Lenin lives. One of these, "And Ilich Will Live," is about little Vasia, the son of two workers, who accompanies his parents to Lenin's funeral. He gazes on Lenin.

> His high, clear forehead in the red coffin no longer thinks,
> And Ilich in his coffin no longer lives,
> But little Vasia's young forehead
> Absorbs Ilich. And Ilich will live.[49]

Lenin Evenings were occasional events. The one-month anniversary of the leader's death was made into an appropriate occasion. So was his birthday, April 22, 1924. For that day provincial departments of Glavpolitprosvet prepared special commemorative programs. The political education department of the Don region, for example, published a booklet of instructions on Lenin Evenings for peasants.[50] These were to be rallies with great emotional appeal. They were to include the recitation of stories and reminiscences about Lenin, a short play, and a selection of verses. The most powerful of these was Maiakovsky's "Bulletin." The poet describes his shock at learning of Lenin's illness:

> No!
>
> the language of thunder cannot be fettered! . . .
> No!
>
> Lenin's will shall not weaken
> In the million-strong will of the RKP . . .
> Lenin's heart shall beat eternally
> In the breast of the revolution.
> No!
> No!
> No-o-o!

Here again is the theme of Lenin's immortality. It was echoed as well in the poem placed just after Maiakovsky's, a tribute to Lenin's funeral. "Shall the proletariat surrender to death?" The answer: "LENIN IS IMPERISHABLE." The Russian, "LENIN-NETLENEN," a play on words, describes Lenin with the very term used to identify the imperishable, undecayed bodies of Orthodox saints.[51]

Was this a spontaneous formulation by a peasant poet who really saw Lenin as a latter-day saint, or did the Don political education department perhaps hire a hack poet and ask him to write something that peasant listeners would find moving? There is no way of knowing what the poet, N. Shalimov, had in mind when he wrote the poem. But professional propagandists chose to recommend it for Lenin's birthday commemoration and thus knowingly decided on the desirable tone for the event. The Lenin Evening was to resemble a gathering of group worship. True, skits and stories lent later Lenin Evenings a recreational mood missing from the January mourning meetings, but generally planners of Lenin Evenings sought to capture or, if necessary, rekindle some of the fervent veneration so often expressed in ritual cadence just after Lenin's death.

This worshipful mood, at once reverential and resolute, was necessary for a successfully functioning cult of Lenin. It was the basso continuo over which the rest of the cult was played out. Veneration, adoration, loyalty, devotion—these were the emotions that Lenin Evenings and other cult rituals were designed to evoke in the populace. No evidence published in the Soviet Union can indicate whether or not they in fact did so. What is likely, however, is that if any part of the population responded to the propaganda of Leninism with the requisite emotions, it was the most impressionable part—the children of Soviet Russia.

Little Leninists

The propagation of Leninism among children was an increasingly important focus of the cult after Lenin's death. The goal was two-fold: the publicized story of Lenin's childhood was to provide for Soviet children an ideal model of energetic, studious little Volodia who always had a highly developed sense of obligation to the narod; and the idealized Ilich—usually called by his patronymic to make him more accessible and familiar—was to personify the regime in the image of a kindly man, all smiles and dimples, who saved Russia and loved children. It was expected that children properly saturated with Leniniana would grow up to be loyal Soviet citizens, their young love for Lenin maturing into a strong devotion to Soviet power. Furthermore, "Grandpa Ilich" was to counteract pernicious home influences by providing an ideal role model against which children could judge their parents.

Classrooms were inundated with Lenin's portraits after his death. Especially widespread were photographs and drawings of Volodia as a toddler, child, and youth, intended to facilitate the child's affection for and identification with Lenin. The same function was to be served by the illustrated biographies of Lenin for children that were published and distributed in large editions. Most of these included at least one drawing of the adult Lenin surrounded by adoring, happy children, conveying the important message that he had loved children and that those he met had loved him. One of the first such biographies was *Our Teacher Lenin,* written in 1924 by Z. Lilina, Zinoviev's wife. It describes the life of a rambunctious child who studied hard and played hard as well, and who early on became interested in social and political questions. In this version, Volodia sat in on political discussions between his older brother Sasha and his Narodovoltsy friends (a total fabrication), and himself in high school formed small circles of schoolfriends and spoke to them of the oppressed poor in Russia (another fabrication). One of the illustrations shows him as a young gimnazist in his uniform, hugging his books and listening intently to two peasants. Another shows him as ruler of Russia, standing amid a group of adolescents. He thus ap-

228   pears in Lilina's biography as both exemplar and protector, lovable boy and loving Grandpa.[52]

Other publications about Lenin for children included writings about him *by* children. Both children's prose and poetry about Lenin contain the clearest available exposition of the emotional content of the Lenin cult as envisioned by its various managers after 1924. The children whose works were selected for publication were expressing feelings and ideas they had learned in school and in youth organizations, or they were revealing sentiments that derived from their home environments. This last was doubtless the case in many of the reminiscences about Lenin presumably composed by children, since those children who met the leader were likely to have as parents high government or party officials whose careers would lead their children on paths that in a literal sense could cross Lenin's.[53] In any event, whatever the source that inspired children's writings on Lenin, the authorities in charge of cult publications obviously selected only those pieces that conformed to a desired mold, that described Lenin as a genius and beloved teacher, kindly, caring, eternal—and as a relic possessing active powers:

> In the middle of Moscow there stands a grave
> Before the Kremlin wall.
> In that grave is our strength,
> Our leader, our dear Lenin.[54]

After Lenin's death, children's writings about him were valued for their purported artlessness, and seen as such effective examples of popular devotion to him that some of the party's most important spokesmen took to citing these writings in their own publications about Lenin destined for adult readers. In 1925 Emelian Iaroslavsky, a prominent party official, revised his lengthy biography of Lenin that had appeared the previous year to include a section, "Children on Lenin," in which he described Soviet children's affection for Lenin, citing their little stories and poems about him; the book even included a child's drawing of a mourning meeting replete with portraits of Lenin and Marx hung on the walls of the meeting hall. In the fall of 1924, Trotsky published an article in *Pravda* about children's literature on Lenin. He admitted that most children's writings about Lenin simply reflected what the little ones had been taught by adults; but he also insisted that these writings

nonetheless expressed a spirit of unusual "freshness." He then proceeded to review a wealth of literary material some of which demonstrates most clearly the successful propaganda of Leninism among
children by 1924. The young authors Trotsky cited had all internal-
ized an idealized conception of Lenin in perfect harmony with his
official persona. For example, a child's biography of Lenin included
the following description: "Lenin liked fishing. On a hot day he
would take his fishing rod and would sit down on the bank of a
river and *all the time he would think how to improve the life of the*
workers and peasants." "That's what Lenin did!" added Trotsky
approvingly.[55] In fact, the little biographer had to be either par-
roting a myth or himself creating one as an embellishment to
those he had already learned. Trotsky's open support of such myth-
making, which he calls evidence of an acute understanding of Lenin,
is a small but concrete example of conscious cult creation by the
man who was still the most widely known political leader in Soviet
Russia.

Only a tiny group of children and adolescents were honored with
the publication of their writings on Lenin, but many were obliged to
ponder on Lenin and actively participate in his cult through the
school system that not only introduced Lenin to its pupils through
readings and illustrations, but also required them to write essays
about him, gather materials for Lenin Corners, and engage in individual group projects honoring his memory.

In a Kazan secondary school, for example, the teachers asked
their students to describe their idea of the best monument to Lenin.
The Kazan students thought up dramatic or elaborate outdoor
monuments in Lenin's honor, designs they introduced with florid
preambles of praise to the leader. "In his grave Ilich remains the
apostle of communism," wrote one student. The youth proceeded to
list the requirements for a proper monument made of Finnish red
marble in the shape of a pentagonal pyramid and topped with a
five-pointed star. Another participant in the school project thought
the monument ought to be made not of red but of black marble, as a
sign of mourning. Still others believed the monument should be a
statue of Lenin in some specified pose. One scenario locates Lenin at
the stern of a ship, "with great difficulty" turning the wheel to the
left through a sea consisting of the heads of tsars, generals, priests,
monks, bureaucrats, peasants, and workers. The workers' heads are

230   on the left, and the closer they are positioned to the ship bearing
      Lenin, the more hopeful the expressions on their faces. The most
      elaborate of these adolescent fantasies was filled with self-conscious
      symbolism:

> Vladimir Ilich stands in a proud pose. There is a desk beside him.
> On it is a pile of various papers and books: this documents the fact
> that he did a great deal of intellectual labor at a desk.
>
> In his hand he holds a crossed hammer and sickle—the union of
> workers and peasants.
>
> Vladimir Ilich's foot treads on the three-headed snake of the
> bourgeoisie. One head of the snake wears a top-hat, another a
> crown, the third a priest's cap.
>
> The snake is crushed, but still shows signs of life; it is in its death
> agony.
>
> C[omrade] Lenin points with his hand to a throne that is off to one
> side, and invites a worker and peasant in front of him to enter boldly
> and sit on the throne.
>
> The worker and peasant are decisively ascending the steps of the
> throne. The worker holds a hammer in his hand, and the peasant—a
> sickle. Both are also carrying high above their heads a red banner—
> the banner of victory. The banner reads: "Workers of the world,
> unite." On the pedestal of the monument gold letters spell out:
> "Eternal memory to the dear leader for freedom Vladimir Ilich
> Lenin."[56]

Young people's projects of Lenin monuments reveal both the extent of popular participation in the cult expected of Soviet citizens
and the visionary range inspired by cult propaganda. Some of the
images the students produced were palpably religious and even ma-
jestic. The fantasy of Lenin sailing through the heads of tsars, on the
one side, and workers on the other corresponds to the Christian vision of the Last Judgment in which the heads of the saved and the
damned, recognizable by their expressions of beatitude or agony,
are huddled beneath the feet of Christ. The project in which Lenin
invites a worker and peasant to share the throne shows him in glorious majesty, striking a proud pose and at the same time bestowing
power on the people as a gift of grace; in this tableau Lenin is the
good tsar, hard working, all-powerful, and generous.

That the students composed such projects indicates that traditional images and concepts of power from prerevolutionary Russia

were firmly implanted in their minds and were grafted onto their perceptions of Soviet power. This should come as no surprise; after all, only seven years had passed since the revolution. That the propagandist who published the projects saw fit to include these in particular might indicate that he judged acceptable any fantasies that portrayed Lenin as great and powerful, no matter what form they took, or that he had poor judgment. But the students' projects also included revolutionary symbols that may have come from old Russia but figured prominently in civil war agitation. The image of Lenin as helmsman, the three-headed snake, the hortatory slogans embroidered onto banners, had become by 1924 symbols familiar to ordinary high school students, the stuff of which they wove their political fantasies. This perhaps testifies to the success of the agitation that, since 1918, had attempted to impress upon the people of Soviet Russia a political symbolism that would stir their loyalties. That the very myths, symbols, and images with which the regime tried to mobilize the country surfaced in student visions of Lenin monuments may indicate either that those symbols had come from the people and continued to inspire them because they were truly indigenous to Russian popular culture, or that agitprop activities had been effective enough, in the six years before Lenin's death, to instil enduring political images in the popular imagination. The evidence does not, in fact, decisively bear out either speculation. It only shows that the Kazan propagandist who decided to publish a summary of adolescent projects honoring Lenin chose the ones he liked best. Or that the teacher chose those that he or she preferred, perhaps having coached the students before making the assignments in the first place.

This raises the larger question of the extent to which the Leniniana dreamed up in the most diverse forms in 1924 and 1925 was spontaneously generated. It is clear why the Kazan students designed projects in honor of Lenin's memory: they were told to. But what about the thousands of other tributes, some of which remained on paper as fantasies, but many of which were realized as poems, drawings, busts, statues, and the like? What (or who) prompted workers, peasants, and artists to make public statements of the most diverse sorts in homage to Lenin? And to what extent were those statements genuine, that is, did they reflect original conceptions or did they conform to models or even directives from above? The

232   complex and, in the end, impenetrable interweaving of politics and true inspiration was fundamental to the intense Lenin cult of 1924 and 1925, when along with party leaders and government and party agitators and propagandists, a broad spectrum of ordinary people, many of whom had never before been actively political, joined in the national celebration of Lenin and thus contributed to the cult of his memory.

Russia Celebrates Lenin

For more than a year after his death Lenin was the subject of an effusion of poems, portraits, busts, monuments, and the most diverse sorts of memorabilia. His face was fired onto porcelain pitchers, teacups, and plates. It appeared on jewelry, on candy wrappers, on cigarette boxes. Institutions of all description continued the rush to take Lenin's name in a behavior pattern that had been set during mourning week. Individuals followed suit; many named their boy babies Vladlen or Vladilen and their newborn girls, Ninel (Lenin spelled backwards). Plans of all sorts were drawn up—plans for Lenin museums, plans to raise money for projects honoring Lenin, plans for monuments, plans to live better, study harder, work more productively. In 1924 more than seventeen million copies of books by and about Lenin and Leninism, comprising almost 16 percent of all Soviet book publications, were printed. In 1925 the figure was even higher.[57]

The press carried articles debating the question of the best way to honor Lenin's memory and printed proposals supposedly sent to newspaper offices by enthusiastic workers:

> Provincial Committees of the Sick and Wounded in the War should each take one male child of an invalid. This child should be brought up in the spirit of Leninism. The boy should bear the surname, "Ilich . . ."

> Every Monday at 6:50, at the moment of the death of V. I. Lenin, everyone who feels love and respect toward the person of Lenin, wherever he may be, at a meeting, school, etc., is obligated to propose to all those present that they should honor the deceased [Lenin] by rising . . .

> (1) To the national flag, add a black stripe or a square as a symbol of perpetual mourning . . .

(2) In the Russian language, replace the word *rabochii* [worker]   **233**
with a word deriving from Lenin.[58]

A Minsk periodical proposed that Sunday be renamed Leninday
(*Leninden'*) and that the day should be dedicated to Lenin's memory
and devoted to the study of Leninism.[59] This proposal was a transparent attempt to replace the sabbath, the Lord's day, with one dedicated to a new god. Whether it was prompted by a religious veneration of Lenin or [something quite distinct but possibly related] a
general antireligious and iconoclastic sentiment, the effect was the
same. Lenin was to take the place of God. He was to replace the tsar
as well in a resolution passed in April 1925 that christened the
northernmost piece of land in Soviet territory "Vladimir Ilich Lenin
Land." The territory had previously been named after Nicholas II.[60]

The published photographs of Lenin were often black-rimmed, as
were many of the posters. Some of the most dramatic posters had a
red and black color scheme to symbolize the requisite formula: Ilich
has died, but Lenin lives. A common poster style included a
drawing or photograph of Lenin's face and a brief biographical
sketch or some rhapsodic verse. These commemorative posters were
often strikingly iconographic in form: a portrait of the mature Lenin
in the center is surrounded by photographs and drawings of various
stages of his life—from toddler to corpse—in the exact manner of
icons that celebrated important moments in the lives of Orthodox
saints. In some cases the iconography reflected the artists' own peculiar preferences. A 1924 poster displaying a montage of drawings
and photographs of scenes from Lenin's life includes as well a separate circle of portraits: in the middle is Gandhi surrounded by the
heads of Christ, Tolstoy, the martyred German Spartacist Karl
Liebknecht, Mohammed, Buddha, and Lenin.[61] Most remarkable is
that not Lenin but Gandhi is the central figure of these titans. This
would indicate that the artist was free to create his own constellation
of saints within the rubric of the Lenin cult. In this respect, in 1924
and (to a lesser extent) 1925, the official Lenin cult gave creative artists of varying talents room to express their individuality in their
glorifications of Lenin—within limits. But the authorities wanted to
reserve the right to set those limits.

In the beginning, immediately upon Lenin's death, no agency supervised or controlled the overall production of artistic renditions of

234   Lenin. Produced in a hurry and often by men and women of little talent, they were often of very poor quality. It was not long before the Funeral Commission took notice of the problem. Ten days after Lenin's funeral, Leonid Krasin complained bitterly about the busts of Lenin that were popping up everywhere. Not a single one bore a satisfactory resemblance to the leader. On the contrary, they looked "simply repulsive." Some of these, Krasin continued angrily, should be destroyed on account of their "disgraceful, I should say even sacrilegious," lack of resemblance to Lenin.[62] Even worse, he said in an article on monuments to Lenin, were busts that bore a *partial* resemblance to Lenin:

> When the sculptor has managed to catch some single feature that reminds you of Vladimir Ilich, but in the rest of the portrayal there is nothing that looks like him, the result can be vulgar and shocking beyond description: instead of the exquisite incomparable head of Vladimir Ilich that has the most interesting structure since that of Socrates, before us is the head of some rickets-ridden shopkeeper or provincial lawyer.

(Krasin apparently missed the irony of the fact that in reality Lenin *was,* by training at any rate, a provincial lawyer.) "One is seized with fear," exclaimed Krasin, at the thought that "hundreds of thousands of such busts" might appear throughout the country, and that "millions of people might forever imagine the features of Vladimir Ilich wearing the grimaces of these monstrosities."[63]

Krasin insisted that the realization of this nightmare be prevented by government decree.[64] His suggestion was speedily adopted. On April 24, 1924, the Central Executive Committee passed a decree prohibiting the reproduction, sale, and public exhibition of portrayals of Lenin in all media (except photographs), including photomontages, posters, paintings, drawings, bas-reliefs, and busts, without the express permission of any one of a number of specifically named subcommittees of the Immortalization Commission. The decree further stated that the originals of all works approved by the committees for distribution would be given to the Lenin Institute for safekeeping. It ended with the warning that it was a criminal action to disobey this decree.[65]

In Moscow the actual judging was done by the Immortalization Commission's executive committee or troika, which was also in charge of the construction of the mausoleum and sarcophagus for Lenin's body and the preservation of the body. The troika consisted of Viacheslav Molotov, its nominal chairman, a rising party functionary who was destined for a career of prominence under Stalin; Avel Enukidze; and Leonid Krasin, author of all its reports.[66] Authorized portraits, posters, and busts of Lenin were put up for sale and advertised. They sold well, judging by foreign visitors' frequent comments on the pervasiveness of such objects. But if many individuals and institutions responded to the sale of Leniniana by buying it, there were some who deplored the practice. Its most strident and vocal critic was the renowned poet Vladimir Maiakovsky.

The author of a number of poems on Lenin, Maiakovsky was in the process of composing his most famous contribution to the cult of Lenin, the epic poem "Vladimir Ilich Lenin," when he came out with a public plea: "Don't Traffic in Lenin!" This article, authored by the poet and possibly also by his colleague Osip Brik, was an editorial written for the journal *LEF* (Left Front in Art) which Maiakovsky edited.

Maiakovsky objected not to the public celebration of Lenin, but to the cheap and vulgar form that celebration was taking. The cult of Lenin, as he saw it, was sullying and destroying Lenin's immortal spirit. The editorial's first page provided a graphic illustration of the practice the poet found so distasteful, a reproduction of one of the many advertisements carried in the contemporary press:

BUSTS

OF V. I. LENIN

plaster, treated copper, bronze,

marble, granite

LIFE-SIZED AND DOUBLE LIFE-SIZED

from the original approved for reproduction

and distribution by the Commission on the Immortalization

OF THE MEMORY OF V.I. LENIN

MADE BY THE SCULPTOR

S.D. MERKULOV [MERKUROV]

————OFFERED BY————

STATE PUBLISHING HOUSE

for state institutions, party and professional

organizations, cooperatives, etc.

EVERY COPY IS AUTHORIZED.

[Items may be] viewed and ordered
IN THE COMMERCIAL PUBLICATIONS DEPARTMENT
Moscow, Rozhdestvenka, 4.
An illustrated prospectus will be sent out for free
on a first-come, first-served basis.
REPRODUCTION AND COPYING WILL BE
PROSECUTED ACCORDING TO THE LAW.

Maiakovsky then went into his dramatic comment:

We are against this.
We agree with the railroad workers from the Kazan RR who asked an artist to decorate the Lenin hall in their club without busts and portraits of Lenin, saying: "we don't want icons."
We insist:—
Don't mechanically punch out Lenin.
Don't print his portraits on posters, on tablecloths, on plates, on mugs, on cigarette-cases.
Don't bronze Lenin.
Don't take from him his living acts and human aspect, which he was able to retain, while directing history.
Lenin is still our contemporary.
He is among the living.
We need him alive, and not dead.
Therefore,—
Learn from Lenin, but don't canonize him.
Don't create a cult around a person, who during his whole life fought against every kind of cult.
Don't traffic in the articles of that cult.
Don't traffic in Lenin![67]

He is among the living. This was the theme of Maiakovsky's own tributes to Lenin: "Komsomolskaia," written at the end of March 1924, and "Vladimir Ilich Lenin," completed in October of that year. In that epic, which describes Lenin's life in the context of Russian revolutionary history, Lenin is at once all-powerful, omiscient, and touchingly human, "the most human of all human beings." He is also immortal. On the very first page of the poem Maiakovsky asserts that "Lenin/ even now/ is more alive than the living." His eternal life resides in the collective: the party and the working class. The poet hails the enthusiasm that turned "Ilich's/ very death/ into/ the greatest/ communist-organizer," meaning the Lenin Enrollment which, in Maiakovsky's portrayal, replaced Lenin with hundreds of thousands of zealous workers. He rejoices in the massive grief that shook Russia when Lenin died, in the popular outpouring of sorrow and solidarity. But at the same time he voices his fear that the multitudinous eulogies to Lenin that rang out across the land would obscure his humanity, and that "rituals,/ mausoleums/ and processions" would drown Lenin's simplicity.[68] This sentiment echoes the editorial in *LEF:* we must glorify Lenin's immortal spirit, but we must take care that this glorification not diminish Lenin. And yet Maiakovsky could not prevent even his own epic poem from being reduced and stripped of its integrity. It was eventually chopped up into little bits and pieces that served as captions for the bland and boring posters of Lenin so widespread in the 1960s and 1970s.

Maiakovsky was not alone in deploring the gross impropriety of much of the Leniniana that appeared just after Lenin's death. As early as February 1924 the newspaper *Rabochaia Moskva* published a letter from a reader who complained that a Ukrainian cigarette factory was putting Lenin's portrait on cigarette packets. The unfortunate result, he said, was that the empty boxes littering the streets were trod upon by pedestrians who were unwittingly stepping on Lenin's face.[69] The authorities moved to prevent such abuses of Lenin's image. In May 1924 the Immortalization Commission published a resolution informing all enterprises that the printing and distribution of Lenin's portrait on cigarette boxes and wrappers, candy wrappers and candy, labels for products of any sort, and all jewelry was "categorically forbidden."[70]

But the vulgarizing of the Lenin cult continued into 1925 as a wave of unveilings of monuments and statues, openings of museums and exhibits, and countless memorial meetings swept the land on the first anniversary of Lenin's death. A full week of ceremonies commemorated that event in the same ritualized style that had characterized mourning week. The same emotional gatherings in all institutions, the same poems and speeches dominating the press, and once again, on January 21, 1925, the nation was mobilized in mass demonstrations culminating in five minutes of total silence. In Moscow there was a "mass pilgrimage" to the Lenin Mausoleum.[71]

All of this was consonant with the canons of Communist Party taste. But at the same time, in 1925, one music critic was horrified to

238   find that a song routinely sung at Lenin Evenings had the melody of a "cabaret romance."[72] In this year two Lenin toys came into production. One was a set of building blocks that could be made into five different portraits of Lenin and one drawing of the Lenin Mausoleum.[73] The other was a cardboard model of the mausoleum that children were supposed to put together according to enclosed instructions.[74] At the end of 1925, a literary critic, Victor Iakerin, published a stinging indictment of the cheap objectification of Lenin he saw all around him: the director of a sausage factory had applied to name his enterprise after Lenin; Lenin's portraits were being displayed in shop windows next to advertisements for liquor; a Moscow firm was selling inkwells in the shape of the Lenin Mausoleum. "From a synonym for the proletarian struggle [Lenin is] turned into a household utensil. How far is this from a primitive skull-chalice?" (The reference is to the Pecheneg tribe whose chieftain killed the Kievan Prince Sviatoslav in the tenth century and made a drinking cup out of his skull.) In the author's judgment, Lenin symbolism had become as decadent as that of Fedor Sologub and other turn-of-the-century symbolist writers.[75]

In this he was very wrong. The refined and self-conscious symbolism of Russian literature was worlds away from the tastelessness that so frequently characterized the Lenin cult of this period. That cult, which had been designed to raise the Russian spirit out of its apolitical torpor, was in fact being absorbed and modified by the ordinary concerns and tastes of ordinary men and women. The party and government agitprop people had shaped their cult rituals and trappings carefully and thoughtfully, hoping to evoke a popular reverence for Lenin according to their own ideas about the culture of the narod. Those party propagandists who were members of the intelligentsia had concocted projects that reflected their manifest distance from the people they were hoping to influence. They presumably expected that Lenin cult rites and symbols that resembled forms of worship in the Orthodox tradition were likely to engage the masses. But—an important question—how deep had been the popular devotion to Christian saints? Had the icon corner been a shrine that inspired genuine feelings of reverence or simply an empty collection of objects, maintained out of habit and possessed of no spiritual dimension? What if the Lenin cult, established with such feverish energy in the winter and spring of 1924, should become a systematic series of routine and meaningless gestures?

By 1925, some critics maintained that this had happened. Singled out for special criticism were the Lenin Corners that had proliferated with great speed. A Glavpolitprosvet official complained that Lenin Corners were widespread but too often were simply decorative, erected with great ceremony and then left to stagnate "like a temple, in which everything should breathe of 'sacred inviolability.' "[76] A number of other critics made the same argument, lamenting the fact that the Lenin Corner had quickly turned into an "iconostasis."[77] There were also complaints that the posters of Lenin displayed in Soviet libraries were trite and that the quality of agitators lecturing on Lenin in the countryside was poor.[78] The designers of the Lenin cult had envisioned a living religion of Leninism. What they got instead was a short-lived enthusiasm that generated kitsch.

In 1924 and 1925 there was an evident popular involvement with Lenin in many quarters, but the emotions that informed it and the causes that inspired it appeared to be far from the pristine devotion to Lenin projected by party and government propagandists. The precise cause of the widespread popular celebration of Lenin's memory is impossible to determine. That a portion of it was generated by the broad agitprop campaign launched shortly after Lenin's funeral is very likely. It is also probable that some of the Lenin-oriented activity was inspired by the constant references to Lenin that filled the press and, in particular, the published speeches of important party figures. With what emotions did the many individuals, both within and outside the party, who hurried to organize Lenin memorial meetings, Lenin Corners, and the like, approach those projects? Zeal? Anxiety? Resignation? Furthermore, how many artists produced drawings, paintings, and posters of Lenin and how many poets wrote verses to him purely out of love and respect for his memory? Again we are confronted with that crucial and imponderable question of the extent to which the cult of Lenin was spontaneous. Certainly the intensity of mourning week and the rapidity with which memorial activities occurred would indicate two things: the agitational apparatus of the party and government was remarkably well organized at a time when little else in the political and economic structure of Soviet Russia was functioning

240   efficiently; and, at the same time, the mourning-week campaign and Lenin's death itself had inspired genuine enthusiasm for Lenin on a mass scale.

After mourning week, with time on the side of the agitprop agencies, the spontaneous element in Lenin cult activities is impossible to prove and difficult even to speculate on. Given Lenin's popularity, especially after the institution of the New Economic Policy, and given also the Russian tradition of showing respect to the dead, it seems highly probable that at least some individuals were moved by genuine feelings of sympathy to dedicate time, money, or labor to honor Lenin's memory. But was it sympathy for Lenin or for the party? Did they perhaps sense that by subscribing to Lenin's collected works, by designing a monument, by suggesting that their factory or village or theater be named after Lenin, they would please their superior, sell a product, keep their job, get promoted? If these were the motivating concerns, then the public outpourings of solidarity with Lenin were not, strictly speaking, genuine, *but* the cult of Lenin was working.

For the cult to operate successfully, many individuals had to support its activities. For this they had to be motivated emotionally. But in terms of the effective operation of the Lenin cult as a system of symbols and rituals that mobilized the populace around the party and state, and that *resembled* a religion, it actually made little difference what the emotions were that prompted popular participation. Indeed, if the authorities had the talent and organizational skills to pressure large numbers of Soviet citizens into believing that demonstrated enthusiasm for Lenin would further their careers, then those authorities had done their job well.

If, on the other hand, the Lenin cult is judged by the standards of a true religion, then the feelings that inspired its participants are very important indeed. In that case it was necessary that Lenin resonate deeply in the lives of Soviet citizens, that he be a source of comfort during troubled times, that they be moved to think about him, read his works, visit the places he lived in, and make pilgrimages to his grave in search of solace and some deep communion with his spirit. In 1924 and 1925, there is no evidence that the Lenin cult functioned as a true religion. It did, however, engage many people and prompt them, for a variety of reasons, to rally around Lenin and the party he personified. And that engagement demonstrates, to a greater or lesser extent, a *fusion* of political and religious images and emotions.

The Lenin cult quickly became an established part of Communist Party ritual, its pervasive elements familiar to the population at large. As early as 1925 there were indications that Lenin and his cult had penetrated the consciousness of uninformed peasants who understood virtually nothing of the new order. In that year, a survey of peasants in Iaroslav province asked them to define a number of terms that had become current after 1917. Some sample definitions: "declee [decree]—this is when the government writes papers"; "camunist, camenist [communist]—one who doesn't believe in God"; "proletaria [proletariat]—poverty." However, despite their utter lack of comprehension of postrevolutionary terminology, those same peasants could identify Lenin and Lenin Corners: "Mars, Karlo-Mars [Karl Marx]—like Lenin"; "corner, red corner—that is potraits [portraits] of Lenin and big written words."[79] In one year, 1924, the propaganda of Leninism had apparently succeeded in at least acquainting these untutored people with Lenin and the most widespread cult structure, the Lenin Corner.

It also succeeded in influencing at least some of the children of the Russian countryside. In 1926 a survey of peasant children in one rural township (*volost'*) of Tver province was conducted. This group of ten-to-twelve-year-olds had no evident political aspirations. For example, when asked what they wanted to do when they grew up, most of the boys wanted to become artisans or teachers, and the girls, teachers or seamstresses. Of the boys only .6 percent wanted to become Communists and the same percentage wished to join the Komsomol. (An identical proportion of boys named their preferred future professions as shepherd and zookeeper.) Despite this lack of political enthusiasm, when the boys were asked, "Whom would you wish to resemble?" a full 15.9 percent answered "Lenin." No other figure, including locally eminent individuals, was as highly esteemed. Of the girls, 6.2 percent hoped to be like Lenin and another 1.7 percent chose Krupskaia as their model. (Of the girls, the largest percentage wanted to resemble their teacher.) The children were also asked to indicate precisely why they wanted to be like the person they had named. The boys who wanted to be like Lenin gave the following sorts of answers: "I have heard that Lenin is a good person. Handsome. Diligent. Wise. Affectionate. He defended the op-

242 pressed and the poor. He loved children very much. He knew lots of things. To live the easy life that Lenin lived. To be at least a little bit like Lenin. To be wise and good. Little Lenin had pretty curls and forehead." These answers demonstrate that among this group of 165 peasant boys Lenin had made a strong impression. Their teachers had doubtless read or told them about Lenin or had assigned children's books about him. And they had seen the fetching photograph of the three-year-old Volodia Ulianov, his smiling face wreathed in blond curls. Of the 120 girls in the survey, those who hoped to resemble Lenin explained their choice in answers that show they perceived him as superhuman: "Learned. He fought for a better life. He ruled the whole world. Very learned. I want to be like the three-year-old Lenin, because he was conscious from infancy."[80]

When the Commissariat of Enlightenment had introduced the propaganda of Leninism among children as a conscious policy, it had posited two long-range goals: children saturated with Leninism were to grow up loyal to the party Lenin personified; and they were to find in him a role model more powerful than their parents. Though it is impossible to know the later political views of the children who participated in the survey described above, it is clear that in the short term, at least, Lenin was capable of serving as an effective role model. It is telling that, while almost 16 percent of the boys wanted to be like Lenin, less than 3 percent hoped to resemble their fathers.[81] The propaganda of Leninism for children was already showing results.

Also apparently effective was the cult of Lenin's body. In the four months after the opening of the Lenin Mausoleum, well over half a million people paid their respects to the leader.[82] Long lines of patiently waiting pilgrims continued to form in the next year and seemed to indicate that the cult was growing. "The Lenin cult has made big strides in the past year," wrote Walter Duranty in September 1925. His article focused on the ever present Lenin Corner, which he called "almost a shrine," and on the "constant throng" of pilgrims regularly seen at the mausoleum. The correspondent interviewed a "typical Communist girl" wearing a black leather jacket and a red kerchief on her head. She said she had visited the mausoleum six times in the previous three months. "She said it helped her somehow—life isn't always easy—and—and—it helped her." "The average simple-minded believer in any faith," said Duranty, "would speak much the same of a pilgrimage to a saint in a temple."[83]

Another campaign launched coincidentally with the propaganda of Leninism was that of antireligious propaganda. In the year of Lenin's death, the first antireligious newspaper, *Bezbozhnik* (The Godless), was founded, together with an organization to manage antireligious campaigns, which in 1925 was named the League of the Militant Godless.[84] The league's propaganda was conducted through published literature, lectures, discussions, exhibits, and group gatherings that were partly recreational. (Among the exhibits were special displays intended to prove that the preserved bodies of Orthodox saints were, in fact, bogus.) Though the party had hoped from the beginning to wean the people away from religion, it went about this delicate business slowly, moving into high gear only when the church itself was split and weakened and the party was sufficiently strong and organized to extend its domain into the realm of spirit. It moved to create secular holidays and rituals as a replacement for the many Orthodox ones that had played such an important role in setting the tempo of traditional rural life. From 1918 on, May Day and November 7 had been celebrated with great fanfare as the high points in the sacred history of the revolution. In 1924, Lenin provided the focus for the new religion.

He also figured in the attempt at national cohesion in the newly formed Union of Soviet Socialist Republics.[85] Among the broad spectrum of national minorities in the country, the propagandists of Leninism worked to promote loyalty to the Muscovite leadership as part of a larger effort to centralize and unify the Soviet Union. The progress was slow. An article published in *Pravda* in January 1925 observed that among certain mountain peoples in Georgia Lenin was looked upon merely as a Russian—"your Lenin." Furthermore, one mountaineer was unimpressed with Lenin's portrait: "He does not look like a brave person. See how he is dressed." These mountain people, explained the author, needed to see Lenin as a big, bold warrior in military uniform. But "there will come a time when in these mountains the Lenin legend will be the life to whose defense these mountaineers will come at the first call."[86]

The Lenin legends were not long in coming. Poems and stories about Lenin had appeared in minority languages well before

244 Lenin's death, and the agitational campaigns of 1924 had inspired a significant number of verses and stories by artists faithful to the party. The efforts by party and government propagandists to collect folklore about Lenin after his death, as part of the propaganda of Leninism, eventually provided the material for an anthology entitled *Lenin in Russian Folk Stories and Eastern Legends*. The year of publication was 1930, and although some of the stories had been printed before and were probably genuine folk creations, most are undated and their genesis remains mysterious. What should one make of an Uzbek story that describes Lenin as having been born "from the moon and stars" whence came his special powers to bestow on the world human happiness?[87] Perhaps it was the product of a simple bard who was inspired to weave Lenin into his traditional cosmology. On the other hand, he could have been consciously creating a colorful devotional piece to curry favor with the authorities. Or the tale could have been fabricated by an editor at the *Molodaia gvardiia* press that published it. In any event, this legend and others like it were printed to demonstrate that the Lenin cult had been assimilated and embraced by remote portions of the population of the USSR.

By 1930 the cult of Lenin may have reached the periphery, making it more extensive than ever before. But in the center, it was fading fast.

The Waning of the Lenin Cult

The broad agitational campaign of 1924 that established the nationwide Lenin cult had been designed so as to give way eventually to a stable propaganda of Leninism. By 1926 it had.

For four more years—until the end of the decade—it survived in a standardized but reduced pattern. Lenin Corners continued to proliferate, but no new campaigns were launched to revive those that were judged to be uninspired. Posters, photographs, and busts of the leader were ubiquitous and took on the sameness of an iconography—the same resolute gaze on Lenin's face, the same bodily gestures and poses. Orthodox iconography had exhibited a similar stylization in the requisite hieratic gaze of Christ, the set hand gestures of various saints, and so on. Lenin museums and exhibits were kept up and new ones opened; in particular his former dwellings (and his Kremlin office) were opened to the public as sites of pilgrimage.

Lenin Evenings, conducted according to a fixed format, were held annually on January 21, Lenin's death day. They were convened in schools, factories, and in party, government, army, and trade union groups of every level. But while these yearly Lenin Evenings were widespread, there is evidence that a portion of them paid little homage to Lenin's memory. Just a few days before the third anniversary of Lenin's death, one of *Pravda*'s editors, Viacheslav Karpinsky, published an article in which he complained that in some clubs Lenin Evenings had turned into recreational events. It seems that in January 1926 certain groups had added to the official part of evening, programs of entertainment, including "artists with a name." The tone of these gatherings was gay rather than properly mournful. Karpinsky urged local party committees to prevent a repeat performance of this in 1927.[88]

The exemplary tone and content of Lenin memorial meetings was provided by the party leaders who gathered in Moscow's Bolshoi Theater before a large bust of Lenin. The January 21 issues of *Pravda*, *Izvestiia*, and other newspapers carried headlines about the anniversary of Lenin's death and printed articles and reminiscences about the leader, accompanied by photographs or drawings. The January 22 issue reported on the memorial speeches of the leaders in the Politburo. One of the most frequently performed occasional rituals of the Lenin cult was the fervent pledge to Grandpa Ilich made by the Young Pioneers upon initiation into that organization.

The Lenin Institute was busy building up the Lenin archive and editing both Lenin's works and *Leniniana,* a publication that meticulously categorized, annotated, and listed Soviet publications by and about Lenin. But after 1925 fewer and fewer annotations were included, and the bibliography was progressively reduced in size as the overall number of works on Lenin began to shrink. By the end of 1926 it had fallen sharply.[89] The 1928 listings, published in 1930, made up a slim volume. After that, the bibliography ceased publication. Throughout the twenties, standardized biographies of Lenin and memoirs by his contemporaries were still available in large editions, as were his published works in collected volumes, individual editions, and thematic anthologies. These last enabled the authors of books and articles on a variety of subjects to make the requisite

246   obeisance to Lenin by citing his views on the given subject (usually at the outset of the work). By 1926 the cult was standardized and controlled from above, allowing little room for the flights of fancy that had added variety to the Leniniana of the earlier period. If this meant, as it doubtless did, that even the possibility of the expression of genuine popular sentiment for Lenin was now precluded, then that course must be interpreted as a deliberate choice made by the men who ruled Russia.

In 1926, for all practical purposes, the party was in the hands of Stalin and his supporters. The diminution and standardization of the cult of Lenin must be interpreted as their conscious policy. Not that they acted purposefully to stem some surging tide of continuing popular devotion to Lenin. There is no evidence of such a spontaneous groundswell beyond January 27, 1924, the day of Lenin's funeral. The subsequent outpouring of Leniniana had been sustained by massive agitation and propaganda efforts. Stalin's machine curtailed those efforts and in so doing reduced the intensity of the Lenin cult in Soviet Russia. With each succeeding year after 1925, a steadily growing preponderance of the books, articles, and published speeches about Lenin, as well as the slogans about him that occasionally appeared in the press, linked him to the current concerns of the party. Leninism versus Trotskyism, Lenin and the struggle against the Right Opposition, Lenin on the construction of a socialist economy—these were the subjects that made up a progressively greater proportion of published Leniniana as the decade wore on. The cult of Lenin came to concentrate less and less on mourning the leader and more and more on using his sanctified memory to fight political battles of the moment.

Those battles, by 1930, were monumental. By then Stalin's incomparable iron rule of the party had annihilated all opposition. The "Great Turn," the massive industrialization and collectivization of Russia, was underway. The state-building process begun in the middle of the decade had culminated with the emergence of a monolithic party machine powerful enough to wage a successful war against its own peasant population in the brutal forced collectivization drive launched in the winter of 1929–30, together with the First Five-Year Plan. By then all political, economic, social, and cultural activities had been harnessed to the needs of the state. And so had the cult of Lenin.

This is readily apparent from the newspaper coverage of Lenin's
death day. *Pravda's* 1929 annual Lenin issue concentrated on
Lenin's views of a socialist economy, including an article by Krupskaia on Lenin and the construction of collective farms. The leitmotif
of the 1929 Lenin celebration was symbolized in a cartoon drawing
by the talented artist, Deni. It showed the Lenin Mausoleum against
a background of factories spewing forth smoke. A worker's arm with
rolled-up sleeve was thrusting out of the factory complex and holding a banner that read: "Let Us Fulfill the Leader's Legacy!"[90] In
1929, the memorial meetings for Lenin were above all celebrations
of party solidarity. On this, the fifth anniversary of Lenin's death, all
party workers were instructed to conduct mass agitation in the propaganda of Leninism. In 1929, this meant "the struggle against de-
viations, vacillations, opportunism." And party members were
directed to lecture city soviets on the theme of the progress made toward the construction of socialism in the previous five years.[91] Gone
was the mournful tone of the mid-twenties. The new mood of the
January 21 holiday was one of determined optimism.

This tone was retained in 1930 and the years following. Under
Lenin's banner, socialism will be built in the USSR! This was
Pravda's message on January 21, 1930. The comparable issue of *Izvestiia* showed Lenin's photograph against a background of factory
construction. And the new book on Lenin advertised for sale in the
January 20, 1930, issue of *Pravda* was entitled *Lenin on Collective
Farms and on the Struggle Against the Kulak*. The next year, on the
anniversary of Lenin's death, his legacy was simply equated with the
Great Turn: "We are building the best monument to Lenin—uninterrupted collectivization."[92] In 1932, again the same message and a
photo-montage of machines and factories setting the background
for Lenin's face imposed on a waving banner.[93] As for the memorial
meetings, the party's Central Committee issued a directive speci-
fying how they should proceed. All party organizations were instructed to hold meetings of workers, collective farmers, and party,
soviet, and trade union organizations. These meetings commemorating the eighth anniversary of Lenin's death were to "illuminate
the success of the workers of the USSR under the guidance of the
Leninist Party in the struggle for Communism based on the legacy
and instructions of Lenin." During the "Lenin Days," continued the
directive, "it is imperative to mobilize workers around the task of

the overfulfillment of the Five-Year Plan in 1932." The published directive concluded with a listing of the main slogans for the eighth anniversary of Lenin's death. The first one reads: "For the fulfillment of the Five-Year Plan in four years, for the successful construction of a socialist society!"[94] Lenin was being edged out of his own Lenin Day. The Great Turn was steamrolling even the modified cult of his memory.

And, in 1933, the Lenin cult as an integrated system of rituals focused on Lenin *alone* was at an end. In that year the commemoration of his death was a glorification of the Five-Year Plan and of its architect, Stalin. The January 21, 1933, issue of *Izvestiia* carried the following headline: "Realizing the legacy and directives of Lenin, the proletariat of the USSR under the leadership of the Party headed by Lenin's best disciple and companion, Com. Stalin, has fulfilled in four years of great labor the Five-Year Plan." Stalin had invaded the sacred sphere of the Lenin cult.

This invasion had begun subtly, almost imperceptibly. The first possible indication came in 1929, on November 7. The special issue of *Pravda* devoted to the October revolution carried a headline that articulated the determination to build socialism in the USSR: "Under the Leninist party of steel." The Russian, *stal'noi leninskoi partii*, sounds something like "Stalin-Leninist Party" (Stalin's pseudonym was derived from the Russian word for steel). Just ten weeks later, on Lenin's death day, *Pravda*'s headline asserted that under Lenin's banner the USSR would build socialism and move "from the peasant's horse to the steel steed of machine industry!" The steel steed—it would be interesting to know who thought to use the adjective *stal'nyi* in both these instances, and whether or not the usage was a conscious attempt to please Stalin. The following scenario seems possible: the headline editor composes the lines, shows them to his superior; the superior glances at the page, then at the editor, and says "godit'sia" (it'll do); they share a knowing look.

However it was generated, this shadowy incursion of Stalin's name into the commemoration of Lenin was coincident with the beginning of Stalin's own personality cult. That cult was already in evidence on December 21, 1929—Stalin's fiftieth birthday—an event marked by an enormous press campaign that splashed page after page with praises of Stalin. Speeches by his lieutenants and birthday greetings sent into the press by the hundreds exalted the party's "glorious leader" and "staunch fighter." The epithets were varied and flamboyant, reflecting the extravagance of the event, which differed strikingly from the incomparably more modest campaign marking Lenin's fiftieth birthday in 1920. One of the most frequently repeated praises of Stalin was an idealized characterization of his close relationship to Lenin. Stalin was Lenin's faithful pupil, companion-in-arms, comrade, best successor.[95] The development of the Stalin cult was enormously complex and multifaceted, but one of the many indicators of its formation was the emphatic placement of Stalin in proximity to the idealized Lenin. This proximity was especially meaningful if it took place on Lenin's territory—the January 21 newspapers.

The Stalin jubilee carried over into the 1930 Lenin ceremonials in a limited but significant way. As part of the December 1929 birthday campaign, the party had instituted a "Stalin Recruitment" of workers who applied to join the party in honor of Stalin. This, of course, was reminiscent of the Lenin Enrollment of 1924, an event whose fifth anniversary had been noted in a long article earlier that year.[96] In January 1930, Stalin's birthday and Lenin's death day were actively honored by workers who pledged to enter the party in commemoration of *both* occasions. The January 20, 1930, issue of *Pravda* printed an article that described the "most advanced workers" as marking "the jubilee of Com. Stalin—the devoted pupil of Vladimir Ilich—by joining the Party" and in so doing also commemorating the sixth anniversary of Lenin's death. In conjunction with this article the paper published a collection of separate listings, summarizing party recruitments by city. For example: "PERM—In connection with the anniversary of Lenin's death and the Jubilee of Com. Stalin, this [party] district received three hundred applications from workers and one hundred fifty from poor peasants in the past one and a half months."

From that point on, Stalin's own cult subsided for a time and then built up gradually and erratically until it emerged in full force in 1933. But he maintained his presence in the yearly Lenin celebrations. On January 19, 1931, it was his book, *On Lenin*, that was advertised in the press; it was published in an edition of 500,000.[97] That same year *Pravda*'s headline in the January 21 issue lauded Lenin's banner and Leninism. Its author—clearly indicated—was I. Stalin.[98] In 1932 there was another front-page slogan (albeit a small

250   one) by Stalin. And in 1933 not only was Stalin portrayed as Lenin's best pupil and heir, but Lenin himself was depicted in a weakened state, quite literally. On January 21 of that year *Pravda*'s first page carried, in large print, the "oath" speech Stalin made on the eve of Lenin's funeral, the speech in which he solemnly swore to fulfill Lenin's legacy. Next to it was an enormous photograph of Lenin that differed markedly from the ones published before on the same occasion. The earlier portrayals of Lenin in the January 21 newspapers had been drawings or photographs of his face, or of him standing in some strong pose or engaging in some activity. The photograph that appeared in 1933 was published for the first time. It was taken in 1922 in Gorki, when Lenin was ill. He is seated in a wicker armchair, his hands crossed and resting on his belly. Lenin looks like a friendly, tired old man—a "harmless icon," as he would have put it. That, presumably, is just how Stalin wanted him to look. Lenin had been stripped of his visible power and of the integrity of his cult.

That process had begun in the second half of the 1920s with the reduction of publications about Lenin, and the diminution of virtually all cult activities. In 1931, the party had openly moved to relegate Lenin to part of a deified trinity, with Marx and Engels. In that year the Lenin Institute ceased to exist as a separate entity. On March 31, 1931, it was merged with the Marx-Engels Institute.[99] The new organization was called the Institute of Marx-Engels-Lenin. The following year that institute began to publish its bibliographical work on published Leniniana, but no separate volume was devoted to works by and about Lenin. They were listed in a general bibliography of 1929 publications on Lenin, Leninism, and the histories of the party, Komsomol, and Comintern.[100] This bibliography was intended as a sequel to *Leniniana,* but after the 1929 listings no more volumes were published.

By 1933, Lenin's cult was at a low ebb and Stalin's was blossoming.[101] That year, on November 7, the American journalist Eugene Lyons took a stroll along several blocks in Moscow and counted the number of exhibited portraits and busts—"political icons," as he called them. He tallied up 103 of Stalin and only 58 of Lenin. Lazar Kaganovich, Stalin's lieutenant, came in third, with 56.[102] The cult of Lenin had provided Stalin with a precedent and a foundation for the creation of a dual cult of Lenin and Stalin. Why did Stalin need to become the more visible object of reverence? In what way could the dead (rather, the "living") Lenin have been a threat to him? An OGPU (secret police) report of 1931 may help to provide an explanation.

In March 1931, the head of the OGPU of the city of Smolensk reported on how the local population responded to the exile of the kulaks, the rich peasants. In general the attitude was favorable, but some workers had a "negative" attitude, reminiscing about the good old days, saying that if Lenin were alive, things would be different. In particular, a certain saddler was reported to have looked at a portrait of Lenin, saying: "There was an exemplary leader. Under him the narod lived high on the hog and everyone was content. But these idiot rulers can't find any way to improve things for the narod. If LENIN were alive, then he would have announced free trade and with that brought [us] over to collectivization, not by means of force, but through a voluntary path, the path of persuasion."[103]

The saddler was probably right. It is difficult to believe that Lenin would have unleashed a forced collectivization drive resulting in the deaths of millions of people, as Stalin did. A cult of Lenin that evoked a *nostalgia* for Lenin was certainly intolerable to the Stalin machine. If popular devotion to Lenin could inspire a critical attitude toward the current "idiot ruler," then that devotion was harmful to the stability of his rule. The idealized Lenin could only be tolerated if he were marching hand in hand with his "faithful companion," Stalin. And that is just what he proceeded to do for the next quarter century.

Epilogue: "Lenin Is Always with Us"

The cult of Lenin did not survive the tenth anniversary of his death. By 1934, the idealized Lenin was relegated to the supporting role of Sacred Ancestor as the cult of Stalin took center stage in Soviet political ritual. For the next two decades Lenin remained an object of organized reverence, but only within the context of the extravagant veneration of his "worthy continuer."

If the Lenin cult of the 1920s was a homely but rousing funeral march solemnly played on ceremonial occasions, the cult of Stalin was an ongoing symphony, in a major key. Its tone was bright and brassy, and its triumphal melodies resonated ever more loudly throughout Soviet Russia even as the purge and terror of the thirties silently ground up their victims. Every available instrument joined in playing endless variations on one theme: Stalin is the source of all our happiness or, as it is said in our party, "Stalin is the Lenin of today."[1]

This watchword of the Stalin cult struck at the very core of Lenin cult mythology. For the cult of Lenin had systematically celebrated his perpetual direct availability to the faithful through their receptivity to him, which itself was evoked by his own power. He emanated that power beyond death through his writings, through a collective appreciation and emulation of his exemplary life, and through his preserved body. Lenin cult rituals had been designed precisely to create an emotional bridge between the people and the leader and to evoke their resolve to continue the work he had undertaken on their behalf.

This dynamic could no longer be operative when Stalin became
Lenin incarnate. The mythology of the Stalin cult made Stalin the
intermediary between Lenin and the people; through Stalin's works,
writings, and person Lenin's spirit was accessible to all. "The genius
of Lenin burns on in Stalin," wrote the Kazakh poet Dzhambul
Dzhabaev.[2] If Stalin was the living Lenin, then the underlying
premise of the Lenin cult—Lenin's immortality qua Lenin—was no
longer functional. In 1938 the children's magazine *Murzilka* published a poem whose very title demonstrates the demise of the living
Lenin:

Lenin Lived

Lenin! Who does not know him?
From the Kremlin, where he soundly sleeps,
To the mountain tops of the blue Altai
The glory of Lenin shines.

Higher than the mountains, wider than every sea,
Heavier than the very earth
Was our people's grief
When he died, our dear one.

Lenin died. But stronger than steel,
Firmer than the flinty mountain races
Came his pupil—splendid Stalin.
He is leading us to victories and happiness.[3]

Although the systematic cult of Lenin was at an end, some individual practices were retained. A number were absorbed into the
Stalin cult, converting the (by then) traditional mode of revering
Lenin into a public veneration of Lenin and Stalin together. This
corresponded to a central tenet of the Stalin cult—that Lenin and
Stalin had always been spiritual brothers, devoted companions, the
closest friends and colleagues. *"Stalin was Lenin's right-hand man,"*
declared the author of Stalin's *Short Biography* in his section on
1917.[4] This purported closeness was repeatedly stressed in biographies and histories during the Stalin years. It resonated in the arts as
well. A typical sculpture from the 1930s showed Lenin and Stalin in
dialogue: both men are standing, and Stalin is the larger, more imposing, and more expansive of the two; he is *explaining* something to
Lenin, whose unprepossessing brow is knit in concentration.[5] Similarly the 1937 film *Lenin in October* (the first nondocumentary film

about Lenin) had Stalin (played by a handsome actor) paternally puffing on his pipe and advising Lenin's every move.

The January 21 holiday continued to elicit the requisite laudatory articles and memorial meetings dedicated to Lenin, but Stalin was as visible as Lenin in the commemorative issues of the newspapers; a photograph of Lenin or of a bas-relief or statue of the dead leader was usually matched by an exact counterpart of his living successor.

Leniniana, particularly visual tributes to Lenin, continued to be produced during the two decades that the Stalin cult was in force, although those productions were greatly outnumbered by the representations of Stalin that were churned out by the millions. Lenin's figure was the subject of a limited number of discrete works, paintings and statues by and large, as distinct from the flood of posters that had covered Soviet Russia after his death. It suited the managers of the Stalin cult that individual items glorifying Lenin should pay obeisance to the founder of Bolshevism, and should find their way into museums, while Stalin should pose with Lenin (or figure alone) in the widely distributed cult artifacts. Sometimes, however, Lenin's life was celebrated in imaginative ways reminiscent of 1924. On the tenth anniversary of his death, for example, a series of memorial stamps commemorated the occasion in a kind of temporal chromatic scale: the one-kopek stamp showed Lenin as a toddler; the three-kopek stamp bore a picture of him as an adolescent in his gimnazium uniform; the five-kopek stamp showed the adult Lenin; and the ten-kopek stamp portrayed him as a leader, addressing a crowd.[6] This series of stamps was reissued in 1944, to mark the twentieth anniversary of Lenin's death.

By that time, all political ritual in Soviet Russia was focused on the immediate goal of defeating the German enemy. Like everyone else, Lenin was pressed into service. The January 21, 1944, issue of *Pravda* carried a slogan proclaiming that Lenin's spirit was inspiring the war effort. In the Red army, said the lead editorial, Lenin's spirit lives on. Lenin is the brilliant "son of the Russian people." This original epithet was consonant with the general tenor of wartime propaganda that was fiercely patriotic, stirring up sentiments of Russian chauvinism (as opposed to loyalty to the Soviet government or working class or Communist Party). During the war Lenin cult rituals were kept to a minimum as the country mobilized all of its energies to survive the horror of invasion.

In July of 1941, just days after the outbreak of war, Lenin's body and the staff of scientists who supervised its continued preservation were evacuated for safekeeping to the city of Kuibyshev. Not until April 1945 was Lenin returned to the mausoleum, which was reopened in September of that year, sporting a new sarcophagus and an additional tribunal. From that tribunal Stalin stood atop the Lenin Mausoleum on revolutionary holidays, expressing his symbolic relationship with the founder of Bolshevism. The dead Lenin was a stepping stone for the living Stalin. But not for long: in March 1953 Stalin joined his erstwhile companion in the Lenin-Stalin Mausoleum.

In 1956, in his "secret speech" delivered to the Twentieth Congress of the Communist Party, Nikita Khrushchev fulminated against the "cult of the individual." He was referring of course to Stalin. "It is impermissible and foreign to the spirit of Marxism-Leninism to elevate one person, to transform him into a superman possessing supernatural characteristics akin to those of a god." "Such a man," he continued, "supposedly knows everything, sees everything, thinks for everyone, can do anything, is infallible in his behavior."[7] With these words of introduction, the party's first secretary silenced the symphony of the Stalin cult and denounced many of the abuses that had made Stalin's rule of Russia an unparalleled nightmare. This was the famous speech that marked the beginning of Khrushchev's daring de-Stalinization campaign, in which he hoped to gather political support by dissociating himself totally from a ruler he could never emulate.

To expose the crimes of Stalin's rule to a roomful of people who had, by and large, been accomplices in those crimes, and who for two decades had perfected the art of ignoring the unmentionable, it was necessary for Khrushchev to construct his argument with the utmost care and to arm himself with the strongest possible weapon. Khrushchev brandished his chosen weapon before describing Stalin's reprehensible behavior. That weapon was Lenin, the only existing (after a fashion) being with sufficient power to topple the man of steel.

Lenin (and Marx before him) was modest and firmly opposed to any hero worship, the first secretary declared. He then proceeded to debunk the myth of Stalin's happy and close relations with Lenin—

the cornerstone of the early Stalin cult—by circulating among the delegates three explosive and hitherto unpublished documents proving that Lenin had been on very bad terms with Stalin during the period of his illness in 1922 and 1923. First, Khrushchev read the "Testament," in which Lenin branded Stalin as "excessively rude" and recommended his removal from the position of general secretary of the party. The other documents were a letter from Krupskaia to Kamenev, complaining of Stalin's abusive behavior toward her, and another from Lenin to Stalin, written just days before his paralytic stroke of March 9, 1923, threatening to break off relations unless Stalin apologized to Krupskaia for his rude assault of the previous December.[8]

The transcript of the congress indicates that the reading of these documents produced a commotion among the delegates. And no wonder. Khrushchev had produced documentary evidence of the "devoted disciple's" maltreatment of Lenin's wife, of Lenin's subsequent dismay, and his sharply negative assessment of Stalin. Khrushchev thus both broke the legendary link between Lenin and Stalin and paved the way for his own attack by indicating that he was belatedly acting on Lenin's own recommendation. Lenin's fears about Stalin's rudeness were justified, Khrushchev announced.[9] And with that he proceeded to condemn Stalin, all the while contrasting his evil rule with Lenin's exemplary behavior. Lenin had governed through persuasion, Stalin through force; Lenin had ruled together with the Central Committee of the party; Stalin had been a dictator; and so on.

In the same breath with the denunciation of Stalin and the cult of the individual, Khrushchev introduced a new cult of Lenin. All legitimate party doctrine was poured back into its original Leninist vessel, a vessel that had been broken by Stalin in an extraordinary drive for power that was matched only by his overweening vanity. Khrushchev accused Stalin of a lack of respect for Lenin's memory. "Were our Party's holy Leninist principles observed after the death of Vladimir Ilich?" he asked rhetorically. And Stalin had committed the grave sin of attempting to minimize Lenin's historical significance in order to inflate his own role in revolutionary history. Stalin wanted the party to think that during the revolution and civil war, he had told Lenin what to do and how to do it. "However," Khrushchev declared, "this is slander of Lenin." Furthermore, the

Palace of Soviets, planned over thirty years earlier as a monument to Lenin, had never been built. Stalin had established the Stalin Prizes ("not even the tsars," Khrushchev observed, "created prizes they named after themselves") but the Lenin Prizes, established in 1925, had never been awarded. "This," said Khrushchev, "should be corrected (*tumultuous, prolonged applause*)."[10]

Some thirteen months before delivering this speech, Khrushchev had prepared the ground for a renewed cult of Lenin, designed not on the black-rimmed model of the twenties but on the showy and sentimental cult of Stalin. On January 11, 1955, he signed a published resolution moving the annual commemoration of Lenin from his death day to his birthday. With this act he inaugurated the slick and cloying cult of Lenin still in evidence today. The resolution provides a lucid exposition of the philosophy underlying the contemporary Lenin cult.

> After Lenin's death the tradition was established of commemorating V. I. Lenin—the great founder and wise leader of the Communist party and Soviet state on the day of his passing—21 January.
>
> In the first years after V. I. Lenin's death, this day was directly linked in the consciousness of the soviet people and Communist party with a sorrowful event—the termination of the life-path of the great leader V. I. Lenin; from this followed the solemn mournful character of the activities observing the bright memory of V. I. Lenin.[11]

The old cult was appropriate for an era that had long since disappeared. In the three decades after Lenin's death, Khrushchev observed, the party and the Soviet people, following the path blazed by Lenin and under the guidance of Stalin, had made gigantic strides toward the construction of socialism and had brought the country onto the road leading to Communism.

> Leninism is the great life-affirming teaching, illuminating the path for the construction of communism. Lenin lives in the great works of the Communist party of the Soviet Union, in the new successes of our soviet Motherland, resolutely moving on the path to communism . . .
>
> The great victories of the soviet people in the construction of a communist society are tied, in the consciousness of the peoples of our country and the workers of the entire world, with V. I. Lenin's name, with his teaching. Therefore, it is now more appropriate to

commemorate V. I. Lenin not on the day of his death, which leaves an imprint of mourning and sorrow, but on the day of his birth—22 April, making this date a holiday that will better correspond to the whole spirit of Leninism as an eternally alive, life-affirming teaching.

The CC of the CPSU resolves:

Solemnly to commemorate V. I. Lenin, the great leader of toilers and the founder of the Soviet socialist state, on the birthday of V. I. Lenin—22 April.

On this day to illuminate broadly the significance of the all-victorious ideas of Marxism-Leninism and the successes attained in the construction of communism. On the eve of the holiday to hold grand meetings of party, soviet, and public organizations, and in addition to have reports and talks about the life and work of V. I. Lenin and about the significance of the ideas of Leninism in the construction of a communist society, in all workplaces, institutions, collective and state farms.[12]

And so, on January 21, 1955, for the first time in thirty years, the press made no mention of the anniversary of Lenin's death, although *Pravda* did carry an editorial entitled "The Victorious Banner of Leninism," lauding the "founder and wise leader of the Communist party." That year, and every year thereafter, Lenin's birthday was celebrated with the requisite meetings, speeches, and attendant press campaign.

The revived cult of Lenin took shape speedily and with careful orchestration. Handbooks and bibliographies told party propagandists what to read about Lenin and once again, as in the 1920s, provided handy collections of writings by Lenin on a variety of subjects.[13] Thousands of publications about him—biographies, reminiscences, laudatory essays—quickly crowded the shelves of Soviet bookstores. Paintings, statues, busts, posters, and little badges were produced in enormous quantities, even as the once ubiquitous Staliniana was fast disappearing from the Soviet political landscape.

In 1961, Stalin himself disappeared from public display. His preserved body was removed from the Lenin-Stalin Mausoleum and buried next to it. This was the climactic moment in the history of de-Stalinization, which reached its peak of intensity in that year as millions of books from the Stalin years and countless busts and portraits were hurriedly moved into the storerooms of libraries and mu-

seums. Lenin's sacred memory and living spirit were called upon to   **259**
eject Stalin from the mausoleum. The medium who conveyed
Lenin's desire to be rid of Stalin was Dora Lazurkina, who made the
following dramatic pronouncement to the delegates of the Twenty-
Second Party Congress in 1961:

> I always carry Ilich in my heart, comrades, and have survived the
> most difficult moments only because Ilich was in my heart and I
> took counsel with him. (*Applause.*) Yesterday I took counsel with
> Ilich and he stood before me as though alive and said: "It is unpleas-
> ant for me to be beside Stalin, who brought such misfortune to the
> party." (*Stormy prolonged applause.*)[14]

In 1930, Stalin had lain Lenin to rest in the granite Lenin Mausoleum as the emerging Stalin cult gradually eclipsed and ultimately
eroded the formalized veneration of Lenin. Now, in 1961, the re-
verse process took place as the immortal Lenin arose to drive Stalin
into the nether regions of the Kremlin wall. Stalin, like the fallen
angel of *Paradise Lost,* assumed a satanic role as Lenin's spirit was
restored to its original exalted status and achieved new heights.

The Lenin cult of the 1960s was far more extensive than the cult
of the late twenties. Its forms repeated earlier ones: the ubiquitous
iconographic representations of his entire life; the idealized biographies resembling the gospels; the reverence toward Leninism as to
sacred writings; the Lenin Corners as local shrines evident in every
public institution; and the Lenin Mausoleum, which continued to
draw crowds into its inner sanctum. In scope this cult fulfilled the
dreams of the Glavpolitprosvet propagandists of 1924. They had
envisioned an ongoing celebration of Lenin that would imprint his
name, face, life story, and doctrine on every Soviet heart and
mind—at least on ceremonial occasions. The cult of the sixties was
so polished and so pervasive that it left no facet of public life un-
touched. And yet it bore such a different tone from the early cult
that a propagandist from the twenties would doubtless have found
greater similarities between the later Lenin cult and the cult of Stalin than between the two Lenin cults.

Khrushchev's cult of Lenin had been cleansed of the funerary
quality that characterized the original. It was a lavish, technicolor
production with a cast of hundreds of thousands: grand, sentimen-

260   tal, and rosy red, every bit the elaborate symphonic creation that for two decades had sung the praises of Stalin. The style in which Lenin was portrayed in the Leniniana of the sixties differed markedly from the stiff and stylized cult creations of the twenties. By and large he came to figure either as a titanic statue, grand and imposing, or as a kindly, approachable figure in soft focus. With increasing frequency he was pictured—in paintings and posters, on lacquer boxes and bric-a-brac—smiling at fluttering birds or giggling children. Stories about him emphasized his humanity, love of family, sense of humor, simplicity, accessibility.

Once again, Lenin was celebrated as an immortal. Once again, the watchword "Lenin lives!" resounded throughout Soviet Russia. But it was rarely prefaced by the reminder that Ilich had died. Pure optimism characterized all cult rituals, speeches, and articles, which linked Lenin's immortal spirit to every achievement of the Communist Party and Soviet government. Annual Lenin celebrations included poems, songs (usually written in a sprightly major key, even the song called "At the Mausoleum"), and declamations that observed the appropriateness of the fact that Lenin's birthday comes in the spring. The emphasis was not on death and salvation but on renewal and resurrection. The ice breaks on Russia's mighty rivers, the first crocuses appear (spring comes late to European Russia), and Lenin is once again reborn to lead the nation to ever greater victories.

The highlight of the yearly birthday celebrations were the parades of Young Pioneers—Lenin's "grandchildren"—sporting badges of Lenin together with bright red neckerchiefs. Indeed, the Lenin cult of the sixties placed special emphasis on the propaganda of Leninism for children. It stressed Ilich's warm love for little ones and took elaborate measures to inculcate in the future citizens of the USSR a familiarity with Lenin and the desire to resemble him in every way. He was the model for all schoolchildren, the subject of countless stories, biographies, poems, songs, projects, organized rituals, and excursions.

For children the main functions of the Lenin cult were exemplary and inspirational. But in its totality the Lenin cult was designed and maintained to serve several functions. As organized veneration of the "founder and wise leader of the Communist Party," it provided that party with legitimacy that was unassailable, not losing a beat when, in 1964, Nikita Khrushchev lost his job to Leonid Brezhnev.

The cult of the sixties was entirely standardized and regulated from above. By completely homogenizing political ritual, it served as an exercise of the party's power to require that all public activity pay heed to the officially sponsored Lenin cult. All authors, for example, had to begin, and indeed did begin, every book with some reference to Lenin. In substance this was, of course, meaningless. But its significance lay in the demonstration that the party could expect a salute from everyone who wished to see his name in print. For a tribute to Lenin was a tribute not to Lenin per se (at least not in the overwhelming majority of instances); it was a mandatory gesture of loyalty to the party and government he founded. The Lenin cult made visible and ubiquitous everything they stood for.

The cult of Lenin aimed to inspire the populace by glorifying a legendary past that would assure the realization of a legendary future—and to cover over the many disappointments of present-day life in the USSR. In the early 1960s the Lenin cult became a major Soviet export. Real competition from the People's Republic of China for the role of leader of the Communist world was still in the future, and Soviet propagandists broadcast their adulation of Lenin worldwide, just as the previous regime had expected the Communist parties of the fraternal socialist nations of East Europe to express reverence for Stalin, which they did, while at the same time imitating the Stalin cult in the emerging cults of their own leaders. In the USSR, Lenin cult propaganda often placed special emphasis on Lenin as a global figure, beloved by the oppressed people of the world. The Soviet press frequently carried photographs of visiting foreign delegations laying wreaths at the foot of the Lenin Mausoleum—the clearest and simplest ritual honor paid to the Communist Party of the Soviet Union.

In 1967, at the celebration of the fiftieth anniversary of the Russian revolution, Lenin of course figured prominently in the lavish celebrations of that event, his gargantuan face gazing above the multitude from the sides of buildings and even from the Moscow heavens, for above the city his portrait was suspended from a balloon and illuminated with lights in the dark of night. (This technique had previously been used at the commemoration of Stalin's seventieth birthday on December 21, 1949; its proximity to the Christmas season had turned Stalin's gleaming face into a Soviet

262   star of Bethlehem.) The symphonic cult of Lenin built up to a cre-
scendo as the Communist Party and Soviet government prepared to
meet its climactic moment—the hundredth anniversary of Lenin's
birth, April 22, 1970.

The Lenin jubilee was a meticulously orchestrated extravaganza,
far exceeding the campaign of 1924 that had established the nationwide cult of Lenin. The centennial's primary slogan was "Lenin is
always with us." Although the eternal nature of Lenin's spirit was its
main message, his spatial pervasiveness was its most striking aspect.
Factories, publishing houses, looms, kilns, lawns, bakeries—everything that could produce artifacts—contributed some manner of
Leniniana for the occasion. The Soviet Union became a giant display case for busts, statues, posters, poems, banners, bric-a-brac, and
commemorative volumes of every description. On April 16, 1970,
Brezhnev himself traveled to the city of Ulianovsk (formerly Simbirsk) to preside over the formal opening of the grand Lenin Memorial built for the occasion around the tiny house in which Vladimir
Ulianov was born. Six days later the Soviet newspapers, which for
weeks had carried daily exhortations to their readers to prepare for
the jubilee, published the speech Brezhnev had delivered on April
21 in the Kremlin's Palace of Congresses to the Central Committee of the party, the Supreme Soviet of the USSR, and the Supreme
Soviet of the Russian Republic. Standing against the backdrop of an
enormous profile of Lenin's head, the general secretary of the Central Committee made his speech while throughout the country thousands upon thousands of meetings involving millions of people
commemorated the centennial of Lenin's birth. Brezhnev entitled
his lengthy address, "Lenin's Cause Lives and Will Conquer."
Lenin was a genius, a titan, the founder of the party, the architect of
the Soviet government. The shimmering future will always recall
that Lenin was the founder of Communist civilization. "For a communist, a Leninist, there is nothing more sacred than to give all his
energy and will to realize the future for which Lenin fought." A
thundering standing ovation followed Brezhnev's speech, which
concluded with the familiar six-word formula taken from Maiakovsky's 1924 poem: "Lenin lived, Lenin lives, Lenin will live!"[15]

THE Lenin centennial had been intended to saturate political, civic,
and cultural life with Lenin. But the celebration was a disaster for

the credibility of Communist propaganda and political ritual. The barrage of Leniniana was so vast and unrelenting that the jubilee took on the appearance of a burlesque performance. Although it is likely that, with the exception of a tiny group of dissidents, the population at large and Communist Party members in particular had a genuine respect for Lenin's talents and a measure of admiration for his achievements, and although the Soviet tradition of marking important anniversaries with great fanfare made Lenin's centennial a unique historical event that deserved a major celebration, the Lenin jubilee had gone too far. Too many slogans and busts, too many speeches, too many articles in every periodical for months and months beforehand, and too many rhapsodic declamations to the immortal Lenin turned an event designed to evoke enthusiasm into one that provoked disdain.

The 1924 campaign had been a rally to tap the genuine popular sentiments of anxiety and sorrow unleashed by Lenin's death. But in 1970 Lenin's birth was indeed a remote event, and besides, like the cult more generally, the jubilee glorified not the birth of the person but the doctrine he had authored, the following he had inspired, the wisdom of his prophecies, and the glowing future his exemplary life had made an ultimate certainty. It was one thing for the party to make its mythology clear, available, and aesthetically pleasing. But to bombard the country with slogans, paraphernalia, and rituals that could have little meaning, with the expectation that people would be happy to jump through Lenin hoops on demand, was simply unrealistic. The observances had been fashioned to evoke expressions of loyalty, which was fine—within limits. But those limits were surely exceeded. Week in and week out in 1970, and throughout the previous year as well, there was no way to escape the ubiquitous trappings of the cult as the jubilee gained momentum. There was no place to go to avoid the reproductions of Lenin's face and figure—except home, where one could relax with friends and a bottle of something pleasant to drink, and enjoy the age-old Russian form of entertainment, the exchange of quips and jokes. In 1970, many of these made fun of the Lenin cult, a bad sign for the organizers of the jubilee.

A department store selling beds for newlyweds, it was said, was displaying a bed for three, since "Lenin is always with us." Another section of the store advertised a new brassiere called "Lenin Hills."

264   (Moscow's Sparrow Hills were named after Lenin in 1924.) A widely recounted anecdote described the results of an official contest for the best statue of Alexander Pushkin: third prize went to a statue of Lenin reading Pushkin; second prize, to a statue of Pushkin reading Lenin; and the first prize was awarded to a statue of Lenin! This story was a particular favorite among the Moscow and Leningrad intelligentsia, for it derided the invasiveness of the Lenin cult, its unwillingness to tolerate any other gods but one. The story that best illuminates the poignant discrepancy between real life in the Soviet Union and the legends fervently upheld by the cult tells of a man seeking an apartment with no success. All his letters to his party committee and even to the Central Committee remained unanswered. Finally, in desperation, he went to the Central Committee in person and asked to see Lenin. "Lenin?" exclaimed the astonished receptionist, "but Lenin died in 1924!" "How come," the old man muttered, "when *you* need him, he's alive, but when *I* need him, he's dead?"

That the authorities were aware that the centennial celebration had exceeded tolerable bounds is clear from the speed with which they moved to reduce the frequency and high-pitched tone of the rituals. Obviously they must have intended to ease up on the Lenin theme after April 23, 1970, but the reduction of the cult was particularly marked and sharp. During the 1970s, even the yearly celebrations marking Lenin's birthday were palpably more modest than those of the previous decade. The author of a Soviet book on Communist ritual explains that the modesty of the Lenin holidays is meant to reflect Ilich's own simplicity.[16] But it seems clear that Soviet propagandists had learned the virtues of moderation only after the 1970 fiasco. That event seems to have made it impossible to rekindle popular interest in most Lenin cult rituals, even once a year.

The 108th anniversary of Lenin's birth in 1978, for example, was a dull and dreary event. It fell on a Saturday, and throughout the Soviet Union people participated in the yearly Lenin subbotnik, the day of labor given to the state (the subbotnik occurs annually on the Saturday closest to Lenin's birthday). In Ulianovsk, a provincial city in which the Lenin celebration is *the* event of the year, town residents began sweeping streets and tending public gardens early on the morning of April 22. The previous evening, the Ulianovsk city committee of the Communist Party and the executive committee of the city Soviet of People's Deputies had held its annual grand celebration in honor of Lenin's birthday. The elegant big hall of the Lenin Memorial, with its polished paneled walls and plush red seats, was filled with invited representatives of party, soviet, trade union, and Komsomol organizations, as well as a delegation of military officers.[17]

It was a supremely boring evening. Party and government dignitaries sat at a long table on the stage as the regional party secretary droned on about Lenin. The dignitaries were so visibly bored that they whispered to each other throughout the speech, and one actually fell asleep, awaking with a start every now and again. Only the first five minutes of the speech concerned Lenin; the secretary quickly moved on to detailing Soviet achievements and finally to railing at Jimmy Carter and the neutron bomb. Indeed, although a huge portrait of Lenin was hung on the wall behind the dais, Lenin himself received little attention at this official gathering commemorating his birth. There was a short dramatic reading about him and the performance of some of his favorite songs, but most of the evening was devoted to a concert of songs and folk dances.

Similarly, the Ulianovsk parade of Young Pioneers held on April 22 was poorly attended and uninspired. A child read a poem about Lenin coming to us at springtime together with the flowers, and balloons of many colors enlivened the huge city square, but on the whole the event was stale and routine. Most aspects of the contemporary Lenin cult have become as empty as the benches set up for the Ulianovsk Pioneers' parade. On the weekend of Lenin's birthday, the well-appointed Lenin Memorial in Ulianovsk had only a moderate number of visitors, most of them groups of tourists from East Europe. Happily for the tourist, Volodia Ulianov was born near the Volga River, and the memorial constructed around his birthplace has a lovely location, looking out on the mighty river and a huge expanse of sky. The museum is filled with displays of Lenin relics. But the heart of the memorial is the Hall of Ceremonies. On its walls glitter a vibrant mosaic of red bands, golden rays, and a hammer and sickle. In the center is a huge white marble statue of Lenin before which initiation rituals are enacted by new members of the Young Pioneers, the Komsomol, and the Red army.

The Lenin museums in Moscow and Leningrad serve these same political functions. Groups of youngsters in white blouses fidget

266   nervously while older children tie red kerchiefs around their necks to mark their admission into the Young Pioneers. The children then raise their right arms before a statue of Lenin and swear to be true to the "precepts of Ilich." This is mandatory cult ritual, and the children are often accompanied by their parents, but few people come simply to visit Lenin museums except in organized groups on guided tours. Packs of schoolchildren, for example, trot through the Central Lenin Museum in Moscow, stopping to listen to the guide intone tired praises of young Ulianov's excellent study habits, as they all gaze at a reproduction of the honor-roll certificate from the Simbirsk gimnazium with Ulianov's name on it.

Cult museums attract few individual visitors, and bookstores cannot find buyers for Lenin's writings, phonograph records of his speeches, or busts that come in all sizes. College students proudly boast to foreigners that they make it a point to forget promptly everything they must learn about Lenin and Leninism in their required courses. The iconographic representations of Lenin, the sacred writings, the commemorative meetings, and the grand Lenin museums appear to evoke little enthusiasm in the contemporary populace.

But some cult rituals and sites do function with evident effectiveness. The cult of Lenin for children is as intense and high-pitched as ever. Journals on the Communist upbringing of children abound with articles on how best to inspire a love for Lenin in little ones, who are deluged from the earliest grades with stories and projects about Lenin. They cannot but be impressed by the legendary Ilich who forms such an important part of their school program.

And there are Lenin shrines that attract crowds of visibly interested visitors. One of these is his boyhood home on old Moscow Street (now Lenin Street) in Ulianovsk. There visitors are allowed only in groups, and some of them appear genuinely animated as they shuffle past the cordoned-off rooms in outsized canvas slippers tied over their shoes (to protect the floor). The house is furnished to approximate the original decor of the Ulianov household during the time of the family's residence there, 1878–1887. The tour guides tell anecdotes about young Vladimir Ulianov and his family, and there is none of the usual concomitant lecturing on party history. This, combined with the personal aura that infuses an actual residence, helps differentiate the house-museum from other Lenin museums. The house in which Lenin died, located in Gorki, some thirty kilometers from Moscow, is a museum that successfully communicates a mood of extreme solemnity, and visitors exhibit the appropriate deportment.

Without a doubt, the most successfully functioning pilgrimage site of the Lenin cult is the stately Lenin Mausoleum in Moscow. It is the central locus of political ritual. Party and government leaders gather on its tribunal on revolutionary holidays. It also serves as an official spiritual center. Contemporary Soviet writings on the Lenin Mausoleum call it a "sacred" place that "provides an inexhaustible source of revolutionary energy."[18] It is to the mausoleum that Soviet cosmonauts come before their space flights to gather courage, and after their return to give thanks. And it is customary for newlyweds to lay flowers outside the mausoleum directly after their weddings. The demeanor of visitors to the mausoleum is serious and respectful. Even during the long wait most stand silently or chat in low tones, and admonish restless children who skip and jump to relieve the tedium. Once inside the mausoleum, all eyes are riveted on the body that rests, awash in light, on an ornate bier in the center of a dark gray chamber. Since its completion in 1930, tens of millions of visitors have patiently waited on long queues for their permitted eighty seconds with the embalmed body of the founder of Bolshevism.

WESTERN observers have typically derided the Lenin cult on the grounds that it is the secular religion of a state that professes atheism. But surely one can find in the Soviet system of government—as in other systems—far more glaring incongruities between action and profession. The cult of Lenin developed during a desperately confused period in early Soviet history. Its story is at once rational and bizarre, funny and tragic, vulgar and, if not sublime, then at least supremely human. After all, ritual has always and everywhere played an important role in politics. What country has not venerated its past heroes?

The Lenin cult celebrates a dead leader rather than a living one, and this distinguishes it from those of most other Communist leaders because the real Lenin is not able to abuse the enormous power with which he has been imbued. His cult therefore seems extravagant and primitive, but harmless. And yet the Lenin cult is called upon to legitimize Soviet policy and to glorify the fatherland with

268   all its defects; indeed the cult is meant to provide the vision of a higher reality that obliterates the need to confront those defects. This intention is expressed in the widespread slogan: "Lenin is more alive than all the living."[19] In an odd way the Lenin cult provides a dramatic reversal to Oscar Wilde's *The Picture of Dorian Gray*. In that story a man retains his youthful beauty while his portrait gradually takes on the ugly marks of his sordid life. The cult of Lenin celebrates an immortal exemplary leader, while his living successors in the Kremlin bear the burdens of age and of power.

Notes

Selected Bibliography

Index

Notes

1. Russian Roots of the Lenin Cult

1. "Vae, puto deus fio." Robert Graves's translation of Suetonius reads: "Dear me! I must be turning into a god." *The Twelve Caesars* (London, 1957), p. 261.

2. Lily Ross Taylor, *The Divinity of the Roman Emperor* (Middletown, Conn., 1931), pp. 53–57. See also L. Cerfaux and J. Tondriau, *Le Culte des souverains dans la civilisation gréco-romaine: un concurrant du christianisme* (Tournai, 1957). See also Keith Hopkins, *Conquerors and Slaves* (Cambridge, Eng., 1978).

3. Taylor, *Divinity of the Roman Emperor*, pp. 7–8. See also L. R. Farnell, *Greek Hero Cults and Ideas of Immortality* (Oxford, 1921).

4. Crane Brinton, *A Decade of Revolution, 1789–1799* (New York and London, 1934), p. 157.

5. Quoted in Seymour Martin Lipset, *The First New Nation* (New York, 1963), p. 21.

6. Marcus Cunliffe, *George Washington, Man and Monument* (New York and Toronto, 1958), p. 21.

7. I have drawn on the definition of religion formulated by Clifford Geertz in *The Interpretation of Cultures* (New York, 1973), pp. 87–125.

8. Stepniak [S. M. Kravchinskii], *The Russian Peasantry: Their Agrarian Condition, Social Life and Religion* (New York, 1888), p. 218.

9. Vasilii Vasil'ev, "Istoriia kanonizatsii russkikh sviatykh," *Chteniia v Imperatorskom Obshchestve istorii i drevnostei rossiiskikh pri Moskovskom universitete*, III.166 (1893), p. 10.

10. E. Golubinskii, *Prepodobnyi Sergei Radonezhskii i sozdannaia im Troitskaia Lavra* (Moscow, 1892), pp. 36–37.

11. E. Golubinskii, *Istoriia kanonizatsii sviatykh v russkoi tserkvi* (Moscow, 1903), p. 302.

12. Fyodor Dostoevsky, *The Brothers Karamazov*, trans. David Magarshak, (Baltimore, 1958), II, 386.

13. Michael Cherniavsky, *Tsar and People: Studies in Russian Myths* (London and New Haven, 1961), pp. 13–14.

272

14. George P. Fedotov, *The Russian Religious Mind* (New York, 1960), pp. 105, 110.

15. Ernst H. Kantorowicz, *The King's Two Bodies: A Study in Medieval Theology* (Princeton, 1957), pp. 7–9, citing Edmund Plowden, *Commentaries or Reports* (London, 1816), 212a and 213.

16. On the influence of Agapetus on Russian monarchical theory, see Ihor Ševčenko, "A Neglected Byzantine Source of Muscovite Political Ideology," in Michael Cherniavsky, ed., *The Structure of Russian History* (New York, 1970), pp. 80–107. Cited quotation appears on p. 83.

17. For a stimulating discussion of naive monarchism, see Daniel Field, *Rebels in the Name of the Tsar* (Boston, 1976), pp. 1–29.

18. Ibid., pp. 17–18.

19. Cited in ibid., p. 1.

20. Michael Cherniavsky, "The Old Believers and the New Religion," *Slavic Review,* 25 (March 1966), 1–39.

21. For a discussion of the "just" tsar in Russian folklore, see V. K. Sokolova, *Russkie istoricheskie predaniia* (Moscow, 1970), chap. 3.

22. Field, *Rebels,* p. 5.

23. Ibid., p. 12.

24. Iu. M. Sokolov, *Russkii fol'klor* (Moscow, 1941), p. 354.

25. Ibid., p. 353.

26. For the Kuz'mich legend, see Lev Liubimov, *Taina Imperatora Aleksandra I* (Paris, 1938). See also his "Taina startsa Fedora Kuz'micha," *Voprosy istorii,* no. 1, 1966, pp. 209–215.

27. D. N. Loman, *Tsar' osvoboditel', tsar'-muchenik Imperator Aleksandr II. Chtenie dlia naroda* (St. Petersburg, 1898).

28. *Pribavleniia k tserkovnym vedomostiam,* no. 30, July 26, 1903, p. 1127.

29. This is one of the main themes of Daniel Field's *Rebels.*

30. Walter Sablinsky, *The Road to Bloody Sunday: Father Gapon and the St. Petersburg Massacre of 1905* (Princeton, 1976), p. 346.

31. Field suggests that the monarchy was not able to use it effectively even before 1905.

32. I. A. Bunin, *Okaiannye dni* (Berlin, 1935), p. 58.

33. Isaiah Berlin, *Russian Thinkers* (New York, 1978), p. 124.

34. Anna Akhmatova, *Stikhi i proza* (Leningrad, 1977), p. 18.

35. Konstantin Mochulsky, *Dostoevsky, His Life and Work* (Princeton, 1967), p. 639.

36. The phrase, by N. A. Ishutin, is quoted in Franco Venturi, *Roots of Revolution* (New York, 1960), p. 331.

37. Nikolai Valentinov (N. V. Vol'skii), *The Early Years of Lenin,* trans. Rolf H. W. Theen (Ann Arbor, 1969), p. 135.

38. Ibid., p. 10.

39. Quoted in ibid., p. 199.

40. Ibid., p. 98.

41. Richard Stites, *The Women's Liberation Movement in Russia* (Princeton, 1978), p. 144.

42. Valentinov, *Early Years*, pp. 104–105.

43. Nicolas Berdyaev, *The Origin of Russian Communism* (Ann Arbor, Michigan, 1960), p. 90.

44. James H. Billington, *The Icon and the Axe: An Interpretive History of Russian Culture* (New York, 1966), p. 504.

45. *The Oxford Book of Russian Verse* (Oxford, 1947), p. 221.

46. Alexander Blok, *Selected Poems*, intro. and ed. Avril Pyman (Oxford, 1972), p. 182.

47. For an imaginative essay on Fedorov, see Peter Wiles, "On Physical Immortality," *Survey*, 56 (July 1965), 125–143; 57 (October 1965), 142–161. For an essay that observes the influence of Fedorov in the Soviet period, see S. V. Utechin, "Bolsheviks and their Allies after 1917: The Ideological Pattern," *Soviet Studies*, 10 (October 1958), 129–135.

48. N. Fedorov, *Filosofiia obshchago dela*, ed. V. A. Kozhevnikov and N. P. Peterson (Moscow, 1913), III, 7.

49. The resolution also charged V. D. Bonch-Bruevich with editing a newspaper entitled *Sredi sektantov* (Among Sectarians). V. I. Lenin, *Sochineniia*, 4th ed., vol. 6 (Moscow, 1946), p. 431.

50. *Rassvet*, no. 1 (Geneva, 1904).

51. N. Valentinov, *Vstrechi s Leninym* (New York, 1953), pp. 217–218.

52. For two excellent articles concerning Lunacharsky and *bogostroitel'stvo*, see Jutta Scherrer, "La Crise de l'intelligentsia marxiste avant 1914: A. V. Lunačarskij et le *bogostroitel'stvo*," *Revue des Etudes slaves*, 51.1–2 (1979), 207–215; and "Culture prolétarienne et religion socialiste entre deux révolutions: les 'Bolcheviks de gauche'," *Europa*, 2.2 (Spring 1979), 67–90.

53. George L. Kline, *Religious and Anti-Religious Thought in Russia* (Chicago and London, 1968), pp. 116–117; Sheila Fitzpatrick, *The Commissariat of Enlightenment* (Cambridge, Eng., 1970), pp. 2–3.

54. A. V. Lunacharskii, *Velikii perevorot* (Petrograd, 1919), p. 31.

55. Ibid., p. 30.

56. Ibid., p. 18.

57. A. V. Lunacharskii, "Osnovy pozitivnoi estetiki," *Ocherki realisticheskogo mirovozzreniia*, ed. S. Doratovskii and A. Charushnikov (St. Petersburg, 1904), pp. 181–182.

58. A. Lunacharskii, *Religiia i sotsializm* (St. Petersburg, 1911), II, 228.

59. A. Lunacharskii, "Budushchee religii," *Obrazovanie*, no. 10, 1907, p. 14.

60. Fitzpatrick, *Commissariat*, pp. 3–4.

61. A. Lunacharskii, *Religiia i sotsializm* (St. Petersburg, 1908), I, 228.

62. Lunacharskii, "Budushchee religii," p. 23.

63. Lunacharskii, *Religiia i sotsializm*, I, 104.

64. Lunacharskii, *Velikii perevorot*, p. 31.

65. A. V. Lunacharskii, "Eshche o teatre i sotsializme," *Vershiny* (St. Petersburg, 1909), p. 213, cited in Kline, *Religious and Anti-Religious Thought*, p. 120.

66. Robert C. Williams, "Collective Immortality: The Syndicalist Origins of Proletarian Culture, 1905–1910," *Slavic Review*, 39 (September 1980), 390.

274 67. Letter, Lenin to Gor'kii, November 13 or 14, 1913, in V. I. Lenin, *Polnoe sobranie sochineniia,* 5th ed., vol. 48 (Moscow, 1970), p. 228.

2. Vladimir Ilich Ulianov-Lenin

1. Nikolai Valentinov (N. V. Vol'skii), *The Early Years of Lenin,* pp. 9–10.
2. N. Valentinov (N. V. Vol'skii), *Vstrechi s Leninym,* pp. 158–159.
3. A. Elizarova, "Vospominaniia ob Aleksandre Il'iche Ul'ianove," part 1, *Proletarskaia revoliutsiia,* no. 1, 1927, p. 89.
4. Valentinov, *Early Years,* p. 17.
5. A. Elizarova, "Vospominaniia ob Aleksandre Il'iche Ul'ianove," part 2, *Proletarskaia revoliutsiia,* no. 2–3, 1927, p. 285.
6. Valentinov, *Vstrechi s Leninym,* pp. 90–91.
7. Elizarova, "Vospominaniia," pp. 285–287.
8. D. Delarov, "Kak ia poznakomilsia s sem'ei Ul'ianovykh," *Sever* (Vologda), no. 1, 1924, p. xvi.
9. Elizarova, "Vospominaniia," pp. 95–96.
10. I. Kh. Laliants, "O moikh vstrechakh s V. I. Leninym za vremia 1893–1900," *Proletarskaia revoliutsiia,* no. 1, 1929, p. 49.
11. *A. I. Ulianov. Sbornik* (Moscow, 1927), p. 346.
12. Valentinov, *Vstrechi s Leninym,* p. 108.
13. Ibid., pp. 107–108.
14. Ibid., p. 107.
15. A. G. Rashin, *Formirovanie rabochego klassa Rossii* (Moscow, 1958), pp. 24–25.
16. The only accurate translation for this appellation would be "adherents of the defunct People's Will organization," so it is best to use the Russian term.
17. Letter to F. Sorge, November 5, 1980, in Karl Marx and Friedrich Engels, *Werke,* vol. 34 (Berlin, 1966), p. 447, cited in Richard Pipes, *Struve: Liberal on the Left, 1870–1905* (Cambridge, 1970), p. 46. Marx's Russian translators were G. A. Lopatin and N. F. Danielson.
18. V. I. Lenin, "Chto delat'?" *Polnoe sobranie sochinenii,* 5th ed., vol. 6, pp. 180–181.
19. Richard Pipes, "The Origins of Bolshevism: The Intellectual Evolution of Young Lenin," in Richard Pipes, ed., *Revolutionary Russia* (Cambridge, 1968), p. 29n.
20. Ibid., p. 32n.
21. Ibid., p. 34; for sources on Skliarenko, see p. 34n.
22. V. V. Vodovozov, "Moe znakomstvo s Leninym," *Na chuzhoi storone,* no. 12, 1925, p. 176.
23. Ibid.
24. Pipes, "Origins of Bolshevism," pp. 36–37.
25. Vodovozov, "Moe znakomstvo," p. 176. In 1903 in Kiev he continued to voice the same prediction to Valentinov (Valentinov, *Early Years,* p. 156).
26. Vodovozov, "Moe znakomstvo," p. 176.

27. Richard Pipes, *Social Democracy and the St. Petersburg Labor Move-* **275** *ment, 1885–1897* (Cambridge, 1963), p. 44.

28. G. M. Krzhizhanovskii, *O Vladimire Il'iche* (Moscow, 1924), pp. 12–13.

29. Pipes, *Social Democracy*, pp. 53–54.

30. Lenin, "Kak chut' ne potukhla 'Iskra'?" *Polnoe sobranie sochinenii*, vol. 4, pp. 334–335. See a thoughtful discussion of the incident in Leopold H. Haimson, *The Russian Marxists and the Origins of Bolshevism* (Cambridge, 1955), pp. 139–141.

31. Lenin, "Kat chut' ne potukhla 'Iskra'?" pp. 346–347.

32. Lenin, "Chto delat'?" pp. 106–107, 127.

33. Valentinov, *Vstrechi s Leninym*, pp. 54–55.

34. Lenin, "Chto delat'?" p. 24.

35. Bruce Mazlish, *The Revolutionary Ascetic* (New York, 1976), pp. 111–156.

36. Adam Ulam, *The Bolsheviks* (New York, 1965), p. 171.

37. Krzhizhanovskii, *O Vladimire Il'iche*, pp. 8, 26.

38. Mazlish contends that Lenin's unrelenting insistence on constant work was his self-cure for the Oblomovism from which he—like all Russians—suffered. *Revolutionary Ascetic*, p. 144.

39. Lenin, *Polnoe sobranie sochinenii*, vol. 47, p. 10.

40. Krupskaia later recalled how hard Lenin found it to break with Martov. N. K. Krupskaia, *O Lenine: Stat'i i rechi*, comp. Liudmila Stal' (Moscow, 1925), p. 47.

41. A. N. Potresov, "Lenin," *Posmertnyi sbornik proizvedenii* (Paris, 1937), pp. 301–302.

42. Every book on CPSU history and every biography of Lenin contains some account of this event. To name but a few, see Leonard Schapiro, *The Communist Party of the Soviet Union* (New York, 1964), pp. 46–53; Haimson, *The Russian Marxists and the Origins of Bolshevism*, pp. 171–181; J.L.H. Keep, *The Rise of Social Democracy in Russia* (Oxford, 1963), pp. 107–148; Ulam, *The Bolsheviks*, pp. 187–193.

43. Leon Trotsky, *My Life* (New York, 1930), p. 163.

44. A. V. Lunacharskii, *Velikii perevorot*, p. 59. This collection of essays on revolutionary leaders was reprinted, with changes, in 1923 under the title *Revoliutsionnye siluety* (Revolutionary Silhouettes).

45. Trotsky, *My Life*, p. 163.

46. Lunacharskii, *Velikii perevorot*, p. 60.

47. Krzhizhanovskii, *O Vladimire Il'iche*, p. 7. To Lunacharskii, Krzhizhanovskii described Lenin as looking like a "prosperous peasant from Iaroslavl, especially when he is sporting a beard." Lunacharskii, *Velikii perevorot*, p. 61.

48. Valentinov, *Vstrechi s Leninym*, pp. 79, 72–73. According to Valentinov, the appellation *starik* (old man) was an expression of deference to the thirty-four-year-old Lenin. It is conceivable that the term was left over from the identical appellation used to identify the members of Radchenko's St. Petersburg circle in the mid-1890s. In any event, whatever the origin of its use, by 1904 in Valen-

276 tinov's view *starik* was used by Lenin's followers in its Russian sense, to imply wisdom and greatness of spirit.

49. Ibid., p. 75.
50. Lunacharskii, *Velikii perevorot*, p. 66.
51. Potresov, "Lenin," p. 302.
52. Lunacharskii, *Velikii perevorot*, p. 68.
53. Ibid., pp. 67–68.
54. Robert C. Tucker, *The Lenin Anthology* (New York, 1975), p. 195.
55. Ibid., p. 291.
56. Robert C. Tucker suggests that Lenin's powers of persuasion were in fact the real source of his charismatic authority as a revolutionary leader. *Stalin as Revolutionary, 1879–1929: A Study in History and Personality* (New York, 1973), pp. 32–47.
57. Alexander Rabinowitch, *The Bolsheviks Come to Power* (New York, 1978), p. 14. This book makes a most convincing argument about the lack of unity among the Bolsheviks in the summer and fall of 1917.
58. Tucker, *The Lenin Anthology*, p. 313.
59. Rabinowitch, *The Bolsheviks Come to Power*, pp. 178–181, 187.
60. Vladimir Maiakovskii, *Vladimir Il'ich Lenin* (Moscow, 1967), p. 126.
61. See Michael Cherniavsky, ed. and trans., *Prologue to Revolution: Notes of A. N. Iakhontov on the Secret Meetings of the Council of Ministers, 1915* (Englewood Cliffs, 1967).
62. Aleksandr Blok, "Poslednie dni starogo rezhima," *Arkhiv russkoi revoliutsii* (Berlin, 1922) IV, pp. 28–29.
63. Cult lore abounds with memoirs of visits with "Il'ich." For two early ones see "U t. Lenina," *Bednota*, April 23, 1920, and A. I. Gusev, *V gostiakh u Vladimira Il'icha* (Tver, 1921).
64. V. D. Bonch-Bruevich, *Vospominaniia o Lenine* (Moscow, 1965), p. 225.
65. Ibid., pp. 221–222.
66. *Deviatyi s"ezd RKP(b). Protokoly* (Moscow, 1960), p. 184.
67. *Vos'moi s"ezd RKP(b). Protokoly* (Moscow, 1959), p. 182.
68. He held V. R. Menzhinskii by a coat button until the future commissar of finance agreed to accept that post. G. Lomov, "V dni buri i natiska," *Proletarskaia revoliutsiia*, no. 10, 1927, p. 172, cited in T. H. Rigby, *Lenin's Government*, (Cambridge, Eng., 1979), p. 122.
69. Rigby, *Lenin's Government*, pp. 65, 109.
70. Ibid., p. 108.
71. Ibid., p. 112.
72. A. Elizarova, "Stranichka vospominanii o Vladimire Il'iche v Sovnarkome," *Proletarskaia revoliutsiia*, no. 11, 1929, p. 89, cited in Rigby, *Lenin's Government*, p. 75.
73. Rigby, *Lenin's Government*, p. 221.
74. Valentinov, *Vstrechi s Leninym*, p. 86.
75. Ulam, *The Bolsheviks*, p. 442.
76. Maria Ilinichna made this statement on January 28, 1924. *Rabochaia Moskva*, January 30, 1924, p. 3.

77. V. I. Lenin, *Sochineniia*, 4th ed., vol. 35 (Moscow, 1950), p. 272.

78. Lenin, *Polnoe sobranie sochinenii*, vol. 37, p. 91.

3. Lenin in Bolshevik Myth, 1917–1922

1. Flysheet versions of the signed decree on land can be seen in the Central Museum of the Revolution in Moscow.

2. Paul Avrich, *Kronstadt 1921* (New York, 1970), p. 12.

3. Lenin, "Chto delat'?" *Polnoe sobranie sochinenii*, vol. 6, pp. 66–67.

4. *Partiino-politicheskaia rabota v krasnoi armii (aprel' 1918–fevral' 1919)*, *Dokumenty* (Moscow, 1961), p. 15; Schapiro, *Communist Party*, pp. 246–247; N. Krupskaia, "Perspektivy politprosvetraboty," *Kommunisticheskoe prosveshchenie*, no. 1, 1922, p. 5.

5. *Agitatsionno-massovoe iskusstvo pervykh let Oktiabria* (Moscow, 1971), pp. 13, 67. See also Richard Stites, "Iconoclasm in the Russian Revolution: Destroying and Preserving the Past," Occasional Paper 147 (1981), Kennan Institute for Advanced Russian Studies, The Wilson Center, Washington, D.C. (unpublished).

6. Lenin, *Polnoe sobranie sochinenii*, vol. 50, pp. 422–423.

7. Ibid., p. 182.

8. L. F. Volkov-Lannit, *Lenin v fotoiskusstve* (Moscow, 1967), p. 106.

9. Lenin, *Polnoe sobranie sochinenii*, vol. 37, pp. 169–172.

10. *Agitatsionno-massovoe iskusstvo*, photograph 50.

11. Maksim Gor'kii, *O russkom krest'ianstve* (Berlin, 1922), pp. 14–15.

12. Lenin, *Polnoe sobranie sochinenii*, vol. 38, p. 79.

13. Charles Sargent Sampson, "The Formative Years of the Soviet Press. An Institutional History," Ph.D. dissertation (University of Massachusetts, Amherst, 1970), p. 93.

14. In fact, it was tiring. She made thirty-four speeches in two months.

15. N. K. Krupskaia, "Na krasnoi zvezde" in her *Pedagogicheskie sochineniia*, vol. 1 (Moscow, 1957), p. 66. For additional information on Krupskaia's summer on the *Red Star* see N. Krupskaia, "Po gradam i vesiam sovetskoi respubliki," *Novyi mir*, no. 11, 1960, pp. 113–130; E. Gerasimov, "Nesluchainye vstrechi," ibid., pp. 131–156; V. P. Voznesenskii, "Na 'Krasnoi Zvezde'," *Vospominaniia o N. K. Krupskoi* (Moscow, 1966), pp. 180–185; S. M. Levidova and S. A. Pavlotskaia, *Nadezhda Konstantinovna Krupskaia* (Leningrad, 1962), pp. 148–162.

16. My discussion of agitation during the civil war is based largely on documents and posters on deposit in the Central Museum of the Revolution, Moscow.

17. "Desiat' zapovedei proletariia," Document no. 12160/4 L113-20 V.b. (Moscow, 1918), Central Museum of the Revolution, Moscow.

18. B. S. Butnik-Siverskii, *Sovetskii plakat epokhi grazhdanskoi voiny 1918-1921* (Moscow, 1960).

19. Document no. 11843/36 L113.20.ch.a. (Moscow, 1918), Central Museum of the Revolution, Moscow.

20. Document no. 11914/9 L113-11L (Moscow, 1918), Central Museum of the Revolution, Moscow.

278

21. Butnik-Siverskii, *Sovetskii plakat,* pp. 598, 588, 612.

22. Krupskaia, "Perspektivy politprosvetraboty," p. 5.

23. S. Ingulov, "Zadachi i perspektivy nashei agitatsii," *Kommunisticheskoe prosveshchenie,* no. 2, 1922, p. 9.

24. See the excellent discussion of this subject in Moshe Lewin, *Lenin's Last Struggle* (New York, 1970), pp. 3–19.

25. Ingulov, "Zadachi i perspektivy," p. 7.

26. Krupskaia, "Perspektivy politprosvetraboty," p. 7.

27. M. N. Goder, "Osnovy obucheniia vzroslykh," *Kommunisticheskoe prosveshchenie,* no. 1, 1922, p. 63.

28. See, for example, the speeches by Smilga, Bubnov, and Glebov in *Shestoi s"ezd RSDRP (bol'shevikov) avgust 1917 goda. Protokoly* (Moscow, 1958), pp. 131, 139, 230.

29. Ibid., p. 121.

30. Ibid., pp. 2–3, 5.

31. Document no. 17637/57b L111-11K, Central Museum of the Revolution, Moscow.

32. M. S. Ol'minskii, "O t. Lenine," *Sotsial-demokrat,* May 26, 1917.

33. M. S. Ol'minskii, "Tov. Lenin," *Vestnik zhizni,* no. 2, 1918, pp. 8–14, reprinted in *Proletarskaia revoliutsiia,* 3(26), 1924, pp. 24–33. For a discussion of this article see pp. 87–88.

34. "Stranichka iz istorii partii," *Soldatskaia pravda* no. 26(13), May 1917, reprinted in *Zapiski Instituta Lenina,* no. 2, 1927, pp. 148–154. The reprint includes phrases that Lenin had crossed out and makes note of those added in his handwriting.

35. It was first published in *Pravda,* April 16, 1927. It appears in his *Polnoe sobranie sochinenii,* vol. 32, p. 21.

36. This suggestion is made by R. M. Savitskaia in "Razrabotka nauchnoi biografii V.I. Lenina," *Voprosy istorii,* no. 4, 1971, p. 4.

37. The foreword appeared in both the American (1922) and the Russian (1923) editions. John Reed, *Ten Days That Shook the World* (New York, 1967, p. xxiv).

38. Ibid., p. 45. Reed uses the Western, Gregorian dating system. I use the Russian, Julian calendar until February 1918, when Soviet Russia adopted the Western system.

39. Ibid., p. 86.

40. Ibid., pp. 125–127.

41. N. K. Krupskaia, "Lenin v 1917 godu," *O Lenine, Sbornik stat'ei i vystuplenii* (Moscow, 1965), p. 54. This article, first published in 1960 (*Izvestiia,* January 20), is a speech delivered by Krupskaia in 1934 at a meeting of students and teachers.

42. M. S. Nappel'baum took the photograph for a collection of Lenin's selected writings published by the Central Committee. Volkov-Lannit, *Lenin v fotoiskusstve,* p. 82.

43. Poster no. 37428-45 (1918), Lenin Library, Moscow.

44. Butnik-Siverskii, *Sovetskii plakat,* p. 688.

45. "Vladimir Ul'ianov (N. Lenin)," *Izvestiia,* November 5, 1917.　　**279**
46. Leontii Kotomka (Zelenskii), "Bortsu," *Pravda,* October 29, 1917.
47. B. Gantsev, "Privet narodnomu vozhdiu," *Soldatskaia pravda,* November 18, 1917, cited in *Lenin v sovetskoi poezii* (Leningrad, 1970), p. 63.
48. *Pravda,* May 4, 1918.
49. Bonch-Bruevich, *Vospominaniia,* p. 318.
50. See, for example, *Petrogradskaia pravda,* August 31, 1918; *Krasnaia gazeta,* August 31, 1918.
51. *Krasnaia gazeta* and *Izvestiia,* August 31, 1918.
52. L. D. Trotskii, "O ranenom," *O Lenine, materialy dlia biografa* (Moscow, n.d.), pp. 151–156. This book has appeared in English translation as Leon Trotsky, *Lenin: Notes for a Biographer,* trans. Tamara Deutscher (New York, 1971).
53. L. Kamenev and L. Trotskii, *Vozhd' proletariata* (Moscow, 1918).
54. L. V. Bulgakova, comp., *Materialy dlia bibliografii Lenina 1917–1923* (Leningrad, 1924), p. 203. The speech was also published simultaneously in French, German, and English. G. Zinov'ev, *Sochineniia,* vol. 15 (Leningrad, 1924), p. 297.
55. This misleading statement was edited out of the later edition of the speech published in 1924 in Zinoviev's collected works, vol. 15, pp. 5–50.
56. Lenin always lived in physical comfort during his emigré years. His Paris apartment in particular was large, light, and elegant. N. Valentinov, *Maloznakomyi Lenin* (Paris, 1972), 59–64.
57. L. Sosnovskii, "K pokusheniiu na tov. Lenina," *Petrogradskaia pravda,* September 1, 1918.
58. Akim Stradaiushchii, "V. Leninu," *Bednota,* September 11, 1918.
59. G. Gulov, "Dorogomu tovarishchu Leninu," *Bednota,* September 17, 1918.
60. F. K–v, "Mirovomu vozhdiu proletariata V. I. Leninu," *Bednota,* September 12, 1918.
61. Iona Brikhnichev, "V. I. Leninu," *Proletarskii sbornik,* bk. 1 (Moscow, 1918), p. 18, cited in M.E.O., "Vozhd' mirovoi revoliutsii. Vladimir Il'ich Ul'ianov Lenin," *Zheleznyi put',* no. 8, March 1919, p. 4.
62. N. Al–ov, "Takova volia proletariata," *Okar'* (Organ moskovskogo okskago oblastnogo komiteta), September 6, 1918.
63. I. Lipatnikov, "Udar v serdtse," *Vestnik glavnago voenno-revoliutsionnago komiteta Moskovsko-Kievo-Voronezhskoi zheleznoi dorogi,* September 9, 1918, p. 1.
64. M. Ol'minskii, "Tov. Lenin," *Vestnik zhizni,* no. 2, 1918, pp. 8–14.
65. E. Iaroslavskii, *Velikii vozhd' rabochei revoliutsii* (Moscow, 1918), pp. 3, 4, 12, 14.
66. The Socialist Revolutionary Party polled more than 50 percent of the vote in the elections to the Constituent Assembly in the fall of 1917.
67. A. M...v [Mitrofanov], *Vozhd' derevenskoi bednoty, V. I. Ul'ianov-Lenin* (Moscow, 1918), p. 14.
68. Bonch-Bruevich attempted to hide the process from Lenin, in view of

280　the leader's reluctance to be photographed, but the photographers managed to make themselves visible and Lenin demanded an explanation of why those men were running down the street with cameras on their shoulders. Bonch-Bruevich, *Vospominaniia,* pp. 358–363.

69. At present it is shown hourly in the Central Lenin Museum in Moscow along with other documentary film clips of Lenin.

70. Bonch-Bruevich, *Vospominaniia,* pp. 337–340.

71. L. Seifullina, "Muzhitskii skaz o Lenine," *Krasnaia nov',* no. 1 (18), January-February 1924, p. 167.

72. The diminutive Mikolashka referred to Nicholas. Peasants often confused the letters "m" and "n." Thus they frequently called an automobile "autonobile" (*avtonobil'*). A. M. Selishchev, *Iazyk revoliutsionnoi epokhi* (Moscow, 1928), p. 214.

73. The Russian phrase: "Neizvestnogo on chinu-zvaniia, bez pashportu, a po prozvaniiu Lenin."

74. Seifullina, "Muzhitskii skaz o Lenine," pp. 162–169.

75. *Izvestiia,* September 3, 1918.

76. "Derevenskaia bednota o tov. Lenine," *Petrogradskaia pravda,* September 21, 1918.

77. M. E., "Ne umiraet solntse," *Tvorchestvo,* no. 7, November 1918, pp. 22–25.

78. M.E.O., "Vozhd' mirovoi revoliutsii. Vladimir Il'ich Ul'ianov Lenin," p. 2.

79. Lunacharskii, *Velikii perevorot,* p. 66.

80. Ibid., p. 69.

81. See p. 45.

82. Lunacharskii, *Velikii perevorot,* p. 65.

83. Lunacharsky's 1919 memoir of Lenin was published in an edition of 13,000.

84. Cited in Robert Vincent Daniels, *The Conscience of the Revolution: Communist Opposition in Soviet Russia* (Cambridge, 1960), p. 113.

85. Cited in ibid., pp. 113–114.

86. In 1918 and 1919 there had been no official celebrations of Lenin's forty-eighth and forty-ninth birthdays.

87. *Pravda,* April 23, 1920. This speech was reprinted in Trotsky, *O Lenine,* pp. 145–150.

88. *Pravda,* April 23, 1920.

89. Ibid.

90. Ibid.

91. *Bednota,* April 23, 1920.

92. Akop Akopian, "V. I. Lenin," Toktogul, "Chto za mat' rodila takogo syna, kak Lenin!", *Lenin v sovetskoi poezii* (Leningrad, 1970), pp. 73–76.

93. *Pravda,* April 23, 1920.

94. Adrian Vechernii, "Vozhdiu mirovoi revoliutsii," *Vlast' truda* (Irkutsk), April 23, 1920, cited in *Lenin v sovetskoi poezii,* pp. 79–80.

95. V. V. Maiakovskii, "Vladimir Il'ich," *Sochineniia*, vol. 1 (Moscow, **281** 1965), pp. 172–174. The poet first read this work at a meeting of publishers honoring Lenin on April 28, 1920; it was first published in *Krasnaia gazeta*, November 5, 1922.

96. *Bednota*, April 23, 1920.

97. V. I. Nevskii, *V. I. Ul'ianov (N. Lenin)* (Moscow, 1920).

98. I. Khodorovskii, *V. I. Lenin, velikii vozhd' proletarskoi revoliutsii* (Kazan, 1920).

99. The speeches were published in *Pravda* and *Izvestiia* on April 24, 1920. They were also republished as a separate volume in an edition of 100,000: *50-letie Vladimira Il'icha Ul'ianova-Lenina* (Moscow, 1920).

100. *Pravda*, April 24, 1920.

101. Lenin, *Polnoe sobranie sochinenii*, vol. 51, p. 272.

102. S. Leningradskii, *Lenin sredi krest'ian derevni Kashino* (Moscow, 1924), pp. 23, 19.

103. "Pis'ma krest'ian v sviazi s konchinoi V. I. Lenina," *Voprosy istorii*, no. 7, 1968, p. 122.

104. A. V. Lunacharskii, "Shtrikhi," *Lenin—tovarishch, chelovek*, 2nd ed. (Moscow, 1963), p. 179.

105. *Lenin: Sobranie fotografii i kinokadrov*, vol. 1, *Fotografii 1874–1923* (Moscow, 1970), pp. 178–179.

106. Volkov-Lannit, *Lenin v fotoiskusstve*, p. 33, citing P. A. Kholodova, "Rodnoi i blizkii," *Rabochie i krest'iane Rossii o Lenine* (Moscow, 1958), p. 335.

107. *Leninskii sbornik*, vol. 34 (Moscow, 1942), p. 439.

108. Lenin, *Polnoe sobranie sochinenii*, vol. 54, p. 429. The resolution was accepted by the Politburo on July 31, 1920.

109. M. Gor'kii, "Vladimir Il'ich Lenin," *Kommunisticheskii internatsional*, no. 12, 1920, pp. 1929–1936; ibid., "Pis'mo M. Gor'kogo k G. Uellsu," p. 2207.

110. Poster no. 4416-55, Lenin Library, Moscow.

111. William Reswick, *I Dreamt Revolution* (Chicago, 1952), pp. 56–57.

112. Walter Duranty, *I Write as I Please* (New York, 1935), p. 226.

113. Gor'kii, *O russkom krest'ianstve*, pp. 43–45.

114. For an excellent discussion of the Kronstadt rebellion, see Avrich, *Kronstadt 1921*.

115. Ibid., pp. 172–177; *Izvestiia* cited on p. 177.

116. Ibid., pp. 178–179.

117. N. Valentinov (N. V. Vol'skii), *Novaia ekonomicheskaia politika i krizis partii posle smerti Lenina*, ed. J. Bunyan and V. Butenko (Stanford, 1971), p. 88.

118. Ibid.

119. Daniels, *Conscience of the Revolution*, pp. 137–153.

282   **4. Illness and Immortality**

1. Adam Ulam, *The Bolsheviks,* p. 553.

2. V. N. Rozanov, "Zapiski vracha," *Vospominaniia o Lenine,* vol. 2 (Moscow, 1957), p. 342.

3. Ulam, *The Bolsheviks,* p.555.

4. "Stranichka iz dnevnika," written January 2; "O kooperatsii," written January 4 and 6; "O nashei revoliutsii," written January 16 and 17; "Kak nam reorganizovat' Rabkrin," written January 23; "Luchshe men'she, da luchshe," written February 6.

5. L. A. Fotieva, *Iz zhizni V. I. Lenina* (Moscow, 1967), p. 279.

6. Rozanov writes that when there seemed to be a bit of improvement in his condition, *"against all medical logic* the thought unconsciously took shape in my mind: and what if it should all turn out well and Vladimir Il'ich ... would become able to work again" ("Zapiski," p. 345; italics added).

7. Cited in Ulam, *The Bolsheviks,* p. 559.

8. Lenin, *Polnoe sobranie sochinenii,* vol. 45, p. 485.

9. For a discussion of Lenin's relationship with Stalin, see Moshe Lewin, *Lenin's Last Struggle,* and Ulam, *The Bolsheviks.*

10. N. Valentinov (N. V. Vol'skii), *Novaia ekonomicheskaia politika i krizis partii posle smerti Lenina,* pp. 185–187. Henceforth this work is cited as Valentinov, *NEP.*

11. *Bednota,* April 22, 1922.

12. Valentinov, *NEP,* p. 36.

13. David Shub, *Lenin: A Biography* (Baltimore, 1966), p. 428.

14. *Pravda,* April 28, 1922.

15. *Pravda,* June 4, 1922.

16. *Pravda,* June 18, 1922.

17. *Pravda,* July 29, 1922.

18. "Tov. Lenin na otdykhe," supplement to *Pravda,* September 24, 1922.

19. *Pravda,* November 7, 1922. There was no mention of any illness in *Pravda* and *Izvestiia* during the rest of 1922.

20. "Stranichka iz dnevnika," *Pravda,* January 4, 1923; "Kak nam reorganizovat' Rabkrin," *Pravda,* January 25, 1923.

21. *Izvestiia,* March 14, 1923.

22. *Pravda,* March 16, 1923.

23. *Pravda,* March 17, 1923; March 18, 1923.

24. *Pravda,* March 23, 1923.

25. *Pravda,* March 23, 1923.

26. *Pravda,* April 2, 1923; April 5, 1923.

27. *Pravda,* April 11, 1923.

28. *Pravda,* April 22, 1923.

29. *Pravda,* April 25, 1923.

30. *Pravda,* April 22, 1923.

31. *Pravda,* April 29, 1923, contained a bulletin stating that the catarrh had

diminished significantly; *Pravda,* May 1, 1923, that the catarrh had disappeared; **283** *Pravda,* May 3, 1923, that Lenin's condition had become satisfactory.

32. *Izvestiia,* April 26, 1923.
33. "Vladimir Il'ich lives and is overcoming his serious illness." *Pravda,* August 30, 1923.
34. *Izvestiia,* August 30, 1923.
35. *Izvestiia,* October 8, 1923.
36. *Pravda,* October 21, 1923.
37. *Pravda,* December 16, 1923.
38. Supplement to *Pravda,* November 7, 1922.
39. Although Lenin wrote it in early February, his article, "Better Fewer But Better" was published in *Pravda* on March 4, 1923, and was dated March 2.
40. Valentinov, *NEP,* pp. 46–53.
41. Trotskii, "O bol'nom," *O Lenine,* pp. 159–161; italics added.
42. N. Babakhan, "Marksizm i leninizm," *Pravda,* April 6, 1923.
43. Materialist, "Truslivyi opportunizm budushchego professora," *Pod znamenem marksizma,* no. 2–3, 1923, pp. 218–222.
44. Lenin's article is called "Novye khoziaistvennye dvizheniia v krest'ianskoi zhizni." The article by S. Mitskevich is "Pervye literaturnye raboty V. I. Ul'ianova-Lenina," *Izvestiia,* March 14, 1923.
45. *Pravda,* April 6, 1923.
46. Mikh. Pavlovich, "Lenin, kak razrushitel' narodnichestva" *Pod znamenem marksizma,* no. 4–5, 1923, p. 157.
47. G. Zinov'ev, "Piat' let," *Pravda,* August 30, 1923.
48. N. Kuz'min, "Molodezh—ni na shag ot 'Leninizma,' " *Iunyi proletarii,* no. 4(48), March 1923, p. 5.
49. *Dvenadtsatyi s"ezd RKP(b). Stenograficheskii otchet, 17–25 aprelia 1923 g.* (Moscow, 1923), p. 149.
50. *Dvenadtsatyi s"ezd RKP(b), 17–25 aprelia 1923 goda. Stenograficheskii otchet* (Moscow, 1968), p. 537.
51. Ibid., pp. 1–3.
52. Ibid., p. 479.
53. Ibid., p. 6.
54. *Izvestiia* and *Pravda,* April 4, 1923.
55. *Biulleten' Instituta V. I. Lenina pri TsK RKP,* no. 1, 1923, p. 31.
56. *Pravda,* August 22, 1923.
57. *Pravda,* August 14, 1923.
58. *Pravda,* August 22, 1923.
59. *Pravda,* August 23, 1923.
60. *Pravda,* September 4, 1923.
61. *Pravda,* October 26, 1923. A governing board of Kamenev, Liadov, and Arosev was also established.
62. *Pravda,* October 27, 1923.
63. *Pravda,* October 30, 1923.
64. A. Arosev, "Institut V. I. Lenina," *Proletarskaia revoliutsiia,* no. 11, 1923, p. 273.

284

65. Volkov-Lannit, *Lenin v fotoiskusstve*, p. 106.

66. Many of these are on display at the Central Lenin Museum in Moscow.

67. *Izvestiia*, April 26, 1923.

68. Lenin, *Polnoe sobranie sochinenii*, vol. 45, p. 298.

69. *Pravda*, August 31, 1923.

70. Z. Bogomazova, "Tsentral'nyi Dom Krest'ianina v Moskve," *Kommunisticheskoe prosveshchenie*, no. 6, 1922, pp. 99–101.

71. *Izvestiia*, August 30, 1923.

72. *Ugolok V. I. Ul'ianova Lenina. Pervaia sel'sko-khoziaistvennaia i kustarno-promyshlennaia vystavka SSSR* (Moscow, 1923). See also T. Shepeleva, "Sel'skokhoziaistvennaia vystavka 1923 g.," *Krasnyi arkhiv*, no. 100, 1940, p. 91.

73. The biographer was S. I. Mitskevich. *Pravda*, July 17, 1923.

74. Ibid.

75. *Izvestiia*, August 30, 1923.

76. *Pravda*, September 1, 1923.

77. *Izvestiia*, August 28, 1923. Lenin's name was also being used to raise money for an airplane that was dubbed "samolet Il'icha." A table was set up at the exhibition, selling Il'ich medals; the money went toward building the plane. *Pravda*, September 8, 1923.

78. Georgii Shidlovskii, "Lenin—mificheskoe litso," *Proletarskaia revoliutsiia*, no. 3, 1922, p. 334.

79. "Obrazets togo, kak nel'zia pisat' biografii," *Molodaia gvardiia*, no. 3, 1923, pp. 237–238. The biography in question, "Vladimir Il'ich," was written by I. Chebotarev and published in *Iunyi proletarii*, no. 1 (1922).

80. The maligning of Fedor Kerensky was of course prompted by the fact that he was Alexander's father.

81. A. V. Lunacharskii, *Revoliutsionnye siluety* (Moscow, 1923), p. 11.

82. *Pravda*, August 30, 1923.

83. *Izvestiia*, March 14, 1923.

84. P. N. Lepeshinskii, "Po sosedstvu s Vladimirom Il'ichom," *Lenin*, ed. D. Lebed' (Kharkov, 1923), p. 76.

85. She asked him why he had "two faces," one in front and one in back. "That is because I do a lot of thinking," Lenin answered. Ibid., p. 77.

86. B. Gorev, "Lenin," *Lenin*, pp. 39–41.

87. Lunacharskii, *Revoliutsionnye siluety*, p. 11.

88. *Izvestiia*, August 30, 1923.

89. *Pravda*, November 2, 1923.

90. *Bednota*, November 30, 1923.

91. G. Zinov'ev, "Pokushenie na T. Lenina," *Prozhektor*, August 31, 1923, p. 7.

92. *Pravda*, August 30, 1923.

93. *Pravda*, November 7, 1923.

94. Jack London, *Love of Life and Other Stories* (New York and London, 1907), pp. 3–42.

95. N. K. Krupskaia, "Chto nravilos' Il'ichu iz khudozhestvennoi literatury," N. K. Krupskaia, *O Lenine, sbornik stat'ei i vystuplenii*, ed. V. S. Dridzo

(Moscow, 1965), p. 96. First published in *Narodnyi uchitel'*, no. 1, 1927, pp. 4–6.

96. V. Osipov, "Nekotorye cherty kharaktera V. I. Lenina vo vremia ego bolezni," *Krasnaia letopis'*, no. 2(23), 1927, p. 244.

97. *Izvestiia*, January 20, 1924.

5. The Nation Mourns

1. *Pravda*, January 24, 1924, p. 4. Lenin's death of course unleashed a flood of articles in the Soviet press. Since each issue in the week after he died contains so many pertinent articles, notes for Chapters 5 and 6 contain page numbers of the citations.

2. *New York Times*, January 23, 1924.

3. *Pravda*, January 24, 1924, p. 4.

4. *New York Times*, January 23, 1924.

5. *Izvestiia*, January 24, 1924, p. 1.

6. Michael Farbman, *After Lenin* (London, 1924), p. 56; "Russia After Lenin—Will Soviet Survive?" *New York Times,* January 27, 1924.

7. *Otchet komissii TsIK SSSR po uvekovecheniiu pamiati V. I. Ul'ianova (-Lenina)* (Moscow, 1925), p. 9. The other members were Voroshilov, Enukidze, Zelensky, Molotov, Muralov, Lashevich, Bonch-Bruevich, Sapronov, and Avanesov.

8. Bonch-Bruevich left memoirs about his work on the Funeral Commission in his *Vospominaniia o Lenine*, pp. 422–437.

9. In 1919 this hall was for the lying-in-state of Iakov Sverdlov.

10. Bonch-Bruevich, *Vospominaniia*, p. 422.

11. *Pravda*, January 30, 1924, p. 1.

12. Bonch-Bruevich, *Vospominaniia*, p. 427.

13. *Petrogradskaia pravda*, January 24, 1924, p. 1. One volume of Stalin's works has a calendar of the author's activities in the back of the book, which states that Stalin was among those who carried the coffin out of the house on January 23. I. V. Stalin, *Sochineniia*, vol. 6 (Moscow, 1947), p. 418.

14. Reswick, *I Dreamt Revolution*, p. 72.

15. There is some similarity between these ceremonials and those for Alexander III, who died in 1894. The emperor's death came while he was attempting a cure in Livadia (near Yalta). When the train bearing Alexander's body edged into the Petersburg station, an orchestra began playing funeral music ("Kol' slaven") and all banners were lowered. Then the music stopped as prayers were said and everyone bared their heads. At the Pavletsky station in Moscow, obviously no prayers were chanted for Lenin, but part of the custom carried over.

16. *Petrogradskaia pravda*, January 24, 1924, p. 4.

17. A. Abramov, *Mavzolei Lenina* (Moscow, 1969), p. 45.

18. Ibid.

19. *Petrogradskaia pravda*, January 24, 1924, p. 4.

20. *Description des funérailles de feu l'Empereur Nicholas I de glorieuse mémoire précédée d'un aperçu historique sur les funérailles des tsars et des em-*

286   *pereurs de toutes les russies et de quelques autres souverains européens* (St. Petersburg, 1856), p. 7.

21. A special volume, *Leninu, 21 ianvaria 1924* (Moscow, 1925), contains photographs of 1,070 of these wreaths.

22. According to Krupskaia, "day and night people went by (750,000 went by), looked at Il'ich and wept"; I. A. Armand, "Vospominaniia o Vladimire Il'iche Lenine," *Vospominaniia o Vladimire Il'iche Lenine* (Moscow, 1970), IV, 330. Zinoviev put the figure at 700,000; *Pravda*, January 30, 1924, p. 1. A Moscow correspondent estimated that 7–8,000 people were admitted to the hall every hour—as many as 200,000 every twenty-four hours; *Petrogradskaia pravda*, January 25, 1924, p. 2.

23. *New York Times*, January 24, 1924.

24. Bonch-Bruevich, *Vospominaniia*, p. 429.

25. *Izvestiia*, January 27, 1924, p. 2; Bonch-Bruevich, *Vospominaniia*, p. 428.

26. Farbman, *After Lenin*, p. 57.

27. Valentinov, *NEP*, pp. 89, 88.

28. *Izvestiia*, January 24, 1924, p. 1.

29. *Pravda*, January 30, 1924, p. 1.

30. *Petrogradskaia pravda*, January 26, 1924, p. 3; see also January 24, 1924, p. 3 for another example of "boundless grief."

31. See, for example, *Petrogradskaia pravda*, January 25, 1924, pp. 4 and 5; January 26, 1924, p. 5.

32. *Pravda*, January 30, 1924, p. 1.

33. *Petrogradskaia pravda*, January 25, 1924, p. 2.

34. This commission was formed on January 23, 1924, and included in its membership A. S. Bubnov and N. I. Smirnov. *Otchet komissii*, p. 23.

35. A. N. Kotyrev, *Mavzolei V. I. Lenina* (Moscow, 1971), p. 23.

36. *Izvestiia*, January 26, 1924, p. 1.

37. *Petrogradskaia pravda*, January 26, 1924, p. 1.

38. Ibid.

39. Ibid., p. 5. The article makes a point of mentioning that this statement was made by workers who were not members of the party.

40. Ibid., p. 4.

41. Ibid., p. 4.

42. Ibid., January 25, 1924, p. 5.

43. Ibid., January 26, 1924, p. 5. The article in which this statement is contained is entitled, "Damnation to the Murderers!"

44. Published in *Smolenskaia pravda* and cited in Robert Payne, *The Life and Death of Lenin* (New York, 1964), p. 640.

45. Trotsky later wrote that at the end of February 1923 Stalin informed him, Zinoviev, and Kamenev that Lenin had summoned him and asked for poison. While his shocked listeners insisted that complying with Lenin's wishes would be out of the question, Stalin kept repeating, "the Old Man is suffering." Trotsky thus implies that Stalin may have been instrumental in bringing about Lenin's death; Leon Trotsky, *Stalin: An Appraisal of the Man and His Influence,*

trans. Charles Malamuth (New York, 1941), pp. 376–377. But as Valentinov cor- **287**
rectly points out, it was not in keeping with his disposition for Lenin to despair
and ask for poison, no matter how sick he was. It was much more characteristic of
him to battle for life, like the hero of the Jack London story that Krupskaia read
to Lenin just before his death; for Valentinov's views, see his *NEP*, p. 86. As for
Stalin's having somehow killed Lenin, there is no evidence whatsoever. We know
that Lenin suffered from extreme arteriosclerosis and that his father died of the
same disease at the same age. It is of course conceivable that Stalin played a role
in Lenin's death in an indirect way. Just before the stroke of March 9, 1923, the
relationship between Lenin and Stalin became very tense (see Lewin, *Lenin's
Last Struggle*). It can be conjectured that the extreme anxiety resulting from
Lenin's perception of Stalin's behavior at that time may have helped to bring
about the terrible stroke from which he never recovered.

46. *Pravda* ran a continuing list of provincial party and government organizations that sent in resolutions of grief. By January 27, the list numbered 438.

47. *Petrogradskaia pravda,* January 26, 1924, p. 3.

48. *Petrogradskaia pravda,* January 25, 1924, p. 4.

49. *Pravda,* January 26, 1924, p. 4.

50. *Petrogradskaia pravda,* January 25, 1924, p. 4.

51. *Petrogradskaia pravda,* January 26, 1924, p. 4.

52. Ibid. The paper listed not only how much money was received in all but
how much was contributed by each factory. This made certain that contributing
funds to this account should become a competitive matter.

53. Ibid.

54. *Petrogradskaia pravda,* January 25, 1924, p. 5. The building of a fine
Lenin memorial appears to have been a matter of civic pride in Petrograd. This is
undoubtedly true of other cities as well; each wanted to demonstrate both its loyalty and its status through such a project.

55. *Petrogradskaia pravda,* January 26, 1924, p. 3.

56. Ibid., p. 4.

57. *Petrogradskaia pravda,* January 25, 1924, p. 4.

58. Ibid.

59. *Petrogradskaia pravda,* January 26, 1924, p. 5.

60. Sometimes parts of the Mozart Requiem were played. One such occasion was a meeting of performing artists held in Petrograd's Marinsky Theater.
Petrogradskaia pravda, January 25, 1924, p. 4.

61. "You fell victims in the fated struggle/ For your boundless love for the
people./ You sacrificed all that you could for them,/ For their lives, their honor,
their freedom."

62. *Petrogradskaia pravda,* January 26, 1924, p. 3.

63. *Petrogradskaia pravda* was so eager to be successful in urging people to
join the party that it even so headlined articles *not* describing pledges. "Collectively—into the ranks of the RKP," read the headline of an article that made no
mention of anyone's joining the party ranks. January 25, 1924, p. 3.

64. *Petrogradskaia pravda,* January 25, 1924, p. 4.

288   65. See, for example, *Petrogradskaia pravda,* January 26, 1924, p. 3.

66. For a discussion of the Bolshevik collective ideal as expressed in the arts, see René Fueloep-Miller, *The Mind and Face of Bolshevism: An Examination of Cultural Life in Soviet Russia* (New York, 1928), pp. 1–37.

67. "Lenina net," *Pravda,* January 24, 1924, p. 2.

68. "K partii. Ko vsem trudiashchimsia," *Izvestiia,* January 24, 1924, p. 2.

69. The Young Pioneers numbered only about 10,000 in the beginning of 1924. The Komsomol, on the other hand, had a membership of 623,000 in 1924. Samuel N. Harper, *Civic Training in Soviet Russia* (Chicago, 1929), pp. 46, 66.

70. *Petrogradskaia pravda,* January 26, 1924, p. 2.

71. *Petrogradskaia pravda,* January 25, 1924, p. 3.

72. *Petrogradskaia pravda,* January 26, 1924, p. 4.

73. The fullest discussion of the Lenin Enrollment is provided in T. H. Rigby, *Communist Party Membership in the USSR, 1917–1967* (Princeton, 1968), pp. 110–131. See also E. H. Carr, *The Interregnum, 1923–1924* (Baltimore, 1969), pp. 358–363. For a brief discussion of Trotsky's situation vis-à-vis the Lenin Enrollment, see Isaac Deutscher, *The Prophet Unarmed, Trotsky: 1921–1929* (New York, 1965), pp. 135–136.

74. Leonard Schapiro explains this phenomenon by observing that, as the apparatus of the party bureaucracy was increasing in size and complexity, it required members with a higher level of education than that offered by the proletariat. A survey of 15,000 officials in 1921 found that just over a third were of proletarian origin (*Izvestiia tsentral'nogo komiteta rossiiskoi kommunisticheskoi partii* [*bol'shevikov*], no. 39, March 1922). Besides, by this time, a sizable proportion of older Communists of proletarian origin had left the party and had been replaced by white-collar elements, Schapiro, *Communist Party,* pp. 237–238.

75. Since the absolute number of workers was growing as a result of the gradual economic recovery that characterized the post-civil war period, the proportion and influence of worker Communists within the working class was further diminished. Rigby, *Communist Party Membership,* p. 117.

76. *Pravda,* January 19, 1924, p. 5.

77. See pp. 157–159.

78. *VKP(b) v rezoliutsiiakh* (Moscow, 1941), p. 561. The Lenin Enrollment added some 200,000 workers to the ranks of the party, increasing its membership by more than 40 percent. In January 1924 the party consisted of 472,000 members. Rigby, *Communist Party Membership,* p. 52.

79. Carr, *The Interregnum,* pp. 362–363.

80. There are many articles describing such requests in *Petrogradskaia pravda,* January 24, 25, and 26, p. 5.

81. *Petrogradskaia pravda,* January 24, 1924, p. 5.

82. Ibid., p. 3.

83. Ibid.

84. *Pravda,* January 27, 1924, p. 4.

85. See, for example, the article describing the meeting of the workers of the Krasnyi Tkach factory (*Petrogradskaia pravda,* January 25, 1924, p. 5); the article about the meeting of the students and teachers of the Institute of Medicine and

Radiology (January 26, 1924, p. 5); the article describing the gathering of the   **289**
Twentieth Military Division (January 26, 1926, 1924, p. 5).

86. *Leniniana*, no. 1, 1924 (Moscow-Leningrad, 1926), p. 266, citing *Krasnaia gazeta*, no. 20, p. 5.

87. A cursory list of a few of these renamed institutions: the Zinoviev Mill, the Zinoviev Printing Works, the Zinoviev Polytechnical School, the Zinoviev Paper Factory, the Uritsky Palace, the Uritsky Railroad, the Kalinin Sawmill, the Bebel Workers' School, the Dzerzhinsky Polytechnical Institute of Communications, the Dzhaparidze Factory.

88. *Petrogradskaia pravda*, January 24, 1924, p. 4.

89. *Petrogradskaia pravda*, January 26, 1924, p. 2.

90. This speech as well as the others delivered at the meeting was summarized in *Pravda*, January 27, 1924, p. 3. The full texts of all the speeches were first published in *Pravda*, January 30, 1924, pp. 5–6, and January 31, 1924, p. 4.

91. Isaac Deutscher, *Stalin: A Political Biography* (New York, 1967), pp. 269–272; Carr, *The Interregnum*, pp. 353–355; Schapiro, *Communist Party*, p. 282.

92. Adam Ulam suggests that the "purple prose" of the speech made it rather ridiculous at the Congress of Soviets, but that it would not have been out of keeping had it been delivered at Lenin's funeral. *Stalin: The Man and His Era* (New York, 1973), p. 235.

93. There is one exception: a speech written by Krupskaia sometime in 1924 and first published in 1965 in a collection of her writings on Lenin; *O Lenine, Sbornik stat'ei i vystuplenii*, ed. V. S. Dridzo, 2nd ed. (Moscow, 1965), pp. 11–12. This speech, the handwritten original of which is reproduced in the book, was in the central party archive of the Institute of Marxism-Leninism. It is dated simply "1924." Robert McNeal, who includes an English translation of the speech in his biography of Krupskaia, contends that it was definitely meant to be a funeral oration. He cites as evidence the fact that the editor of the volume in which it is published chose to place it *before* the speech that Krupskaia did make on January 26, 1924. McNeal's more important evidence, however, is the ritualistic form of the speech itself; in this respect it is similar to Stalin's speech. The first part of the speech is a series of descriptions of Lenin, each beginning with his name: "LENIN was the foe of tsars, landlords and capitalists, the foe of oppressors. LENIN was the closest friend of working men and women, peasant men and women, the friend of all toilers." After nine such phrases, Krupskaia enumerates eight precepts that constitute Lenin's legacy: "1. To further strengthen the fraternal union of workers and peasants. 2. To strengthen and improve their power—Soviet power. 3. To unite more closely around the Communist Party." And so on. This speech ends on a hortatory note, in capital letters: "Unswervingly forward, to the life of light, to socialism, to communism! We shall fulfill Lenin's legacy!" McNeal suggests that this extraordinary speech, so unlike Krupskaia's usual style, was never delivered because "all speeches had to be cleared with Dzerzhinsky's commission, which decided that only Stalin was to be permitted to interpret Lenin's legacy." *Bride of the Revolution: Krupskaya and Lenin* (Ann Arbor, 1972), p. 241.

94. One example is an article entitled "We Swear!" (*Klianemsia!*). Most of

290   the article consists of a series of vows: "We all swear, as one person, we all swear—workers, peasants, and members of the Red army—to fight to the end for our Leninist fighting Red Banner. We swear . . . not to allow any faint-hearted vacillations, not under any circumstances." The article conveys the message of the Petrograd Soviet, which swore to strengthen the nation and to be Leninist in all of its struggles and its work. *Petrogradskaia pravda*, January 24, 1924.

95. *Petrogradskaia pravda*, January 25, 1924, p. 4.

96. *Pravda*, January 27, 1924, p. 3.

97. *Pravda*, January 31, 1924, p. 4.

98. These resolutions were published in *Pravda*, January 27, 1924, p. 4.

99. Leon Trotsky, *My Life*, p. 500.

100. Ibid., p. 509.

101. Ibid.

102. Ibid., p. 499.

103. Ibid., p. 509.

104. Trotsky quotes this passage from his wife's notes in *My Life*, p. 511.

105. *New York Times*, January 28, 1924.

106. Daniels, in *Conscience of the Revolution*, p. 236, quotes this passage, citing Duranty, *I Write as I Please*, pp. 225–226.

107. Stalin, *Sochineniia*, vol. 6, pp. 418–419.

108. *Pravda*, January 30, 1924, p. 1.

109. My description of the funeral is based mainly on *Pravda*, January 30, 1924.

110. "LENIN vezde vsiudu bezrazdel'no s nami." From a photograph of the Leningrad delegation standing by its banner (Kotyrev, *Mavzolei Lenina*, p. 43). Some other banners read: "Lenin's grave is the cradle of freedom for mankind." "Il'ich has died, but he lives in the hearts of workers." "Lenin has died, but his cause will live on for centuries."

111. *New York Times*, January 28, 1924, p. 1.

112. *Pravda*, January 27, 1924, p. 5.

113. *New York Times*, January 28, 1924, p. 1.

114. *Mo-gi-la Le-ni-na . . . Ko-ly-bel' svo-bo-dy . . . Vse-go che-lo-ve-che-stva Pravda*, January 30, 1924, p. 3.

115. Kotyrev, *Mavzolei Lenina*, p. 41.

116. The head of the Moscow ambulance department announced that on the day of Lenin's funeral 3,196 people were treated for frostbite, hysteria, and fainting. *New York Times*, January 30, 1924.

117. Abramov, *Mavzolei Lenina*, p. 60.

118. *Pravda*, January 30, 1924, p. 1.

119. *Petrogradskaia pravda*, January 26, 1924, p. 1.

120. *Petrogradskaia pravda*, January 25, 1924, p. 3.

121. *Petrogradskaia pravda*, January 26, 1924, p. 1.

122. Duranty remarks on this in his coverage of the events (*New York Times*, January 28, 1924.

123. F. A. Brokgaus and I. A. Efron, "Pogrebenie khristianskoe," *Entsiklopedicheskii slovar'*, vol. 24 (St. Petersburg, 1898), p. 42.

6. The Body and the Shrine

1. *Petrogradskaia pravda,* January 25, 1924, p. 2.
2. Ibid., p. 5.
3. Tatiana Maiskaia, "U groba," *Izvestiia,* January 26, 1924, p. 4.
4. "Chto-b Il'icha unichtozhit'—smert' takoi eshche net." Guzdev-Slesar', "Dlia kogo on umer," *Petrogradskaia pravda,* January 25, 1924.
5. This is part of a statement made by a worker to a gathering of the Komsomol. Ibid., p. 5.
6. January 24, 1924, p. 1.
7. D. Manuil'skii, "Lenin i epokha," *Lenin, 1870–1924* (Kharkov, 1924), p. 9.
8. Reprinted many times, this poem was first published in *Molodaia gvardiia,* no. 2–3, 1924, pp. 10–14.
9. *Petrogradskaia pravda,* January 25, 1924, p. 2.
10. Em. Iaroslavskii, *Zhizn' i rabota V. I. Lenina* (Moscow, 1924), p. 237.
11. *Pravda,* January 27, 1924, p. 2.
12. It would be naive to think that the Ilich-Lenin formulation reflects the mere prompting of Sosnovsky's heart.
13. P. Stuchka, "Nash Il'ich," *Pravda,* January 27, 1924, p. 1.
14. Ibid.
15. Iu. Steklov, "Mogila Lenina," *Izvestiia,* January 27, 1924, p. 1.
16. *Pravda,* January 30, 1924, p. 1.
17. *Pravda,* January 26, 1924, p. 2.
18. The team consisted of Professors O. Foerster, V. P. Osipov, A. A. Deshin, V. S. Veisbrod, V. V. Bukak; Drs. F. A. Guetier, P. I. Elistratov, V. N. Rozanov, V. A. Obukh; and Commissar of Health N. Semashko. *Izvestiia,* January 25, 1924, p. 3.
19. *Petrogradskaia pravda,* January 26, 1924, p. 1.
20. See the detailed autopsy report in *Izvestiia,* January 25, 1924, p. 3. Related articles can be found in *Petrogradskaia pravda,* January 25, 1924, pp. 1, 2, and January 26, 1924, p. 2; *Izvestiia,* January 25, 1924, p. 1.
21. *New York Times,* January 26, 1924. On a certain level, Duranty may be right. We have seen that throughout the period of his rule and illness, Lenin was portrayed as a man beloved by the people, their "Ilich." The publication of the minutiae of what was inside him might be a demonstration that the leadership wanted the people to feel that nothing would be hidden from them, that the people had the right to know all.
22. Valentinov, *NEP,* p. 87.
23. Ibid.
24. A few days after the autopsy, on January 25, Lenin's heart and brain were sent to the Lenin Institute. Also sent was a bullet from the 1918 attempt on his life which had not been removed from his body until now. It was expected that Lenin's brain would be used as the subject of study. Scientists would be enabled to study the finest specimen of a brain of a person of great intellect, explains an article published shortly after Lenin's death. "Issledovanie mozga V. I. Lenina," *Otchego bolel i umer V. I. Lenin* (Leningrad, 1924), p. 31. On the day be-

292   fore the funeral, Lenin's brain was photographed. Professor Abrikosov was given the task of finely sectioning the brain so that it could be studied under the microscope.

25. Armand, "Vospominaniia o Lenine," pp. 329–330.

26. *Izvestiia,* January 24, 1924, p. 1.

27. *Izvestiia,* January 25, 1924, p. 1.

28. Cited in Shub, *Lenin,* p. 438.

29. *Pravda* and *Izvestiia,* January 24, 1924, p. 1.

30. *Petrogradskaia pravda,* January 26, 1924, p. 2.

31. N. Semashko, "Chto dalo vskrytie tela V. I. Lenina," *Izvestiia,* January 25, 1924, p. 1.

32. N. Semashko, "Otchego bolel i umer V. I. Lenin," *Otchego bolel i umer V. I. Lenin,* p. 6.

33. Maria Alexandrovna Ulianova died in 1916.

34. Semashko, "Chto dalo vskrytie tela V. I. Lenina," *Izvestiia,* January 25, 1924, p. 1. Abrikosov concurred that Lenin's form of arteriosclerosis is often based on hereditary factors. Like Semashko he pointed out that Lenin's father died of the same condition and added that fatty deposits can begin to collect in the arteries in one's childhood. He was much more circumspect than Semashko in his discussion of acquired factors and how they affect the disease. He never implied, as did the commissar of health, that Lenin died from thinking too hard about the revolution. Abrikosov simply said that mental strain and worry tend to exacerbate arteriosclerosis. *Petrogradskaia pravda,* January 25, 1924, p. 2.

35. Ibid.

36. Semashko, "Otchego bolel," p. 6.

37. Ulam, *The Bolsheviks,* p. 518.

38. *Petrogradskaia pravda,* January 24, 1924, p. 5.

39. *Otchet komissii TsIK SSSR po uvekovecheniiu pamiati V. I. Ul'ianova (-Lenina),* p. 42.

40. Valentinov, who quotes this story in his memoirs, explained that it originated with Bukharin but that he himself had heard it elsewhere. This lessens its evidential weight but only somewhat, since Valentinov was a very careful scholar and would have retold the story only if he had trusted the reliability of his source. The meeting described probably took place in late October or early November of 1923. Valentinov, *NEP,* pp. 90–92.

41. E. O. James, *Christian Myth and Ritual: A Historical Study* (Cleveland and New York, 1965), p. 190.

42. "Resurget igitur caro, et quidem omnis, et quidem ipsa, et quidem integra" (Tertullian, *De carnis resurrectione,* p. 63). Cited in Norman O. Brown, *Life Against Death: The Psychoanalytic Meaning of History* (New York, 1959), p. 309.

43. *Pravda,* June 13, 1924, p. 4; *Izvestiia,* June 13, 1924, p. 4.

44. Bonch-Bruevich, *Vospominaniia,* p. 435.

45. This number originates in the Old Testament. The body of Joseph was embalmed for forty days: "And forty days were fulfilled for him; for so are fulfilled the days of embalming" (Genesis 50:3).

46. *Pravda,* January 26, 1924, p. 4; *Izvestiia,* January 26, 1924, p. 1.   **293**

47. *New York Times,* January 26, 1924.

48. *Petrogradskaia pravda,* January 26, 1924, p. 2.

49. *Izvestiia,* January 27, 1924, p. 1.

50. *Izvestiia,* January 29, 1924, p. 1.

51. Armand, "Vospominaniia o Lenine," p. 330.

52. McNeal, *Bride of the Revolution,* pp. 241–242.

53. Ibid., p. 242.

54. *Pravda,* January 30, 1924, p. 1.

55. Bonch-Bruevich, *Vospominaniia,* p. 435.

56. McNeal, *Bride of the Revolution,* p. 242.

57. Bonch-Bruevich, *Vospominaniia,* p. 435.

58. *Rabochaia Moskva,* January 26, 1924.

59. Bonch-Bruevich, *Vospominaniia,* pp. 435.

60. *Pravda, Izvestiia,* and *Petrogradskaia pravda,* January 30, 1924, p. 1.

61. *Pravda,* June 13, 1924, p. 4; *Izvestiia,* June 13, 1924, p. 4.

62. Bonch-Bruevich, *Vospominaniia,* p. 435.

63. The delay was largely due to conflicts between the Egyptian government and the British who were financing and directing the excavation under Lord Carnarvon.

64. *New York Times,* February 7, 1923.

65. Some years later these stories inspired *The Mummy,* the famous horror film starring Boris Karloff.

66. *Izvestiia,* January 29, 1924, p. 1.

67. K. S. Melnikov, "V komissiiu po postroike mavzoleia V. I. Lenina," July 15, 1924 (Melnikov archive), cited in S. Frederick Starr, *Melnikov: Solo Architect in a Mass Society* (Princeton, 1978), p. 249.

68. See Chapter 1.

69. M. Ol'minskii, "Kriticheskie stat'i i zametki," *Proletarskaia revoliutsiia,* no. 1, 1931, pp. 149–150.

70. On the connection between Krasin and the Lenin cult, see Nina Tumarkin, "Religion, Bolshevism and the Origins of the Lenin Cult," *Russian Review,* 40 (January 1981), 35–46.

71. *Pravda,* February 3, 1924, p. 5.

72. Kotyrev, *Mavzolei Lenina,* p. 56.

73. *Izvestiia,* March 4, 1924, p. 6.

74. Kotyrev, *Mavzolei Lenina,* p. 62.

75. Starr, *Melnikov,* p. 83. The restaurant was called "The Ravine."

76. *Otchet komissii,* p. 36.

77. S. O. Khan-Magomedov, *Mavzolei Lenina, istoriia sozdaniia i arkhitektura* (Moscow, 1972), pp. 55–56.

78. *Otchet komissii,* p. 43.

79. *Pravda,* June 13, 1924, p. 4; B. I. Zbarskii, *Mavzolei Lenina* (Moscow, 1945), pp. 30–31.

80. Dr. George Curtis, Medical Examiner, City of Boston, telephone interview, March 1975.

294   81. Zbarskii, *Mavzolei Lenina*, p. 31.

82. Ibid.

83. Ibid., p. 32.

84. Ibid., pp. 32–33.

85. *Izvestiia, Pravda,* and *Leningradskaia pravda,* March 25, 1924, pp. 1, 2.

86. *Izvestiia,* March 25, 1924, p. 1.

87. *Izvestiia,* July 31, 1924, p. 4; *Bol'shaia sovetskaia entsiklopediia,* vol. 9, 1952, p. 97. Abramov in *Mavzolei Lenina* claims that Vorobev had been working for many years on embalming and had studied the subject intensively, but no contemporary source mentions this.

88. This group included P. I. Karuzin, Ia. G. Zamkovskii, A. L. Shabadash, and A. N. Zhuravlev. *Izvestiia,* March 25, 1924, p. 1.

89. Ibid.

90. Zbarskii, *Mavzolei Lenina*, p. 38.

91. Ibid., p. 24.

92. *New York Times,* August 4, 1924, p. 2.

93. Zbarskii, *Mavzolei Lenina*, pp. 39–40.

94. *New York Times,* April 28, 1924.

95. *Otchet komissii,* p. 42.

96. The brief announcement was published in *Pravda* and *Izvestiia* on March 25, 1924.

97. Two and one half months, to be more precise.

98. *Pravda* and *Izvestiia,* June 13, 1924, p. 4.

99. The first team of experts consisted of Professors Melnikov-Razvedenkov, Tonkov, and Iatsuty, and the second of Commissar Semashko, Professor Rozanov, and Dr. Savelev. *Izvestiia,* July 25, 1924, p. 5, and July 27, 1924, p. 5.

100. The full commission consisted of F. E. Dzerzhinsky, A. S. Enukidze, L. B. Krasin, K. E. Voroshilov, V. A. Avanesov, V. D. Bonch-Bruevich, N. A. Semashko, V. P. Vorobev, B. I. Zbarsky, A. L. Shabadash, P. I. Karuzin, V. N. Rozanov, A. N. Zhuravlev, Ia. G. Zamkovsky, A. P. Savelev, N. F. Melnikov-Razvedenkov, V. N. Tonkov, K. E. Iatsuty, and A. Belensky. *Izvestiia,* July 27, 1924, p. 5.

101. *Otchet komissii,* p. 45.

102. *Izvestiia,* July 27, 1924, p. 5.

103. Immediately upon completion of the embalming, Vorobev, who had headed the project, was given the title of *zasluzhennyi professor*. In 1927 he received the Lenin Prize. In 1934 he was awarded the Order of Lenin and made a member of the Academy of Sciences of the Ukrainian SSR. In 1935 he was made a member of the Central Executive Committee of the Ukrainian SSR. Vorobev's collaborators also received honors for their work. *Izvestiia,* July 27, 1924, p. 5; Abramov, *Mavzolei Lenina*, p. 116. Zbarsky, Vorobev's closest colleague who continued to supervise the preservation of the body after Vorobev's death in 1938, was also publicly rewarded for his work. In 1944 he was made a state prize laureate, and in 1945 he was awarded the title of Hero of Socialist Labor.

Kotyrev, *Mavzolei Lenina,* p. 139.   **295**

104. Bonch-Bruevich, *Vospominaniia,* p. 433.

105. Kazimir Malevich, "Iz knigi o bezpredmetnosti," Malevich Archive, Stedelijk Museum, Amsterdam (January 25, 1924), p. 20. Notes from this archive were kindly provided by Robert C. Williams.

106. Ibid., pp. 7–8.

107. Shchusev was a well-known architect. In 1919 he contributed to the plans of the restoration of Moscow and was the chief architect of the 1923 Agricultural and Industrial Exhibition held in Moscow. In 1922 he was president of the Moscow Architectural Society. Kotyrev, *Mavzolei Lenina,* p. 32.

108. Bonch-Bruevich, *Vospominaniia,* p. 434.

109. Khan-Magomedov, *Mavzolei Lenina,* p. 48.

110. Bonch-Bruevich, *Vospominaniia,* p. 436.

111. Ibid. The dramatic interior of the crypt was designed by the artist I. I. Nivinsky.

112. *Izvestiia,* February 7, 1924, p. 2.

113. *Izvestiia,* February 3, 1924, p. 2.

114. *Izvestiia,* February 7, 1924, p. 2.

115. Kotyrev, *Mavzolei Lenina,* p. 70.

116. *Izvestiia,* February 3, 1924, p. 2.

117. *Pravda,* February 22, 1924, p. 4.

118. Besides Krupskaia's statement of January 30, 1924, this article of February 22 is the only public protest against the mausoleum and the embalming in the contemporary central press.

119. *Otchet komissii,* p. 36.

120. *Izvestiia,* March 5, 1924, p. 6; March 11, 1924, p. 6.

121. For a detailed discussion of the Linin Mausoleum from an architectural point of view, and for photographs, drawings, and plans of the edifice, see Kotyrev, *Mavzolei Lenina,* pp. 71–86, and Khan-Magomedov, *Mavzolei Lenina,* pp. 61–71.

122. Abramov, *Mavzolei Lenina,* p. 79.

123. *Izvestiia,* May 11, 1924, p. 4.

124. *Trinadtsatyi s"ezd RKP(b), Mai 1924 goda. Stenograficheskii otchet* (Moscow, 1963), p. 34; *New York Times,* May 25, 1924.

125. *Pravda,* June 13, 1924, p. 4; Zbarskii, *Mavzolei Lenina,* p. 41.

126. *New York Times,* June 20, 1924.

127. *Izvestiia,* June 19, 1924, p. 3.

128. Each *raion* of Moscow was assigned a particular day of the week for its visitation. Visitors from out of town could go on any day. Individual citizens could not enter the mausoleum; they had to be part of a district group. The Lenin Mausoleum was to be open three hours a day, except when there were conferences or congresses in Moscow; then it was to be open four hours. *Izvestiia,* July 30, 1924, p. 4; July 31, 1924, p. 6.

129. *Izvestiia,* August 2, 1924, p. 4.

130. Walter Duranty thought that the design and rich color made the decor

296 resemble that of a fashionable American bar or a French cabaret. *New York Times,* August 4, 1924.

131. Ibid.

132. Ibid.

133. Ibid.

134. Theodore Dreiser, *Dreiser Looks at Russia* (New York, 1928), p. 31.

135. *New York Times,* January 30, 1924.

136. Doubtless the most charming of these is Robert Service's "The Ballad of Lenin's Tomb." In this humorous poem, Service tells the story of a man who witnessed someone throwing a bomb at Lenin's body, destroying it completely. Soon afterward, another body appeared in the Lenin Mausoleum: "So stern and firm it mocks the worm, it looks/ like wax . . . *and is./* They tell you he's a mummy—don't you make/ that bright mistake./ I tell you—he's a dummy; aye, a fiction/ and a fake." *Bar-room Ballads* (New York, 1940), pp. 88–89.

137. "Lenin," *Lenin-Märchen: Volksmärchen aus der Sowjetunion* (Berlin, 1929), pp. 32–34; "Pis'ma krest'ian v sviazi s konchinoi V. I. Lenina," *Voprosy istorii,* no. 7, 1968, p. 123.

138. Adrian Vechernii, in the anthology *Il'ichu* (Irkutsk, 1924), p. 9, reprinted in *Lenin v sovetskoi poezii,* p. 199.

139. Rodion Akul'shin, "Tri skazki," *Novyi mir,* no. 11, 1925, pp. 124–127.

140. See Chapter 1.

141. Lunacharskii, *Velikii perevorot,* pp. 43–44.

142. George L. Kline, *Religious and Anti-Religious Thought in Russia,* p. 123.

143. A. V. Lunacharskii, *Lenin* (Leningrad, 1924), pp. 22, 31–32.

144. *Styk* (Moscow, 1925), p. 90, reprinted in *Lenin v sovetskoi poezii,* pp. 329–330. Predsovnarkom is the contracted form of chairman of the Council of People's Commissars.

145. *Otchet komissii,* p. 37.

146. Ibid.

147. Ibid., p. 38.

148. Kotyrev, *Mavzolei Lenina,* pp. 104–108.

149. *Otchet komissii,* p. 38.

150. Kotyrev, *Mavzolei Lenina,* pp. 110–113.

151. I. Iaroslavskaia, "Tribuna naroda," *Khudozhnik,* no. 4, 1970, p. 58.

152. The monument was pictured on a commemorative poster published that year (Lenin Library, Moscow). Its caption, "Lenin—steel and granite," might mark the very beginning of a dual Lenin-Stalin cult, since the Russian *stal'* (steel) forms the basis for Stalin's pseudonym.

153. Khan-Magomedov, *Mavzolei Lenina,* p. 91.

154. Zbarskii, *Mavzolei Lenina,* p. 44.

155. Valentinov, *NEP,* p. 89.

156. Kotyrev, *Mavzolei Lenina,* p. 118.

157. Ibid., p. 123.

158. *Pravda,* November 10, 1930.

159. *Pravda,* November 11, 1930.

7. Lenin's Life After Death

1. See Chapter 3.

2. See Tucker's thoughtful analysis of the succession issue in his *Stalin as Revolutionary,* pp. 304–324.

3. Ibid., p. 306.

4. *Pravda,* December 20, 21, 1923.

5. For a detailed account of the conflict among the leaders and their repeated references to Lenin, see Carr, *The Interregnum,* pp. 292–366, and his *Socialism in One Country, 1924–1926,* (New York, 1960), II, 3–75. See also Schapiro, *The Communist Party of the Soviet Union,* pp. 282–308, and Daniels, *Conscience of the Revolution,* pp. 235–252.

6. *Pravda,* February 12, 1924. See also Ulam's analysis of the speech in *Stalin,* pp. 238–239.

7. *Pravda,* April 26, 30; May 9, 11, 14, 15, 18, 1924. See Tucker's discussion of these lectures in *Stalin as Revolutionary,* pp. 317–324.

8. Leon Trotsky, *Lenin: Notes for a Biographer,* pp. 52–53, 119. "It smells of revolution," said Lenin of the government's name.

9. *Leningradskaia pravda,* June 13, 1924. Carr also takes note of Zinoviev's attack on Trotsky (*Socialism in One Country,* pp. 5–6).

10. Some of these are reprinted in his *Sochineniia,* vol. 15, pp. 146–288.

11. *Trinadtsatyi s"ezd RKP(b). Mai 1924 goda. Stenograficheskii otchet,* p. 37.

12. K. Popov, "O propagande i izuchenii leninizma," *Kommunisticheskoe prosveshchenie,* no. 1, 1924, p. 60. By the beginning of March 1924, 183,000 people, mostly workers "from the bench," had been recruited into the party. G. Zinov'ev, "Leninskii prizyv i nashi zadachi," *Bol'shevik,* no. 1, 1924, p. 16.

13. Popov, "O propagande i izuchenii leninizma," p. 61; N. Kolesnikova, "God propagandy leninizma," *Kommunisticheskoe prosveshchenie,* no. 1, 1925, p. 87.

14. Popov, "O propagande i izuchenii leninizma," p. 61.

15. Ibid., p. 62.

16. A. Ryndich, "Leninizm i sovpartshkola," *Kommunisticheskoe prosveshchenie,* no. 1, 1924, p. 67.

17. B. Glak., "Il'ich v klubakh RKSM," *Kommunisticheskoe prosveshchenie,* no. 1, 1924, p. 117.

18. Ryndich, "Leninizm i sovpartshkola," pp. 63–64.

19. Popov, "O propagande i izuchenii leninizma," pp. 62–63.

20. *Rabochaia Moskva,* March 14, 1924.

21. Jeffrey Brooks, "Discontinuity in the Spread of Popular Print Culture, 1917–1927," Occasional Paper 138 (1981), Kennan Institute for Advanced Russian Studies, The Wilson Center, Washington, D.C. (unpublished).

22. E. Khlebtsevich, "Massovoi chitatel' o sochineniiakh V. I. Lenina," *Kommunisticheskoe prosveshchenie,* no. 1, 1925, pp. 150–152.

23. Brooks, "Popular Print Culture," p. 16, citing M. I. Slukhovskii, *Kniga i derevnia* (Moscow-Leningrad, 1928), p. 81.

24. One of the widely read biographies of Lenin available just after his

298   death was a revised version of a speech that Grigory Zinoviev made in the wake of the assassination attempt on Lenin's life. E. Khlebtsevich, "Kakie proizvedeniia Lenina bol'she vsego chitaiutsia v bibliotekakh," *Kommunisticheskoe prosveshchenie*, no. 1, 1924, p. 165.

25. G. Okulova, "Izba-chital'nia (Pri svete zavetov Lenina)," *Kommunisticheskoe prosveshchenie*, no. 1, 1924, p. 127.

26. Khlebtsevich, "Kakie proizvedenii a Lenina," p. 165.

27. M. Smushkova, "Propaganda leninizma cherez biblioteku," *Kommunistcheskoe prosveshchenie*, no. 1, 1924, p. 122.

28. N. Krupskaia, "O kul'turnoi rabote v derevne," *Kommunisticheskoe prosveshchenie*, no. 2, 1924, p. 3.

29. Okulova, "Izba-chital'nia," pp. 127, 129.

30. E. Khlebtsevich, "Sobiranie proizvedenii ustnogo tvorchestva rabochikh, krest'ian i krasnoarmeitsev o Lenine," *Kommunisticheskoe prosveshchenie*, no. 1, 1924, pp. 118–120.

31. F. Lukoianov and M. Rafail, eds., *Rabkory o smerti Il'icha: sbornik pisem, stat'ei i zametok rabkorov, sel'korov i voenkorov o smerti V. I. Lenina* (Moscow, 1925), pp. 66, 70–71.

32. A. Bubnov and Rafes, "Izuchenie leninizma v Krasnoi armii (Instruktsiia Politicheskogo Upravleniia Revoliutsionnogo Voennogo Soveta SSS Respublik)," *Kommunisticheskoe prosveshchenie*, no. 1, 1924, p. 72.

33. Ibid., p. 69.

34. Krupskaia, "O kul'turnoi rabote v derevne," p. 4.

35. Bubnov and Rafes, "Izuchenie leninizma v Krasnoi armii," p. 70.

36. See, for example, *Pamiatka krasnoarmeitsu-otpuskniku* (Novonikolaevsk, 1922); *Pamiatka krasnoarmeitsu strelkovoi divizii* (Kaluga, 1923); *Pamiatka krasnoarmeitsu 9-ii Donskoi strelkovoi divizii* (Rostov-on-Don, 1923).

37. *Pamiatka otpuskniku* (Novonikolaevsk, 1924).

38. Bubnov and Rafes, "Izuchenie leninizma v Krasnoi armii," p. 71.

39. V. Vitkich, *Leninskie ugolki v Krasnoi armii* (Moscow, 1925), pp. 5–9.

40. Ibid., pp. 12–13, 41.

41. Ibid., p. 13.

42. *Lenpalatka territorial'naia* (Kharkov, 1925), p. 18.

43. V. Menzhinskaia, "Ugolki Lenina," *Kommunisticheskoe prosveshchenie*, no. 1., 1924, p. 101.

44. Ibid., p. 105.

45. Iu. V. Grigor'ev, *Ugolki Lenina v zhilishchnykh tovarishchestvakh* (Moscow, 1924), pp. 3–7.

46. E. Sh., "Leninizm v rabochikh klubakh," *Kommunisticheskoe prosveshchenie*, no. 1, 1924, p. 100.

47. P. Budkov, "Propaganda leninizma v klube 'Krasnyi luch,' " *Kommunisticheskoe prosveshchenie*, no. 1, 1924, p. 163.

48. *Vecher pamiati V. I. Lenina v rabochem klube: sbornik materialov* (Moscow, 1924), pp. 72–73.

49. Ibid., pp. 25, 65.

50. *Klubnye vechera v derevne. Materialy k vecheram pamiati Lenina* (Ros-   **299**
tov-on-Don, 1924).

51. Ibid., pp. 48–49.

52. Z. Lilina, *Nash uchitel' Il'ich* (Moscow, 1924).

53. Lenin did not as a rule seek out the company of small children, not, in any event, until illness incapacitated him in 1922–23.

54. S. Margolis, "Ego mogila," in V. N. Shul'gin and K. T. Sverdlov, *Chas Lenina v shkole: kniga dlia chteniia v trudovoi shkole I stupeni* (Moscow, 1924), p. 53.

55. Trotsky, *Lenin: Notes for a Biographer*, pp. 190–191.

56. M. Kamshilov, "Izuchat' Lenina—znachit izuchat' zhizn'," *Put' prosveshcheniia*, no. 4–5, April–May 1924, pp. 114–122.

57. *Leniniana*, no. 1, 1924 (Moscow-Leningrad, 1926), pp. x–xi; in 1925 the published copies of books by and about Lenin totaled 20, 898, 727. *Leniniana*, no. 2, 1925 (Moscow-Leningrad, 1927), p. v.

58. *Pravda*, February 13, 1924; February 15, 1924.

59. Khobanov, "Vmesto voskresen'ia Leninden'," *Zvezda* (Minsk), cited in *Leniniana*, no. 1, 1924, p. 442.

60. *Izvestiia*, April 22, 1925.

61. Poster Collection, Lenin Library, Moscow.

62. *Pravda*, February 7, 1924.

63. L. B. Krasin, "O pamiatnikakh Vladimiru Il'ichu," *O pamiatnike Leninu* (Leningrad, 1924), p. 13.

64. Ibid., pp. 18–19.

65. *Otchet komissii TsIK SSSR po uvekovecheniiu pamiati V. I. Ul'ianova* (*-Lenina*), pp. 39–40.

66. In 1924 the executive troika judged 405 paintings, drawings, posters, and photographs of Lenin and of these approved all but 26. But of the 126 busts and sculptures it reviewed, it rejected 74, more than half. In accordance with the Central Executive Committee decree, the originals of the approved works were sent to the Lenin Institute, and rejected pieces were banned from public display (ibid.).

67. "Ne torguite Leninym!" *LEF*, no. 1(5), 1924, pp. 3–4. Sometime after its original printing in the spring of 1924, the editorial was evidently deemed inappropriate for public consumption and was removed from extant copies of the journal. But its title remained in the table of contents, and the copy that the publisher had sent to the Lenin Library in Moscow retained the editorial. I am grateful to Lars Kleberg for giving me his illuminating article, which quotes the editorial in its entirety. Lars Kleberg, "Notes on the Poem *Vladimir Il'ič Lenin*," in Bengt Jangfeldt and Nils Ake Nilsson, eds., *Vladimir Majakovskij: Memoirs and Essays* (Stockholm, 1978), pp. 166–178.

68. Vladimir Maiakovskii, *Vladimir Il'ich Lenin* (Moscow, 1970), pp. 5, 200, 8.

69. *Rabochaia Moskva*, February 22, 1924.

70. *Leningradskaia pravda*, May 7, 1924.

71. *Izvestiia*, January 22, 1925.

300   72. S. Korev, *Obzor muzykal'nykh proizvedenii dlia Leninskikh vecherov* (Moscow, 1925), pp. 8–9. The author's distress seems slightly misplaced, since it was quite common for Russian revolutionary and political songs to have delightfully inappropriate melodies.

73. *Izvestiia*, March 25, 1925.

74. *Lenin u detei; Mavzolei V. I. Lenina. Model' dlia skleivaniia*, described in *Leniniana*, no. 2, 1925, p. 422.

75. Victor Iakerin, "Ob izpol'zovanii imeni Lenina," *Krasnaia nov'*, no. 9, 1925, p. 280.

76. A. Shneer, "K voprosu ob organizatsii krasnykh ugolkov (po lichnym nabliudeniiam)," *Kommunisticheskoe prosveshchenie*, no. 1, 1925, p. 117.

77. *Rabochaia pravda* (Tiflis), October 29, 1925; *Bakinskii rabochii* (Baku), no. 20 and no. 50, 1925. Summaries of these articles are provided in *Leniniana*, no. 2, 1925, pp. 441, 446, 450.

78. I. Ts-kii, "Lenin v bibliotechnym plakate," *Knigonosha*, no. 5(86), 1925; E. Shifron, "Agitatsionnyi pokhod v derevniiu. (K nedele Lenina)," *Krasnaia Tataria* (Kazan), no. 6, 1925, cited in *Leniniana*, no. 2, 1925, pp. 469, 464.

79. A. M. Selishchev, *Iazyk revoliutsionnoi epokhi* (Moscow, 1928), pp. 214–217.

80. A. M. Bol'shakov, *Derevnia 1917–1927* (Moscow, 1927), pp. 264–275.

81. Ibid., p. 271.

82. To be exact, 664, 122. *Otchet komissii*, p. 41.

83. *New York Times*, September 3, 1925.

84. David E. Powell, *Antireligious Propaganda in the Soviet Union* (Cambridge, 1975), p. 35.

85. The USSR was formed in 1923, and its constitution was ratified on July 6 of that year.

86. "Pshavy i khevsury o Lenine," *Pravda*, January 21, 1925.

87. "Ot mesiatsa i zvezdy rodilsia Lenin," A. V. Piaskovskii, *Lenin v russkoi narodnoi skazke i vostochnoi legende* (Leningrad, 1930), pp. 68–69.

88. *Pravda*, January 18, 1927.

89. *Leniniana*, no. 3, 1926, (Moscow-Leningrad, 1928), preface (page unnumbered).

90. *Pravda*, January 20, 1929.

91. *Pravda*, January 5, 1929.

92. *Izvestiia*, January 21, 1931.

93. *Pravda*, January 21, 1932.

94. *Izvestiia* and *Pravda*, January 21, 1932.

95. See Tucker, *Stalin as Revolutionary*, pp. 462–487 and, for a detailed account of the terminology used in the Stalin jubilee, see James Lee Heizer, "The Cult of Stalin, 1929–1939" (Ph.D. dissertation, University of Kentucky, 1977).

96. The author was Emelian Iaroslavsky. *Pravda*, January 12, 1929.

97. *Pravda* and *Izvestiia*, January 19, 1931.

98. *Pravda*, January 21, 1932.

99. *Uchitel'skaia gazeta*, November 20, 1980.

100. *Ezhegodnik leninskoi i istoriko-partiinoi bibliografii,* vol. 1 (Moscow, **301** 1932).

101. For a discussion of Stalin's role in the development of his cult, see Robert C. Tucker, "The Rise of Stalin's Personality Cult," *American Historical Review,* 84 (April 1979), 347–366.

102. Eugene Lyons, *Moscow Carrousel* (New York, 1935), pp. 40–41.

103. Smolensk Archive, Harvard University Library, WKP 159, p. 2.

Epilogue: "Lenin Is Always with Us."

1. *Stalin: k shestidesiatiletiiu so dnia rozhdeniia* (Moscow, 1940), p. 67.

2. Quoted in Iu. M. Sokolov, *Russkii fol'klor,* p. 549.

3. Quoted in Felicity Ann O'Dell, *Socialisation through Children's Literature: The Soviet Example* (Cambridge, Eng., 1978), p. 156.

4. *Joseph Stalin: A Short Biography* (Moscow, 1941), p. 32.

5. The sculpture was the work of G. Mikhaltsov. A photograph is included in Iu. M. Sokolov, ed., *Samoe dorogoe: Stalin v narodnom epose* (Moscow, 1939), p. 25.

6. These stamps are displayed in the Leningrad branch of the Lenin Museum.

7. Russian Institute, Columbia University, *The Anti-Stalin Campaign and International Communism* (New York, 1956), p. 2.

8. Ibid., pp. 7–9.

9. Ibid., p. 9.

10. Ibid., pp. 20–21, 73–75.

11. *Pravda,* January 11, 1955.

12. Ibid.

13. See, for example, *Ko dniu pamiati V. I. Lenina* (Moscow, 1955); M. N. Talantova, *Chto chitat' o V. I. Lenine* (Moscow, 1956); *V pomoshch propagande V. I. Lenina i literatura o nem* (Moscow, 1959); S. V. Kazakov, *Lenin i teper' zhivee vsekh zhivykh* (Moscow, 1958).

14. *XXII s"ezd kommunisticheskoi partii sovetskogo soiuza. Stenograficheskii otchet,* vol. 3 (Moscow, 1962), p. 121.

15. *Pravda,* April 22, 1970.

16. *Nashi prazdniki* (Moscow, 1977), pp. 28–30.

17. I was also present at the Ulianovsk celebration.

18. *Sovetskaia Belorussiia,* January 20, 1974.

19. Like so many other Lenin cult slogans, this one derives from Vladimir Maiakovskii's epic poem, *Vladimir Il'ich Lenin.*

Selected Bibliography

For the formative years of the Lenin cult, a useful bibliographical source is L. V. Bulgakova, comp., *Materialy dlia bibliografii Lenina, 1917–1923* (Leningrad, 1924). The full-blown Lenin cult of the period 1924–1928 is catalogued in the comprehensive bibliographical journal, *Leniniana,* published in 1926–1930 by the Lenin Institute. Also informative is that institute's own bulletin, *Biulleten' Instituta V. I. Lenina pri TsK RKP,* which began publication in 1923. The official report of the Commission on the Immortalization of the Memory of V. I. Ulianov (Lenin), *Otchet komissii TsIK SSSR po uvekovecheniiu pamiati V. I. Ul'ianova (-Lenina)* (Moscow, 1925), contains valuable information about mourning week, Lenin's funeral, and the preservation of his body. On these subjects the contemporary press is also useful. The best accounts are in *Petrogradskaia pravda, Pravda, Izvestiia, Rabochaia Moskva,* and *The New York Times.* The most important source for the "propaganda of Leninism" campaign of 1924 is issue 1(13), 1924, of *Kommunisticheskoe prosveshchenie,* the organ of the Commissariat of Enlightenment's Political Education Department. The numerous articles it contains are not listed separately below.

A large assortment of posters of Lenin is available in the poster collection (*plakatnyi fond*) of the Lenin Library in Moscow. Posters and other cult artifacts are also on display in the Central V. I. Lenin Museum in Moscow and on deposit in Moscow's Museum of the Revolution, whose staff is knowledgeable and helpful.

The following listing is a selection of works cited in the notes.

Abramov, A. S. *Mavzolei Lenina.* Moscow, 1969.
Agitatsionno-massovoe iskusstvo pervykh let Oktiabria. Moscow, 1971.
Akul'shin, Rodion. "Tri skazki." *Novyi mir,* 11 (1925): 120–127.
Arosev, A. "Institut V. I. Lenina." *Proletarskaia revoliutsiia,* 11 (1923): 269–274.
Avrich, Paul. *Kronstadt 1921.* New York, 1970.
Berlin, Isaiah. *Russian Thinkers.* New York, 1978.
Billington, James, H. *The Icon and the Axe: An Interpretive History of Russian Culture.* New York, 1966.
Bol'shakov, A. M. *Derevnia 1917–1927.* Moscow, 1927.

304   Bonch-Bruevich, V. D. *Vospominaniia o Lenine.* Moscow, 1965.

Brooks, Jeffrey, "Discontinuity in the Spread of Popular Print Culture, 1917–1927." Occasional Paper 138, Kennan Institute for Advanced Russian Studies, The Wilson Center, Washington, D.C., 1981.

Bunin, I. A. *Okaiannye dni.* Berlin, 1935.

Butnik-Siverskii, B. S. *Sovetskii plakat epokhi grazhdanskoi voiny 1918–1921.* Moscow, 1960.

Carr, E. H. *The Interregnum, 1923–1924.* Baltimore, 1969.

——— *Socialism in One Country, 1924–1926,* vol. 2. New York, 1960.

Chebotarev, I. N. "Vladimir Il'ich." *Iunyi proletarii,* 1 (1922): 37–39.

Cherniavsky, Michael. *Tsar and People: Studies in Russian Myths.* New Haven, 1961.

Cunliffe, Marcus. *George Washington, Man and Monument.* New York, 1958.

Daniels, Robert Vincent. *The Conscience of the Revolution: Communist Opposition in Soviet Russia.* Cambridge, Mass., 1960.

Description des funérailles de feu l'empereur Nicholas I de glorieuse mémoire précédée d'un aperçu historique sur les funérailles des tsars et des empereurs de toutes les russies et de quelques autres souverains européens. St. Petersburg, 1856.

Deviatyi s"ezd RKP(b). Protokoly. Moscow, 1960.

Duranty, Walter. *I Write as I Please.* New York, 1935.

Dvenadtsatyi s"ezd RKP(b). Stenograficheskii otchet, 17–25 aprelia 1923 g. Moscow, 1923.

Elizarova, A. "Obrazets togo, kak nel'zia pisat' biografii." *Molodaia gvardiia,* 3 (1923): 237–238.

——— "Vospominaniia ob Aleksandre Il'iche Ul'ianove." Part 1, *Proletarskaia revoliutsiia,* 1 (1927): 70–124; part 2, 2–3 (1927): 278–316.

Ezhegodnik leninskoi i istoriko-partiinoi bibliografii, vol 1. Moscow, 1932.

Fedorov, N. *Filosofiia obshchago dela,* ed. V. A. Kozhevnikov and N. P. Peterson. Moscow, 1913.

Field, Daniel. *Rebels in the Name of the Tsar.* Boston, 1976.

Fitzpatrick, Sheila. *The Commissariat of Enlightenment.* Cambridge, Eng., 1970.

Fotieva, L. A. *Iz zhizni V. I. Lenina.* Moscow, 1967.

Geertz, Clifford. *The Interpretation of Cultures.* New York, 1973.

Golubinskii, E. *Istoriia kanonizatsii sviatykh v russkoi tserkvi.* Moscow, 1903.

Gor'kii, Maksim. *O russkom krest'ianstve.* Berlin, 1922.

——— "Pis'mo M. Gor'kogo k G. Uellsu." *Kommunisticheskii internatsional,* 12 (1920): 2207.

——— "Vladimir Il'ich Lenin." *Kommunisticheskii internatsional,* 12 (1920): 1928–1936.

Grigor'ev, Iu. V. *Ugolki Lenina v zhilishchnykh tovarishchestvakh.* Moscow, 1924.

Gusev, A. I. *V gostiakh u Vladimira Il'icha.* Tver, 1921.

Haimson, Leopold H. *The Russian Marxists and the Origins of Bolshevism.* Cambridge, Mass., 1955.

Heizer, James Lee. "The Cult of Stalin, 1929–1939." Ph.D. dissertation, University of Kentucky, 1977.

Iakerin, Victor. "Ob izpol'zovanii imeni Lenina." *Krasnaia nov'*, 9 (1925):   **305**
    280–281.
Iaroslavskaia, I. "Tribuna naroda." *Khudozhnik*, 4 (1970): 56–60.
Iaroslavskii, E. *Velikii vozhd' rabochei revoliutsii.* Moscow, 1918.
—— *Zhizn' i rabota V. I. Lenina.* Moscow, 1924.
Ingulov, S. "Zadachi i perspektivy nashei agitatsii." *Kommunisticheskoe pros-veshchenie*, 2 (1922): 7–14.
Kamshilov, M. "Izuchat' Lenina—znachit izuchat' zhizn'." *Put' prosveshcheniia*, 4–5 (1924): 114–125.
Kantorowicz, Ernst. *The King's Two Bodies: A Study in Medieval Theology.* Princeton, 1957.
Khan-Magomedov, S. O. *Mavzolei Lenin, istoriia sozdaniia i arkhitektura.* Moscow, 1972.
Khlebtsevich, E. "Massovoi chitatel' o sochineniiakh V. I. Lenina." *Kommunist-icheskoe prosveshchenie*, 1 (1925): 150–152.
Khodorovskii, I. *V. I. Lenin, velikii vozhd' proletarskoi revoliutsii.* Kazan, 1920.
Kleberg, Lars. "Notes on the Poem *Vladimir Il'ič Lenin.*" In Bengt Jangfeldt and Nils Ake Nilsson, eds., *Vladimir Majakovskij: Memoirs and Essays.* Stockholm, 1978.
Kline, George L. *Religious and Anti-Religious Thought in Russia.* Chicago, 1968.
Klubnye vechera v derevne. Materialy k vecheram pamiati Lenina. Rostov-on-Don, 1924.
Kolesnikova, N. "God propagandy leninizma." *Kommunisticheskoe prosve-shchenie*, 1 (1925): 86–88.
Korev, S. *Obzor muzykal'nykh proizvedenii dlia Leninskikh vecherov.* Moscow, 1925.
Kotyrev, A. N. *Mavzolei V. I. Lenina, proektirovanie i stroitel'stvo.* Moscow, 1971.
Krupskaia, N. K. "Na krasnoi zvezde." In N. K. Krupskaia, *Pedagogicheskie so-chineniia*, 1 (1957): 56–67.
—— "O kul'turnoi rabote v derevne." *Kommunisticheskoe prosveshchenie*, 2 (1924): 3–5.
—— *O Lenine, sbornik stat'ei i vystuplenii*, ed. V. S. Dridzo. 2nd ed. Moscow, 1965.
—— *O Lenine, stat'i i rechi*, comp. Liudmila Stal'. Moscow, 1925.
—— "Perspektivy politprosvetraboty." *Kommunisticheskoe prosveshchenie*, 1 (1922): 5–9.
Krzhizhanovskii, G. M. *O Vladimire Il'iche.* Moscow, 1924.
Laliants, I. Kh. "O moikh vstrechakh s V. I. Leninym za vremia 1893–1900." *Proletarskaia revoliutsiia*, 1 (1929): 38–70.
Lane, Christel. *The Rites of Rulers: Ritual in Industrial Society—The Soviet Case.* Cambridge, Eng., 1981.
Lebed', D., ed. *Lenin.* Kharkov, 1923.
—— *Lenin, 1870–1924.* Kharkov, 1924.
Lenin, V. I. *Polnoe sobranie sochinenii*, 5th ed. 55 vols. Moscow, 1967–1970.
Lenin: Sobranie fotografii i kinokadrov, 2 vols. Moscow: 1970–1972.

306 *Lenin—tovarishch, chelovek,* 2nd ed. Moscow, 1963.

Lenin v sovetskoi poezii. Leningrad, 1970.

Leningradskii, S. *Lenin sredi krest'ian derevni Kashino.* Moscow, 1924.

Lenin-Märchen: Volksmärchen aus der Sowjetunion. Berlin, 1929.

Leninu, 21 ianvaria 1924. Moscow, 1925.

Lenpalatka territorial'naia. Kharkov, 1925.

Lewin, Moshe. *Lenin's Last Struggle.* New York, 1970.

Lilina, Z. *Nash uchitel' Il'ich.* Moscow, 1924.

Lukoianov, F., and M. Rafail, eds. *Rabkory o smerti Il'icha: sbornik pisem, stat'ei i zametok rabkorov, sel'korov i voenkorov o smerti V. I. Lenina.* Moscow, 1925.

Lunacharskii, A. "Budushchee religii," part 1. *Obrazovanie,* 10 (1907): 1–25.

―――― *Lenin.* Leningrad, 1924.

―――― "Osnovy pozitivnoi estetiki." *Ocherki realisticheskogo mirovozzreniia,* ed. S. Doratovskii and A. Charushnikov. St. Petersburg, 1904: 8–182.

―――― *Religiia i sotsializm,* 2 vols. St. Petersburg, 1908 and 1911.

―――― *Revoliutsionnye siluety.* Moscow, 1923.

―――― *Velikii perevorot.* Petrograd, 1919.

Maiakovskii, Vladimir. *Sochineniia,* vol. 1. Moscow, 1965.

―――― *Vladimir Il'ich Lenin.* Moscow, 1967.

Materialist. "Truslivyi opportunizm budushchego professora." *Pod znamenem marksizma,* 2–3 (1923): 218–222.

Mazlish, Bruce. *The Revolutionary Ascetic.* New York, 1976.

McNeal, Robert H. *Bride of the Revolution: Krupskaya and Lenin.* Ann Arbor, 1972.

M. E. O. "Vozhd' mirovoi revoliutsii. Vladimir Il'ich Ul'ianov Lenin." *Zheleznyi put',* 8 (1919): 2–4.

Mitrofanov, A. M. *Vozhd' derevenskoi bednoty, V. I. Ul'ianov-Lenin.* Moscow, 1918.

Nashi prazdniki. Moscow, 1977.

Nevskii, V. I. *V. I. Ul'ianov (N. Lenin).* Moscow, 1920.

O pamiatnike Leninu. Leningrad, 1924.

O'Dell, Felicity Ann. *Socialisation through Children's Literature: The Soviet Example.* Cambridge, Eng., 1978.

Ol'minskii, M. "Kriticheskie stat'i i zametki." *Proletarskaia revoliutsiia,* 1 (1931): 148–152.

―――― "Tov. Lenin." *Vestnik zhizni,* 2 (1918): 8–14; reprinted in *Proletarskaia revoliutsiia,* 3 (1924): 24–33.

Osipov, V. "Nekotorye cherty kharaktera V. I. Lenina vo vremia ego bolezni." *Krasnaia letopis',* 2 (1927): 236–247.

Otchego bolel i umer V. I. Lenin. Leningrad, 1924.

Pamiatka otpuskniku. Novonikolaevsk, 1924.

Pavlovich, M. "Lenin, kak razrushitel' narodnichestva." *Pod znamenem marksizma,* 4–5 (1923): 157–182.

Piaskovskii, A. V. *Lenin v russkoi narodnoi skazke i vostochnoi legende.* Leningrad, 1930.

Pipes, Richard. "The Origins of Bolshevism: The Intellectual Evolution of Young Lenin." In Richard Pipes, ed., *Revolutionary Russia*. Cambridge, Mass., 1968: 26–52.

—— *Social Democracy and the St. Petersburg Labor Movement, 1885–1897*. Cambridge, Mass., 1963.

"Pis'ma krest'ian v sviazi s konchinoi V. I. Lenina." *Voprosy istorii*, 7 (1968): 118–124.

Potresov, A. N. *Posmertnyi sbornik proizvedenii*. Paris, 1937.

Powell, David E. *Antireligious Propaganda in the Soviet Union*. Cambridge, Mass., 1975.

Rabinowitch, Alexander. *The Bolsheviks Come to Power*. New York, 1978.

Reed, John. *Ten Days That Shook the World*. New York, 1967.

Reswick, William. *I Dreamt Revolution*. Chicago, 1952.

Rigby, T. H. *Communist Party Membership in the USSR, 1917–1967*. Princeton, 1968.

—— *Lenin's Government*, Cambridge, Eng., 1979.

Russian Institute, Columbia University. *The Anti-Stalin Campaign and International Communism*. New York, 1956.

Savitskaia, R. M. "Razrabotka nauchnoi biografii V. I. Lenina." *Voprosy istorii*, 4 (1971): 3–19.

Schapiro, Leonard. *The Communist Party of the Soviet Union*. New York, 1964.

Seifullina, L. "Muzhitskii skaz o Lenine." *Krasnaia nov'*, 1 (1924): 162–169.

Selishchev, A. M. *Iazyk revoliutsionnoi epokhi*. Moscow, 1928.

Ševčenko, Ihor. "A Neglected Byzantine Source of Muscovite Political Ideology." In Michael Cherniavsky, ed., *The Structure of Russian History*. New York, 1970: 80–107.

Shestoi s"ezd RSDRP (bol'shevikov), avgust 1917 goda. Protokoly. Moscow, 1958.

Shidlovskii, Georgii. "Lenin—mificheskoe litso." *Proletarskaia revoliutsiia*, 3 (1922): 333–334.

Shneer, A. "K voprosu ob organizatsii krasnykh ugolkov (po lichnym nabliudeniiam)." *Kommunisticheskoe prosveshchenie*, 1 (1925): 115–119.

Shul'gin, V. N., and K. T. Sverdlov. *Chas Lenina v shkole: kniga dlia chteniia v trudovoi shkole I stupeni*. Moscow, 1924.

Smuta noveishego vremeni ili Udivitel'nye pokhozhdeniia Vani Chmotanova. Paris, 1970.

Sokolov, Iu. M. *Russkii fol'klor*. Moscow, 1941.

—— *Samoe dorogoe: Stalin v narodnom epose*. Moscow, 1939.

Sokolova, V. K. *Russkie istoricheskie predaniia*. Moscow, 1970.

Stalin: k shestidesiatiletiiu so dnia rozhdeniia. Moscow, 1940.

Starr, S. Frederick. *Melnikov: Solo Architect in a Mass Society*. Princeton, 1978.

Stites, Richard. "Iconoclasm in the Russian Revolution: Destroying and Preserving the Past." Occasional Paper 147, Kennan Institute for Advanced Russian Studies, The Wilson Center, Washington, D.C., 1981.

—— *The Women's Liberation Movement in Russia*. Princeton, 1978.

Trinadtsatyi s"ezd RKP(b). Stenograficheskii otchet. Moscow, 1963.

308 Trotsky, Leon. *My Life*. New York, 1930.

———— *O Lenine, materialy dlia biografa*. Moscow, n.d. [1924].

Tucker, Robert C. *The Lenin Anthology*. New York, 1975.

———— "The Rise of Stalin's Personality Cult." *American Historical Review*, 84 (April 1979): 347–366.

———— *Stalin as Revolutionary, 1879–1929: A Study in History and Personality*. New York, 1973.

Tumarkin, Nina. "Religion, Bolshevism and the Origins of the Lenin Cult." *Russian Review*, 40 (January 1981): 35–46.

Ugolok V. I. Lenina. Pervaia sel'sko-khoziaistvennaia i kustarno-promyshlennaia vystavka SSSR. Moscow, 1923.

Ulam, Adam. *The Bolsheviks*. New York, 1965.

———— *Stalin: The Man and His Era*. New York, 1973.

Valentinov, Nikolai (N. V. Vol'skii). *The Early Years of Lenin*, trans. Rolf H. W. Theen. Ann Arbor, 1969.

———— *Maloznakomyi Lenin*. Paris, 1972.

———— *Novaia ekonomicheskaia politika i krizis partii posle smerti Lenina*, ed. J. Bunyan and V. Butenko. Stanford, 1971.

———— *Vstrechi s Leninym*. New York, 1953. In English, *Encounters with Lenin*, trans. Paul Rosta and Brian Pearce. London, 1968.

Vasil'ev, Vasilii. "Istoriia kanonizatsii russkikh sviatykh." *Chteniia v Imperatorskom Obshchestve istorii i drevnostei rossiiskikh pri Moskovskom universitete*, III.166 (1893): 1–256.

Vecher pamiati V. I. Lenina v rabochem klube: sbornik materialov. Moscow, 1924.

Vitkich, V. *Leninskie ugolki v Krasnoi armii*. Moscow, 1925.

Volkov-Lannit, L. F. *Lenin v fotoiskusstve*. Moscow, 1967.

Vos'moi s"ezd RKP(b). Protokoly. Moscow, 1959.

Vospominaniia o Vladimire Il'iche Lenine. 3 vols. Moscow, 1956–60.

Zbarskii, B. I. *Mavzolei Lenina*. Moscow, 1945.

Zinov'ev, G. "Leninskii prizyv i nashi zadachi." *Bol'shevik*, 1 (1924): 14–21.

———— *Sochineniia*. Vol. 15, *Vladimir Il'ich Ul'ianov-Lenin*. Leningrad, 1924.

Index

Abrikosov, A. I., 169, 176, 179
Agapetus, 7
Agitation, 64–74, 97–99, 101–102, 126, 142, 213–232, passim. *See also* Propaganda
Agitation and Propaganda Department (Central Committee; Agitprop), 66, 73, 97, 101, 119, 123, 213
Akhmatova, Anna, 13
Akselrod, Pavel, 36, 37, 42, 43
Alexander the Great, 1
Alexander I, 10, 199
Alexander II, 10, 16, 28, 31, 84
Alexander III, 28
Alexandra, Empress, 10
All-Russian Agricultural and Domestic-Industrial Exhibition (1923), 116, 117, 126
Andrei Bogoliubsky, Saint, 6, 108
Apocalypse, 18–20
"April Theses" (Lenin), 48–49, 98
Armand, I. A., 177
Arosev, A., 124
Arteriosclerosis, 59, 113, 169
Autopsy, Lenin's, 169–173
Avenarius, Richard, 20

Babakhan, N., 120
Batiushka (little father). *See* "Naive monarchism"
Bednota (newspaper), 83, 98, 100, 114
Bednyi, Demian, 80, 99, 216
Belinsky, Vissarion, 13–14, 42
Belyi, Andrei, 18

Bentham, Jeremy, 184
Berdiaev, Nikolai, 18
Bezbozhnik (newspaper), 243
Biographies of Lenin, 3, 24, 27, 87, 95, 101–102, 128–129, 142, 216, 259; by children, 229; for children, 227–229; by Iaroslavsky, 88, 166, 228; by Krupskaia, 76–77; by Lilina, 227; by Nevsky, 101–102; by Olminsky, 75–76, 87; by Peasant Department of Central Executive Committee, 88–90; *Pravda* and *Izvestiia* coverage of Lenin's illness and death, 115–118, 135; by Reed, 77–79; speech to Kazan Soviet (1920), 102; by Zinoviev, 82
Birthday, Lenin's, 95–103, 226, 249, 257, 260, 262
Birthday, Stalin's, 249, 261, 264
Blok, Alexander, 18
Bloody Sunday (1905), 10–11, 134
Body, Lenin's, 3, 164, 168–169; cult of, 242; embalming, 173–182 passim, 183, 195; evacuated during World War II, 225; reembalming, 185–189
Body, Stalin's, 258
Bogdanov, A. A. (Malinovsky), 20, 22, 45, 108, 181
Bogostroitel'stvo, 20, *See also* God-building
Bolsheviks, bolshevism, 3, 12, 19–20, 21, 22, 36, 40, 41, 42, 43, 44, 45, 47–53, 65, 69, 74, 76, 82, 83, 86, 181
Bonch-Bruevich, Vladimir Dmitrievich, 19, 63, 80, 90, 136, 176, 189, 200

Index